THE WORLD'S MOST
NOTORIOUS
MEN

CHANCELLOR
PRESS

This 2001 edition published by
Chancellor Press, an imprint of Bounty Books,
a division of Octopus Publishing Group Ltd,
2-4 Heron Quays, London E14 4JP

Reprinted 2002, 2003 (twice), 2004

The material in this book has previously appeared in
The World's Greatest Crooks & Conmen
(Hamlyn, Octopus Publishing Group Ltd, 1997)
The World's Greatest Trials
(Hamlyn, Octopus Publishing Group Ltd, 1997)
The World's Greatest Secrets
(Hamlyn, Octopus Publishing Group Ltd, 1991)
The World's Greatest Lovers
(Octopus Publishing Group Ltd, 1985)
The World's Worst Murders
(Bounty, Octopus Publishing Group Ltd, 2001)
The World's Greatest Sex and Scandals
(Bounty, Octopus Publishing Group Ltd, 2001)
The World's Most Evil Men
(Hamlyn, Octopus Publishing Group Ltd, 1997)
The World's Greatest Unsolved Mysteries
(Bounty, Octopus Publishing Group Ltd, 2001)
The World's Greatest Cranks and Crackpots
(Hamlyn, Octopus Publishing Group Ltd, 1997)

ISBN 0-7537-0464-1
ISBN 13 9780753704646

Produced by Omnipress, Eastbourne

Printed in Great Britain

Contents

Twentieth-Century Tyrants

Idi Amin

The dimming of the street lights on the warm, tropical nights in Kampala was always an accurate barometer of the morale of the people in Uganda.

Privileged visitors, arms salesmen and foreign diplomats in the two showpiece hotels would grumble loudly when the cocktail bars were plunged into darkness and the elevators jammed between floors.

But the uncomplaining residents of Kampala would leave the unlit cinemas and cheap little coffee shops in fearful silence to go home and spend a sleepless night behind barricaded doors.

Fitful blackouts in the power supply were a sign that Uganda's President Idi Amin had just completed another busy day of butchery. The drop in the voltage usually meant only one thing . . .

That the hydro-electric generators at Owens Falls Dam, 40 miles west of Kampala, were once again clogged with rotting corpses.

Despite the constant boat patrols on Lake Victoria, the source of the waters of the Nile, the maintenance engineers couldn't hope to spot every dead body swept by the currents towards their filter grids. They had allies helping them to scavenge the lake clear of the harvest of murder victims: the teeming colonies of crocodiles. But even these voracious reptiles became bloated and lazy. The pickings were too rich for them.

Time after time the generators had to be shut down and the water inlets cleared of that day's toll of death, usually 40 or 50 bodies in a 24-hour period.

In eight years of ruling his country in a torrent of blood and terror, Idi Amin had 500,000 of his fellow Ugandans ruthlessly and systematically butchered. He ordered the grisly mutilation of one of his own wives. He killed crusading clergymen, nosy journalists, his own diplomats and a helpless, frail, elderly hijack hostage. He even tasted the flesh of some of his victims in a cannibal ritual.

He killed political opponents, real and imagined, to stay in power. And he killed countless ordinary men and women for profit, sometimes for the sake of a few hundred pounds.

He personally supervised the actions of Uganda's 'State Research Bureau', an organization which was a cross between the Gestapo and Murder Incorporated, dealing in state-sponsored torture, contract killing, drug running and currency smuggling.

For almost 100 years, the fertile land of Uganda had been part of the British Empire, 'The Pearl of Africa' according to its colonial administrators. Spread over the hills and valleys of a high plateau, its gentle climate makes it a pleasant garden nudging the Equator. It had enormous strategic value, but when the 'wind of change' blew through Africa the pressure for independence for Uganda became irresistible.

An astute lawyer and professional politician, Milton Obote became the first Prime Minister when he triumphed in the hastily organized elections in 1962. His first priority was to forge some sort of unity among the 14 million Ugandans who owed more allegiance to their tribal chiefs than to any government in Kampala.

The ruling edicts of some of the chiefs of the 40 different tribes of Uganda often seemed to carry more authority than the decisions of any ballot-box government. Mindful of this, Obote, a member of the minority Langi tribe, appointed the powerful ruler of the Buganda tribe, King Freddy, as President of Uganda. The Buganda tribe, largely anglicized by colonial commissioners and missionaries, were the largest single tribal group. They considered themselves an elite.

But, in placating them, Milton Obote earned himself the

growing distrust of all the other tribes. Shortly after independence, however, he began slowly to reduce the powers of King Freddy.

By 1966 Buganda tribesmen were agitating more and more violently for Obote's overthrow. He needed to pit some military muscle against them and chose the deputy commander of the arm, Idi Amin.

Amin had all the qualifications. He was an outsider, a Kakwa tribesman from the furthest-flung province of Uganda, bordering Sudan. He was a Moslem who spoke virtually no English and was only semi-literate. He wouldn't be loath to dish out some rough justice to the Bugandans.

A former sergeant in the King's African Rifles, Amin was the ex-heavyweight boxing champion of Uganda, a hulk of a man who, at 6ft 4in tall and weighing more than 20 stone, easily dominated his fellow Ugandan Army staff officers.

His British commanding officer before independence had enthusiastically earmarked Amin as 'a tremendous chap to have around'. Although he was tough and swaggering, he was slow-witted and had never shown even the slightest tendency to try to grasp the complexities of politics.

Amin responded swiftly and energetically to the task the Prime Minister had given him. Using a 122mm gun mounted on his personal Jeep, he blew gaping holes in King Freddy's Palace. The Bugandan leader, warned of the danger just before the attack, fled into hiding and eventually made his way to Britain, where he died in lonely exile.

For the next four years, Idi Amin was the Prime Minister's trusted strong-arm man. Milton Obote was calm and relaxed when he flew off to Singapore in January 1971 to attend a Commonwealth Conference. He was about to fly home to Uganda when he heard the news on the radio . . . Idi Amin had just mobilized the army and declared himself the country's new ruler.

The overgrown village bully turned military chief had decided that if he was to to do the dirty work in Uganda he might just as well install himself as its supreme authority.

Milton Obote went into exile, having learned an embarrassing political lesson. For the people of Uganda, cautiously celebrating his overthrow, the experience was to be painful to the point of torture and death.

Amin's first move was to pacify tribal enemies and buy valuable breathing space. He persuaded Buganda leaders that he himself had actually tipped off King Freddy and given him time to flee to safety. He arranged for the release of many political prisoners detained by Obote and had the body of the dead tribal King flown back from Britain for a ceremonial burial.

Amin was deeply affected by the ritual outpouring and lavish expense of the Buganda tribesmen at the burial ceremony. The experience was to be put to hideous use later.

Amin them moved against the most potent potential threat to his new power – the officers of the Ugandan army.

He announced a new programme of army restructuring and began by ordering 36 senior officers, Langi and Acholi tribesmen, to report to Makindye Prison for training in internal security. Disgruntled, but seduced by the thought of forming part of a government of military men instead of politicians, the officers arrived at Makindye. They were locked in cells and bayonetted to death.

The former army chief-of-staff, Brigadier Suleiman Hussein, was arrested and taken to yet another prison where he was beaten to death with rifle butts. His head was severed and taken to Amin's new palatial home in Kampala where the President reserved it in the freezer compartment of his refrigerator.

In two widely separated army barracks, at Mbarara and Jinja, the elite of the officer corps were lined up on the parade ground to take a salute from an armoured column. The tanks swept across the square, swung into line-abreast formation and crushed most of the officers to death. Those left alive were used for target practice by riflemen. At another barracks, the remaining staff officers were herded into a briefing room for a lecture by Amin. As they saw his gleaming black Mercedes sweep into the square, the doors of the room were locked from the outside and grenades were lobbed through the windows.

Within five months Amin had killed most of the trained professional officers in his army. Yet the news was kept secret from the Ugandan people, who were simply told that a few disloyal officers had been courtmartialled and executed. To make up the gaps in the ranks, Amin promoted fellow Kakwa tribesmen. Cooks and drivers, mess orderlies and wireless operators became majors and colonels overnight.

But the word of the massacres had filtered out to two inquiring Americans. Nicholas Stroh, son of a wealthy Detroit brewer and a former writer for the *Philadelphia Bulletin* newspaper, was working as a freelance journalist in Africa. He joined forces with another American, Robert Siedle, a sociologist at Makere University in Kampala, to start asking questions about the army massacres.

At Mbarara barracks they were granted an interview with the new commander, Major Juma Aiga, a former taxi driver who had won an instant army commission. When their persistent questioning became too much, Major Aiga telephoned President Amin. His reply was terse: 'Kill them'.

Both men were gunned down on the spot and a few days later Aiga was openly driving around Kampala in Stoh's Volkswagen car. When the American embassy demanded an investigation into the disappearance of the two men, they got nowhere.

As Amin went off on his first foreign trip as a head of government, he had already broken the backbone of the Ugandan army. He was all-powerful, but he returned from his journeys to Israel and Britain empty-handed. His outright demands to both countries for millions of pounds in cash donations were refused. And the word went round the tight community of international diplomacy that the new President was not just a stupid, arrogant man. He was mad and dangerous.

Within a year Uganda was bankrupt. Amin's reaction was to order the Bank of Uganda to print millions of worthless banknotes to pump into the economy. All that remained of the reserves of the US dollars and sterling was made available for his personal use.

In Kampala the price of a bar of soap rose to £6, two weeks' wages for the average worker on the coffee plantations which were among the country's few sources of income.

Temporary salvation was offered by one other extravagant dictator, Libya's Colonel Gaddafi. The price was one Amin was only too happy to pay for their newly formed alliance. As Libyan money poured into Kampala to keep the country barely afloat, Amin kept his side of the bargain. He ranted and raved against the State of Israel and kicked out the small group of skilled Israeli engineers employed on the construction projects which formed Israel's limited aid to Uganda.

Angered and hurt, the Israelis pulled out with their bulldozers and a meticulous mass of paperwork and blueprints. The documents included one slim volume which was later to help make history – the plans of Israel's last gift to Uganda, the new passenger terminal, control tower and runway layout of Entebbe Airport.

Amin, anxious to prove to Gaddafi that he was a worthy protégé, opened an office in Kampala for the

Palestine Liberation Organization with full diplomatic status. He capped it by pronouncing his admiration for his political hero, Adolf Hitler. As Amin drew up plans for a memorial to Hitler in the centre of Kampala, the world began to realize that some awful disaster was beginning to unfold.

They didn't have long to wait.

The Libyan money was barely propping up Uganda, and now Amin had hundreds of his chosen henchmen on the payroll of his new police force, the State Research Bureau. He bought their loyalty with lavish gifts of money and expensive cars, luxuries like videotape recorders and whisky and clothes imported from London and Paris.

One hot August night in 1972, dinner guests at Amin's palace, State House in Entebbe, were shocked and revolted when he left the table and returned from the kitchen with the frost-encrusted head of Brigadier Hussein from the freezer. In a ranting fit of rage, Amin screamed abuse at the severed head, heaving cutlery at it, and then ordered his guests to leave.

Two nights later he turned up unexpectedly in eastern Uganda and announced that God had appeared to him and told him that Uganda's population of 50,000 Asians, mainly tradesman and merchants, doctors and nurses, were causing all Uganda's economic problems. He ordered them to leave the country within 90 days.

For the next three months Amin's voice could be heard on Uganda radio, making a daily countdown to his deadline. Although most of the Asians had lived in Uganda for generations, forming the backbone of the nation's commerce, they fled in terror, leaving behind their homes, offices, shops and plantations.

In November that year, Amin gave away the choice businesses to his friends and cronies. Pharmacies and surgeries were handed over to motor mechanics from the State Research Bureau, textile warehouses were given to

Research Bureau telephone operators and army corporals. Within weeks the shops were deserted, their stocks sold and the shelves never filled again . . . and the men of the State Research Bureau wanted to be paid again.

With no money or property left to meet their demands, Amin gave them the only asset he had left, the lives of his fellow Ugandans.

It was the most bestial mass-murder contract in history. Amin gave his bureau torturers the licence to kill for profit.

He knew the tradition of Ugandans, their deep reverence for the last remains of dead relatives and how they will spend every last Ugandan shilling of their money and part with anything of value to recover the body of a loved one for burial. In many of the tribes 'body finders' will earn rewards by tracking through the bush to find some father or son who had died in some remote cattle grazing area or drowned in the fast-flowing waters of the Nile.

The State Research Bureau became the killers – and the body finders.

Cruising through the streets of Kampala in their imported cars, wearing their 'uniform' of gaudy silk shirts and bell-bottom trousers, they openly arrested ordinary townspeople. And at their headquarters, only a few hundred yards from Amin's palatial home, they ruthlessly butchered their victims.

As the corpses piled up in the basement cells of the three-storey building, other Research Bureau jailers were despatched to tell grieving families that their loved ones had disappeared after being arrested and were feared dead. For a body-finding fee of £150, or every last possession the family owned, the State Research murderers drove the widows and weeping sons and daughters to a lush forest on the outskirts of Kampala.

Almost every gulley and bush concealed a dead body. On many nights, as many as 100 families made the grisly trip. The bodies not reclaimed were thrown into Lake Victoria, useless assets written off as a 'business' loss until they floated through the sluiced gates of the Owens Falls Dam and the hydro-electric generators.

But the executions by firing squads at the Research Bureau became a problem. The neighbouring French Embassy staff complained directly to Amin about the constant gunfire throughout the night. Amin, sinking deeper and deeper into depravity, discussed a solution with the head of the Bureau, Lieutenant Isaac Malyamungu.

Malyamungu, a gatekeeper at a textile factory before Amin made him a government official, was a notoriously sadistic killer. Before executing the mayor of the provincial town of Masaka, he had paraded the badly mutilated man through the streets carrying his own amputated genitals in his hands. Now he and Amin calmly came up with the answer to the problem of maintaining the horrendous flow of lucrative killings without the disturbing, continuous rattle of gunfire. The murder victim would be kept alone in the basement, while another prisoner was offered the promise of reprieve if he would batter the solitary man to death with a 16lb sledgehammer.

Terrified and pleading for their lives, few prisoners were brave enough to refuse the offer. But, once they had carried out their sickening task, the roles were changed. The unwilling executioner, usually sobbing and demented, would be left alone. He would become the solitary man, while in the cell next door another Ugandan was being given the sledgehammer and the heartless promise of life if he would repeat the procedure.

Even as the death toll rose, Amin still found time to indulge in personal episodes of unbelievable horror.

In March 1974 he went through a simple Moslem ritual to divorce three of his four wives. He accused them of meddling in his affairs and ordered them out of his home.

Three months later one of the young ex-wives, Kay Amin, died in an apartment in Kampala as the result of a clumsy abortion attempt. She had been four months pregnant. Amin, in a state of fury, rushed to the mortuary to see her body. A few minutes later, quiet and unemotional, he gave a series of orders to the hospital surgeons and then left.

Two hours later he returned and satisfied himself that his orders had been carried out. Then he strode into the hospital morgue with his most junior wife, Sarah, and six-year-old Aliga Amin, the young son of Kay.

'Pay close attention to what you see,' he roared at them. 'Kay was a wicked woman, now look at what has become of her.'

Kay Amin's mutilated torso lay on the operating table. Her head and all her limbs had been amputated. Now her head had been reversed and sewn back on face down on her torso. Her legs had been neatly sutured onto her shoulders and her arms attached firmly to her bloodstained pelvis.

The swaggering arrogance of Idi Amin came to an end on 4 July 1976, although his brutality was to continue for almost another three years.

On 28 June an Air France airliner hijacked by a team of Palestinians arrived at Entebbe Airport. The plane had been en route from Tel Aviv to Paris when it had been commandeered shortly after a stop-over in Athens. It carried some 300 passengers.

In the heart of an African country governed by a Hitler-worshipper, their hostages far from any hope of rescue, the Palestinians confidently drew up their demands while Amin looked on, basking in the world limelight.

Amin helped to draft the blackmail demand that all the passengers would be killed in 48 hours if 53 Palestinian prisoners in jail in Israel and Europe were not released. As international tension mounted, the deadline was extended until the early hours of 4 July, and passengers who were not Jewish were allowed to go.

Two days before the deadline, as the terrified hostages were huddled in the passenger terminal, one elderly Londoner, Dora Bloch, who held dual British-Israeli nationality, choked on a piece of food and was driven 20 miles from the airport to hospital in Kampala.

But, as Idi Amin was being seen worldwide on television badgering the hostages in the passenger lounge, the Israeli engineers in Tel Aviv unlocked a filing cabinet and began to pore over the vital blueprints of the airport they had helped to build.

Up and down the east coast of Africa an incredible international humanitarian conspiracy began to take shape. Shortly after midnight on 3 July, a task force of Israeli Air Force planes filled with commandoes came swooping over Lake Victoria. In silent co-operation they had been allowed to refuel and fly through the radar screens of Kenya, Uganda's neighbour.

The Israeli planes, guided by their own blueprints, landed swiftly and taxied to the precise spot in the terminal buildings where the hostages were being held. In less than an hour they took off again with the rescued hostages, leaving 20 of Idi Amin's troops dead and the seven hijackers killed on the spot. They also took with them the bodies of two of their own men caught in the crossfire.

But elderly Dora Bloch remained behind in hospital in Kampala, frail and barely able to breathe. Amin decided to vent his fury on her.

Sixteen hours after the Entebbe rescue mission, British High Commissioner Peter Chandley was allowed to visit Mrs Bloch. He tried to reassure the frightened woman and left the hospital briefly to prepare some food for her.

Shortly after he left, two State Research Bureau officials crashed through the doors of the hospital ward. They pistol-whipped the frail widow and dragged her down three flights of steps. Half an hour later they dumped her bullet-riddled body in a field on the outskirts of Kampala.

When the High Commissioner returned to the hospital, Amin simply announced that Mrs Bloch had gone the day before, returned to the airport under escort before the Entebbe Raid.

Idi Amin's last desperate mad gamble to hold the reins of power collapsed in April 1979. To scare the Ugandan people into submission, he claimed that the country was threatened by a bloody invasion from its southern neighbour, Tanzania.

To give substance to his fantasies, he ordered small contingents of his troops across the Tanzanian border on raids against the 'invaders'. Such provocation was too much for Tanzanian President Julius Nyrere. His soldiers repelled the attacks and then drove deep into Uganda. They were welcomed with open arms by the long-suffering Ugandans as they advanced swiftly towards Kampala.

In one final broadcast, Idi Amin urged his troops to join him in a last stand at the town of Jinja, near the Owens Falls Dam. The soldiers didn't turn up. But then neither did Idi Amin. He had fled in his personal aircraft to the safety of Libya to seek sanctuary with his ally Colonel Gaddafi.

Five years after his overthrow, Idi Amin was still safely living in luxury in a private suite of a hotel in Saudi Arabia, the guest of the Moslem royal rulers of that country.

He would still rant about his return to Uganda and his self-appointed role in international politics. But this time no one was listening.

Prime Minister Milton Obote was back in power in Kampala. The country still suffered the ravages of the long years of Amin's tyranny. But the power supply flowed smoothly from the Owens Falls Dam hydro-electric generators, and the crocodiles in Lake Victoria had only the birds' nests in the swamps to prey on for a decent meal.

Pol Pot

He has a broad, chubby face with sparkling, grandfatherly eyes and thick lips which split into a toothy, genial grin. He looks slightly comical, an impression not dispelled by his peculiar name, Pol Pot. But there is nothing funny about Pol Pot . . . he is a tyrannical fanatic responsible for the coldly calculated extermination of three million people.

Pol Pot spent just four years on the world stage, as the shadowy leader of Kampuchea (formerly Cambodia) after the overthrow of President Lon Nol in 1975. Yet in that short period he virtually destroyed a nation – all for the sake of an unworkable creed that he imposed unyieldingly on a starving and terrorized population. Under his rule, a once-beautiful country became known as 'The Land of the Walking Dead'.

Little is known of Pol Pot's background, and what is known could easily have been the invention of his propaganda machine. It is said that he was brought up in a peasant community in Cambodia's Kampong Thom province and was educated at a Buddhist temple where, for two years, he was a monk. In the 1950s he won a scholarship to study electronics in Paris where, like so many other students at the time, he found it fashionable to espouse left-wing causes.

Also in Paris in the 1950s was another left-wing Cambodian student, Khieu Samphan, who used his political science courses to formulate an extraordinary philosophy of rural revolution. His theory was that, to rid itself of the vestiges of colonial rule and to avoid capitalist exploitation, Cambodia must regress to a peasant economy – without towns, without industry, without currency, without education.

It is unlikely that Pol Pot and Khieu Samphan ever met

in Paris. But back among the Khmer people of Cambodia, they teamed up and set about making Khieu's crackpot creed come true, using as their instrument the newly formed and Chinese-backed Communist Party of Kampuchea.

After a decade of political intrigue and rural guerrilla warfare, in 1975 the communists finally overthrew President Lon Nol and became masters of the capital, Phnom Penh. By now the party was known as the Khmer Rouge. Khieu Samphan became its figurehead. But the real power lay in the hands of the former peasant from the provinces, Prime Minister Pol Pot. And he immediately turned political daydreams into horrific, brutal, uncompromising reality.

The capital was emptied. As many as three million of its citizens were stripped of all they possessed and were ordered out of their homes. Irrespective of whether they were old, sick, pregnant, crippled, newly born or dying, they were marched into the countryside and herded into vast communes of as many as 10,000. No town was left inhabited. Even villages were emptied of their people. Everybody had to work in the fields.

Of course, not everyone could. The aged and the ill died of exhaustion. The young died of starvation. And the crippled and the lame were clubbed to death.

Living in malaria-ridden swamps, with no proper shelter or sanitation, the new 'peasants' were frogmarched into the paddy fields to work a minimum of 11 hours a day. They were fed a daily bowl of gruel and a morsel of dried fish. They worked nine days on and one day off . . . but that tenth day of rest was taken up with political indoctrination. Children began their working lives at the age of seven.

Not only did the Khmer Rouge abolish towns and communities, they also abolished families, splitting up husbands and wives and placing them in different co-operatives. They also abolished personal property, apart from the one sleeping mat and one pair of black overalls handed out no more than once a year. Since there was no property and no trade, there was no need for money, so they abolished that too.

Because there was no education apart from political indoctrination, Pol Pot abolished schools and colleges. All books were burned. With education thereby shown to be non-essential, he abolished the educated classes – and had them murdered by the tens of thousands. Also eliminated, by the bayonet or pickaxe, were priests, political reactionaries, prison inmates and the defeated soldiers of ex-President Lon Nol.

Anyone who complained, or even questioned the system, would be instantly executed by clubbing. Special offenders, like those starving peasants found cannibalizing dead bodies, would be buried up to their heads in the ground and left to die. Their heads would then be cut off and stuck on stakes as a warning to others.

The extermination continued for four years, with no hope of help from the outside world. Refugees reaching neighbouring countries told stories of horrors that were unbelievable. Yet, with no diplomatic ties, no travel, not even a postal service, the renamed nation of Kampuchea was an impenetrable armed camp seemingly set on the genocide of its own people.

The world's repugnance was unheeded; protest appeared futile. In March 1978, Britain reported Kampuchea to the United Nations Commission On Human Rights. The Khmer Rouge's embassy in Peking issued a hysterical response, saying: 'The British Imperialists have no right to speak of the rights of man. The world knows well their barbarous and abject nature. Britain's leaders are living in opulence on top of a pile of rotting corpses while the proletariat have only the right to be unemployed, to steal and to become prostitutes.' There was little chance of a reasoned debate . . . and indeed Pol Pot's ministers sent their regrets that they could find no one with the time to spare to attend the United Nations human rights hearings.

Predictably, it was military might, not moral right, that brought the overthrow of Pol Pot and his murderous henchmen. Vietnam signed a pact with Kampuchea's only ally, China, and in 1978 Vietnamese forces which had been skirmishing with the Khmer Rouge for years launched a full-scale invasion. The Chinese did not step in to aid Pol Pot, and in January 1979 his regime fell to the invading Vietnamese. So swift was his overthrow that the chubby little despot had to flee for Phnom Penh in a white Mercedes limousine only two hours before the first of Hanoi's troops arrived.

Pol Pot fought on from his power base among his dedicated followers in the countryside. He formed the Khmer People's National Liberation Front and announced a hypocritical manifesto promising political and religious freedom. Khieu Samphan remained titular head of the Khmer Rouge. In a rare interview with foreign journalists in 1980, he said the mistakes made by his regime were mainly in implementation of policy. For instance, he said, over-zealous commune leaders had often forgotten to give workers their one day off in ten. As for the massacres, he said: 'To talk about systematic murder is odious. If we had really killed at that rate, we would have no one to fight the Vietnamese.'

No one will ever know the truth about how many Khmers died of disease, starvation, neglect, brutalization, murder or massacre. But, in June 1979, Foreign Minister Ieng Sary admitted to three million deaths since the Khmer Rouge came to power. As there were only eight million Khmers in the pre-revolutionary census, it was pointed out by journalists that this did not seem a good record for a four-year-old government. The Minister was apologetic. He had an explanation. The orders from Pol Pot had been 'misunderstood.' The massacres had, he said, been 'a mistake'.

'Emperor' Bokassa

For a brief period just before the 'coronation' of self-styled Emperor Jean Bedel Bokassa it seemed as if some glimmer of humanity might be creeping into his tyrannical madness. Important diplomats and influential international businessmen from many parts of the world were preparing to attend his spectacular enthronement ceremony in Bangui, capital of the land-locked Central African Republic, the sprawling former French colony in the heart of the continent.

At the beginning of December 1977, as rehearsals began for the great event, Bokassa had locked himself away in his palace 50 miles outside the capital watching endless reruns of a film which had been specially flown to him from London. The film showed the majesty and splendour of the coronation of Britain's Queen Elizabeth. Bokassa, a violent, squat, ugly little man, seemed to be genuinely moved by the scenes of the splendid pageantry and the spontaneous, heart-felt joy and devotion of the Queen's loyal subjects.

His own coronation, he decided, would be a similarly historic occasion. Even if he couldn't hope to win the hearts of the people he ruled, at least his guests couldn't fail to be impressed. Apparently on a whim, he ordered the governor of Bangui Prison to select a dozen prisoners for more humane treatment. They were to be moved to less cramped cells, given better food than the other inmates and allowed some fresh air in the prison yard. Some prison guards even talked excitedly of a partial amnesty to celebrate the coronation. The prisoners,

Bokassa promised, wouldn't be in jail much longer.

Then Bokassa busied himself again supervising the last-minute preparations for the ceremony. The Government of France, headed by his frequent holiday guest, President Valéry Giscard d'Estaing, had generously provided him with credit of £1 million to buy a fleet of Mercedes limousines for his guests and to equip their ceremonial escort with 200 new BMW motorcycles.

It mattered little to the 58-year-old dictator that his country ranked as one of the poorest in the world, with barely 10 per cent of the two million population able to read and write and more than a quarter of their children dying of disease and malnutrition before they reached their first birthday.

He planned to spend £10 million in a 48-hour spectacular binge, a regal extravaganza to rival the coronation of his 'hero', the Emperor Napoleon. President Bokassa himself would assume the title Emperor Bokassa and his bankrupt country would be grandly renamed The Central African Empire.

Many political leaders had no stomach for his lunacy and returned their gold-lettered invitation cards with scant apologies for their absence. Even the formally polite British Foreign Office were blunt and rude when they refused to attend. American President Jimmy Carter, outraged by Bokassa's insane claim to Napoleonic grandeur, promptly responded by cutting off all aid to the country.

Bokassa was unrepentant. His rag-tag army formed most of the unenthusiastic onlookers at the triumphal parade through Bangui where the new Emperor would ride in a gilded carriage drawn by eight white horses along the city's only two miles of paved road.

The coronation went ahead with all the panoply of crowns and ermine robes in the sweltering African heat, and the guests were treated to a mouth-watering imperial banquet in Bokassa's palace at Berengo.

Protected by screens of bullet-proof glass in a land-scaped garden amid fountains and ornate ivory carvings, they were pampered by uniformed servants who brought them elaborately cooked dishes specially imported from the workshops of the master designer, Berardaud of Limoges.

Some of the French and African diplomats, and the Italian and German businessmen, seemed ill at ease in the absurd splendour of their bizarre surroundings. They would have felt distinctly more queasy if they had realized the origins of some of the tastiest morsels served up to them on the Limoges porcelain.

Bokassa had kept his promise to the prison governor. The inmates who had been given food, fresh air and exercise had found their new privileges short-lived. As soon as they had been restored to near normal health, they had been killed, expertly butchered and served up to the unsuspecting guests at Bokassa's celebration feast.

His obsession with the trappings of the power and grace of the age of Napoleon were flattering to many of his French VIP visitors. At least most of them found his mania for all things French to be understandable. His character had been moulded by his long years as a soldier in the French colonial army, where all new recruits were thoroughly indoctrinated in the glories of French history and the awesome achievements of its finest soldier, Napoleon Bonaparte.

In 1960, when the French gave independence to the Republic, an area almost as large as France itself, most of them were glad to be rid of the task of governing its vast, arid waste. There was some embarrassed amusement in 1966 when Colonel Bokassa seized power in a coup from the Republic's civilian government and began to boast of his devotion to France. He swore undying loyalty to French President Charles de Gaulle, whom he lovingly called 'Papa'. The French Government responded with generous aid in return for some minor business concessions and a military foothold in a strategic part of Africa.

In 1975, the new French President Valéry Giscard d'Estaing took advantage of Bokassa's welcome to make several big-game hunting trips to his private game reserve, an area covering most of the eastern half of the country.

There were reports that Bokassa was never slow to shower his visitors with lavish gifts, including fistfuls of diamonds, one of his country's few precious resources, which should have gone to help alleviate the crushing poverty of its people.

By the time Bokassa was in the full grip of his 'imperial' mania, the soaring price of oil had made the country's only other asset, uranium deposits, look like a promising commercial prospect for French developers. Wary of growing evidence of Bokassa's brutality, the French uneasily indulged his regal fantasies while keeping a discreet eye on his appetite for power and showmanship. Within two years of his ludicrous coronation, he had become more than a posturing embarrassment to Paris. He was a bloodthirsty, dangerous liability.

Apparently determined to transform his dusty capital city into a model of French 'provincial' fashion, Bokassa ordered the barefoot schoolchildren of Bangui's only high school to buy expensively tailored school uniforms to be worn at all lessons. Their parents could hardly afford to buy the textbooks their children needed if they were to have even a basic education. And it hadn't passed unnoticed that the Emperor owned the only clothing factory which produced the school uniforms. It was yet another impossible order from the Emperor which they couldn't obey even if they wanted to. No one foresaw the consequences.

President Bokassa, who had seen his demands for national opera, ballet and art societies dismissed by his wary people, had at one time seemingly grown accustomed to being ignored. But *Emperor* Bokassa, the Napoleon-worshipper, expected every order to be carried out without question.

Two hundred ragged schoolchildren were rounded up by the 'Imperial Guard'. Bokassa gathered them in the yard of Bangui Prison, swaggering among them with his gold-topped cane, bullying the overawed, frightened pupils. 'You will not need school uniforms as long as you stay in prison,' the Emperor screamed at them. Under the threatening guns of the guards, the children were herded into the already overcrowded cells.

Over the next few weeks the killings began. One by one the children were led from the cells for 'school uniform inspection' . . . and mercilessly beaten to death.

News of the mass murders finally reached the disbelieving ears of the officials of the French Embassy in Bangui. At first they couldn't bring themselves to accept the evidence. But witness after witness from the prison repeated the same story. And Paris finally woke up to the fact that Jean Bedel Bokassa was more than a comic-opera Emperor with his crown and robes and sceptre. He was a monster.

For the honour of France, for the sake of common decency, the Emperor had to go.

The opportunity came a month later when the demented Emperor left Bangui for a visit to another dictator Colonel Gaddafi of Libya. As Bokassa stepped off his plane in Tripoli, he learned a lesson in the true French art of power politics and military muscle which would have delighted his long-dead hero Napoleon.

At his home in Paris where he had lived since being ousted by Bokassa, African politician David Dacko was roughly shaken awake by French Secret Service agents and given a prepared speech to rehearse and memorize before being bundled into a waiting car. Ten hours later he stumbled from a French military jet at Bangui and asked the French Foreign Legion troops who had landed immediately after him to help him to a 'spontaneous' humanitarian overthrow of the evil Bokassa.

Within 24 hours the 'Empire' was effectively back under French control. The deposed Emperor went into exile from Libya to the Ivory Coast in West Africa and then to a run-down château in an unfashionable Paris suburb.

The hardened Legionnaires who searched the grounds of the prison had the grim task of uncovering the mass grave which held the bodies of the dead schoolchildren.

Later, when they stormed the Emperor's Napoleonic palace, they found the bones of another 37 children lying on the tiled floor of the Olympic-standard swimming pool. Lounging at the poolside were the predators who had enjoyed the grisly feast, Bokassa's four pet crocodiles. And, in the cold storage rooms of the palace kitchens, they found the half-eaten remains of another dozen unnamed victims who had been served up at the Emperor's dining table only the week before.

As the uniform-obsessed Emperor began a new career in exile as a supplier of khaki suits to African tourist boutiques, President Giscard d'Estaing announced in Paris that he had sent a personal cheque for £10,000, the value of the diamonds given to him as gifts, to a charity school for children in Bangui.

Papa Doc

Many tyrants have held power over nations by preying on simple human emotions, such as fear of invasion by hostile neighbours or nationalistic pride in conquest over weaker countries. Others have kept themselves in government by rigged elections or by armed suppression of their own downtrodden populations.

But only one modern dictator has ever managed to keep his people enslaved through a grisly combination of machine-gun and mysticism – the force of a vicious police state and an unholy alliance with the Devil and his legions of demons, ghosts, vampires and zombies.

In the era that saw astronauts land on the moon and orbiting laboratories in space, President 'Papa Doc' Duvalier still ruled the republic of Haiti by bullets and black magic, by real live bogeymen who carried very real automatic pistols and by a supernatural 'police force' of living skeletons raised from the dead. Millions of Haitians who suffered the terrors of his 15 years of brutal dictatorship are convinced that he still reigns beyond the grave, controlling his country's destiny from within the gates of hell.

The bitter irony of the plight of the 5 million inhabitants of Haiti is that their struggling nation was once hailed as the most progressive in the Caribbean, a proud democracy which showed the way for other countries to free themselves from exploiters and foreign rule.

Haiti shares the island of Hispaniola with the Dominican Republic, and its lush and rolling sub-tropical forests were one of the wondrous sights of the New World for explorer Christopher Columbus when his ship foundered and was wrecked there in December 1492. It was an inauspicious start for a new nation. And over the centuries the people of that island have paid a terrible price for its accidental introduction to the adventurers from the Old World.

By the end of the 16th century most of the original population of Arawak Indians had been wiped out. Many fell victim to newly introduced European diseases. The survivors were literally worked to death on the plantations of their new Spanish masters. When the Spaniards moved on, there was little left to plunder for the next occupants, the rapacious pirates who used Hispaniola as their base for marauding, murder and looting. The buccaneers who controlled the whole western part of the island renamed their territory using its original Indian name – Haiti.

They were soon ousted by a new set of colonial rulers, the French, who revived the plantation system and peopled Haiti with black slaves captured on the west coast of Africa and packed into stinking hulks for the voyage to their new 'home'. The wretched slaves brought with them only two possessions – hatred of their new oppressors and their age-old belief in African witchcraft and demons. The first of these was to lead to uprisings so passionate and violent that even the all-conquering Emperor Napoleon eventually had to concede defeat in 1804; and Haiti, with its short history of bloodshed and superstition, became the first independent black-governed republic in the world.

Over the years this unhappy land lurched from one incompetent or greedy regime to another. From 1915 to 1934 it was occupied by US Marines. There followed a string of provincial presidents, mostly mulatto descendants of mixed French-negro marriages, each being toppled in the midst of scandal and crisis which only made the already poverty-stricken population more miserable.

But in 1957 a popular new president emerged: François Duvalier, known to his friends and foes alike as 'Papa Doc'. Duvalier was a trained doctor, working on a US medical aid scheme before he turned to politics. Since they provided almost the only source of income for Haiti, the Americans were pleased to see a a modern man of medicine as the new ruler. But the black peasants who formed 95 per cent of the population welcomed him for a totally different reason.

To them, Duvalier was not so much a doctor as a medicine man and a pure descendant of African slaves. They were enthralled by his open boast that he was a skilled witch doctor with experience in the dark practices of their voodoo religion, a mixture of French-inspired Christianity and ancient African superstitions. Papa Doc promised that through witchcraft and black-magic ritual he would summon the Devil himself to share his power with all the voodoo worshippers of Haiti. On a more practical note, to placate the more educated political opposition, he vowed that the millions of dollars in American aid would be used to raise living standards. At that time, only 10 per cent of the population were literate, the national income averaged £1 per week, and most Haitians died of malnutrition and disease by the age of 35.

Within a few years of gaining control, Papa Doc made it plain he would share his power with no one. Most of the finance from the United States was funnelled into his own private bank accounts while he lived in seclusion in his palatial presidential mansion. In 1961 he declared himself President for life and ordered the ill-disciplined Haitian Army to murder scores of political opponents. Their bodies were strung up on lamp-posts around the capital, Port-au-Prince, with bloody voodoo symbols engraved on their corpses.

They had been killed, Papa Doc warned, by the forces of 'Baron Samedi', the avenging zombie of witchcraft. Baron Samedi, a hellish figure dressed in a black hat and a suit of mourning, was a voodoo demon, a soul raised from the dead to prowl the earth and carry out the wishes of the Devil.

To ensure that his own army was in fear of him, Duvalier raised a secret police force, the Ton Ton Macoute – voodoo bogeymen who swore allegiance to him as the supreme witch doctor. The 10,000 members of the Ton Ton were given the task of killing hundreds of army officers who were threatening rebellion against the bloodthirsty tyrant. In return they were given free reign to terrorize the countryside, looting and stealing from the starving peasants, carrying out murders which were always staged to bear the hallmarks of terrifying religious ritual.

The savagery of Papa Doc and his declaration of the grotesque cult of voodoo as Haiti's official national religion looked certain to prove his downfall. In the United States, recently elected President John F. Kennedy reacted with fury and indignation. Reflecting the civilized world's revulsion with Papa Doc's depravity, Kennedy announced that American aid to Haiti would cease as long as the Devil-worshipper was in power. It was thought to be only a matter of time before the pangs of hunger of the Haitians overcame the fear of demons and zombies. As the rumblings of discontent grew, even the gunmen of the Ton Ton Macoute were hard pressed to silence the increasing number of voices raised in anger against Duvalier.

For Papa Doc there was only one source of help to which he could turn. With power slowly beginning to slip from his grasp, he announced that he had performed a nightmarish voodoo ceremony to raise the Devil from hell to put a curse on the American President. Six weeks later, John F. Kennedy died as a result of an assassin's bullets in Dallas.

In Haiti the news was greeted with stunned despair. Nothing could shake the belief of terrified Haitians that the trigger of the assassin's gun had been pulled by the bony finger of the grinning zombie, Baron Samedi. Now Duvalier found new ways to bleed his people dry –

literally. Still grasping for American dollars, he used the Ton Ton Macoute to round up thousands of Haitians daily and march them to medical centres in the capital, Port-au-Prince. There, each was given a week's wages of £1 in exchange for a litre of blood. The blood was flown to America and sold for transfusion at £12 a litre.

Papa Doc continued to rule supreme in Haiti. Any challenge to his power was met swiftly by the murder squads of the Ton Ton Macoute. In 1971, dying of diabetes and heart disease, he altered the constitution of Haiti to allow his podgy playboy son Jean-Claude, known as Baby Doc, to assume the mantle of power . . . Papa Doc had been President for life. Now he was trying to ensure that his devilish dynasty survived even after his death.

Joseph Stalin

Bolshevik bullets finally ended 400 years of repressive rule by Russia's Tsars. Nicholas II, gunned down with his haemophilic son Alexei in the cellar of a house in Ekaterinburg in July 1918, had fought to the last against what he called the 'senseless dream' of the people having a say in how their lives were governed. Bolstered in his belief in absolute autocracy by the sinister 'mad monk' Rasputin, he allowed ruthless henchmen to try to silence with savagery the growing clamour for basic human rights.

Chief of Police Vyacheslav von Plehve mounted pogroms in Kishiniov and Gomel to 'drown the revolution in Jewish blood'. Minister of the Interior Peter Stolypin executed so many people for political offences – 5,000 in less than two years – that the gallows were nicknamed Stolypin's Necktie. And on Bloody Sunday, 22 January 1905, when riflemen and Cossack horsemen killed 150 defenceless men, women and children and injured a thousand more by brutally attacking a peaceful protest march to the St Petersburg Winter Palace, the Tsar's only question was: 'Have they killed enough?'

But there was by then no way that the revolution could be prevented. All it needed was a catalyst . . . and that came with the carnage of World War I, in which Russia lost vast tracts of land and 4 million men.

By 1916 abysmal leadership and terrible suffering had sapped the army's strength. And a year later, when soldiers and sailors garrisoned near St Petersburg sided with the strikers protesting at food shortages, inflation and corruption, the Tsar was forced to abdicate. The dreaded Ochrana, the secret police who maintained his reign of terror, were disbanded. Land confiscated from the rich was given to the peasants. Workers were promised an eight-hour day. Genuinely free elections were called. To the suddenly unsuppressed masses, Utopia seemed theirs.

But the revolutionaries had inherited a bitter legacy. In maintaining power at all costs, the Tsars had neglected the nation's interests. Revolutionaries like Lenin, returning from exile, knew from first-hand experience in Europe how backward the country was. 'Our task,' Lenin told his Politburo colleagues, 'is to take the lead of the exhausted masses who are wearily seeking a way out and lead them along the true path, along the path of labour discipline . . .'

But Lenin died in 1924, having taken only a few steps along that path. And his successor was to turn the democratic dream into a blood-soaked nightmare of tyranny on a scale that even the most sadistic Tsars never contemplated. In just 30 years of power, Stalin killed more people than the Tsars had accounted for in four centuries. He turned a popular revolution based on ideals of freedom and equality into a totalitarian dictatorship maintained solely by terror. Although in the process he turned the Soviet Union into one of the world's two great super-powers, and extended its empire far beyond the boundaries established by the Tsars, even the communists who succeeded him denounced his monstrous excesses.

The dying Lenin had warned the communist Central Committee against Stalin, the shoemaker's son who had robbed banks in his native Georgia to raise funds for the Bolshevik cause, and rose to become party General Secretary in 1922. Lenin urged his colleagues to find someone 'more tolerant, more loyal, more polite, more considerate, less capricious,' and added: 'Comrade Stalin has concentrated boundless authority in his hands and I am not sure whether he will always be capable of using that authority with sufficient caution . . .'. The party hierarchy did what they could, appointing Comrades Zinoviev and Kamenev to share leadership with Stalin. But already he was too powerful to be shackled. Adroit manoeuvring of the Politburo power blocs enabled him to demote, expel, even exile all potential rivals. By 1928 he was undisputed master of Moscow. Nikolai Bukhanin, one of Lenin's closest aides, confided to a friend when he was ousted: 'Stalin is a Genghis Khan who will kill us all.' It was a chillingly accurate prediction.

Stalin decided to accelerate Russian development. Huge new coal, iron and steel complexes were built all over Russia at a tremendous cost in human life. One of the American engineers called in as a consultant said: 'I would wager that Russia's battle of ferrous metallurgy alone involved more casualties than the Battle of the Marne.'

The programme was partly financed by swingeing taxes on richer peasants, the kulaks, who had been allowed by Lenin to sell surplus food to ease shortages. Dogmatic Stalin allowed no such 'deviations'. Soon the kulaks lost not only the right to sell but also their land and their livestock. Stalin announced the elimination of the kulaks as a class. Millions were ordered to join vast state-run collective farms. Millions more were herded to towns to become forced labour in the new state-owned factories.

Others disappeared into the growing network of 'corrective labour camps', the harsh 'Gulags' much later exposed by writer Alexander Solzhenitsyn. More than 25 million were forcibly evicted. More than three million were killed.

Stalin – the revolutionary name meant 'Man of Steel' – imposed his Marxist will on all walks of life. The party and government bureaucracies were purged of 'unreliable' workers – 164,000 Moscow civil servants were kicked out in 18 months. Church publications were suppressed, church buildings confiscated and the leaders exiled or jailed. Local nationalism in satellite states was dismissed as another 'deviation' and ruthlessly eradicated. Writers were subjected to intense censorship to ensure they wrote only work to inspire the proletariat. 'Where else do they kill people for writing poetry?' one artist asked plaintively. The grip of the secret police, the OGPU, tightened over everyone. Internal passports were reintroduced to make keeping track of people easier. Often, alleged enemies of the state were quietly liquidated without troubling the courts. After all, the OGPU were working for a man who said: 'The death of a man is a tragedy; the death of a thousand is a statistic.'

Statistically the first five-year plan was a success. By 1935 industrial production was four times greater than in 1913. But progress had been bought at a staggering cost. Results of a census in 1937 were so appalling they were suppressed. Two years later experts estimated that Russia's population was an astounding 20 million short of what it should have been. Emigration and famine were factors, but Stalin's purges and the breakneck pace of industrialization accounted for many millions more. Historian E.H. Carr wrote: 'Seldom perhaps in history has so monstrous a price been paid for so monumental an achievement.'

In November 1932 Stalin's wife Nadezhda Alliluevna

committed suicide with a revolver. At one time she had helped Stalin, telling him secrets learned from her job as a confidential clerk in Lenin's private office. Now she was appalled at his increasingly brutal nature. He had become a foul-mouthed drunkard prone to violent rages, abusing underlings and indulging in debauched delights to test their loyalty. One one occasion he rolled five slim tubes of paper and stuck them on his secretary's fingers. Then he lit each like a candle and grinned as the man writhed in agony, not daring to remove them. Nadezhda's death removed one of the few remaining checks on Stalin's absolute authority. Their daughter Svêtlana said later: 'It deprived his soul of the last vestiges of human warmth.'

Then, in December 1934, a young communist shot dead party secretary Sergei Kirov in St Petersburg – which had been renamed Leningrad. Stalin instantly ordered the security services to speed up cases against people accused of executing or preparing to execute acts of terror. And he told courts to carry out death sentences immediately, since the government would no longer consider petitions for possible pardons. The ruling, as Nikita Khrushchev later said, was 'the basis for mass acts of abuse against socialist legality.'

Stalin now began moving against old revolutionary colleagues. Zinoviev, Kamenev, Bukhanin and OGPU chief Yahoda were just four of the prominent communists accused of conspiring against the state in a series of show trials which lasted from 1936 to 1938. Astonishingly, they all pleaded guilty, perhaps through loyalty to the revolution, but more probably because they had been broken by torture and warned that their families would suffer if they caused a stir. By 1939, of the 139-strong Central Committee, 98 had been shot, and every member of Lenin's Politburo except Stalin himself and Trotsky, exiled in 1929, had been condemned by the courts.

New massive purges began throughout society. The

Red Army leadership was more than halved. Naval top brass was devastated. The Communist Party rank and file was cleansed of intellectual idealists who put principles before the new politics of power, privilege and practicalities. Ruthless sycophants took their places, men with whom Stalin felt more secure. The secret police were shaken up and renamed the NKVD, under notorious Beria. Even secret agents abroad, including spies who recruited and controlled English traitors Philby, Blunt and Burgess, were summoned back to Moscow and eliminated. Stalin, who knew more than most about conspiracy, saw plots everywhere. Others had to die because they knew too much about his private misdeeds.

More than 500,000 people were summarily shot. Millions more were tortured and incarcerated. Even President Kalinin's wife spent seven years in a prison camp to guarantee her husband's behaviour.

The purges suddenly ceased in 1939. With the promise of a new, liberal constitution, people began to breathe more easily. But their relief was short-lived, for World War II was about to begin . . .

To the war-weary nations allied against the Nazis, Soviet Marshal Stalin was avuncular Uncle Joe, a hero helping America and Britain end the evil of Hitler. Winston Churchill posed for photographs with him at the Yalta summit, and told journalists Stalin's life was 'precious to the hopes and hearts of us all'. He added: 'I walk through this world with greater courage when I find myself in a relation of friendship and intimacy with this great man.' It was not a sentiment shared by many of the millions who entered the war under Stalin, or the peoples he subjected during the hostilities. For Stalin's smiles at Yalta concealed a cruel and calculating nature prepared to condone and commit war crimes at least as evil as those of the enemy, and an ambition which was already bent on betraying the leaders who sang his praises.

Stalin had already betrayed the Allies once when, in August 1939, he had signed a non-aggressive pact with Hitler. It was a cynical deal between a man who secretly planned to murder 30 million Slavs and a man who was already well on his way to doing so. Under its terms, the NKVD and the Gestapo compared notes on dissident refugees. Jewish prisoners in Soviet Gulags were swapped for concentration-camp inmates Stalin wanted to get his hands on. Germany was allowed to use Murmansk as a submarine base and Russia supplied the Nazis with vital war materials. Most importantly for Stalin, he was given a free hand in certain areas to extend his reign of terror.

The Red Army marched into the Balkan states, ostensibly to preserve their neutrality. When Finland refused to hand over strategically useful land and islands, Stalin invaded to force the transfer at gunpoint. But it was Poland, a traditional enemy of Russia for centuries, which was most callously abused. The two dictators had drawn a line down the middle of the independent state. When Hitler invaded from the west, forcing Britain and France to declare war, Stalin's troops went in from the east, taking cruel advantage of Polish preoccupation with the Nazi attack. More than a quarter of a million Polish officers and men were captured – and 14,000 were never seen alive again.

In all the captured countries, the sinister NKVD arrived soon after the army had established control. They eliminated political and cultural leaders who might stand in the way of Stalin's planned Russification of the different nationalities. Millions were transported to the remote wastelands of Russia. Others were simply shot. So were Russians returned from captivity by the Finns. Stalin had no time for Soviet soldiers who failed him.

The fate of some of the missing Poles was revealed in 1943. The bodies of 4,000 officers were unearthed in shallow graves beneath a grove of young conifers at

Katyn, near Smolensk. Most had their hands tied behind their backs and bullet wounds in the back of their necks. A few had smashed skulls. Some had straw sawdust stuffed in their mouths, to kill them while saving ammunition. What happened to the remaining 10,000 who vanished has never been conclusively established, but some experts suspect they were loaded on barges and drowned in the White Sea by the NKVD. The missing included 800 doctors and 12 university professors.

Stalin was able to indulge himself in such blood-letting against his own and other peoples because he trusted Hitler. But, by late 1940, the Führer was the master of mainland Europe, and able to prepare for the move he had planned all along: Operation Barbarossa, the invasion of Russia.

When Hitler's troops crossed the border at dawn on 22 June 1941, Stalin was stunned. For 11 days he did nothing as the Red Army, weakened by purges and assured by their leader that invasion was impossible, fell back in disarray. But Stalin was eventually stung into action, when it became clear that many of his subjects were not resisting the Nazis, but welcoming them as liberators.

Long-silent church bells rang out in occupied towns as a religious people, denied the right to worship for years, joyously assembled for services. Civilians began hoping for the freedoms promised in 1917. Even the Jews, victims of Stalin's anti-semitism, responded willingly to Nazi posters asking them to register with the invaders. Nobody dreamed that Hitler could be as murderous a master as Stalin. Disillusioned Russian troops surrendered in droves. In less than six months, the invading army of just over 3 million captured nearly 4 million of the Red Army.

But Hitler and his army threw away their chances of capitalizing on Russian misery. Freed towns were soon appalled at the cruelty of the occupying forces. Hitler himself refused to allow nearly 800,000 Russian volunteers to fight for him against Stalin under rebel general Alexander Vlasov. And when Stalin appealed over the radio to 'his friends' the Russian people they rose heroically to throw off the Nazi yoke.

Yet, while his troops were battling back with courage, and Stalin was appealing to the Allies to send him battalions of reinforcements or to invade Europe to open a second front, the NKVD were waging war on the Russian people. Fearful of anyone who might try to topple him for his earlier savagery or for his military mistakes, Stalin launched yet another great purge. Army officers were killed by the hundred. Gulag inmates were slaughtered by the thousand. Potential 'enemies of the people' were massacred in every area that might fall into German hands. In his book *Stalin's Secret War*, Count Nikolai Tolstoy wrote: 'At Lvov, as the Soviet 4th Army battled against odds to save the city, the NKVD was working for a week with machine guns, grenades and high explosives in its frantic effort to liquidate thousands of Ukrainian prisoners. Thousands more were being transferred east under heavy armed guard.'

The Germans knew how Stalin dealt with Ukrainians. They had uncovered a mass grave of 9,000 bodies, clinically laid head to toe to save space, in the Ukrainian town of Vinnitsa, population 70,000. Again, most had their hands bound and bullet wounds in the back of the neck. Nazi propaganda chief Paul Joseph Goebbels was making a rare excursion into truth when he said: 'If the Germans lay down their arms, the whole of eastern and south-eastern Europe, together with the Reich, would come under Russian occupation. Behind an iron screen, mass butcheries of people would begin, and all that would remain would be a crude automaton, a dull fermenting mass of millions of proletarians and despairing slave animals knowing nothing of the outside world.'

Slowly the Red Army pushed back the Germans and

began pursuing them beyond Russia's borders. At their Yalta summit, the Allied leaders had agreed how to divide the spoils, once Hitler was forced into unconditional surrender. American forces held back to allow Stalin's troops to take Prague. In Poland, the Russians roused the Warsaw resistance via radio to attack their German oppressors and help the liberating army. Then the advance was halted for several days, giving Nazis time to kill as many Poles as possible.

By the end of the war, Stalin had added parts of Finland, Romania and Czechoslovakia, half of Poland and East Prussia, and most of the Baltic States to the Soviet Union. He had also established sympathetic buffer states in the rest of Czechoslovakia, Hungary, Bulgaria and Romania. And, by entering the fighting against Japan after America dropped its A-bombs, he legitimized his annexation of the Kurile Islands, Sakhalin Island and parts of Mongolia. His sinister rule now stretched from the South China Sea to the River Elbe in Germany. And, just as Goebbels predicted, mass butchery began behind heavily policed borders.

Beria's NKVD took savage revenge on anyone suspected of collaborating with the Nazis. Whole peoples from outlying areas – the Crimean Tatars, Kalmyks, Karachi-Balkars, Chechens – were transported to starvation in Siberia and Central Asia. Russian soldiers, returning either from captivity or victorious invasion, were thoroughly vetted. Those impressed by what they had seen in the West were shot or incarcerated. Stalin could not allow anyone to spread the word that the capitalist masses actually enjoyed a better standard of living than his Soviet proletariat. Even heroes suffered. Author Alexander Solzhenitsyn, twice decorated for bravery as an artillery officer, vanished into a Gulag for eight years for 'insulting Stalin'. In the new satellite countries, loyal Marxist-Leninists were executed or jailed after show trials and the communist parties purged of anyone not proved to be a committed Stalinist.

But details of the most terrible retribution leaked out only years later. At Yalta, Western leaders agreed to return to Stalin not just prisoners of war but all refugees from his iron rule. The list ranged from Soviet citizens and soldiers who had tried to fight Hitler to White Russians who had fled after the civil war ended in 1921. More than three million desperate escapees were in Western hands in 1945. But by 1948 almost all had been forcibly repatriated. Britain alone sent 30,000. At Scarisbrook camp on Merseyside, one man hanged himself rather than fall into Stalin's clutches. Another cut his throat as he was led towards a ship on Liverpool dockside. In Rimini, Italy, British soldiers forced reluctant returnees to board trains at gunpoint. One man beat his brains out with a stone. Another was shot by troops as he tried to break free.

Back in the USSR, thousands of the helpless hostages were marched straight off boats and trains into makeshift execution yards. At ports on the north coast and in the Crimea, Soviet Air Force planes flew low to try to drown the sound of shooting. Those who escaped the quayside massacres were bundled into closed trains for a lingering death in the Gulags.

If Western governments hoped such sacrifices would satisfy Stalin, they were in for a shock. Instead of planning for peace, he ordered exhausted Russia into massive rearmament. Iron and steel production was trebled. Coal and oil targets were doubled. Hundreds of captured German scientists and technicians were forced to try to bridge the technology gap between the USSR and the West. The growing army of Moscow moles abroad was ordered to steal the secrets of the A-bomb. And the Soviet communist party was purged of anyone who refused to toe the hard-line Stalinist policy of cold war.

But the man hell-bent on imposing his brand of Soviet slavery on free nations was now a prisoner of his own terror. Otto Kuusinen, a Finn who knew Stalin better than most, said: 'The more ruthless and cold-blooded he became, the more he lived in an almost insane fear of his life.' Stalin's daughter Svêtlana described her father as being 'as bitter as he could be against the whole world. He saw enemies everywhere. It had reached the point of being pathological, of persecution mania.'

Even in the Kremlin, Stalin wore a special bullet-proof vest. Tunnels were dug to link his office with other government buildings. Moscow's underground railway was secretly extended to his villa at Kuntsevo. When forced to appear above ground, Stalin used only an armour-plated car with bullet-proof windows 3 inches thick. NKVD squads checked out every route, and lined the roads when their leader drove past. All Stalin's food came from farms run by the NKVD. It was analysed by a special team of doctors, served by bodyguards posing as waiters, and always tested for poison by companions before Stalin took a mouthful. His tea had to come from specially sealed packs which were used just once, the rest being thrown away. When the woman who always prepared his tea was spotted taking leaves from a pack with a broken seal, she was thrown into Lubianka Prison.

But even a man as powerful as Stalin could not cheat death for ever. On 5 March 1953, he collapsed with a cerebral haemorrhage, aged 73, apparently in a fury because some of the Politburo opposed his plans to transport thousands of Soviet Jews to wasteland near the Chinese border. According to Czech defector Karel Kaplan, he had even more sinister plans in mind. Kaplan, who fled to the West in 1976, reported that in 1951 Stalin told leaders of the East European satellite states to prepare for all-out war to occupy western Europe 'in three or four years at the most'.

Stalin had taken Russia from the wooden plough to the nuclear age in 30 years. He had caught up with the advanced countries who had spent centuries making the transition. But, in the process, the lives of more than 20 million Soviet citizens had been sacrificed. Another 14 million were still in Gulag camps when he died. Count Nikolai Tolstoy wrote that, in a nation of 200 million people, 'scarcely a family had been untouched by tragedy'. It was too much even for the stomachs of those who succeeded Stalin as Soviet leaders.

The NKVD apparatus of fear, which had mushroomed to 1.5 million men and women, was slimmed down and renamed the KGB. Beria and other powerful aides were shot within months of their patron's death. In 1956 Nikita Khrushchev accused the man for whom he had once worked of unjustified harshness against 'punished peoples' and Russians captured by the Nazis. He also attacked Stalin for killing 'many thousands of honest and innocent communists'. And he added: 'Arbitrary behaviour by one person encouraged and permitted arbitrariness in others. Mass arrests and deportations of many thousands of people, execution without trial and without normal investigation created conditions of insecurity, fear and even desperation.'

Slowly Stalin slipped from public adulation in Russia as revelations about the means he used overshadowed the ends he achieved. In 1961 his remains were removed from the Red Square mausoleum and buried outside the Kremlin walls. His entry in Soviet encyclopaedias shrank. In 1977 his name had vanished from the national anthem, though Lenin's stayed. But the most telling blow was a name change which symbolized the passing of two of the world's most repressive regimes. The Volga town of Tsaritsyn had been retitled Stalingrad in honour of Stalin's gallant defence of it during the Russian civil war. Within a few years of his death, it became known as Volgograd.

Merciless
Despots

Attila the Hun

Mass slaughter, rape and pillage were an integral part of life for most of northern Europe for centuries. Though the Greeks and Romans established the Mediterranean as the cradle of civilization, it was constantly rocked by murderous incursions by barbarian hordes from the north. Greek historian Herodotus, born in 484 BC, described savage Scythians living north of the Black Sea who skinned opponents to make coats, sawed off the top of their skulls to make drinking cups and drank the blood of their victims. Wild Goths swept south from Sweden, and in AD 410 sacked Rome in a six-day orgy of rape and killing. Vicious Vandals reached the city fewer than 50 years later after storming through Germany, Gaul, Spain and North Africa, leaving death and destruction in their wake. Saxons, Franks and Vikings were other warlike and unmerciful raiders. But of all the brutal barbarians who terrorized Europe none struck greater fear into men's hearts than a tribe whose roots were in the harsh steppes of Mongolia.

The Huns were wild horsemen driven out of their homeland by the Chinese in the 2nd century AD. They rode west, conquering and cold-bloodedly massacring any tribe that stood in their way. Eventually they settled north of the river Danube, between the Volga and the Don, and established uneasy détente with neighbouring Romans, even helping the legions subdue troublesome tribes. Rome paid the Huns' King Ruas an annual tribute of 350 pounds of gold, but in return took hostages as a guarantee of good behaviour. The king's nephew, Attila, born in AD 406, spent part of his youth as a hostage in Italy. It was invaluable experience for a leader whose bloodthirsty campaigns were to earn him the title 'Scourge of God'. Attila the Hun was 27 when King Ruas died. At first he ruled jointly with his brother Bleda, strengthening the kingdom by defeating Teutonic tribes like the Ostrogroths and Gepidae. By AD 444 he had complete control of the territory known today as Hungary and Romania. And he was absolute ruler after having his brother murdered. Now his ruthless ambition was ready to take on the Romans. The plaintive plea of a damsel in distress gave him the pretext for war.

Honoria, sister of Roman emperor Valentinian III, caused a scandal by having an affair with a court chamberlain and getting pregnant. Valentinian had her sent off to Constantinople, where she lived with religious relatives, virtually a prisoner. Frustrated and bored, she smuggled her ring together with a message for help to Attila at his camp near Budapest, offering herself as his bride if he rescued her. The Hun chieftain already had as many wives as he needed, but he made the most of the request. He asked Valentinian for Honoria's hand – and half the Roman Empire as dowry. Rejected, he unleashed a furious onslaught.

His hordes swept south, through Macedonia – now mostly part of Greece – to the gates of Constantinople in AD 447. The Romans bought him off, increasing their yearly tribute to 2,100 pounds of gold, and paying a heavy indemnity for withdrawal. Attila went home with his booty, but four years later he led a vast army of Huns, Franks and Vandals across the Rhine into Gaul.

Town after town was ravaged and razed, but, as the unscrupulous barbarians were about to storm the city of Orléans, the city was saved by the arrival of Roman legions allied to an army of Visigoths. Attila withdrew to the plains near Châlons-sur-Marne and prepared for battle. It lasted all day, with appalling carnage on both sides. One eye-witness later described the hand-to-hand fighting as 'ruthless, immense, obstinate'. The Visigoth king was just one of the thousands slaughtered. But Attila was forced to retreat back beyond the Rhine. Historians describe the battle as one of the most crucial ever. Had the Romans not won, they say, Europeans might today have slant-eyed, Mongol-like features.

Attila was bloodied but unbowed. A year later his men again swarmed south into Italy. Aquileia, the major city in the province of Venetia, was completely destroyed after appalling atrocities against its inhabitants. The Hun hordes swept on to the Adriatic sea, slaughtering the civilians of Concordia, Altinum and Padua before burning their properties. Frightened refugees fled to the islands and lagoons where horsemen could not follow. There they established the city we know as Venice.

The power-crazed heathen turned his army towards the Lombardy plain and Milan, plundering and pillaging until northern Italy was devastated. As Rome itself was threatened, Pope Leo I courageously left the Vatican for a personal interview with the irresistible invader. Attila, his fury subdued by such a bold move, agreed to lead his men home, though he talked menacingly of returning if Honoria's wrongs were not righted.

But there were to be no more atrocities from the most ruthless despot the world had then known. On 15 March AD 453, he hosted a gigantic banquet to celebrate the taking of yet another wife, the beautiful virgin Ildico. That night, as he tried to consummate the marriage, an artery burst, and bloodthirsty Attila bled to death.

Genghis Khan

Nearly 800 years after Attila's demise, Europe was reeling from the onslaught of another Mongol conqueror whose callous cunning and cruelty have never been matched. He was born in 1162 and named Temuchin after a tribal chief his father Yesukai had just defeated. At the age of 13,

Yesukai's death in an ambush plunged the boy into the terror and treachery of tribal infighting. But he proved equal to every challenge. He cold-bloodedly killed one of his brothers in a dispute over a fish. He slaughtered every man, woman and child in a tribe of nomads who dared to kidnap his wife. And though his rivals battled bitterly – one boiled 70 of his followers alive in cooking pots – by the spring of 1206 Temuchin was powerful enough to impose his power on all the Mongol tribes. He summoned leaders of dozens of warring factions to a conference on the banks of the river Onon and proclaimed himself their chief. He also took a new name – Genghis Khan, which meant perfect warrior.

China was first to feel his wrath. The Kin Tartars ruled the northern half of the country, and had been glad to accept when Genghis offered them some of his troops to suppress troublemakers. In 1211 that move rebounded on them. The troops had gained a comprehensive knowledge of the land inside the Great Wall, and even subverted sentries at some of the gates. The Mongol armies poured south, besieging and sacking cities, trampling and burning crops. By 1214 Genghis Khan controlled almost all the country north of the Yellow River. He offered the Kin emperor peace, adding: 'It will be necessary that you distribute largess to my officers and men to appease their fierce hostility.' Two royal princesses were among the prizes the Mongol armies carried home. But within a year they were back, ruthlessly besieging the few cities that had survived the previous invasion.

Genghis Khan's empire was soon secure, ruled by a regime of fear which meant instant death to any rebel. The savage warlord now looked to the west and his neighbours the Khwarizms. Their vast territories stretched from the Ganges to the Tigris, and included present-day Turkistan, Iran and northern India. Genghis sent envoys to Shah Mohammed, promising peace and proposing trade. The reply seemed favourable. But, when the first caravan of 100 Mongol traders arrived in the border town of Otrar, governor Inaljuk had them all massacred as spies. Furious Genghis sent more envoys, demanding the governor's extradition. Mohammed beheaded their leader and sent the rest home minus their beards. The insult was to cost the Shah his kingdom – and bring unprecedented horror to Europe's door.

More than 400,000 Khwarizm troops were strung along the Syr Daria river to repel the invasion, but they were like lambs to the slaughter when the Mongol armies struck in a three-pronged attack. One army attacked in the south, threatening the strategic cities of Bukhara and Samarkand. Two others crossed the mountains to the north and be-sieged Otrar. A bitter battle ended with the errant governor being executed as painfully as possible – molten metal was poured into his eyes and ears. Then, while one army turned south to link up with the first near Bukhara, 40,000 men led by Genghis Khan vanished into the vast Kizylkum desert. They re-emerged behind Bukhara and behind the enemies' lines. The Shah fled as the city suffered the Mongol victory rites. Its mercenary defenders were slaughtered, and the civilians ordered what was left of the walls to allow uninterrupted looting. Then the women were raped in front of their families, craftsmen were taken as slaves and the remaining residents put to the sword.

The terror-struck Khwarizms had no answer to the Mongols' devastating military efficiency. Their infantry was helpless against the hordes of horsemen who unleashed waves of arrows which decimated defenders, then moved in to finish them off ruthlessly with their carved sabres and lances. If a city or a pass seemed too secure, the Mongols would appear to retreat, then turn and scatter their pursuers with savage ferocity. As they moved further into Khwarizm territory, they herded crowds of captives in front of them as a human shield. Giant catapults, manned by up to 100 Mongol warriors, hurled rocks at city walls. Other defences were breached by means of a weapon unknown to the West, gunpowder.

Towns which opened their gates to the invaders were spared. Those that fought, like Samarkand, were not. The Mongols arrived in May 1220 to find a garrison of 50,000 men well dug in. When the attackers pretended to flee, the defenders poured after them and were cut to ribbons. When half the mercenaries deserted to Genghis Khan, the civilians surrendered, leaving soldiers besieged in the citadel. They were starved out and killed – then the turncoat mercenaries were massacred for treachery. Nearly 30,000 civilians were herded away to form a living shield at the next siege.

At Urgenj, the Mongols slaughtered every man and took the women and children as slaves before breaching dykes to flood the burning ruins. In Termez, every body was cut open after Genghis discovered that one old woman had swallowed some pearls. At Nisa, Genghis's son Tulé had all the inhabitants' hands tied behind their backs, then watched them die in a hail of arrows. At Merv, the poor were beheaded while the rich were savagely tortured to reveal the whereabouts of their treasures. When Nishapur surrendered, the severed heads of the residents were arranged in three gruesome pyramids of men, women and children.

Shah Mohammed had been broken by the speed and savagery with which his empire had been destroyed. He fled to a village on the Caspian Sea, and died of pleurisy. Genghis pursued his son and successor, Jelaleddin, south through Afghanistan, slaughtering hundreds of thousands of innocent civilians as he went. When his quarry took refuge with the Sultan of Delhi, the Mongols ravaged Lahore, Peshawar and Melikpur before turning northwest again. News had reached Genghis that the people of Herat, spared after surrendering without a fight, had deposed the governor he installed. A six-month siege by 80,000 men ended the rebellion. Then a week of unbridled murder meted out the punishment. Thousands of corpses lay in the rubble of the city when Genghis at last headed for home. He had unfinished business with the Tangut tribe, who had declined to send troops to aid his Khwarizm campaign. He vowed to exterminate them all.

But both age and weakness following a hunting accident were finally to achieve what no foe could manage. Genghis Khan was besieging the Tangut capital of Ninghsia in August 1227 when he fell ill and died, aged 65. His will named his son Ogotai as successor, but the warlord's aides decided that the death must remain secret until Ogotai was safely in command. The final victims of the man described by one historian as the 'mightiest and most bloodthirsty conqueror of all time' were the innocent souls who accidentally spotted the funeral procession as it headed for the burial ground in the valley of Kilien. Without exception, they were put to the sword.

Genghis Khan left an empire stretching from the China Sea to the Persian Gulf. But trembling neighbours who hoped his death would spare them further conquest were sadly mistaken. For the mighty Mongol had fathered a dynasty of ruthless rulers almost as callous and cruel. And they had their own ambitions to extend their legacy.

Genghis's successor, Ogotai, spent his first years in power consolidating his grip on China and extending his empire in Korea. Then his avaricious eyes strayed westward again. The Mongol warriors surged through central Asia, laying waste to the cities of Tiflis and Ryazan, in Georgia, and massacring the inhabitants. Moscow, then an insignificant wooden township, was quickly taken. At Koselsk, revenge for an earlier reversal resulted in such a carnival of death that the laughing invaders renamed the town Mobalig, 'city of woe'. Finally Kiev, known as 'the mother of cities', was battered into submission. The residents were slaughtered and the buildings razed.

Now the Mongol army split. One of Genghis Khan's old lieutenants, Subatai, led a three-pronged assault on Hungary, aiming to rendezvous with the rest of the army at the Danube. But first the armies of Poland, Germany and Bohemia had to be prevented from coming to the aid of Hungary's fearsome Magyars. The rest of the invasion force swarmed into Poland, moving at a pace which staggered generals accustomed to slow-moving traditional battle strategy. The Poles were routed at Szydlow and the Germans at Liegnitz. The Bohemians beat a hasty retreat. In less than a month the Mongols had covered 400 miles, won two decisive battles, captured four major cities and cleared the way to the main objective – Hungary.

Hungarian King Bela IV had massed his men to meet Subatai at the Danube. But the Mongol commander declined to fight on ground which did not suit his horsemen. He began a calculated retreat to the Sajo river, and for six days the Hungarians followed, being lured further from their stronghold and reinforcements. Then Subatai turned for a savage dawn attack. Most of Bela's army was still asleep. By midday, more than 70,000 Magyars had been massacred. 'They fell to the left and right like leaves in winter,' wrote one chronicler. 'The roads for two days' journey from the field of battle were strewn with corpses as the rest tried to flee.'

Subatai stormed Budapest while part of his force chased King Bela to the Adriatic coast, burning and destroying everything in their path. On Christmas Day 1241 he led his forces across the iced-up Danube and took the city of Esztergom. But, as Europe waited in trepidation for the next move, the Mongols again turned back. News had reached them that Ogotai was dead, and a bitter battle for succession was likely. No one wanted to miss it.

It was ten years before Genghis Khan's grandson Mangu,

son of the tyrant Tulé, emerged as undisputed Mongol leader. Unrest in Persia, fostered by the Ismailites, prompted him to send his brother Halagu to the Middle East to storm the strongholds of a sinister sect known as the Assassins. Halagu rode on to Baghdad, then the major city in the region. After resisting for a month, the city surrendered in February 1258. Halagu's marauders massacred everybody inside, trampling the sultan to death under horses. They set fire to the city, then turned towards Syria. Aleppo was sacked, Damascus surrendered, and Halagu was about to attack Jerusalem when, once again, a single death prevented thousands. The news was received that Mangu had died, and the horsemen rode home.

Mangu's brother was Kubla Khan, celebrated in Coleridge's verse. Alone among the family, he treated captives humanely and banned indiscriminate massacres. For 34 years he concentrated on conquests in the East, in southern China, Tibet and Vietnam. He even tried to invade Japan without success. After his death, the empire fell apart as his heirs squabbled. Even the Chinese cast off the Mongol yoke as the Ming Dynasty forced the wild warriors back to their Mongolian homeland.

Tamerlane the Great

The world had not heard the last of the merciless Mongols. In 1336 a boy called Timur was born at Kesh, near Samarkand. He was the great-great-grandson of Genghis Khan and conceived the desperate dream of rebuilding his forefather's empire, by then divided into a multitude of smaller principalities. Locals nicknamed him Timur i Leng, or Timur the Lame, because of a disability which made him limp. But the world remembers him as Tamerlane the Great, a wicked warmonger with a savage sadistic streak.

At 33 he usurped the Transoxian throne at Samarkand and gained the power base he needed for his conquests. Superb military management earned him mastery of Persia, Turkistan, the Ukraine, the Crimea, Georgia, Mesopotamia and Armenia. Governors who appealed to him for help frequently found themselves betrayed once he had restored their realms. He dethroned a rival khan to occupy Russia, then over-ran India, leaving behind a trail of carnage all the way to Delhi, where he reduced the city to rubble and massacred 100,000 inhabitants.

Like his ancestors, Tamerlane, tall with a huge head and white-haired from childhood, found that fear was no way to establish allegiance among the peoples he conquered. Revolts in the growing empire were frequent, but repressed ruthlessly. Whole cities were destroyed out of spite and their populations slaughtered. Massive towers or pyramids of skulls were constructed for the emperor's enjoyment. Twice he had thousands of opponents bricked up alive for agonizingly slow suffocation and starvation. Another time he hurled all his prisoners to their deaths over a cliff.

After his Indian campaign, Tamerlane stormed into Syria to settle old scores with leaders who refused to help in his earlier wars. Aleppo was seized and sacked and Damascus occupied in 1400. Baghdad, still smarting from Halagu's atrocities a century earlier, was devastated again by fire, and 20,000 people were put to the sword. In 1402 Tamerlane unleashed his wrath on Anatolia – now Turkey – and beheaded 5,000 Ottoman fighters after one siege. Their sultan was killed in captivity in a barbarous iron cage.

The nightmare return to the depravity of an earlier age ended only with Tamerlane's death. His hordes were on their way to attack China when, in January 1405, he fell ill while camping on the Syr Daria river and died. By a bizarre twist of fate, it happened at Otrar – the town whose governor had unwittingly sparked off the fury of the Mongols under Genghis Khan nearly 300 years earlier when he executed 100 traders. Millions had since paid the Mongol's bloody price for that rash act.

Ivan the Terrible

In July 1662, a mob of 5,000 angry Russians marched to the palace of Tsar Alexis in the suburbs of Moscow. Poor harvests and a long war with Poland had exhausted their patience over harsh taxation, currency devaluation and corrupt officialdom, and they extracted a promise from the Tsar that he would act on their grievances. But his solution to the problems was not what they had in mind. According to historian V.O. Klyuchevsky, 'Tsar Alexis called on the streltsy (musketeers who formed the Tsar's bodyguard) and his courtiers for assistance, and an indiscriminate slaughter ensued, followed by tortures and executions. Hundreds were drowned in the River Moskva and whole families were exiled permanently to Siberia.'

Alexis was pious and artistically minded. He tried to leave government to ministers. But he had been born into a succession of Tsars who inherited absolute rule from the Mongols – and were equally merciless about maintaining it. Any challenge to their authority was met by torture, exile and execution. The loyalty of a few select aristocrats was bought with land and honour. The peasants (90 per cent of the population) were shackled in medieval-style serfdom – denied education, the right to change jobs, even the right to choose their own marital partners. If they grew restless about their lot, soldiers and a secret army of informers soon brought them back into line with bloodshed. For four centuries, the Tsars ruled Russia by fear. And few rulers inspired more fear than Ivan the Terrible.

Ivan, born in August 1530, was an orphan by the age of eight. His father Vasily, Grand Duke of Moscow, died when he was three. Five years later his mother Elena, who acted as Regent, was poisoned. After that, Ivan was to claim that he received 'no human care from any quarter'. Vicious power battles between leading families marked his early years. Ivan was used as a pawn by rival factions wrestling for control, only to lose it, in a succession of bloodbaths. He watched one of his uncles being carried off to his death by a Moscow mob in one uprising. But he quickly learned how to fight back. He was just 13 when he ordered his first assassination. Then he threw the body of his victim, a troublesome Shuisky prince, to his dogs.

In 1547, Ivan had himself crowned Tsar and, at a parade of the nation's most beautiful and eligible virgins, he selected himself a bride – 15-year-old Anastasia. She produced six children for him, but only two were still alive when she died in 1560. Their deaths, plus the loss of his wife's calming influence and the trauma of his childhood, may all have played a part in the horrors that followed.

First Ivan banished his closest advisers, his personal priest Father Silvestr, and nobleman Alexei Adashev, accusing them of plotting to kill Anastasia. Then he left Moscow for virtual monastic seclusion in the provinces. All sections of the community begged him to return, fearing a power vacuum. Ivan agreed – but only if he was allowed to govern without any interference. When his terms were accepted, he split the nation into vast sections. In one, he was absolute master. The rest of the country was to be governed for him by bureaucrats.

Now Ivan unleashed unprecedented terror on his people, using the sinister oprichniki. They were black-cloaked riders on black horses, whose saddles carried the symbols of a broom and a dog's head. With unbridled fury, they slaughtered anyone suspected of opposition to Ivan, and settled scores from the turmoil of his teenage days. More than 4,000 aristocrats were purged. The Staritsky family, relatives of Ivan but potential rivals for power, were wiped out. When Metropolitan Philip, leader of the Orthodox Church in Moscow, condemned the oprichniki's attacks and refused to bless the Tsar, the ruthless riders tracked him down and savagely executed him.

Ivan himself often took part in their orgies of rape, torture and death. And his rage really ran wild when an informant told him civic leaders of Novgorod, then Russia's second city, were planning rebellion. Without bothering to check the allegation, which was almost certainly untrue, Ivan led his oprichniki north, pillaging and plundering aristocratic homes, monasteries and churches within 50 miles of the city.

Having laid waste to the fields that fed Novgorod, he then built a wooden wall around the metropolis to prevent anyone from fleeing. And for five weeks he watched, or took part in, wholesale slaughter.

Husbands and wives were forced to watch as their partners – and sometimes their children – were tortured. Many women were roasted alive on revolving spears. Other killings were treated almost as sport. One German mercenary wrote: 'Mounting a horse and brandishing a spear, he (Ivan) charged in and ran people through while his son watched the entertainment . . .'

Though Soviet scholars have claimed recently that no more than 2,000 people died, Western historians put the total toll in the annihilation of Novgorod at over 60,000. And Ivan's sadistic savagery there, and at Pskov, also suspected of plotting rebellion, certainly had an effect on later opponents. When he invaded neighbouring Livonia, one besieged garrison blew themselves up rather than fall into his cruel clutches.

In 1572 Ivan suddenly disbanded the oprichniki and banned all mention of them. Throughout his life, his sadism alternated with periods of manic religious depression, when he would publicly confess his sins and don sackcloth. So perhaps genuine shame ended the six-year reign of terror. Perhaps an attack on Russia from the south by Turks forced him to call off internal vendettas. Or perhaps his assassins had eliminated almost everyone Ivan wanted out of the way.

Ivan got away with his ruthless rule because he had the support of the Orthodox Church. Western Europe was undergoing the religious crisis of the Reformation, and Orthodox leaders were terrified of free-thinking Protestantism which would weaken their hold on the unthinking masses. In exchange for a hard line on all religious dissent, including burning for 'heresy', the Church backed the Tsar and became an effective propaganda machine on his behalf. When peasant revolts were crushed with total brutality, the causes and the consequences were never attributed to Ivan. They were blamed on the corruption or excessive zeal of those who worked for him.

For a few Russians, Ivan was not so terrible. They were the people granted lands and power in the territories the Tsar added to his empire, north of the Black Sea and in Siberia. But the wars that won them, and campaigns which won nothing, forced an ever-increasing tax burden on Russian landowners and their peasants. And, by the end of Ivan's reign, English ambassador Giles Fletcher was reporting to London: 'The desperate state of things at home maketh the people for the most part to wish for some foreign invasion, which they suppose to be the only means to rid them of the heavy yoke of his tyrannous government.'

In fact there was another way – Ivan's death. It came in March 1584, three years after he killed his son and heir Ivan with a spear during a quarrel. A life of licentiousness – six more wives and innumerable mistresses – had left the Tsar riddled with disease. As British trader Sir Jerome Horsey put it: 'The emperor began grievously to swell in his cods, with which he had most horribly offended above 50 years, boasting of a thousand virgins he had deflowered and thousands of children of his begetting destroyed.' Ivan collapsed and died as he prepared to play a game of chess.

Yet even his departure did not spare Russia agony. His heir's death left Ivan's imbecilic son Theodore as successor and he soon proved hopelessly unable to govern. The country was plunged into 30 years of chaos, which included occupation by the armies of both Poland and Sweden, before the Romanovs – relatives of Ivan's wife Anastasia – were able to reimpose the authority of the Tsars.

Historians still dispute whether Tsarist Russia's most bloodthirsty tyrant was consciously bad or completely mad. Some seek excuses in his traumatic childhood. Others blame a painful spinal defect for his excesses. It was nearly 350 years before Ivan the Terrible found sympathetic consideration from someone who believed his oprichniki had played a 'progressive role', someone who claimed his only mistake was not taking his purges further. That sympathizer was Joseph Stalin. And, as the earlier chapter on Stalin shows, he did not make the same 'mistake'.

The Ottoman Sultans

Turkey was known as the sick man of Europe throughout the 19th century. Crisis followed crisis – one culminated in the bloody Crimean War – as the continent's superpowers bolstered the weak and crumbling regime of the once-great Ottoman Sultans to prevent rivals like Russia from seizing Constantinople and threatening trade routes. Then the outraged Western world learned that Turkey was even sicker than they feared – but in a very different sense.

Like the Mongols before them, early Ottoman armies

conquered mercilessly. Massacres of captives were commonplace, an accepted aspect of warfare. And by 1588 – the year Spain's Armada was routed by England – the Sultans ruled an empire which circled most of the Mediterranean. It stretched from the Red Sea port of Aden to Budapest and Belgrade, from the Crimea north of the Black Sea to Algeria. Huge chunks of present-day Hungary, Poland and Russia shared the same masters as the people of Greece, Egypt, Tunisia, Libya, Lebanon, Syria, Israel, Yugoslavia, Romania and Bulgaria. Any revolts among the 30 million subjects were ruthlessly suppressed.

But the absolute power of the Sultans not only corrupted them, it blinded them to the changing world outside their realms. In 1876 a rebellion in Bulgaria was repressed with traditional carnage. Ottoman troops ran amok in an orgy of killing, and more than 12,000 men, women and children were slaughtered. But by then the Western world had newspapers, and millions were appalled to realize that medieval-style tyranny still went on in the 'modern' age. Historians were to discover that such tyranny had run virtually unchecked for 350 years – and would carry on well into the 20th century.

The sinister Sultans had more reason than most absolute rulers to be paranoid about plots. A strong tradition of strangulation by deaf mutes, using silk bowstrings, existed inside the walls of their Grand Seraglio palace. Mahomet the Conqueror (1431–81) formulated a law by which his successors as Sultan had 'the right to execute their brothers to ensure the peace of the world'. It was designed to stop disputes over succession. But, when Mahomet III took the throne in 1595, his father Murad III's prowess in the harem meant that he had to murder 19 brothers, all aged under 11, and throw seven pregnant concubines into the Bosporus tied up in sacks.

Thereafter, close male relatives of the incoming Sultan

were locked up in a windowless building within the grand Seraglio complex until the Sultan's death called them to the throne. Cut off from the outside world, with only deaf mutes and sterilized concubines for company, many were completely deranged when they came to power, sometimes after more than 30 years of incarceration. It was 1789 before the practice was abolished – and, by then, madness was in the blood of the Ottoman dictators.

Suleiman the Magnificent, who ruled from 1520 to 1566, is regarded by most historians as the last great Sultan. In 1526 he seized more of Hungary, massacring 200,000 – 2,000 were killed for his enjoyment as he watched from a throne – and taking 100,000 slaves back to Constantinople. Three years later, when Vienna stubbornly refused to surrender, he scoured the surrounding countryside and selected the most nubile girls for Turkey's harems. Then he threw hundreds of unwanted peasants on a gigantic fire in view of the city walls. Such 'sanity' in the name of military strength was succeeded by a dynasty of Sultans who were weak, debauched, indecisive or insane – or sometimes all four.

Suleiman's son Selim II was a drunkard, despite the proscription of alcohol by the Koran, and decided to wrest Cyprus, source of his favourite wine, from its Venetian rulers. His soldiers sacked Nicosia, slaughtering 30,000. When the key fortress of Famagusta fell after a two-year siege, the Turks promised to spare the heroic garrison – then killed them all. Their commander was flayed alive, then paraded in front of the Turkish troops, his body stuffed with straw. Venice, Spain and Austria retaliated with the humiliating naval triumph of Lepanto, at which 50,000 Turks died. But the Ottomans still held Cyprus when, in 1574, Selim lost his footing climbing into his bath after a drinking session, and died from a fractured skull.

His son, Mahomet III, the man who killed his 19 young

brothers, was a man with a fiery temper who enjoyed the sight of women's breasts being scorched off with hot irons. Osman II, who ruled for less than a year before his 1618 murder, enjoyed archery – but only if his targets were live prisoners-of-war or page boys. And while these two, and a string of insignificant Sultans, indulged themselves the empire began to fall to pieces. Neglect and oppression ravaged the countryside, with tax income tumbling as famine laid waste to whole areas. The rigid disciplines which had made the Ottoman empire strong were also disintegrating.

Murad IV, a savage, dark-eyed giant, tried to reimpose them when he took over in 1623. After the Janissaries, the Sultan's special army, forced him to sack the chief minister and 16 other officials, he later avenged himself for their impudence by having more than 500 of their leaders strangled in their barracks. Then he set about the rest of the nation, as author Noel Barber records in his excellent book, *Lords Of The Golden Horn*:

'Murad quickly found a simple panacea for the ills of the country. He cut off the head of any man who came under the slightest suspicion. In 1637 he executed 25,000 subjects in the name of justice, many by his won hand. He executed the Grand Mufti because he was dissatisfied with the state of the roads. He beheaded his chief musician for playing a Persian air. He liked to patrol the taverns at night and if he caught anyone smoking he declared himself and executed the offender on the spot. When he caught one of his gardeners and his wife smoking, he had their legs amputated and exhibited them in public while they bled to death.'

A Venetian who added a room to the top of his house was hanged because Murad thought he had done it to spy on the Sultan's harem. A Frenchman who arranged a date with a Turkish girl was impaled. And, according to Barber, Murad 'spent hours . . . exercising the royal prerogative of taking ten innocent lives a day as he practised his powers with the arquebus on passers-by who were too near the palace walls. On one occasion he drowned a party of women when he chanced to come across them in a meadow and took exception to the noise they were making. He ordered the batteries to open fire and sink a boatland of women on the Bosporus when their craft came too near the Seraglio walls . . .'

Murad's atrocities were not confined to home. In 1638 he led his troops to the Persian capital, Baghdad. After a six-week siege, during which he sliced in half the head of a Persian champion in single-handed combat, he ordered the massacre of the defending garrison of 30,000 men, women and children.

But Murad was the last of the all-conquering Ottoman despots. His son Ibrahim's most notable conquest was deflowering the virgin daughter of the Grand Mufti, Turkey's highest religious leader. Then, when one concubine from his harem was seduced by an outsider, he had all 280 girls tied in weighted sacks and thrown into the Bosporus. Even Constantinople, which could forgive its Sultans almost anything, could not condone that. The Grand Mufti took revenge by organizing a coup which toppled Ibrahim, then had him, his mother and his favourite lover strangled.

The Ottoman armies had long lost their invincible reputation. In 1683 an alliance of European forces crushed another attempt to take Vienna. In 1790 the Russian forces of Catherine the Great took Ismail, 40 miles north of the Black Sea, and dropped the corpses of 34,000 fallen Turks into the Danube through holes in the ice. In 1827, a six-year war, with massacres on both sides, ended with the Greeks winning independence. Egypt achieved a large measure of self-government.

The Ottoman empire was in steady decline. Elsewhere in the world, such events as the French Revolution, the American Constitution, with its declaration of rights, the Industrial Revolution, a more general right to vote and the introduction of newspapers had all helped foster an awareness of human rights which forced governments to act more humanely. But in 1876 the Ottoman Sultan showed just how far behind the tide of civilization his country had fallen.

In that year, the Bulgarians, who had been part of the Ottoman empire for nearly 500 years, revolted – and Sultan Abdul Aziz unleashed the bloodlust of unpaid troops who were rewarded only by what they could loot. Within days 12,000 men, women and children were dead and 60 villages burned to the ground. The Sultan gave the commander of the troops a medal.

The carnage in the town of Batak was witnessed by American journalist J.A. MacGahan and, when his report appeared in the *Daily News*, the stunned world had its first eye-witness account of an Ottoman atrocity. 'On every side as we entered the town were the skulls and skeletons of woman and children,' he wrote. 'We entered the churchyard. The sight was more dreadful. The whole churchyard for three feet deep was festering with dead bodies partly covered. Hands, legs, arms and heads projected in ghastly confusion . . . I never imagined anything so fearful. There were 3,000 bodies in the churchyard and the church. In the school 200 women and children had been burnt alive . . . no crime invented by Turkish ferocity was left uncommitted.'

Western governments at first refused to accept the reports, labelling them 'picturesque journalism'. But, when Britain sent an investigator from the Constantinople embassy, he told Whitehall the troops had perpetrated 'perhaps the most heinous crime that had stained the history of the present century'. Ex-Prime Minister William Gladstone issued a pamphlet describing the Turks as 'the great anti-human specimen of humanity'. The storm of worldwide protest caused a coup which installed Abdul Aziz's drunken nephew Murad as Sultan. His reign lasted three months, until he was declared insane, and his brother Abdul Hamid II took over.

Abdul was so paranoid about possible plots that he built an entire village, designed only for his safety. Behind the barricades he kept loaded pistols in every room – two hung beside his bath – and constructed glass cupboards which, when opened, blasted the room with bullets from remote-controlled guns. He personally shot dead a gardener and a slave girl whose sudden movements alarmed him. He countered the growing revolt of the Young Turks with a network of spies and a torture chamber under a cruel executioner who delighted in slowly drowning broken men.

But his most astonishing act was to order the monstrous slaughter of the Armenians, a minority race whose homeland was in the northeast of the dwindling empire, close to the Russian border. He regarded the business-minded Armenians much as Hitler later regarded the Jews. First he banned the word 'Armenian' from newspapers and school books. Then he told Moslems they could seize Armenian goods – and kill the owners if they resisted.

Clearly, Abdul had learned nothing from the 1876 atrocities. And his massacres were far worse. It was cold-blooded, premeditated genocide. For days a bugle at dawn and dusk called the faithful to murder. Nearly 100,000 Armenians were killed. And Westerners witnessed the terror in Trebizond, where every Christian house was plundered before the owners were ritually slaughtered, their throats cut as if they were sheep. Those who jumped into the river to flee were caught and drowned by Moslem boatmen. At Urfa 3,000 men, women and children were roasted alive in the cathedral after seeking sanctuary. Sultan Abdul noted every detail as his spies sent detailed reports.

If the Sultan hoped to curry favour with his people, using racial prejudice to blind them to the economic ruin of his empire, he was sadly mistaken. Many Moslems felt only shame, labelling him Abdul the Damned. And this time it was not only Europe that was outraged. Two Armenian professors at an American missionary school were arrested, taken in chains for trial for printing seditious leaflets, and sentenced to die. America was scandalized. Finally, when 7,000 Armenians were slaughtered in Constantinople in reprisal for a band raid carried out by 20, every European power signed an open telegram to the Sultan. If the massacres did not end at once, it read, the Sultan's throne and his dynasty would be imperilled.

Sultan Abdul Hamid survived to celebrate his Silver Jubilee as the new century dawned. But he was now an obsolete leftover from another age. And, in 1908, the Young Turks – whose numbers had influence had been growing, first in exile, then in Turkey – seized power. The Sultan was exiled to Salonika and his brother, a stooge figurehead, was installed as constitutional monarch. Sacks of gold and precious gems, a fortune in foreign bank accounts and shares in international companies were discovered at Abdul's palace, all obtained with money milked from the Turkish treasury.

The repressive rule of the Ottomans had finally ended. But if the Turks and the West thought they had seen the end of evil and tyranny they were in for a shock. For in 1915 Enver Bey, one of the three Young Turk leaders, ordered a new massacre of Armenians, even more ruthless than that of the Sultan. Using the excuse that some Armenians had collaborated with the Russians during World War I battles – Turkey fought on the Kaiser's side –

he made his brother-in-law Djevet Bey governor of the region, with orders to exterminate the Christians.

The inhabitants of more than 80 villages were rounded up and shot. Thousands of women were raped. Men were tortured, often by having horseshoes nailed to their feet. One official admitted he 'delved into the records of the Spanish Inquisition and adopted all the suggestions found there'. More than 18,000 Armenians were sent on a forced march of exile across the Syrian desert to Aleppo. Then Kurdish rebels were encouraged to attack them. Only 150 women and children reached Aleppo, 70 days after setting out.

The official British report on the atrocities, presented to Parliament, estimated that, of two million Armenians in Turkey in 1915, a third died and another third fled to Russia. The American Ambassador in Constantinople asked Enver Bey to condemn his underlings for the outrages. To his astonishment, the callous leader accepted responsibility for everything that had taken place. His co-leader, Taalat Bey, said it was unwise to punish only those Armenians who had actually helped the Russians 'since those who are innocent today might be guilty tomorrow'. And he had the audacity to ask the American Ambassador for a full list of Armenians covered by US insurance companies. As their relatives were probably dead, he said, life-assurance payments should go to the government.

Enver, Talaat and Djevet fled in November 1918, denounced for choosing the wrong side in a war which cost Turkey half a million battle casualties and for profiteering in food at a time of famine. The victorious Allies took control in Constantinople. The empire was now smashed, and Turkey pushed back almost to its present borders. But, to head off feared Italian territorial ambitions, the Allies allowed the Greeks to occupy the port of Smyrna. Revenge for centuries of repression resulted in massacres of Turks – and fuelled the fury that, in atoning for wrongdoing, would make Turkey once again an international outcast.

Patriot Mustafa Kemal was the focus for Turkish anger at the Allied occupation, and the loss of Smyrna. Though he was courtmartialled and sentenced to death in his absence, his support grew, and the Allies were unable to control his rebel forces. Finally the Greeks offered their army to restore order. In 1920 their campaign pressed the Turks back. But in August 1921 Mustafa's men won a three-week battle along a 60-mile front at Sakkaria river. The Greeks fled towards the coast. The following year, reinforced by arms from France, Italy and Russia, the Turks again routed their most bitter foes, forcing them back to Smyrna. In September, Mustafa arrived in triumph at the port, and decreed that any Turkish soldier who molested civilians would be killed.

But within hours the Greek Patriarch had been torn to pieces by a Turkish mob, under the eyes of the town's new commander. Mass looting, raping and killing began, Turkish troops methodically moving from house to house in the Greek and Armenian areas in the north of the town. 'By evening dead bodies were lying all over the streets,' said one American witness. Worse was to come. On Wednesday 13 September, Westerners saw squads of Turkish soldiers setting fire to houses in the Armenian quarter using petroleum. The wind spread the flames northwards, and thousands of flimsy homes were engulfed. Five hundred people perished in a church set ablaze deliberately. The reek of burning flesh filled the air. Tens of thousands fled to the waterfront, pursued by a rapidly growing wall of fire. In the bay lay warships from Britain, America, Italy and France. They were there to protect their nationals – but they had strict orders to maintain neutrality in the war between Greek and Turk. The sailors watched in horror as the inferno changed the colour of the sea and silhouetted the throng of helpless refugees on the wharfs. Then, at midnight, they heard what one described as 'the most awful scream one could ever imagine'.

Humanity over-rode orders next morning, when a massive rescue attempt began. Mustafa Kemal had said as he watched the fire: 'It is a sign that Turkey is purged of the traitors, the Christians, and of the foreigners, and that Turkey is for the Turks.' Three days after the blaze began, he announced that all Greek and Armenian men aged between 15 and 50 were to be deported inland in labour gangs. Women and children had to be out of Smyrna by 30 September or they too would be rounded up. He was later persuaded to extend the deadline by nearly six days. Military and merchant ships performed a miracle, ferrying nearly 250,000 people to safety. No one has ever been able to say how many corpses were left behind, though most estimates start at 100,000.

Mustafa Kemal always maintained that the Greeks and Armenians started the great fire of Smyrna. But a report for the American State department said all the evidence pointed to an attempt by the Turks to hide evidence of 'sack, massacre and raping that had been going on for four days'.

Mustafa, oddly, later changed his name to Kemal Atatürk and instigated massive reforms throughout the government and society which finally dragged Turkey into the 20th century. The last vestiges of the scourge of the Ottomans were buried for ever.

For God, King and Country

The Borgias

It was a city where the brazenly licentious indulged in perverse orgies and incestuous relationships, where ambitious and greedy men grabbed power and personal fortune by bribery and extortion, and where anyone who stood in their way was ruthlessly eliminated. Yet the city where all this happened was not the hub of a barbarian empire. This citadel of sin was the Vatican City in Rome. And the evil masterminds putting vice before virtue, riches before religion and power before piety were the Pope, Alexander VI, alias Rodrigo Borgia, and his illegitimate son Cesare.

For centuries, the Catholic Church was the only Christian faith in Europe. But its monopoly on salvation brought corruption. It sanctioned merciless killing in crusades against so-called heathen-races who worshipped other gods. It exterminated as heretics all who dared question its edicts about the world and life. And it amassed immense wealth by charging a high price for forgiveness of sins. By the 15th century, the Pope was not only a religious leader, but a powerful political force. Secular rulers in the confusing cluster of small states that made up the Italian peninsula competed for his favours and support – and his requests, backed by the threat of excommunication if they were refused, were compelling even for the strongest kings and princes.

Rodrigo Borgia was well grounded in the intrigues and intricacies of the Holy See long before he assumed its highest office. In April 1455, his mother's brother became Pope Calixtus III. Rodrigo, born 24 years earlier at Xativa, near Valencia in Spain, was immediately made a bishop, and quickly progressed up the Catholic hierarchy, to cardinal and vice-chancellor. He served in the Curia under five Popes.

But behind the façade of faith, hope and chastity, Rodrigo was busy seducing as many young virgins as he could lay his hands on. A highly sexed, handsome charmer, he could not resist the temptations of the flesh and one of his brazen open-air orgies earned him a reprimand from the Pope. In 1470 he began a torrid romance with a 28-year-old beauty, Vanozza dei Catanei. She bore him three sons, Giovanni (1480), Cesare (1476) and Goffredo (1481), and a daughter, Lucrezia (1480), before he tired of her and fell for the charms of the 16-year-old Giulia Farnese. For appearances' sake, he had Giulia betrothed to his young nephew – but forbade the boy to consummate the marriage.

When Pope Innocent VIII died in 1492, Rodrigo was one of three contenders to become Pontiff. On the first poll, the electoral college of cardinals voted for Giuliano della Rovere, the successor nominated by Innocent. But Borgia began handing out huge bribes and promised delegates luxurious palaces and lucrative posts if he was chosen. On 10 August he duly became Pope, taking the name Alexander VI.

Instantly he showered his illegitimate children with riches. Cesare, aged just 16, was appointed Archbishop of Valencia. A year later he became a cardinal. But the titles meant little to the ambitious teenager. He was furious that his older brother had been given command of the Papal army. Cesare rode disdainfully round Rome, fully armed, with a succession of shapely mistresses at his side. He canoodled outrageously in public with his sister Lucrezia. And he rivalled his father's scandalous sexual exploits. When Sanchia, promiscuous teenage daughter of the King of Naples, arrived at the Vatican as a prospective bride for Goffredo Borgia, both the Pope and Cesare made a rigorous check on her credentials between the sheets of their own beds.

Rodrigo's reign began in an embarrassing fashion.

When King Ferrante of Naples died, the new Pope recognized the king's son Alphonso, father of saucy Sanchia, as successor. But the French King, Charles VIII, thought he had a better claim – and invaded Rome to prove it. Rodrigo grovelled and agreed to let Charles take Cesare along as a hostage on his journey south to the Naples coronation. But Cesare slipped away during the trip, returned to Rome and helped his father form an anti-French alliance with the rulers of Spain, Milan and Venice. Charles, afraid of being cut off from his homeland, scurried back to France and Alphonso was reinstated.

The Borgias then set about punishing those who had helped Charles to humiliate them. Cesare seized some Swiss mercenaries who had broken into his mother's home during the French occupation of Rome, and tortured them unmercifully. Rodrigo ordered the people of Florence to arrest and torture Girolama Savonarola, a puritan monk who had denounced corruption in the Church and had welcomed Charles as a redeemer arrived to restore Catholicism's old values. The Florentines responded with enthusiasm, because the kill-joy cleric had forced them to abandon their carefree carnivals. He was stretched on the rack 14 times in one day during weeks of persecution before being publicly hanged. His body was then burned.

The Pope sent his son Giovanni off with the army to attack the fortresses of the Orsini family, who had also collaborated with the French. But he proved a hopeless general and returned to Rome in disgrace early in 1497 after losing a battle against the foes he was supposed to punish. Months later, on 14 June, he dined with his mother and brother Cesare. The two men left separately on horseback. Next morning Giovanni's body was dragged from the river Tiber. He had been stabbed nine times.

Giovanni's assassin was never caught, and officially the murder remained a mystery. But wagging tongues noted that one man gained more from the death than most – younger brother Cesare. It meant he could give up the religious positions he held so reluctantly and become the Pope's political and military strong man. That was good news for the Pope, too. Rodrigo could send Cesare away from Rome on business and quell the growing clamour of scandalized gossip. The cardinal's sexual proclivities – he found young boys as alluring as girls, and was far from discreet about his flings with either sex – were the talk of the town. Most embarrassing was his continuing affair with his own sister, Lucrezia. She was placed in a convent when her first husband fled for fear of Cesare's jealous rages. But six months later, after visits from Cesare and his father, she became pregnant. The baby boy was later taken to the Vatican and made heir to the Borgia fortune.

Cesare's new duties took him first to Naples, then to France. The new French King, Louis XII, wanted to annul his marriage and wed his mistress. Rodrigo agreed. In return, Cesare was made Duke of Valentinois and given a bride, the 16-year-old sister of the King of Navarre. More importantly, he was offered French armed help to subdue rebellious nobles in northern Italy and carve out a kingdom for himself in Romagna, south of Venice. The joint invasion began in 1499.

Cesare proved as cunning and unscrupulous in war as he had proved in love. When he crushed the forces of Caterina Sforza and captured her castle at Forli, he insisted that she also surrender her body to him. He wrote a gloating description of their love-making to his father in Rome before confining her in a convent. He took the town of Faenza after stubborn resistance by a population devoted to their 18-year-old master, Astorre Manfredi. The teenager agreed to surrender only after he was promised that his life would be spared. But Cesare sent him to Rome and had him horribly tortured, then killed.

Friends and allies of Cesare had as much to fear from

77

him as from their foes. He betrayed the trust of the Duke of Urbino, marching his men past the city, then doubling back to launch a surprise attack. He appointed a ruthless governor to rule his new lands in Romagna – but when protests about the man's cruelty became impossible to ignore, he had him hacked in two and left on display in Sesena town square. Soon even some of Cesare's lieutenants were alienated by the reign of terror imposed by their morose, unsympathetic leader. Afraid that he might reclaim estates he had given them, they began plotting against him with princes he had deposed. Cesare learned of the conspiracy and lured some of the unsuspecting plotters to a banquet at the town of Senigallia. When they arrived, unarmed, they were seized. Two were instantly strangled.

Cesare's costly campaigns were funded by the Pope. Rodrigo sold cardinal's hats to wealthy aspirants, some of whom died mysteriously only months later, leaving their estates to the Vatican. He declared the year 1500 a Jubilee, which meant pilgrims prepared to pay would receive total absolution for their trespasses. As an added inducement, he announced the unveiling of a 'secret holy door' in St Peter's, which was only ever revealed once every 100 years. Grateful and gullible sinners paid handsomely for the rare privilege of viewing the door, which had been cut in the wall shortly before their arrival.

Rome's death rate rose every time Cesare returned from his territorial conquests. He answered insults, real or imagined, with murder. Many of his homosexual partners were also found poisoned, or dragged from the Tiber with fatal knife wounds. The Venetian ambassador wrote: 'Every night four or five murdered men are discovered – bishops, prelates and others – so that all Rome is trembling for fear of being destroyed by the Duke Cesare.' Then, in 1500, Cesare's fiery passion for sister Lucrezia led to a sensational killing.

Rodrigo had quietly annulled his daughter's first marriage after her husband fled Cesare's jealousy. And, in the wake of the scandal over Lucrezia's baby, the Pope had rushed her to the altar with Alphonse, Duke of Bisceglie and the brother of Sanchia. Sadly, Lucrezia had genuinely fallen in love with him. That infuriated Cesare, who still preferred his sister's embraces to those of his wife.

In July 1500, Alphonse was walking across St Peter's Square after sharing supper with the Pope when a gang of thugs disguised as pilgrims attacked him with knives. He survived, though seriously wounded, and was given a room near the Pope's quarters to ensure his future safety. Lucrezia nursed him devotedly. But one night, having left his bedside briefly, she returned to find him dead. Amazingly, Cesare confessed to strangling him, saying the Duke had earlier tried to murder him with a crossbow. But no action was taken. And in less than two weeks Cesare was again forcing his attentions on his grief-stricken sister. Their incestuous liaison continued until Rodrigo arranged another match for Lucrezia, with the Duke of Ferraro's son. On their last night together before she left for the nuptials, Cesare arranged a special treat in his Vatican room – 50 local socialites rolled naked on the floor, scrambling for hot roasted chestnuts tossed to them by the illicit lovers.

But the debauched days of the unholy Borgia alliance were numbered. In August 1503, Rodrigo and Cesare both fell ill with malaria after attending a party thrown by a cardinal in a vineyard just outside Rome. Within a week the 72-year-old Pope was dead. And Cesare, who knew that all his power derived from his father's protection, was too weak to look after his own interests.

For a while he had reason to hope that he could still maintain power. Rodrigo's successor as Pope was an ineffectual old man who bore no grudge against Cesare.

But he died just one month after taking office. Unluckily for Cesare, the old man's successor was Giuliano della Rovere, who still resented his defeat by Rodrigo in the election of 1492.

Cesare was arrested and forced to relinquish his Romagna kingdom. He left Rome for Naples, then under Spanish rule, hoping to be allowed to build a new power base. Instead he was again arrested, for disturbing the peace of Italy, and sought sanctuary with his brother-in-law, the King of Navarre. But, on 12 March 1507, he was wounded leading a siege of the town of Viana during a territorial dispute with Spain. His captors showed him as much mercy as he had shown his own victims – they stripped him naked and left him to die of thirst.

The Conquistadores

Christian fervour reigned in Catholic Spain in the 16th century. The dreaded Inquisition spread its bloody tyranny, the entire Dutch people were excommunicated and an invasion Armada was sent to convert Protestant England. But missionary mania was not confined to Europe. When explorers sailed home with news of distant lands across the Atlantic full of strange peoples and untold riches, armed expeditions set out to claim them for King and Pope. Natives of the Caribbean, Mexico and Central America were conquered and tamed in the name of Christ. Then the discovery of the Pacific Ocean opened up fresh horizons.

In 1527 a Spanish galleon investigating the new sea captured a balsa raft crammed with beautiful gold and silver objects studded with precious gems. The natives crewing the raft were the first clue to an unexpected and extraordinary civilization which had prospered in total isolation from the known world – the Incas. And the cargo they carried was enough to condemn their well-ordered empire to destruction. For, although Spanish conquistadores, led by Francisco Pizarro, justified their invasion as a crusade for God and the Bible, they committed every sin in the book in pursuit of their real aim – treasure.

Pizzaro, illegitimate son of a soldier from Trujillo, had spent 30 years in the new world subjugating 'savages'. Though an important member of Panama's Spanish community, he had not yet found the crock of gold that would make his fortune. With seizure of the Inca raft, he saw his chance. He obtained royal permission to explore and conquer Peru. Dominican monk Friar Vicente de Valverde was to go with him as 'protector' of the Indians.

The expedition left Panama in December 1530. Pizarro established a coastal base, killing the local chief to intimidate nearby natives, then moved inland with 168 soldiers, 62 on horses. He could not have arrived at a better time for Spain. Disease had ravaged the Inca court, killing the Inca himself, Huayna-Capac, and his heir. Two more of his sons, Huascar and Atahualpa, had begun a civil war for control of the empire, which stretched 3,000 miles through Chile, Bolivia, Ecuador and south Colombia as well as Peru. The conquistadores found towns in ruins and Indian corpses dangling from trees as they pressed up into the mountains.

Atahualpa, who commanded the area of Peru where the Spanish had landed, was none too pleased when his scouts reported that the strangers were pillaging the countryside as they advanced. But he sent the conquistadores gifts and invited them to meet him at Cajamarca. His army was camped beyond the town, and Atahualpa told Pizarro's envoys he would visit their leader in the town's central square next day. But when he arrived, carried on a litter by 80 men and surrounded by thousands of unarmed natives, the conquistadores stayed hidden in the buildings around the square. Friar Valverde emerged with an interpreter, carrying a cross and a Bible, and began explaining his religion to the baffled chief. Then he handed Atahualpa the book. But the Incas did not understand writing. They worshipped the sun, and claimed their images of it spoke to them. When the pages of the Bible did not speak, Atahualpa threw the book to the ground. The furious priest screamed for the insult to be avenged – and Pizzaro unleashed a brutal and carefully planned ambush.

'The Spaniards began to fire their muskets and charged upon the Indians with horses, killing them like ants,' Inca nobleman Huaman Poma told chroniclers. 'At the sound of the explosions and the jingle of bells on the horses' harnesses, the shock of arms and the whole amazing novelty of the attackers' appearance, the Indians were terror-stricken. The pressure of their numbers caused the walls of the square to crumble and fall. They were desperate to escape from being trampled by horses and in their headlong fight a lot of them were crushed to death. So many Indians were killed that it was impractical to count them.' After two hours of horrific slaughter, nearly 7,000 natives were dead and thousands more maimed by sword slashes. All 80 carriers of Atahualpa were massacred, but he himself was spared. Pizarro needed him alive as insurance for the invaders' safety until reinforcements arrived.

The captive Inca noted the conquistadores' glee as they ravaged his camp for treasure, and made a shrewd offer. He would buy his freedom by filling a room 22 feet (6.7m) long by 17 feet (5.1m) wide with treasure, to a depth of 8ft (2.4m). He would fill it once with gold and twice with silver. Pizarro accepted, promising to restore Atahualpa to his stronghold at Quito as long as he instigated no plots against the Spanish. The Inca told the invaders where to find his temples and directed a scouting party to his capital, Cuzco. It returned with 285 llamas loaded with gold and silver stripped from palaces, tombs and holy places. Other treasure trains poured in from all over the empire. Pizarro crushed jars, jugs and sculptures so the room would hold more. Then he set up furnaces to melt all the precious metals into bars. There were 6 tons (6,096kg) of 22-carat gold and 12 tons (12,192kg) of silver, a total then worth nearly £3 million.

Atahualpa, confident of release, had secretly continued his civil war, having his troops kill Huascar and two of his half-brothers. But all he was doing was playing into Pizarro's hands by weakening the empire's chances of ever repelling the invaders. Pizarro had no intention of letting the Inca go. Now he had Atahualpa's treasure, he planned to march on to Cuzco with recently arrived reinforcements, and could not afford to take the native leader along as a magnet for possible attacks. Rumours of an approaching Inca army, out to rescue their chief, were the excuse Pizarro needed. He sent out search parties to check the reports. But before they returned Atahualpa was dead. Condemned without trial for treason, he was tied to a stake on 26 July 1533, and told he would be burned alive unless he became a Christian. He agreed to be converted, taking the name Francisco in honour of Pizarro. Then he was garrotted.

The death caused a furore in Spain and its other colonies. In Madrid the King was angry that a fellow royal had been illegally executed. The governor of Panama said Atahualpa had 'done no harm to any Spaniard'. But Pizarro survived the storm. He reasoned, rightly, that the crown's one-fifth share of all booty would calm humanitarian qualms.

The march to Cuzco started uneventfully. The invaders were going through Huascar country, and locals welcomed the death of Atahualpa. They were trusting, gentle people – their homes did not have doors, let alone locks – and were in awe of the magnificent appearance of the newcomers. Having never seen horses before, some thought mount and rider were one being. Others believed the armour-plated conquistadores, white-faced and wearing strange beards, heralded the return of their sun god Viracocha. They were to pay for their naïveté by losing their wealth, their land, their women, their religion – and, for thousands, their lives.

The first armed opposition to Pizarro's men came 17 months after he landed in Peru. Troops loyal to Atahualpa attacked at Jauja, 250 miles north of Cuzco. But they were trying to fight cavalry armed with pistols, lances and steel swords using only clubs, bronze axes and stone sling-shots. The native forces were routed by charging horses and mercilessly pursued and cut down as they fled. When the futile ambushes continued, Pizarro burned captive commander Chulcuchima alive, accusing him of inspiring the raids. The Inca general defiantly refused to spare himself agony by becoming a Christian.

The town of Cuzco welcomed the Spanish as liberators. And Huascar's son Manco welcomed them most. He was ready to collaborate if they made him Inca. Pizarro willingly installed him, then organized systematic looting of the empire's richest city. Temple walls, priceless statues, jewels and vases buried with the dead, even a unique artificial garden of intricate golden plants, were melted down. A young priest who watched with horror wrote: 'Their only concern was to collect gold and silver to make themselves rich . . . What was being destroyed was more perfect than anything enjoyed or possessed.' But clerical concern at the abuse of a peaceful people in the Church's name could not stop it. As the governor of Panama reported to the King: 'The greed of the Spaniards of all classes is so great as to be insatiable. The more the native chiefs give, the more the Spaniards kill or torture them to give more.'

Reports of the riches available in the Inca land sparked

off a gold rush in other colonies. In Puerto Rico, the governor banned anyone leaving. When he caught a boatload of would-be treasure-hunters, he flogged them and cut off their feet. But still new adventurers reached Peru, committing atrocities in the race to get rich quickly.

Pedro de Alvarado marched into northern Peru, chaining up hundreds of native porters from the tropical coastal areas and watching them die cruelly in the icy Andes. Men, women and children were killed and towns were sacked, and local chieftains were hanged, burned or thrown to dogs when, under torture, they refused to divulge the whereabouts of treasure. Sebastian de Benalcazar burned the feet of chiefs to force them to reveal treasure troves. In one village, where all the men had fled to join Inca armies, he massacred the remaining women and children because there were not enough riches to satisfy his cravings. It was 'cruelty unworthy of a Castillian' according to the official chronicler of the Peruvian conquest. Other Spaniards buried native chiefs up to their waists in pits to try to force them to give away the hiding places of gold. When they would not – or could not – they were flogged, then buried up to their necks before being killed.

Reports of cruelty flooded into Cuzco, angering the Inca Manco. He also had personal reasons to regret collaborating with the Spanish. The town was in the control of Pizarro's brothers, Juan, Hernando and Gonzalo, after Francisco left for the coast to found the new city of Lima. The Inca was continually pestered to reveal more treasure caches. His mother and sisters were raped. Then Gonzalo stole his wife. Such humiliation of himself and his people was more than the proud prince could stand. He and his elders decided to rebel. In 1535 he slipped out of the town at night, but was recaptured by horsemen and returned in chains. Spaniards urinated on him and tortured him, burning his eyelashes with a candle. But a year later he successfully escaped, determined to make the invaders pay for treating him so disgustingly.

Manco had secretly mobilized a vast native army, and began deploying it with a devastating effect. He lured Cuzco's cavalry to nearby Calca, allowing them to seize a treasure train. While they counted their plunder, thousands of natives surrounded Cuzco, diverting irrigation canals to flood fields, making them impossible for horses to operate on. It was the start of a four-month siege. Three squads of Spaniards marching to the rescue were wiped out by native ambushers, who hurled giant boulders down deep gorges to knock them off tortuous mountain paths. Spaniards in Jauja were all killed in a dawn raid. But the conquistadores hit back with subterfuge and savagery to quell the rebellion.

Four shaved off their beards and blacked their faces to appear like Indians. Then, with the help of a native traitor, they got into an inaccessible fortress and opened the gates for colleagues to run amok. Hundreds of Indians leapt to their deaths off cliffs to escape Spanish swords. Morgovejo de Quinones, riding to relieve Cuzco, decided to avenge the death of five Spanish travellers by herding 24 chiefs and elders of a nearby town into a thatched building, then setting light to it and burning them alive. When the encircled horsemen in Cuzco broke out to attack a native fortress – Juan Pizarro was killed by a sling stone in the raid – so many Indians leapt from the battlements that the last to jump were cheated of death because the bodies piled beneath them broke their fall. More than 1,500 natives still in the fort were put to the sword. Conquistadores led by Gonzalo Pizarro surprised an Indian army and massacred the men. Those who plunged into a lake to try to escape were pursued by horsemen and 'speared like fish'.

Horror and mutilation were deliberately used by the

Spanish to demoralize their foes. Hernando Pizarro ordered that all women caught near battlefields were to be killed. They were the Inca soldiers' wives and mistresses. When brother Gonzalo captured 200 Indian fighters, he paraded them in the square at Cuzco and sliced off all their right hands. Then he sent them back to their comrades as 'a dreadful warning'. Later male captives had their noses cut off. Women who escaped death had their breasts chopped. In the Huaylas area, Francisco de Chaves instituted a three-month reign of terror. Homes and fields were destroyed, men and women burned or impaled, and 600 children aged under three were slaughtered.

The final blow to Manco's hopes came when an army led by his commander Quizo tried to take Francisco Pizarro's capital, Lima. Cavalry devastated the foot soldiers as they advanced across the coastal plain, and the horsemen massacred survivors of the charge as they fled towards safety in the mountains. Quizo and 40 fellow generals were among the dead.

Manco now realized he could not save Peru from the Spanish. More than 20,000 of his people had died trying. He retreated to Vilcabamba, a desolate valley screened by misty crags, and escaped his pursuers by hiding with forest Indians. But the Spaniards caught his wife, Cura Ocllo. And Francisco Pizarro took out his anger on her. Pizarro had proved during the siege of Lima that he had no qualms about killing women. Atahualpa's sister Azarpay was his prisoner there. He suspected her of encouraging the native attackers and had her garrotted. He had an even worse fate in mind for Cura Ocllo.

The poor woman only escaped rape at the hands of her escort soldiers by smearing herself with excrement. When she reached Cuzco, where Pizarro was waiting for news of the pursuit of the Inca, she was stripped naked, tied to a stake and savagely beaten. Finally she was loaded into a basket and floated on a river which flowed into

Vilcabamba, so the Inca could see the fate of his spouse. It was yet another horror to appal decent-minded Spaniards. One called it 'an act totally unworthy of a sane Christian gentleman'. Sadly, such acts were becoming all too common in the conquest of Peru.

But Pizarro's days were numbered. The lure of gold had led Spaniards to fight each other. Hernando Pizarro was recalled to Spain and jailed for garrotting without trial Diego de Almagro, one of the first conquistadores, who had rebelled for a bigger share of the booty. On 26 June 1541, Almagro's followers took revenge. Twenty of them stormed Francisco Pizarro's Lima palace and stabbed him to death. Another victim of the raid was the cruel child-killer Francisco de Chaves. Friar Vicente de Valverde, the man who had helped dupe Atahualpa, panicked at the death of his patron Pizarro and took a ship for Panama. On an island off Peru, he was captured by cannibals and eaten.

Pizarro had succeeded in his quest. Contemporaries praised him for acquiring more gold and silver than any other commander the world had seen. But the religious cause which justified his exploits played little part in his epitaph. His achievements were best summed up in the coat of arms awarded him by the King of Spain when he made him a marquis. It showed seven native chiefs with chains round their necks, and a shackled Atahualpa, his hands delving into two treasure chests.

Pizarro's passing did not end the suffering his invasion inflicted on Peru. And deaths resisting his takeover accounted for just a fraction of the estimated five million drop in the empire's native population between 1530 and the end of the century. The other reasons were spelled out damningly in John Hemming's authoritative book, *The Conquest of the Incas*. They were:

Disease: Peruvians had no immunity to European ailments such as smallpox, measles, the plague. Epidemics raged uncontrollably. The town of Quito lost 30,000 in just one.

Neglect: Preoccupied by gold and silver, the Spaniards failed to maintain precious irrigation canals, agricultural terraces, roads and bridges. Where the Incas filled communal storehouses for times of hardship, the Spanish merely looted them.

Hunger: As well as taking the natives' precious metal, the conquistadores and their successors seized, slaughtered and sold at ridiculously cheap prices their herds of llama. Harvests were also grabbed for cheap sale.

Exploitation: Francisco Pizarro had divided the nation into vast estates. Natives living on them had to provide annual tribute – gold, silver, livestock, grain, potatoes, eggs, salt, timber, utensils, clothing – whether the land provided them or not. Get-rich-quick landlords increased their demands until many natives worked all year just to provide the tribute, with no time or energy to look after their families. Many became wandering vagabonds to escape impossible obligations.

Plantations: Indians from the snowbound Andes were herded down to humid forests to harvest lucrative crops of coca, the plant that provides cocaine. They died in their thousands from heat and coca-related diseases.

Expeditions: Greedy Spaniards followed up every every rumour of another rich El Dorado, however remote the gold was said to be. Hundreds of natives were chained to act as porters. They died like flies from exhaustion, exposure or abuse.

Forced labour: Giant silver and mercury mines were set up by the Spanish, and natives from catchment areas up to 600 miles wide were forced to work them. Conscripts chipped at narrow, unsafe faces for six days at a stretch, sleeping in the fetid air of the galleries, full of acrid smoke from tallow candles which were the only lighting. Toxic gases containing arsenic added to the toll of exhaustion, heat and bad diet in the mercury mines. A monk,

Domingo de Santo Tomas, called the mines 'the mouth of hell, into which a great mass of people enter every year, and are sacrificed by the greed of the Spaniards to their god'. But the carnage was too profitable to stop. The royal fifth of the annual output at the Potosi silver mine alone came to 4½ tons (4,550kg).

Yet, according to John Hemming, none of these evils was the biggest killer. The main cause of death, he says, was 'profound culture shock'. The Inca people had lived without money in a benevolent welfare state which cared for them. Now, after decades of fighting, they were expected to work for cash wages by a government which cared nothing for them. Hemming quotes an Inca elder as saying: 'The Indians, seeing themselves dispossessed and robbed, allow themselves to die and do not apply themselves to anything as they did in Inca times.' They lost the will to live – and procreate. The birth rate fell as dramatically as the death toll rose.

The Madrid government tried to impose liberal laws, but the settlers rebelled – once led by Gonzalo Pizarro – insisting it was their right to exploit the land they had won as they thought fit. Rather than risk losing the flow of the New World riches, the King made concessions. The exploitation went on.

The final nails in the coffin of the Inca empire were driven in by Francisco de Toledo, who arrived as Viceroy in 1569. In two years, 1.5 million natives from isolated farms and villages were forcibly uprooted and settled in towns where they were easier to convert and control. Then the Church began a drive against native religions, seizing leaders, smashing relics and rooting out rites. And the last Inca King was captured and killed.

The murder of a Spanish messenger, trying to deliver letters to the new Inca, Tupac Amaru, was the excuse Toledo needed to invade Vilcabamba, the mysterious last refuge of the Peruvian royal family. Native sticks and stones were no match for the cannons and muskets of the 250-strong Spanish force. The Inca and his generals were caught as they tried to flee through the forests, and dragged to Cuzco in chains. Tupac Amaru was accused of ruling a heathen state which allowed heathen practices and raided Spanish Peru. He was also charged with specific murders, including that of the messenger. Despite pleas for mercy from all over Peru, and despite an astonishing public admission that the Inca religion of sun worship was a sham, Tupac Amaru was beheaded in front of vast, emotional crowds. It was almost 40 years to the day since the death of his great-uncle Atahualpa.

Toledo wanted to rid Peru of all Inca influence. He married princesses to Spaniards against the girls' wills, and sentenced several relatives of Tupac Amaru to Mexican exile – a decision over-ruled by Madrid. But all his efforts were in vain. Over 200 years later, when Peruvians successfully fought for independence from Spain, one of their heroes was Jose Gabriel Condorcanqui Tupac Amaru – great-great-great-grandson of the last Inca.

Pirates:
Evil on the High Seas

The Venetian ambassador to London, Giovanni Scaramelli, wrote to his city's Doge and senate in 1603: 'How just is the hatred which all peoples bear to the English, for they are the disturbers of the whole world. The whole strength and repute of the nation rests on its vast number of corsairs. To such a state has this unhappy kingdom come, that from a lofty religion has fallen into the abyss of infidelity.'

Scaramelli was writing home in dismay at the

realization that a mighty nation had granted a licence to criminals to guard its furthest colonial frontiers and boost its revenues. Those criminals called themselves corsairs, privateers, buccaneers or, grandly, 'the brethren of the coast'. In reality, they were no more than pirates. In the service of the English Crown, carrying no-questions-asked commissions, they were seaborne merchants of death and destruction.

Since the early 16th century, deserters, felons and shipwrecked smugglers had been abandoned to their fate on the coasts of the Caribbean islands, mainly Cuba, Jamaica and Hispaniola. They lived off wild pigs, the meat of which they cured by smoking long strips over wood-and-dung fires. The dried meat was known as *boucan* and the wild men of the islands were termed *boucaniers*.

Through trade with passing ships, they acquired an arsenal of weapons, which they used to good effect in raids on the ill-defended colonial outposts – mainly Spanish – then being established throughout the islands. They drank a fearsome mixture of rum and gunpowder, wore trousers of uncured rawhide and shirts stained with pigs' blood. They must have smelt revolting and looked like savages. They certainly struck fear into the hearts of the Spaniards . . . with good reason.

In the first half of the 17th century, these buccaneers took to the sea. They stole small boats or fashioned canoes from hollowed tree trunks and sailed out of coves to attack Spanish shipping. The buccaneers would manoeuvre outside the line of fire of the Spanish guns, then race in close under constant covering fire and clamber aboard the sterns of the great galleons. Captured ships would be looted and occasionally impounded into the service of the attackers. The age of the pirate was born.

With names like Roche Braziliano, Red Legs Greaves, Pierre le Grand and Montbars the Exterminator, they harried Spain's treasure fleets and repeatedly sacked her outposts in the Central American isthmus, torturing the inhabitants without mercy until they revealed their hidden hoards. Most feared among them was a Breton captain, François Lolonois.

At the head of an army of 700 men, Lolonois razed Maracaibo to the ground and rampaged through what is now Nicaragua, lining Spanish prisoners before him and slaughtering them a dozen at a time for the sheer fun of it. According to one chronicler, Lolonois once 'grew outrageously passionate in so much that he drew his cutlass, slashed open the heart of a poor Spaniard and, pulling it out, began to gnaw it, saying to the rest that he would serve them all alike if they did not talk'. Among his other delights, Lolonois would 'cut a man to pieces, first some flesh, then a hand, an arm, a leg, sometimes tying a cord around his head and with a stick twisting it till his eyes shoot out, which is called woolding'. Lolonois met a fittingly unpleasant fate himself, being torn limb from limb by Indians.

The ease with which the buccaneers were able to relieve the Spanish of the gold they had themselves stolen from the natives of Central and South America ushered in a new and, if anything, even bloodier age of piracy. For, under the guise of a crusade against Popery, Britain entered the arena and effectively gave its citizens a free hand in ravaging, robbing and persecuting neighbouring colonies with whom they were not even at war. These sea-going criminals were issued with commissions which were no more than licences to kill.

Foremost among them was Henry Morgan, a farmer's son born in Llanrhymney, Glamorgan. How he got to the West Indies is not known. He may have been transported, he may have been an indentured servant or he may have arrived in 1655 with Oliver Cromwell's army. In 1663 his uncle, Sir Edward Morgan, was appointed Deputy Governor-General of Jamaica and, although there is no evidence, it is likely that this valuable family connection helped the young Welshman launch his piratical career. For Jamaica's Government House was the principal source of buccaneers' commissions, handed out freely under the guise of guarding the colony against Spanish 'invasion'. In return for the commissions, the governor, the notoriously corrupt planter Sir Thomas Modyford, and his deputy received their own 'commission' – a share in the pirate plunder.

First records of Morgan's activities date from 1665 when he was involved in skirmishes with the Spanish in Costa Rica. Two years later, despite a British peace treaty with Spain, Modyford authorized Henry Morgan to assemble a fleet of 12 ships and to sweep the Spanish colonies for booty.

Morgan gained a reputation for barbarity. In Puerto del Principe, Cuba, he systematically tortured the townspeople until he was satisfied no hidden treasures remained. Then he sailed south to the Panama isthmus where he launched an ambitious attack on the impressively fortified town of Portobello. His men scaled the walls of the town by forcing captured priests and nuns up the scaling ladders as a human shield.

Morgan's savage rampage almost came to an early end in 1669 when, about to raid Maracaibo, he called all his captains and senior officers to a council of war aboard his flagship, the *Oxford*, in Port Royal harbour. Midway through the discussions, the *Oxford* was torn apart by an explosion in the powder magazine. Two hundred men, including five captains, died. Among the council of war, only Morgan and 25 others survived – watching horrified as everyone on the opposite side of the chart table was blown to bits. Morgan was unharmed but his reputation was dented.

The following year Morgan determined to restore his prestige and to ensure riches that would last him a lifetime by carrying out a single, dramatic raid on the richest city of the West. He planned to attack 'the Cup of Gold' – Panama City itself.

In 1670, ignoring yet another newly signed treaty between Spain and Britain, Henry Morgan assembled more than 2,000 men and 36 ships, victualled his fleet by sacking a dozen or more townships and set sail for Panama. En route he stopped at Providence Island where the governor agreed to surrender if Morgan staged a mock attack using gunpowder but no ammunition. This charade over and the garrison town sacked, the fleet sailed to the mouth of the River Charge, which breaches the Darien isthmus, and took the sentinel Fort San Lorenzo with the loss of 100 buccaneers.

The city of Panama was only 50 miles away but they were 50 miles of disease-ridden swamp and dense jungle inhabited by unfriendly natives. After five days his men, starving and shot by Indians, urged him to turn back and relaunch the attack with greater supplies. Morgan refused. The Spanish withdrew before them, burning villages and leaving the pirates without food or fresh water. The invaders ate cats, dogs and their own leather bags before, on the tenth day, they reached Panama, routed the defenders on the plains outside the city and burned it to the ground.

The looting of Panama and the murder, rape and torture of its inhabitants produced an unrecorded fortune. But the men who had gone through hell for Henry Morgan got little reward. Morgan claimed that the booty had been far less than expected – and accordingly gave his men pathetically small hand-outs for their sacrifices. Even the widows of those who had died in his service were cheated of their agreed recompense by Morgan. The only people satisfied with the share-out were the expedition's principal backers, some of the captains . . . and Morgan himself.

Rich and famous, he was ordered to England by King Charles II to serve a period of so-called 'detention' for what was known as 'the crime of Panama'. It was no more than a feint to appease the angry Spanish. Morgan spent two years in London, a hero fêted by society, before returning in 1674 to Jamaica as Sir Henry Morgan, Lieutenant-Governor, plantation-owner and justice of the peace. As such, he sat in judgement on many pirates and sentenced them to prison, and to death, without mercy – this, despite his own continuing financial links with the pirate trade. He died a rich man in 1688.

The lessons in terror and barbarity of François Lolonois and Henry Morgan were well learned by the pirates who followed them in the early years of the 18th century. Monstrous Edward Teach (better known as Blackbeard) was a sadistic psychotic who ravaged the West Indies and America's eastern seaboard under the protection of North Carolina's corrupt governor. Dashing, dandified Bartholomew 'Black Bart' Roberts was reported to have treated prisoners with 'barbarous abuse . . . some almost whipped to death, others had their ears cut off, others fixed to yardarms and fired at as a mark'.

But the pirates' crimes often seem in retrospect to have been overshadowed by a more insidious evil – on the part of the corrupt, greedy authorities who not only tolerated but encouraged pirate activities.

The example of royal duplicity and hypocrisy displayed by Charles II and his loyal servant Henry Morgan was exceeded by their immediate successors: King William III and a New York-based privateer called Captain Kidd. In 1695 the King granted 'to our trusty and well-beloved William Kidd' two commissions, one to seize French shipping and the other to subdue piracy (a euphemism for the confiscation of booty from other privateers). For this the King expected a 'commission' of his own of 10 per cent of the haul. After Kidd's share the remainder would go to the expedition's backers – a syndicate of bankers, peers and Whig politicians including the Lord Chancellor and the First Lord of the Admiralty.

Kidd little needed the adventure or the money. Born in Greenock, Scotland, in 1645, the son of a Presbyterian minister, he had already made his mark and his fortune as a privateer against the French in the West Indies. He had then settled in New York, married a wealthy widow and retired to a mansion in Wall Street. It was only his wish to give evidence to a British Board of Trade inquiry about the corrupt practices of an arch enemy, New York's Governor Benjamin Fletcher, that brought Kidd to London and to the attention of the King.

In 1696 Kidd, duly commissioned, sailed from England to New York, where he recruited a crew from among pirates who had once worked for Governor Fletcher. He then sailed south, around the Cape of Good Hope to the Indian Ocean, on a buccaneering rampage that brought protests from almost every major maritime nation. The British Government were forced to tear up his royal commissions and order his capture. Dismayed when he herd the news, Kidd fled to the West Indies, lost most of his plunder to mutinous crews and ended up in Boston, throwing himself upon the mercy of the authorities.

The man who had the power of life or death over Kidd at that stage was the new Governor of New York, the Earl of Bellomont. The noble Earl had got the job with the help of Kidd's evidence against his predecessor. He had also been one of the secret backers of Kidd's expedition. Yet Bellomont had the captain clapped in irons and thrown into a dungeon for six months before sending him back to Britain to stand trial. Bellomont meanwhile appropriated the £14,000 which was all that Kidd had left of his haul from the South Seas.

On 23 May 1701, drunk and insensible, William Kidd was hanged at Wapping and his body suspended in chains 'to serve as a greater terror to all persons from committing the like crimes'.

François Lolonois and Henry Morgan were among the most pitiless, brutal and bloodthirsty pirates who ever put to sea – but the unfortunate Captain Kidd was very different. Though his actions were certainly criminal, the real evil was displayed by those who, to line their own pockets, secretly and hypocritically authorized piracy and murder . . . and who, when their plot began to rebound on them, covered their traces by sending the instrument of their greed to the gallows. They were men like the duplicitous New York Governor and Irish peer, the Earl of Bellomont; the Lord Chancellor, Sir John Somers; the First Lord of the Admiralty, Edward Russell, later Earl of Orford; the Master of Ordnance, the Earl of Romney; Secretary of State, the Duke of Shrewsbury – and the King himself, William III.

As Kidd told the judge at his trial: 'It is a very hard sentence. I am the innocentest person of them all, only I have been sworn against by perjured persons.' It was his last appeal to those evil men in high office – and it went unheeded.

Marat and Robespierre: Evil in the Name of Liberty

Hailing the almost bloodless start of the French Revolution, Honoré-Gabriel Riqueti, Comte de Mirabeau, said in May 1789: 'History has too often recounted the actions of nothing more than wild animals . . . Now we are given hope that we are beginning the history of man.' But, within five years, that hope had been wiped out by one of the world's worst outbreaks of mass murder. Frenchmen freed by negotiation from almost feudal tyranny turned into brutal, barbaric beasts on the pretext of achieving liberty, equality and fraternity. And the most poignant epitaph for Mirabeau's dream was the anguished cry of a fallen revolutionary as she was led to the guillotine: 'Oh liberty, what crimes are committed in your name.'

The Revolution erupted when public patience with the King's absolute power to impose taxes and laws ran out. Louis XVI and the privileged nobility were forced to make concessions to democracy and individual freedom. But each concession merely made the increasingly strong citizens greedy for more. 'The difficulty is not to make a Revolution go, it is to hold it in check,' said Mirabeau shortly before his death in 1791. For, as the people realized they had the power of life or death, negotiation was abandoned for naked force. After the storming of the Bastille, symbol of the old regime's authority, revolutionaries advocating cautious progress were drowned by the clamour of radical factions urging war on France's neighbours and dissidents at home. Then a more sinister voice demanded massacres.

Jean Paul Marat was not even French – his father came from Sardinia, his mother was Swiss. But, when the revolution began, he abandoned his career as a scientist and doctor to become one of Paris's most vitriolic pamphleteers. His early extremism was unpopular, and several times he was forced into hiding. Once, when he took refuge in the city sewers, he contracted a painful and unpleasant skin disease, which added to his bitter persecution complex. But, as the mob became increasingly impatient with a Revolution which seemed to be doing nothing to reduce raging inflation and food shortages, and with leaders who were prevaricating over the fate of Louis and his hated Austrian wife Marie Antoinette, Marat's messages began to find a receptive audience. And he spoke with chilling clarity. 'In order to ensure public tranquillity,' he wrote, '200,000 heads must be cut off.'

On 10 August 1791, an armed procession of 20,000 Parisians marched towards the royal residence, the Tuileries. The King and Queen, and their two children, were smuggled out by elected representatives and taken to the National Assembly building for protection. The Palace's Swiss Guards held the mob at bay until their ammunition ran out. They surrendered – but the mob was in no mood for mercy. More than 500 soldiers were slaughtered with pikes, bayonets, swords and clubs. Another 60 were massacred as they were marched away as captives. Palace staff, even cooks, maids and the royal children's tutor, were slashed to pieces as the Parisians ran riot. Bodies were strewn in rooms and on staircases. The grounds were littered with corpses. And onlookers were sickened to see children playing with decapitated heads. Women, 'lost to all sense of shame, were committing the most indecent mutilations of the dead bodies, from which they tore pieces of flesh and carried them off in triumph'.

The hideous orgy of bloodlust instantly brought fears of a backlash from royalists or counter-revolutionaries. Marat had the answer. Many opponents of the Revolution were already packed in the jails of Paris, and might break out to seek revenge. 'Let the blood of the traitors flow,' wrote Marat. 'That is the only way to save the country.' Hysteria was whipped up by pamphlets warning of a plot to assassinate all good citizens in their beds. In September, the good citizens took steps to make that impossible.

A party of priests who had refused to take a new vow severing their allegiance to Rome were being escorted to prison in six carriages. A mob ambushed them, plunging swords through the carriage windows to wound and mutilate indiscriminately. Then, at the gates of the jail, another mob was waiting. When the convoy arrived, and the priests tried to dash inside for safety, they were slaughtered. Soon afterwards, a bunch of thugs burst into a convent where 150 more priests were being held, along with an archbishop. He was stabbed first. Then the others were killed in pairs, and their bodies thrown down a well.

Over the next week, gangs broke into jails, prison hospitals and mental asylums all over Paris, massacring inmates with swords, axes and iron bars. Only prisons for prostitutes and debtors were spared. Women were on hand with food and drink for the executioners. Drunken killers held mock trials for some of the victims. One woman awaiting trial for mutilating her lover had her breasts cut off and her feet nailed to the floor before being burned alive. Marie Thérése de Savoie-Carignan, Princesse de Lamballe, a friend of Marie Antoinette, was stripped and raped. Then her body was ripped to pieces. A leg was stuffed into a cannon, her head was stuck on a pole, and her heart cut out, roasted and eaten.

Ghastly scenes of grisly glee were reported as the piles of corpses built up. Drunken women sat watching the debauched death-dealers, laughing and applauding at each new depravity. Some pinned cut-off ears to their skirts as gruesome souvenirs. Others drank aristocratic blood handed round by the killers, or dipped bread in it. Men sat on bloodied bodies, smoking and joking while they rested from their labours. In six days, during which the gutters ran red, half the prison population, nearly 1,200 people, were murdered. And those who took a day off work to join the extermination squads were paid compensation for lost wages by delighted leaders of the Paris Commune.

The excesses appalled many of the most radical revolutionaries. But Marat was unrepentant. He signed a letter sent by the Commune to its counterparts in provincial towns, explaining that the 'act of justice' was 'indispensable in order to restrain by intimidation the thousands of traitors hidden within our walls'. And the letter went on: 'We do not doubt that the whole nation will be anxious to adopt this most necessary method of public security; and that all Frenchmen will exclaim, with the people of Paris, "We are marching against the foe, but we will not leave these brigands behind us to cut the throats of our children and wives".' Republicans in many towns took that as their cue to match the capital's atrocities by massacring the inmates of their own jails.

In January 1793, the revolution reached the point of no return. The elected national assembly, now called the Convention, unanimously condemned Louis XVI to death for trying to 're-establish tyranny on the ruins of liberty'. He was executed in the Place de la Révolution, formerly the Place de Louis XV. Within weeks, every major country in Europe had declared war on France, and civil war raged as peasants resisted compulsory call-up to the armed forces.

Minister of Justice Charles Danton set up a Revolutionary Tribunal to try to maintain order and avoid atrocities like the September massacres. 'Let us be terrible to prevent the people from being terrible,' he thundered. But Convention moderates believed the people would stay terrible as long as Marat was free to incite them. They ordered that he be tried by the Tribunal. To their consternation, he was cleared. Carried back to the parliament in triumph by the mob, he forced through a decree ordering the arrest of 22 of his accusers.

Marat did not savour his victory for long. On 13 July 1793, he was at home, wrapped in towels in a copper bath to ease the pain of his skin affliction, when a young girl arrived, claiming to know of moderates who were plotting an anti-leftist coup against Marat's party. 'They will all soon be guillotined,' Marat assured her as he jotted down the names. But the girl, Charlotte Corday, was not what she seemed. She suddenly drew a knife from her cleavage and stabbed Marat. He fell dying as aides manhandled Charlotte to the ground. She seemed oblivious to their blows. 'The deed is done,' she shouted. 'The monster is dead.'

But once again the moderates had miscalculated. Marat the monster became the mob's martyr. All over France, streets and squares were named after him. More than 30 towns changed their name to his. And his death did not divert the revolution from the path of blood. For an even more evil man had taken over leadership of the lethal extremists, a man prepared to sacrifice even the parents of his godson at the altar of his ambitions.

Maximilien Robespierre, a cold, humourless barrister from Arras, was despised by many of his fellow revolutionaries for his fastidious appearance and his squeamishness at the sight of bloodshed. Yet by 1793 the dapper lawyer who shunned public executions because they corrupted the human soul was the most feared man in France. And he used his power, as chief of the ironically named Committee of Public Safety, to institute one of the most cruel reigns of terror in history.

Robespierre's committee directed the Revolutionary Tribunal in eradicating enemies of the Republic. France was still in danger of invasion by its European neighbours, and Robespierre could justify early severity on those grounds. He ruled that all foreign nationals not living in France on 14 July 1789 – the day the Bastille was stormed – should be arrested. And he executed the most famous foreigner on French soil – Austrian-born Queen Marie Antoinette. Charges against her included conspiracy with her brother, the Austrian Emperor, and incest with her son. Though she denied them all, she followed her husband to the guillotine on 16 October 1793.

Soon the dreaded tumbrils were speeding almost daily to the scaffold in the Place de la Révolution bringing new victims. Pierre Vergniand, former President of the Revolutionary parliament, had warned: 'It is to be feared that the Revolution, like Saturn, will end up by devouring its own children.' Now his prophecy was coming true. He was among 20 moderates accused and condemned to death at a show trial. One stabbed himself to death in the courtroom with a concealed dagger – but his lifeless body accompanied his luckless colleagues for ritual decapitation next day.

More than 3,000 Parisians followed them to the blade. They included former royal mistress Madame Du Bary, accused of mourning the executed king while she was in London; a general who 'surrounded himself with aristocratic officers and never had good republicans at his table'; an innkeeper who 'furnished to the defenders of the country sour wine injurious to health'; a gambler who insulted patriots during a card game dispute; and a man who rashly shouted 'Vive le Roi' after a court jailed him for 12 years for another offence. Author Christopher Hibbert, in his authoritative book *The French Revolution*, says alleged speculators and hoarders died for 'starving the people' and one man paid the penalty 'for not giving his testimony properly'.

Vast crowds watched the executions, eating, drinking and laying bets on the order in which each batch of victims would lose their heads. English writer William Hazlitt reported: 'The shrieks of death were blended with the yell of the assassin and the laughter of the buffoons. Whole families were led to the scaffold for no other crime than their relationship; sisters for shedding tears over the death of their brothers; wives for lamenting the fate of their husbands; innocent peasant girls for dancing with Prussian soldiers; and a woman giving suck . . . for merely saying, as a group were being conducted to slaughter, "Here is much blood shed for a trifling cause."'

The Place de la Révolution guillotine was so busy that, according to author Hibbert, people living in nearby Rue Saint-Honoré – ironically the street where Robespierre had lodgings – complained that the smell of stale blood from the stones was a health hazard and consequently lowered the value of their houses.

Outside Paris, the vicious purges were even worse. 'The whole country seemed one vast conflagration of revolt and vengeance,' wrote Hazlitt. More than 14,000 people died as sadists and butchers in positions of office in the provinces made the most of Robespierre's instructions. Others killed to keep up with them, afraid they might be labelled weak or counter-revolutionaries. At Lyons, the Committee of Public Safety mowed down 300 convicted prisoners with a cannon. At Bordeaux a woman who wept when her husband was guillotined was forced to sit beneath the blade while his blood dripped onto her. Then she too was beheaded.

At Nantes, Jean-Baptiste Carrier was busy earning himself immortality as one of the worst brutes in the annals of infamy. Mass-killer Carrier, a lawyer like Robespierre, found the guillotine too slow for his taste. He packed victims into barges, towed them to the middle of the river Loire, then drowned them. Some couples were stripped naked and strapped together, face to face. Men waited with hatchets on the shore, to make sure no one got away. More than 2,000 people died in the river. Ships setting sail brought corpses up with their anchors, and the water became so polluted that catching fish in it was banned.

Carrier was also a child-killer. The guillotine was un-satisfactory – tiny heads were chopped in half because the necks were too small a target for the blade. And one executioner collapsed and died from the trauma of beheading four little sisters. So Carrier had 500 children taken to fields outside the town, where they were shot and cudgelled to death. But disease cheated the butcher of some of his prey. An epidemic swept through his overcrowded prisons, killing 3,000 inmates.

Millions of Frenchmen lived in terror of the midnight knock on the door that spelt arrest. Robespierre's spies were everywhere, and his assistants ensured that the pace of persecution never slackened. 'Liberty must prevail at any price,' declared Louis de Saint-Just, nicknamed Robespierre's Angel of Death. 'We must rule by iron those who cannot be ruled by justice,' he ordered. 'You must punish not merely traitors, but the indifferent as well.'

Early in 1794 Robespierre arrested more than 20 Convention members suspected of being critical of the way their Revolution was going. One of them was Camille Desmoulins. Robespierre was godfather to his son, but that made no difference. Desmoulins had said: 'Love of country cannot exist when there is neither pity nor love for one's fellow countrymen, but only a soul dried up and withered by self-adulation.' He named no names, but everyone knew who his target was. Saint-Just hit back: 'A man is guilty of a crime against the republic when he takes pity on prisoners. He is guilty because he has no desire for virtue.' Desmoulins died – and so did his 23-year-old widow, because she appealed to Robespierre for mercy.

Danton, too, was among this consignment of children of the Revolution to be devoured. Robespierre had decided that the notorious womanizer could never be a fit champion of freedom. Danton confided to his friends that he would not fight his accuser, because 'far too much blood has been shed already'. He added: 'I had the Revolutionary Tribunal set up. I pray to God and men to forgive me for it.'

With his main potential rivals purged, Robespierre again stepped up the slaughter. The Committee of Public Safety decreed that death was henceforth the only sentence it would impose. Defence lawyers, witnesses and preliminary investigations were all banned, and an official said: 'For a citizen to become suspect, it is now sufficient that rumour accuses him.' Hundreds more aristocrats were executed – 1,300 in Paris in one month alone. 'At the point we are now, if we stop too soon we will die,' Robespierre told the Convention. 'Freedom will be extinguished tomorrow.'

But, in the Convention, more and more delegates shared

Danton's belated repugnance at the killings – and, at last, summoned the courage to resist Robespierre. For 24 hours the Convention was split, with both sides drawing up indictments to arrest their opponents. Finally, the vote went against Robespierre, Saint-Just and 18 of their closest associates. But in the confusion troops detailed to escort Robespierre to jail proved loyal to him, and installed him in a safe house. The Convention summoned more soldiers to recapture him. When they burst in, a shot smashed Robespierre's jaw. Next day, 28 July 1794, he was in agony as the Revolutionary Tribunal he had used so lethally sentenced him and his aides to death. Hours later, the tumbrils took all the arrested men to the guillotine, pausing momentarily outside Robespierre's lodgings while a boy smeared blood from a butcher's shop on the door. Robespierre was the last to die. When his turn came, a woman screamed at him: 'You monster spewed out of hell, go down to your grave burdened with the curses of the wives and mothers of France.'

The new Revolutionary regime avenged itself on Robespierre's followers. Many were executed after trials – Carrier was guillotined on 16 November – and hundreds more were lynched in jails all over the country. The people's Revolution was at last over.

The French had paid a bloody price for allowing the likes of Marat and Robespierre to lead them towards their dream of liberty, equality and fraternity.

Reverend Jim Jones

It is just possible that the Reverend Jim Jones set out to be a loving religious leader who would champion the cause of the poor and the oppressed.

Certainly, thousands of sincere worshippers, inspired by his message of brotherhood and justice, flocked to join his faithful congregation. Politicians and civic leaders hailed Jones as a selfless, tireless worker whose personal sacrifices pointed the way towards building a better society for millions in the United States.

But somewhere along the line it all went grotesquely wrong.

Jones changed from Good Shepherd to tyrant, from benign pastor to brutal torturer. In the end he led nearly 1,000 of his followers into a nightmare in a tropical jungle in South America with the promise of building them a paradise on earth. And, when concerned relatives began to plead for an investigation into the plight of the faithful in the jungle settlement of Jonestown, he had the inquiring visitors assassinated to stop them telling the outside world the truth about the living hell he had created in the name of social progress and humanity.

As his religious empire came crashing down under the weight of the terrible suffering he had inflicted on his own followers, he ordered them to commit mass suicide.

Chanting and singing his praises, elderly women and young couples cheerfully drank the deadly arsenic potion of 'holy water' he offered them. Loving parents fed their children a sweet mixture of poison and lemonade. And, for those whose nerve failed them, the elders of Jones's church were ready to slit their throats or put a .38 bullet in their heads. The whole congregation died.

Jim Warren Jones was born on 13 May 1931 in the small farming town of Lynn, Indiana, and he was doomed to grow up a lonely child. His father was a World War I veteran who suffered a disabling lung disease and who could only contribute a meagre government pension towards the support of his family. Embittered and partly crippled, he reserved most of his strength for the fiery rallies of his favourite political cause, the racist Klu Klux Klan.

Jones's mother, Lynetta, was forced to take a factory job to make ends meet. As an adult, Jones was to claim that she was a full-blooded Cherokee Indian. Certainly he took his dark complexion and handsome features from her. And it was obvious from an early age he felt compelled to spread a different message from that of his father's racial hatred. Only an average student at school, he showed an unusual zeal for Bible studies. While his schoolmates demonstrated their energy on the football field, the Jones boy would stand on the porch of the family's run-down home and preach sermons at passers-by.

In 1949, at the age of 18, he took a part-time job as a hospital porter in nearby Richmond to support himself through religious studies at Indiana University. He also married hospital nurse Marceline Baldwin, four years his senior. The following year, although not yet an ordained minister, he became a pastor at a church in Indianapolis and helped to run its racially integrated youth centre.

For the next ten years, Jones suffered abuse at the hands of Indiana's racial bigots. Even the more conservative members of the church where he served protested his plans to welcome black worshippers into their midst. Eventually Jones quit, but not before he had learned a valuable lesson about human behaviour. Members of the congregation who had only been lukewarm about their young pastor had closed ranks and rallied round him when Jones was attacked by outsiders. The message was clear: even people who who don't enthusiastically share each other's beliefs can become loyally bound together if they feel threatened by a common enemy.

With money from his followers he eventually bought his own church, grandly named 'The People's Temple', in a run-down part of Indianapolis which changed from a poor white area to a black ghetto. He preached racial integration and equality, not because it was fashionable, but because he honestly believed in it.

He and his wife adopted seven children, black, white and Asian. Boasting of his mother's Cherokee blood, he called himself 'biracial'.

Now that his new parish was to consist of mainly black churchgoers, he set out to study the style and technique of black preachers who commanded rapturous devotion from their flocks. And in Philadelphia he watched one black preacher who held his congregation absolutely spellbound. Father Divine was a hellfire-and-damnation orator, faith healer and showman who lived a life of luxury on the offerings of totally trusting followers who even believed his claims to be able to raise the dead. Jones was enthralled – and decided to test the level of allegiance of his own churchgoers.

Overnight the campaign of racist abuse against him mysteriously reached a sinister climax. He claimed he had been concussed when a Klan member smashed a bottle in his face on his doorstep. A stick of dynamite thrown into his garden caused a tremendous explosion but no damage or injuries. Newspaper reports, based mainly on information supplied by Jones himself, told of how he bravely stood up to the threats against himself and his family.

In recognition of his courageous stand, the mayor of Indianapolis appointed Jones to a £3,000-a-year job on the city's Human Rights Commission. And his congregation, feeling their young pastor to be beleaguered, gave him their unswerving devotion. Jones decided the time had come to weld the congregation even more tightly together with a common fear that was more terrifying than the threat of racism.

In 1960, when the country was going through 'nuclear war fever', millions of worried Americans built backyard nuclear-fallout shelters. A popular magazine ran a tongue-in-cheek article, claiming to be a scientific survey of the 'ten safest places to live in the event of a nuclear war'. Jones seized on the idea as a perfect trial of how thoroughly he could rule the lives of his followers. Two of the safest 'bolt-holes' from nuclear destruction were

reported by the magazine to be Belo Horizonte in Brazil
and the rural backwoods of Ukiah in California, 120 miles
north of San Francisco.

The Reverend Jones suddenly announced to his church
members that he had experienced 'a personal vision of the
nuclear holocaust' and he told them they should be
prepared to follow him to distant pastures to escape.
Leaving abruptly with his family, at church expense, for a
visit to Brazil, he ordered them to be ready to sell up their
homes and withdraw their savings from their banks.

Jones returned from his South American trip unimpressed by Brazil but curiously interested in the
prospects of the tiny, newly independent country of
Guyana where he had stopped over for a few days. The
former British colony, now a left-wing socialist republic,
fulfilled many of his dreams of social justice, he told his
congregation. As an afterthought, he added that his
terrible premonition of the nuclear holocaust had receded
for the time being.

Emboldened and flattered by the number of devotees
who had already put their homes up for sale just because
of his 'premonition', Jones decided the option of fleeing
from civilization should be held for a future emergency. If
they believed in him enough to let his fantasies rule their
lives, he reckoned, they would believe in just about
anything he told them. Now was the ideal time to launch
himself into the lucrative faith-healing market.

The healing services were spectacular, profitable and
fraudulent. In a religious frenzy, Jones would pass among
the 'sick' and 'crippled' newcomers to his church, laying
his hands on them. Selected patients would then leap
joyously to their feet, saying their injuries and diseases
had been totally cured.

But, when Jones's inner circle of church officials began
to claim that he had raised 40 followers from the dead,
newspapers and the State Board of Psychology began to

take a close interest.

The time had come to make a quick move before the press and local authorities began to pry too deeply. The ideal bolt-hole proved to be in California's Redwood Valley, near Ukiah, one of the so-called 'nuclear safe zones'.

California of the mid-1960s provided the perfect camouflage for the People's Temple. The arrival of 300 religious enthusiasts preaching love and peace blended in neatly with a culture which had more than its fair share of 'flower children', 'peaceniks' and hippy communes.

For his so-called People's Temple to grow and flourish it only remained for Jones to convert the two potential troublemakers, civic busybodies and the press, into allies. He succeeded almost overnight. Temple members who became hard-working shop assistants and farm labourers were always the first to volunteer to work unpaid hours organizing local charities. The churchgoers acted as foster parents to take in scores of problem children from orphanages. Jones himself wooed local politicians until he was elected as foreman of the county grand jury and director of free legal services.

Jones now had hundreds of supporters whose regard for him had been cleverly nurtured from respect to allegiance, from devotion to mindless blind loyalty. One shortcut for him to bring about social justice, he explained to them, was to work tirelessly in elections and canvassing to get him more political power – and to hand over most of their earnings to him.

With the dollars pouring in and the People's Temple a respectable state-registered, tax-exempt, religious organization with the worthiest ideal, he was ready for the big time.

Jones and his flock left the backwoods for the bright lights of San Francisco. Their reputation as an industrious band of do-gooders quickly followed them as Jones set up a new Temple in downtown San Francisco. The membership swelled to 7,500.

City officials, impressed by Jones's boundless energy and his flair for organization, soon turned over to him part of their welfare programme and his Temple took over the task of dispensing thousands of free hot meals in their dining hall every day. No one realized that among the grateful recipients of the meals were many of Jones's own followers who had handed over to him their wages, their savings and even their social-security payments.

In 1976 a naïve local political worker who feared an embarrassingly small turnout at a meeting for Rosalynn Carter, wife of Presidential candidate Jimmy, asked Jones for help to swell the numbers at the election rally. Jones packed the hall with his supporters and received a standing ovation from the crowd. The next day the papers ran his photograph with Rosalynn Carter and, when Jimmy was duly elected, Jones received an invitation to the Presidential inauguration in Washington.

In the eyes of the local community he was a pillar of respectability. He openly boasted about funnelling hundreds of thousands of dollars from his Temple funds to South America to aid starving children in Guyana.

But the first defectors from his Temple began to tell a different story. They spoke of Jones's long tirades about sex during his sermons and how he demanded that happily married couples should be forced to divorce each other and remarry partners he had chosen for them among his inner circle of church elders.

They revealed how Jones insisted that, as their spiritual leader, he had the right to have sex with any woman or girl in the congregation and how he forced them to submit to his sexual demands.

They gave details of how browbeaten Temple members were made to confess publicly to imagined sins of homosexuality. And they revealed how young children

113

were cruelly beaten on a platform in the Temple by Jones
to 'make them show respect'. Young girls were made to
take part in 'boxing matches', outnumbered by teams of
bigger, stronger opponents who knocked them senseless.
Other children vanished into a private room to meet 'the
blue-eyed monster'. No sounds of beatings came from the
room, only the screams of the young victims and the
crackling noise of an electric cattle prod which sent surges
of high-voltage electricity through their bodies.

And, all the time, hundreds of thousands of dollars
poured into the Temple funds.

Many San Francisco newspapers had been the proud
winners of hefty cash bonuses from Jones through his
Temple awards for 'outstanding journalistic contributions
to peace and public enlightenment'. Even the local police
department had benefited from his generous donations to
the widows and orphans of officers killed in the line of
duty.

There was a deep sense of disappointment in the
highest circles, even up to the level of President Carter in
the White House, that Jones the civic hero might just be a
vicious crackpot.

As the bubble began to burst, Jones put into action his
escape plan. The millions of dollars he had salted away in
Guyana had already been put to use buying a lease on
20,000 acres of jungle and swamp near Port Kaituma on
the country's Caribbean coast. A pavilion had been built
as headquarters of 'Jonestown' and dormitories were
ready for 1,000 followers to join Jones in setting up a 'new,
just, socialist society'.

Amazingly, 1,000 loyal volunteers did go with him to
Jonestown in November 1977, and San Francisco's
politicians breathed a sigh of relief that a growing scandal
had removed itself to a place 2,000 miles from their
doorstep. But they reckoned without the tenacity of one
tough, independently minded Congressman who wasn't

prepared to leave the scandal uncovered.

Fifty-three-year-old Leo Ryan was a politician who believed in confronting problems first-hand. He had left the comfort and safety of his plush Congress office to spend time in the solitary security jail, to see for himself the treatment of prisoners. And he had worked under cover as a teacher in ghetto schools to expose failures in the education system.

When worried constituents told him they feared many of their loved ones – husbands and wives, sons and daughters – had discovered the truth about Jones in Guyana but were held there against their will, Ryan pressured the US State Department to force a reluctant Guyanese Government to allow him to fly to Jonestown to speak to Temple members himself.

Accompanied by a group of newspaper and television reporters, he arrived by chartered plane at the settlement on 17 November 1978 and walked straight into the lion's den. Jones himself was holding court in Jonestown's central pavilion. Locked away in a strongroom at the rear were 1,000 American passports which he had taken from his followers. Armed guards patrolled the outskirts of the remote settlement – 'to keep away bandits', Jones explained to the Congressman. Settlement pioneers were gaunt and hungry, but most of them appeared to be still fanatically devoted to Jones.

Ryan was characteristically blunt. Addressing a meeting of the worshippers, under the gaze of the Jonestown armed guards, he explained: 'I am sure there are some of you who think this is the best thing that has ever happened to you in your lives.' He was drowned out by a crescendo of shouting and cheering. 'But I promise if any of you want to leave you can come with me under my personal guarantee of protection.'

There was sullen silence.

Jones was seething. Any defectors who left with the

Congressman would tell the truth about Jonestown as soon as they were away from the power of his evil spell. The façade cracked a little when one volunteer stepped forward.

That night Ryan was allowed to stay in Jonestown to talk to the settlers. The party of journalists was sent packing, to stay in Port Kaitumu, 6 miles away. When they got there, TV reporter Don Harris reached into his pocket for a note which had been secretly thrust into his hand in Jonestown. It bore four names and the plaintive cry for help: 'Please, please get us out of here before Jones kills us.'

The following day, when the journalists returned, Ryan was waiting for them with 20 terrified worshippers who wanted to leave. One by one Jones hugged them as they lined up to ride in an earth-moving truck through the jungle to the airstrip. But there were too many of them for the small plane to carry in one trip and Ryan bravely volunteered to stay behind until the plane could make a second journey.

Then there was a scuffle and a spurt of blood, followed by a grisly cheer. One of Jones's elders had pulled a knife and accidentally slashed himself as he tried to stab Ryan. The journalists pulled the bloodstained Congressman aboard the truck and roared away towards the airfield. They were still trembling beside the runway, briefing the pilot, when a tractor drove though the undergrowth onto the concrete. A volley of shots rang out from the men on the tractor. Ryan was killed instantly, his face blown off. Don Harris, the TV reporter, died as he took the full force of a blast from an automatic rifle. His cameraman was killed as he filmed the scene. A young photographer from the *San Francisco Examiner* was slain in a hail of bullets.

To add to the horror, one of the Jonestown 'defectors' suddenly pulled a gun from his shirt and began pumping bullets at the pilot. It was carnage.

At the settlement, the Reverend Jim Jones called his loving congregation around him for the last time. 'I warned you this would happen,' he told them, sobbing. 'We were too good for this world. Now come with me and I will take you to a better place.'

There was some crying and praying as the elders of the People's Temple struggled from the pavilion carrying huge vats of poison laced with Kool-Aid soft drink. Gospel singing began as the mesmerized followers queued up to drink the cups of death.

The babes-in-arms died first, the poison squirted into their helpless mouths with syringes. Then the children, then their parents.

When Guyanese troops arrived the next day, they found the corpses of entire families with their arms locked around each other in a last loving embrace.

Jones himself lay sprawled with a bullet in his brain. The People's Temple had held its last prayer meeting.

One devotee had left behind a suicide note addressed to Jim Jones. It said: 'Dad, I can see no way out, I agree with your decision. Without you the world may not make it to Communism. I am more than tired of this wretched, merciless planet and the hell it holds for so many masses of beautiful people. Thank you for the only life I've known.'

Congressman Leo Ryan had a more fitting epitaph for Jones. Just before he died in the airstrip massacre, he was interviewed by the television crew. His last words, faithfully preserved on their tape-recorder, found under the pile of bodies, were: 'Jim Jones talks a lot about love, brotherhood and humanity and his faith and the power of religion. But never once did I hear him mention God.'

The Nazis

Hitler:
the Making Of A Monster

There was nothing to set the young Adolf Hitler apart from his schoolmates. He was a studious lad, his report cards showing regular columns of A grades. He was seldom absent, his stern father saw to that. If his teachers had any criticism of his work, it was that his mind tended easily to wander. He could not concentrate for long on a single subject. He was a bit of a dreamer.

In later years, a glorious legend would be carefully fabricated about young Adolf's school days in Austria. That he was born a leader whom his classmates followed instinctively. That, as well as extraordinary artistic gifts, he was also possessed of a formidable political understanding. And that, at the age of 11, he gained an 'insight into the meaning of history'. All bunkum, of course. The true character of Adolf Hitler was subordinated to the Nazis' needs to make a myth, a superman and a master race. And buried so well that today psychiatrists can only guess at the boy's mental and emotional state.

Yet, at the turn of the century, *someone* should have had an inkling that there was something a little different about the blue-eyed, dark-haired, impish youngster with the intense gaze who sat scribbling at a desk in a drab secondary school in the Austrian town of Linz. Someone should have seen into the dark depths of his young mind when the pattern of his future – and therefore the future of the entire world – was being settled.

That very someone could have prevented the making of a monster, and he failed. That man was his father.

Alois Hitler was a customs official in the Austrian town of Braunau-am-Inn, close to the border with Bavaria. He was a stern man and the young Adolf had little close affection for him. Alois had risen from the most modest background to a position of lower-middle-class respectability, adopting along the way a severe conservatism, a self-conscious caution and a strict, pedantic, pompous attitude towards his job and his family. He felt that he had a great deal to be proud of and even his long-suffering colleagues had to admit that he had achieved much in life.

Alois Hitler's father had been a poor country miller who had apprenticed his son to a cobbler while still a child. Alois married young but details of his first wife are scant. His second wife, Franziska Matzelberger, bore two children before dying of consumption. He married for a third time but tragedy still dogged him. Klara Hitler produced two children who died in infancy. A third child, a son, was born at Braunau at 6.30pm on 20 April 1889, and survived. He was given the name Adolf.

There were to be two further children. Another son, Edmund, died at the age of six, causing an early trauma in the elder brother Adolf's life. Then came a sister, Paula, who survived.

Apart from the death of his brother, there was a further detail of family history that was to plague Adolf Hitler throughout his life. It was that his father had been born out of wedlock. This resulted in the wholly erroneous claim, loudly proclaimed by political opponents in the 1930s and by the Allies during World War II, that Adolf himself was illegitimate and that his real name was Schicklgruber. The stigma stuck despite the fact that Hitler's father's birth had subsequently been legitimized by the marriage of Hitler's grandfather to the unmarried mother, Maria Schicklgruber.

There is believed to have been conflict between Adolf Hitler and his father Alois throughout the boy's school days. Faithfully protective of his mother, Adolf found his father a boorish brute. There were stories of young Adolf having to support his drunken father home from late-night drinking houses and of having to watch his mother being verbally abused by her husband. There is some doubt about these tales but there is every indication that, while adopting many of his father's middle-class prejudices, Adolf nevertheless detested the man. And in return Alois Hitler, the one man whose behaviour could have changed the boy's character, showed no interest in his dreaming son's high-flown aspirations.

Adolf was 14 when his father died and the family moved to Linz where Klara managed to keep herself and her two children on a government pension. It was here that Hitler decided his future lay as an artist. The fact that his talent was slight did not dissuade him and in 1907, at the age of 18, he travelled to Vienna to pursue his calling.

It is here again that fact and fiction diverge. According to the Nazis' rewriting of the history books and Hitler's own romanticized version of events, Adolf struggled in poverty, living the life of a typical garret-dwelling artist while, in pavement cafés, he pursued a soul-deep search for a political philosophy that would lead him to his destiny.

What Hitler was doing in Vienna was somewhat less romantic. Having quarrelled fiercely with his mother, who wanted him to pursue his studies, the pampered Hitler persuaded her to give him a generous allowance. He then approached the Vienna Academy of Art which, after viewing his test drawings, firmly rejected his application to become a student. At his second attempt a year later, he was not even offered a test for entry. He had no greater luck at the Academy of Architecture, where he was told that he had not completed to an adequate level his studies back at Linz.

The vision of himself at this time of his life later presented by Hitler soon became even more ludicrously divorced from reality when just before Christmas 1908 his mother died. Adolf was genuinely distraught but her demise did mean that he could pursue his sojourn in the cloud-cuckoo-land he had created for himself with even greater ease. He was provided with a healthy inheritance, including the proceeds of the sale of Klara's house in Linz. On top of this, he claimed part of his mother's continued pension on the basis that he was still a full-time student – an act which was no less than fraud.

Hitler now spent his time lounging around cafés and joining in any and every discussion on politics and philosophy. There would also be visits to the opera, an occasional water-colour, the writing of a never-to-be-performed play. But most of the time his life was idle and unproductive as he used up the money that his late father had spent all his life amassing.

At this stage in his life, he did not have a single close friend. And, despite stories of an assault on an artist's model and of his contracting syphilis from a prostitute, there is no indication of an interest in women. The well-known syndrome of bullying father and cossetting mother may have produced an Oedipus complex, making it difficult for him to form such relationships.

What he was acquiring, however, was a fierce unremitting hatred of the Jewish people. In classic style, the self-blame that should have been brought to bear on his own failures was transferred to another 'guilty' party. The Jews were an easy target in the early years of the twentieth century as more and more of their peasant communities in Russia and eastern Europe were driven west by the pogroms being conducted against them. Hitler encountered these dispossessed people in his early, jobless days and, like others before and since, blamed the immigrant minority for taking work away from the 'more deserving' majority. Other traits that characterized his later life revealed themselves at this time . . . his inability to establish ordinary human relationships, his hatred of the establishment and his sudden, passionate, ranting outbursts. He was beginning to live in a fantasy world to evade the reality of his own failure.

In 1912 Hitler's inheritance ran out and he took a job on a building site, returning at night to a malodorous doss-house. For a few months his lifestyle really did match the accounts later given to an adoring nation. But not for long.

Adolf Hitler was later to relate how he made up his mind to live in the Fatherland, the heart of the German peoples, of whom the Austrians were more than a provincial part. True, in 1913 he moved to Munich – but not for the reason he gave. The cross-border flit was to avoid his conscription into the Austrian Imperial Army. When the Munich police caught up with him and handed him over to the Austrian authorities, he sent a letter to Vienna pleading that he be excused military service. It was unnecessary humiliation as he was shortly afterwards rejected on medical grounds.

In 1914, the event that led to World War I set off the slow time-bomb that exploded into World War II. Through those first hostilities, Hitler, the 25-year-old failed artist, realized that he could become a German hero. He decided that action, not words, would be his way.

Though still an Austrian citizen, he succeeded, through a personal petition to the Kaiser, in joining a Bavarian infantry regiment. Sent to the front, he was employed in what was considered the most dangerous job in the trenches – as a company runner, forever exposed to the machine-guns, shrapnel and sniper fire from across no-man's-land. His valour was redoubtable and he soon gained a Mercury-like reputation as a man immune to enemy bullets. He was decorated twice, the second time with the Iron Cross, first class.

Corporal Hitler avoided bullets but he was unable to escape the greatest horror of that war, mustard gas. It was while he was recovering, half-blinded, in hospital that news of Germany's capitulation came through. Like most of the rank and file of the German army, Hitler believed the armistice to be an act of treason on the part of the politicians and blamed it on a communist and Jewish conspiracy. Still in the army, though certified disabled through gas poisoning, he returned to Munich and became the card-carrying member number five of the newly formed German Workers Party. He attended meetings, became elected to its executive, quit the army and threw himself into the task of recruiting members. He changed the party's title to the National Socialist German Workers' Party – Nazis for short. He adopted the swastika armband and discovered his gift for oratory. He found he could manipulate the minds of the masses.

The machinations that led Hitler to final and supreme power are well documented. There was no steady rise to his eventual position as Führer; his political and brutal struggle was one of Machiavellian successes and sudden disappointments. During one reversal, when he was languishing in Lansberg Prison for his part in the bungled 1923 *putsch* to overthrow the Bavarian government, he wrote the major part of his book *Mein Kampf* (My Struggle) outlining his vision of the future of Germany. This and his other pronouncements gave a clear warning to the races that were to suffer most to avenge the insults, real or imagined, visited on the Fatherland at their hands.

It was a ranting, sometimes unreadable, diatribe against Jews, Slavs, communists, pacifists, gypsies, the mentally ill, the 'subversive' and the 'inferior'. Because of this doctrine of hate, not one life in Europe or throughout most of the world would remain unchanged. The dreaming artist who had no friends, whom no one loved, whose work was derided, who was shunned even by his own father, wrote:

'What we must fight for is to safeguard the existence

and reproduction of our race and our people, the sustenance of our children and the purity of our blood, the freedom and independence of the Fatherland, so that our people may mature for the fulfilment of the mission allotted it by the Creator of the universe.'

It was a creed that was to destroy Germany, sentence eastern Europe to the Russian yoke, cause civilian suffering on a scale never before known, and leave many millions dead.

SS Bloodbath in the Ghettoes

When Hitler's evil genius dreamed up the genocide of the Jews as his 'Final Solution' for the Jewish 'problem', he could have wished for no more willing, obedient and ruthless lieutenants than Heinrich Himmler and Reinhard Heydrich. With cold-blooded relish, they became the most methodical mass murderers of all time, forever seeking 'improvements' in their machinery for massacring an entire race. And they logged their lethal efficiency with the pride of obsequious civil servants.

Himmler's big regret was having been too young to fight in World War I. The Munich schoolteacher's son, born in October 1900, idolized the veterans returning from the front and shared their conviction that their efforts had been foiled by traitors at home. Jews, freemasons, Bolsheviks, Slavs and Poles were all scapegoats for the right-wing radicals whose paramilitary retribution squads flourished under the weak Weimar administration. The young Himmler was carried along with the anti-semitic tide, and saw nothing wrong in the motto that it was better to kill a few innocent people than let one guilty party escape.

He was far from the Nazi ideal of a strong blond Aryan superman. A weak stomach barred him from the traditional Bavarian drinking duels and an attack of paratyphoid in his teens had ruled out strenuous physical work. But his orderly mind and diligent clerical skills made him useful to the organizations springing up in the effort to build a new Germany. He became an invaluable administrator and an effective propagandist.

Himmler was also Hitler's most slavishly sycophantic follower. As the future Führer emerged from political infighting as the strongman of the right, Himmler praised him as the German Messiah, 'the greatest genius of all time'. But it was 1927 before Hitler rewarded 'Loyal Heinrich' with more than a mundane task. Worried that many men in his paramilitary *Sturmabteilung* (SA) were more loyal to their brigade leaders than to him, he set up the rival *Schutzstaffel* (SS) and made Himmler its deputy leader, with orders that his instructions were to be obeyed without question.

At first Himmler had only 280 men to command. But he was shrewd and patient. Slowly he compiled dossiers on enemies of Hitler, real or imagined, and built up his leader's trust by regularly telling him of assassination plots, actual or invented. After two years he became SS chief. But he was still bogged down in Bavaria while the action was switching to Berlin and the north. Then luck presented him the accomplice he needed to achieve his ambitions.

Reinhard Heydrich was also a teacher's son, born at Halle in the Teutoburg Forest in 1904. At the age of 18 he joined the navy. Tall, blond and handsome, he was an expert on the ski slopes and a fine fencer, and a delicate violinist who shared weekends of croquet and chamber music at the home of cultured Admiral Canaris. But at 26 he impregnated the daughter of an influential industrialist and refused to marry her, declaring that any woman who made love before wedlock was not a worthy wife. The navy gave him a dishonourable discharge for 'impropriety', but he was not jobless for long. In October 1931 Himmler appointed him to his personal staff. Heydrich's quick brain and imaginative cruelty, allied to Himmler's plodding thoroughness, produced a deadly double act that would become the most feared combination in Germany.

Hitler's election as Chancellor in January 1933 opened the door to unprecedented power for the SS. Within three months, Himmler set up the first concentration camp, at Dachau, and crammed it with Bavarian communists and other anti-Nazis. Heydrich formed the *Sicherheitsdienst* (SD), a counter-espionage corps, to tighten the net around potential opponents. Its targets included Admiral Canaris, rightly suspected by Heydrich of clandestine contact with the British as war approached. By 1934 Himmler controlled the police of almost every German state. That April he also took over the Gestapo, the secret police network founded by Göring. Heydrich was second-in-command. Two months later, the two organized their first massacre.

Hitler's distrust of the SA had been carefully nurtured by the SS chiefs. Now Himmler and Heyrich stepped up their warnings that an SA coup was imminent. As the damning revelations piled up, angry Hitler summoned SA leaders to a meeting at Bad Wiesse Bavaria. They were marched off to jail and shot. SA supremo Ernst Röhm had been Himmler's patron 12 years earlier, arranging for him to join a paramilitary unit. Himmler had been his flag-bearer in the abortive Munich *putsch* of 1923. But now he had no qualms about ordering the death of his former leader. The Bad Wiesse killings were the signal for the SS to run amok throughout Germany, liquidating prominent politicians on lists meticulously prepared by Himmler and Heydrich. Hitler told the Reichstag that 79 died on the so-called 'Night of the Long Knives'. Most historians put the total of victims at over 500.

Hitler now declared the SS his executive arm, completely independent within the Nazi party. And in May 1935, in an astonishing ruling, the Prussian High Court decreed that actions of the Gestapo could not be contested in court if the secret police were carrying out the will of leadership. Himmler and Heydrich were now beyond all criticism except that of the Führer. The SS was the spearhead for Himmler's drive for racial purity. Applicants had to prove there had been no Jewish blood in their family since 1800. For officers the date was 1750. The SS leadership had to approve marriage between true Aryan types, who were rewarded with gifts for every child. SS men who preferred to remain single took advantage of the *Lebensborn* – a system which enabled them to father children by attractive, racially pure German girls. Most SS personnel were country peasants, for Himmler had a maniacal belief that towns were evil and controlled by Jews. 'Cowards are born in towns', he once said. 'Heroes are born in the country.' But the job Himmler had in mind for his troops was hardly one for heroes.

In October 1938, 17,000 Polish Jews living in Germany were stripped of their citizenship by the Polish Government. Days later, the SS told them that Germany did not want them either. Heydrich organized a massive round-up, and the Jews were taken by truck and train to the Polish border, and dumped in no-man's-land between the two frontiers. The 17-year-old son of one of the victims was in Paris when he heard of the savage treatment. He went to the German embassy, intent on shooting the ambassador. Instead he killed a minor envoy, and was instantly arrested.

Here was a chance Heydrich could not miss. He wrote to every German police chief warning that anti-Jewish demonstrators 'are to be expected' on the night of 9 November, and instructed the officers to inform local political organizers of the rules of the game. No German life or property was to be endangered. And 'synagogues may only be set on fire if there is no danger of fire spreading to adjoining properties'. He added: 'Houses of Jews may only be destroyed, not plundered.'

The 'spontaneous' demonstrations that followed left 35 people dead, nearly 180 synagogues destroyed and 7,500 businesses wrecked. Insurers estimated the damage at more than £3 million. *Kristallnacht* – so called for the amounts of glass smashed – was a clear warning to the Jews of Europe. Those who were able to fled to more friendly countries. Those who could not faced far worse attrocities in the near future.

Before the Nazi invasion of Poland on 1 September 1939, Hitler warned his army generals: 'Things will happen which will not be to your taste. But you should not interfere. Restrict yourself to your military duties.' It was an order Wehrmacht officers, ingrained with a traditional sense of fair play in war, were to find hard to obey. For it was in Poland, the Baltic States and Russia that the full horror of Hitler's policies, ruthlessly implemented by Himmler and Heydrich, was to be revealed.

The SS had paved the way for war by helping Hitler purge his High Command of waverers. Many generals felt the Führer's timetable of invasions too demanding and too dangerous. Some were unwise enough to ask for postponements. Himmler and Heydrich gave Hitler rigged evidence that enabled him to dismiss and replace the 'faint hearts' with men more ready to follow orders blindly. Heydrich then devised a cunning way to check on the loyalty of all Nazi leaders. He set up an exclusive Berlin brothel, Madame Kitty's, and staffed it with the most attractive call-girls in the country. But each bedroom was wired with microphones, and all careless pillow talk was taped.

Heydrich was also the brains behind one of the SS's

most lucrative money-spinning schemes. After the 1938 union with Austria – the SS prepared for it by assassinating Austrian Chancellor Englebert Dollfuss – an Office of Jewish Emigration opened in Vienna. For extortionate sums, Jews could buy exit visas rather than risk death or incarceration in concentration camps. By the end of 1939, 60 per cent of Austrian Jews had sold everything to the SS and fled. A second Office in Prague after the occupation of Czechoslovakia proved equally profitable.

And it was Heydrich who came up with the propaganda ploy to 'justify' invasion of Poland. On the evening of 31 August, a German radio station in the border town of Gleiwitz was attacked by Polish soldiers. They soon withdrew, leaving the area strewn with Polish and German bodies. Next day, as Nazi tanks rolled into Poland, German newspapers justified the move as retaliation for provocation. But the Polish soldiers had been SS men in disguise. And the corpses were inmates from concentration camps, dumped from trucks during the charade.

Within days of the invasion, the Wehrmacht knew that Hitler's warnings had been no joke. SS men were discovered shooting 50 Jews in a synagogue and arrested. Himmler instantly ordered their release. The generals had been told men, women and children would be killed without mercy. At the time it seemed impossible. Now it appeared all too probable. They pleaded for the slaughter to be delayed until the army withdrew once conquest was complete. They feared the world would blame them for any atrocities. But Himmler and Heydrich refused to compromise on the Führer's orders. They began herding Jews behind the high walls and barbed wire of 55 city ghettoes. And Himmler started his duties as head of the Reich's Commissariat for the Strengthening of German Nationhood.

The people of the conquered north were to be evicted to provide land for Germans to farm. In Nazi parlance, this was 'population exchange'. But the euphemism hid a multitude of sins. Himmler spoke of killing 30 million Slavs during the Russian invasion. And of the first year in Poland he said: 'We had to drag away hundreds of thousands of people. We had to have the toughness to shoot thousands of leading Poles, otherwise revenge would have been taken on us later.'

Mass murder was soon second nature to the SS. Nearly 45,000 Jews died in the Polish ghettoes in 1941 alone after Himmler reduced rations to starvation level. On the Russian front, appalled Wehrmacht officers watched units for the military Waffen-SS send hundreds of bullet-ridden bodies tumbling into blood-soaked mass graves. At the war trials in Nuremburg, one SS leader estimated that his squads liquidated 90,000 men, women and children in those 12 months. Ironically, the practice decreased after Himmler witnessed the machine-gunning of 100 helpless captives at Minsk. The man who condemned millions with each stroke of his pen retched at the sight. In future, he ordered, victims were to be eliminated in mobile gas coaches.

Meanwhile, Heydrich had been appointed Reich Protector for Bohemia and Moravia. Within weeks he was known as the Butcher of Prague, as the Gestapo ruthlessly destroyed Czech resistance movements. The Czech premier was condemned to death after a bogus trial. But Czechoslovakian agents were the link between London and a vital spy in the Nazi hierarchy, code-named Franta. Heydrich was getting too close to unmasking him. British intelligence chiefs and the Czech government in exile agreed that Heydrich was too dangerous to live, and parachuted two assassins into the country.

Jan Kubis and Josef Gabcik set their ambush for a hairpin bend on the road that took Heydrich from his country villa to his office in Prague's Hradcany Palace. As the SS chief's Mercedes slowed to negotiate it on 27 May 1942, Gabcik stepped into the road and raised his sten-gun. The trigger jammed. As the car halted, Kubis threw a grenade. Heydrich leapt from the car wielding his revolver. Then he staggered and fell. After a nine-day battle for life, he died in hospital. The SS and Gestapo made 10,000 arrests. But the most brutal reprisal was on the village of Lidice. It was burned to the ground, and all 1,300 male inhabitants were shot.

Himmler was left alone to carry through Hitler's ghastly plans for German supremacy.

'Final Solution' of the Exterminators

Street shootings, starvation in the ghettoes, gassing in rail coaches . . . this was how Jews, communists and other 'undesirables' died by the hundreds of thousands in the 1930s. But still this unprecedented genocide was not fast enough for the coldly efficient masters of the SS. So the concentration camps, established years before to house political prisoners, were turned into extermination camps. Gas chambers and cremation ovens were added. And, to meet demand, new 'purpose-built' camps were erected.

There were 16 extermination camps throughout the Reich but the busiest were in Poland, at Auschwitz and Treblinka. And their sinister efficiency was a tribute to the untiring efforts of Adolf Eichmann.

Born in the Rhineland in 1906 and brought up in Austria, Eichmann was an unemployed travelling salesman before joining the SS as a 'researcher', studying the 'evils' of freemasonry. When Reinhard Heydrich opened the Offices of Jewish Emigration, Eichmann found his niche. By streamlining the bureaucracy, he dealt with more applications than ever before – and thereby raked even more money into the SS coffers. He was so successful in Vienna and Prague that, when Poland was invaded, Eichmann was called to Berlin and appointed chief of the Reich Centre for Jewish Emigration.

But in August 1941 Heydrich told him that the days of milking escaping Jews was over. From now on, the policy was their total extermination.

Eichmann was put in charge of transporting Jews from all over Europe to the death camps. It was his responsibility to round them up and provide the special trains to take them to eternity. Nobody minded much if some died on the way in the overcrowded cattle trucks. Once a train returning to France from Auschwitz was found to contain the bodies of 25 children aged from two to four. Guards at the camp had not bothered to unload the tiny corpses.

Eichmann's hideous success became horrifyingly clear at the Nuremberg trials. Rudolf Hess was commandant at Auschwitz from August 1941 to December 1943. Under cross-examination, he estimated that 2,500 men, women and children died in the gas chambers at that time, and a further 500,000 from starvation or disease. Jews were sent to him from Germany, Holland, France, Belgium, Hungary, Czechoslovakia and Greece as well as Poland. More than 400,000 Hungarian Jews were liquidated in the summer of 1944 alone, he said.

Then Hess clinically drew macabre comparisons between his camp and Treblinka, which dealt mostly with inmates of the Warsaw Ghetto. 'They used monoxide gas, which I considered not particularly effective,' he said. 'I decided to use Zyklon-B, a crystallized prussic acid . . . A further improvement we introduced was that we built gas chambers which could take 2,000 people at once, while the ten chambers at Treblinka only had a capacity of 200 each.'

The Zyklon-B chambers were Eichmann's brainchild, after a painstaking study of the alternatives. They speeded up the business of extermination, enabling 24,000 Jews a day to be eliminated and cremated. The air at Auschwitz was constantly full of the nauseating stench of burning bodies.

The SS exploited every aspect of genocide. Gold rings were ripped from the fingers of corpses, and gold teeth torn out. Bones were ground down for fertilizer. In 1942 all camp commandments received a stunning directive from SS economics chief Oswald Pohl: 'Human hair must be collected. Women's hair can be used in the manufacture of socks for U-boat personnel and for employees of the State railways . . . As to men's hair, it is only of use to us if it has a length of at least 20 millimetres.'

Crude medical experiments were carried out on captive 'guinea pigs' before execution. Sterilizations without anaesthetic, injections to test new drugs and bizarre tests of human resistance to pain, heat and cold were all encouraged. Some patients did not survive for the gas chambers. Yet, in the midst of death, Himmler was concerned about life. He took particular interest in a herb garden just yards from the Auschwitz slaughter houses. He was anxious to help Germans revert to natural foods and remedies.

Utter disregard for human life coupled with concern for seeming trivialities seem the hallmarks of madmen. Yet the most guilty Nazis knew full well that what they were doing was evil and wrong. Eichmann, in particular, always took great care to cover his tracks. And, as the Allied armies closed in on Germany, SS leaders destroyed their carefully compiled dossiers on who had died where. The world might not understand . . .

After July 1944, when Hitler survived a bomb attack by army chief Count Claus von Stauffenburg, Himmler's power was further boosted. In addition to his SS, police and Gestapo responsibilities, he was given command of the vast Reserve Army. Paranoid Hitler could no longer trust a military man with the job.

Himmler knew it was already too late to save Germany. The Allies were consolidating after their D-Day landings, and he was soon trying to save his skin by offering secret peace initiatives to them behind the Führer's back. But that did not stop his brutality. Field marshals and generals convicted of complicity in Stauffenberg's plot were hanged in agony on piano wire strung from butcher's hooks. Would-be deserters from the Reserve Army were warned to remember their families' well-being. They could see the corpses of deserters hanging from trees, with placards pinned to their chests which read: 'I left my unit without permission.'

Even after Hitler's suicide, as the Allies closed in on Berlin, Himmler believed he had a future as a German leader. Only after the Führer's successor, Grand Admiral Dönitz, dismissed him from all his posts as 'politically questionable' did he go to ground. With false papers in the name of Heinrich Hitzinger, and without his glasses and moustache, he tried to lose himself in the huge crowds of refugees and soldiers heading for home in the chaos of beaten Germany. But his civil-service mentality gave him away. He joined a long queue shuffling across a narrow bridge at Meinstedt under the casual scrutiny of British soldiers – and was the only man in the line to volunteer his papers. He was instantly suspected and arrested, though not then recognized.

In prison he confessed his real identity and demanded to be taken to Field Marshal Montgomery. The request was declined. His captors had found one cyanide suicide pill in his clothing, but another was hidden in a dental cavity. As British Intelligence men arrived to interrogate him, he chewed on it. On 26 May 1945, his body was taken to the woods near Lüneburg and buried without ceremony in an unmarked grave. Only the burial detail of five knew where the second most sinister man in the Reich ended his days.

Adolf Eichmann was also arrested in May 1945 – but he was not recognized. When American soldiers stopped him, he was disguised as a Luftwaffe pilot, and the Allies were not too interested in ordinary airmen. Eichmann took advantage of the confusion to slip away and vanish.

It was 1957 before Israeli agents hunting the monster who supervised the murder of six million Jews received their first real lead to his whereabouts. The German secret service passed on a report from a former inmate of Dachau who had emigrated to Argentina after the war. A schoolmate of his daughter had been making violently anti-semitic statements. His name was Nikolaus Klement. And, from the girl's description of the schoolboy's father, the man was convinced he was Eichmann.

The name Klement rang bells in Tel Aviv. Israeli agents had traced the escape routes of 30 high-ranking Nazis via Spain and Italy. One had headed for Latin America on refugee papers issued by Vatican authorities. His name was Ricardo Clementi. Now the Germans had passed on an address for the Klement family – 4261 Chacabuco Street, Olivos, Buenos Aires.

After delicate negotiations with the Argentinian Government, Israeli agents were given permission to put Klement under surveillance. Long-range photographs were sent back to Tel Aviv and shown to death-camp survivors, but none could positively identify the man as Eichmann, and the Israelis dared not make a move without irrefutable proof. Seizing the wrong man would make them an international laughing stock.

Then a bunch of flowers gave the game away. Klement bought them on 21 March 1960, as he left work at the Mercedes Benz factory on the Suarez suburb of Buenos Aires. He was still carrying them when he got off the bus outside his Olivos home. It was enough to finally convince the watchers. They knew 21 March was the Eichmanns' wedding anniversary.

Israeli intelligence chiefs gave the go-ahead for what was later described as one of the world's best-organized kidnappings. Simply killing Eichmann would not have been enough. Ace Nazi-hunter Simon Wisenthal had said, 'If you kill him, the world will never learn what he did. There must be an accounting, a record for history.' On 11 May, Klement was bundled into a car as he got off the bus and driven to a safe house. He was stripped and examined for distinguishing marks. The appendicitis scar, the scar above the left eyebrow and the SS blood group tattooed under the left armpit all proved he was Eichmann.

He was drugged and driven to Buenos Aires airport, his captors posing as nurses and relatives. Forged papers declared him to be an Israeli car-crash victim, fit enough to travel but not to be disturbed. He was waved through to an El-Al jet which had brought Israeli politicians to help celebrate the 150th anniversary of Argentina's independence. Within 24 hours the man the Jews hated most was in Tel Aviv.

His trial began on 12 December 1961. The 15 charges included deporting and causing the deaths of millions of Jews, being party to the murder of thousands of gypsies, and being party to the murder of 91 children. Eichmann claimed that, by streamlining Jewish emigration in the early years of his SS career, he was only doing what Zionists proposed – sending Jews out of Europe to find a new homeland. He said he tried to organize Jewish settlements in Poland and even Madagascar, but was thwarted by others in the Nazi hierarchy. When told in 1941 that the Führer had ordered extermination of the Jews, 'I lost all joy in my work, all initiative, all interest'. Thereafter he simply did his duty and carried out orders.

The Israelis were scrupulous in ensuring a fair trial, and the full procedure of appeals. But, at 11.53pm on 31 May

1962, Adolf Eichmann was hanged at Ramleh Prison, outside Tel Aviv. His defence cut no ice with a people who knew that, when Himmler tried to stop the activity of extermination camps as the end of the war loomed, Eichmann protested violently. They preferred to believe the words of Dieter Wisliceny, executed in Czechoslovakia for war crimes as one of Eichmann's lieutenants. 'He told me in 1944 that he did not care what happened if Germany lost the war,' Wisliceny said. 'He said he would leap into his grave laughing because the feeling that he had five million Jews on his conscience only filled his heart with gladness.'

Klaus Barbie, the Butcher of Lyons

Wartime occupied France was a place without sanctuary for those in fear of the Nazis. The German armies occupied the north. In the south the puppet government of Marshal Philippe Pétain did the Nazis' dirty work for them with an unseemly willingness. And everywhere the SS and the Gestapo ruled by terror.

In greatest fear were the Jews, who knew that unless their identities could be disguised they would end up in transports heading eastward to the terrible death camps like Auschwitz, Mauthausen and Ravensbruck. In the southern part of France, where arrest seemed less imminent, many persecuted families sent their children off to homes in the country, surreptitiously set up as refuges for Jewish infants.

France was dotted with such homes, and generally the local German commanders turned a blind eye to this slight lapse in the otherwise rigid pursuance of the Final Solution to eradicate the Jewish race. But one SS leader thought differently. He was Klaus Barbie, the 'Butcher of Lyons'.

Barbie discovered that a refuge for Jewish children had been established on a large drab, grey house in the centre of the village of Izieu, high in the hills close to France's border with Switzerland. Early in the morning of 6 April 1944 Barbie sent a number of trucks up the steep winding road to the village. Soldiers ordered the children and staff out of the home and into the trucks and they were driven away.

On the night of the raid on the children's home, Klaus Barbie sent a telex message to the Gestapo headquarters in Paris detailing his latest achievement. It read:

'In the early hours of this morning the Jewish children's home, Colonie Enfant, at Izieu was raided. In total 41 children aged from three to 13 were taken. Furthermore, the entire Jewish staff of 10, five of them females, were arrested. Cash and other assets were not taken. transportation to Drancy follows tomorrow. – Barbie.'

Drancy was the 'holding camp' in a Paris suburb, from where two months later the children were transported by cattle train to the most notorious death camp of all, Auschwitz.

Not one of the children survived the gas chambers.

Today on the wall of the grey old house in Izieu there is a plaque bearing the names of all 41 children. It was put there after the war, to remind the people of the region of the blackest period in their history . . . of the valour of the resistance fighters, of the shame of the collaborators who made the Nazis' task so easy, of the terror reign for the SS and Gestapo, and above all of the horrors perpetrated in the name of Hitler by one of his most ardent henchmen, Klaus Barbie.

Thirty-nine years after the capture of the innocents, memories of Barbie's infamy came flooding back. In February 1983 he was expelled from Bolivia and flown to

France to stand trial for crimes against humanity. He was placed in a special wing of St Joseph's Prison, Lyons, while prosecutors sifted through a mountain of evidence to build a damning case against him.

The files reveal a youthful fanaticism that helped build the 'perfect' Nazi. Klaus Barbie was born on 25 October 1913 at Bad Godesberg, near Bonn. He was illegitimate, though his parents later married. He joined the Hitler Youth and at 22 volunteered for the SS (*Schutzstaffell*, or Protection Squads) and he was posted to Dortmund to work in the SS's own elite security branch. There he met Regina Willms and they became engaged. Their marriage was conducted with full SS guard of honour in Berlin in 1940. Two years later, promoted to Oberstürmführer, he was sent to Lyons as head of the Gestapo in the city.

He quickly discovered that his task of 'cleansing' the region of Jews and subversives was far simpler than he had imagined. Collaborators and informers abounded, ready to turn on their own countrymen to win favour, reward and acclaim from their new masters.

Marshal Pétain's puppet government ensured that no more German troops than absolutely necessary were occupied controlling the country. Indeed, the French often enforced law and order more harshly than the Germans. They rounded up Jews for deportation even before being ordered to by the Nazis. Still more thorough in their new duties were French paramilitary units called the Milice who carried out many executions at their masters' behest.

Barbie's headquarters were in Lyons' Ecole Santé Militaire where he installed torture chambers equipped with whips, chains, spiked coshes, electric-shock boxes and welders' torches.

In an astonishing book about the Butcher of Lyons (entitled *Klaus Barbie – His Life And Career*), author John Beattie uncovered some of his horrifying practices.

Barbie installed twin baths at his headquarters, one

filled with near-boiling water, the other with ice-cold water. Prisoners would be ducked in them alternately until they submitted.

Women were stripped, tied down and covered in raw meat. Then Barbie's German shepherd dogs would be set loose on them. Other tortures involved acid injections, burning by blowtorch or being wired up for electric shock treatment.

Author John Beattie traced Barbie's old interpreter, Gottlieb Fuchs, who spoke of the interrogation of a young Jewish boy and girl who adamantly refused to divulge the whereabouts of the rest of their family. In a rage, Barbie picked them up one at a time and smashed their heads against the cell wall.

Fuchs revealed that on another occasion Barbie's over-abundance of zeal lost the Nazis a valuable prisoner. General de Gaulle's top resistance organizer in France, Jean Moulin, was betrayed and captured with eight comrades at a secret meeting in Lyons in June 1942. He was tortured until he passed out and was then dragged by his feet down several flights of stone stairs until his head was battered beyond recognition. He was sent to Germany for further interrogation but died of his injuries.

Barbie's greatest mistake, however, was employing Fuchs as his interpreter. He was a double agent, working for the Allies and feeding information gleaned from Barbie to the Swiss secret service across the border.

Within three months of D-day, the Allies were on the outskirts of Lyons. By then, Barbie's sadistic excesses had reached extraordinary proportions. He would conduct torture sessions seated with a naked woman on his knee, getting a perverted pleasure out of his victims' agonies.

After a café popular with German officers was damaged he took revenge. Barbie ordered a Gestapo raid; five innocent young men were hauled out of the café and shot dead in the street.

He once called local gendarmes to his headquarters to clear out a cellar. They found it piled with the corpses of young men, all machine-gunned, their blood lying deep on the floor.

He took 110 men and women from Montluc prison and had them driven to the village of St Geni-Laval. There, in an upstairs room of an old fort, they were machine-gunned to death until their blood flowed through the ceiling of the room below.

Allied troops entered Lyons on 3 September 1944, but by then Barbie had fled. The Butcher had ruled the city by fear for just 657 days. In that time he had organized the executions of more then 4,000 people, including collaborators who could possibly have borne witness to his crimes.

Barbie laid low at the end of the war, earning a living in Frankfurt from the black market. He kept close touch with other ex-SS men, whose tip-offs saved him from capture on at least one occasion. He thought his luck had run out in August 1946, however, when he was arrested by Americans and driven towards their base in the back of a Jeep. He leaped out of the vehicle which, in the ensuing confusion, crashed into a tree. Barbie was once again a free man.

John Beattie asserts that Barbie spent a period after the war working first for British Intelligence and then the Americans, feeding them information about undercover communist groups. He lived under the name Klaus Altmann in the Bavarian town of Augsburg until 1951 when he, his wife Regina and their two children set sail for South America from the Italian port of Genoa.

They settled in the Bolivian capital, La Paz, where Barbie became a respected businessman, owner of a sawmill and friend of politicians. He was even able to travel abroad on business trips with impunity.

The good life for Klaus Barbie ended in the 1980s. His

son died in a hang-gliding accident and his wife died of cancer. Shortly afterwards a new, more liberal president, Siles Zuazo, came to power, vowing to rid his country of Nazis.

France's constant pressure on the Bolivians to extradite the Butcher bore fruit on 4 February 1983, when Barbie was arrested and told he was to be sent abroad. He was driven to La Paz airport and put on an unmarked transport plane. Barbie was unruffled – until the crew of the plane revealed themselves as French officers. The Butcher of Lyons was on his way to jail in the city where he had imprisoned, maimed and murdered so many innocent people.

The Ones That Got Away With Murder

On 15 May 1984, a cryptic agency dispatch was sent to newspapers. It read: 'Nazi killer Walter Rauff, blamed for the deaths of thousands of Jews in the SS gas chambers during World War II, has died of lung cancer in South America, aged 77.'

An Israeli official who had been fighting for Rauff's extradition said 'God had closed the case'. But there was one man who wished that he, and not God, had been given a chance of concluding the case against Walter Rauff for crimes against humanity. That man was Nazi-hunter Dr Simon Wiesenthal, who believed that Rauff was responsible for the deaths of 250,000 people.

Dr Wiesenthal had long found that his unflagging crusade to bring to justice the surviving Nazi murderers was being hampered by diplomatic stalling and a protective conspiracy on the part of the fast-decreasing band of Hitler's henchmen still on the run.

Rauff, for instance, led a charmed life after the downfall of the Nazis. Like so many of his compatriots, he escaped to South America, ending up in Chile where he ran a meat-freezing plant – quite openly under his own name. On occasions, he even answered letters sent to him by inquisitive journalists.

It was rumoured that Rauff was involved in drug-smuggling in the Punta Arenas area and that at one time he was employed by the right-wing Chilean government as an anti-communist agent.

His hatred of communists is well documented. As commander of the units which provided gas trucks for concentration camps, Rauff was known as Hitler's 'ambulance man'. He had tens of thousands of left-wingers, intellectuals, mental defectives, Jews and others regarded as 'racially undesirable' herded into what looked like Red Cross ambulances. Gas was then released into the airtight trucks until all inside were dead.

Rauff was one of ten names on a list that Dr Wiesenthal produced at the time of the extradition of Klaus Barbie in 1983. The ten names were, he said in a statement from his Jewish Documentation Centre in Vienna, those of Nazis whom he most wished to be brought to justice to fulfil his 'compact with the dead'. The 76-year-old doctor said: 'If I could get all ten, it would be an achievement. But if I could get only Josef Mengele, I think my soul would be at peace.'

Mengele was the Auschwitz concentration-camp doctor who carried out horrifying experiments on humans and was given the title 'Angel of Death' by the inmates. At one time, Wiesenthal believed he had traced Dr Mengele to a remote Mennonite religious community on the border of Bolivia and Paraguay. But, as a registered refugee and a Paraguayan citizen, he was thought to be immune from extradition.

Dr Mengele's qualifications for his infamous work were

impeccable. He was a medical graduate of both Munich and Frankfurt universities, and it was this expertise that won him the post of chief medical officer at Auschwitz where, according to Wiesenthal, he was directly responsible for the deaths of 400,000 people.

Mengele's main preoccupation at Auschwitz was his attempt to prove Hitler's theory of the Teutonic master race. He would alter the hair and eye colouring of human 'guinea pigs' by genetic manipulation. Most of his patients died, were crippled or were blinded.

After the war, Mengele fled to Italy and then Argentina, He eventually settled in Paraguay where he became a naturalized citizen in 1973. Despite the efforts of the Nazi-hunters, he continued to enjoy the effective protection of the Paraguayan Government, although staying constantly on the move to avoid kidnap or assassination attempts.

In 1979 his Nazi friends in the country put about a story that the evil doctor was dead. They even released a photograph of a man on a mortury slab, showing a scar on the right arm where his SS tattoo had been removed. However, Wiesenthal discovered that the body was not Mengele's but that of SS Captain Eduardo Roschmann who sent 80,000 Jews to their deaths in Riga concentration camp.

But neither Rauff nor Mengele were at the top of Dr Wiesenthal's list of most-wanted Nazis. That dishonour went to a man who probably never pulled the trigger on any of his victims, who seldom visited a concentration camp and who may never have witnessed an execution. Heinrich Müller, head of Gestapo, just gave the orders.

Müller was responsible for the deaths of millions of Jews, according to Wiesenthal. Yet the inveterate Nazi-hunter never came close to catching him and often had to admit that he had lost the scent of his hated adversary.

The Gestapo chief was at first thought to have died in the ruins of Berlin. But when his grave was later opened it was found to contain three skulls – none of them Müller's. He is since reported to have been in the Soviet Union, Albania, Spain and Egypt.

Four of Adolf Eichmann's closest aides were on the list. Rolf Guenther was Eichmann's deputy, Anton Burger was his field officer and Josef Schwamberger and Alois Brunner his assistants.

At his trial Eichmann accused Guenther of taking a special initiative in the death camps. Willingly accepting the task of organizing the 'Final Solution', he was sent to Denmark to rid the country of all Jews. So successful was he that he was later asked to advise on similar operations in Hungary and Greece, carrying with him confidential instructions to arrange sterilization, medical experiments and the gassing of concentration inmates.

Guenther disappeared after the war.

Anton Burger was deputy commander of the Resienstadt concentration camp on the German-Czech border. This 'model' camp was open to neutral visitors as a propaganda exercise to dispel stories of mass extermination. But behind the scenes horrific experiments including poisonings, sterilization and abortions were being carried out on inmates.

Burger was arrested after the war. In 1948 he escaped from prison and was never seen again.

Eichmann's third principal aide to escape justice was Alois Brunner, responsible for the deaths of thousands of Jews in Czechoslovakia, Greece and France, where he organized the transportation of Jews to the concentration camps.

After the war Brunner fled to Syria and settled in Damascus under the name of Dr Fisher.

Eichmann's other assistant, Josef Schwamberger, was commander of the Jewish ghetto at Przemysl, Poland, where he is reckoned to have organized the extermination of 15,000 people.

At the war's end, Schwamberger was hidden by the Odessa escape group, then sent to Italy and finally Argentina. In 1973 West Germany requested his extradition and he was arrested – only to be released when extradition was refused due to pressure from local Nazis.

Three other concentration-camp chiefs were on Dr Wiesenthal's list . . .

Friedrich Wartzog was commander of the Polish Lemberg-Janowska camp where he ordered the deaths of 40,000 people. Some of the most damning evidence against him was given by Eichmann at his trial when he spoke of a 'spring of blood gushing from the earth' where executed Jews had been buried.

Prisoners were starved for days, then, if found unfit for work, shot. Camp guards were encouraged to use prisoners for target practice, aiming only for their extremities. Only after they had suffered appalling agonies did an executioner finish them off.

Wartzog, who presided over these horrors, escaped at the war's end and has never been heard of since.

Dr Aribert Heim was director of Mauthausen concentration camp in Austria where prisoners would end up after 'death marches' from other camps like Auschwitz. Survivors said that on these marches people were so hungry that they resorted to cannibalism.

In 1941 the Germans made their first mass arrests in Holland by rounding up 400 Amsterdam Jews and sending them to Mauthausen. According to the Red Cross, only one survived. When Allied troops reached Mauthausen, they discovered the camp's log book which revealed that 35,318 prisoners had died there.

After the war Heim vanished without trace.

Perhaps the most gruesomely intriguing name on Dr Wiesenthal's list is that of Richard Gluecks, Inspector-General of all concentration camps. Less is known about him than almost any other Nazi war criminal, except that he was a Gruppenführer and was head of administration at the Reich Security Head Office which was in overall control of the death camps. Dachau, Buchenwald and Ravensbruck were under his command, as was Auschwitz where more than a million people died.

Like the others, Gluecks vanished at the end of the war.

Despite Dr Wiesenthal's efforts, chances of tracing these missing monsters became slimmer with the years. As was the case with Walter Rauff, death rather than justice is most likely to catch up with the Nazis who got away with mass murder.

The Liquidation of the Warsaw Ghetto

The Nazis had proved that they were capable of mass murder at Babi Yar and numerous other places across occupied areas of the Soviet Union and the Baltic states. At least this suffering was mercifully brief. The torture of the people in the Warsaw Ghetto dragged on for four years and some 500,000 people were lost.

Between 1918 and 1939, the Jewish population of Warsaw became the largest concentration of Jews in Europe and the second largest in the world, after New York. When the Germans occupied the city on 7 September 1939, there were around 380,000 Jews in Warsaw, making up some 30 per cent of the population. The situation grew ugly immediately: many Poles were anti-Semitic and knew what their new German overlords expected of them. Jews soon found themselves subject to kicking and punching on the streets. They were thrown out of their homes and kidnapped for forced labour. Women were raped and people murdered by Polish rowdies as well as by the Germans themselves.

As early as November 1939, the Germans made it clear to the Jews what was going to happen to them. Special 'educational' camps were going to be set up for them. Only one thing would be taught there: how to die.

In the mean time, all Jews had to wear armbands with the Star of David on them. This made it easier for the violent anti-semitic element of the Polish population to know whom to attack. Jews were also issued with identification papers marked prominently with the word 'Jude'. All Jewish assets of over 2,000 zloty per family were confiscated and, later, it became illegal for any Jew to earn more than 500 zloty a month – at a time when the price of bread rose to 40 zloty a pound. It became illegal for Jews to make bread, to buy from or sell to 'Aryans', to own gold or jewellery, to ride on trains or trolleycars or to leave the city without special permits. Jewish doctors were not allowed to treat 'Aryan' patients, nor were Jewish patients allowed to seek the help of 'Aryan' doctors.

Jews were regularly robbed, beaten and murdered on the streets, with no sanction against their assailants. They lived in constant fear of the only punishment for even the slightest infraction of the regulations – death. However, even carefully obeying the rules was no protection, as the regulations were constantly being tightened. Jews were persecuted, humiliated and subjected to ruthless acts of terror. All Jews bore responsibility for what any one Jew did. Hence, early in November 1939, all 53 of the male inhabitants of an apartment house at 9 Nalewski Street were summarily shot because one of the tenants had struck a policeman.

Actions such as these sent a wave of panic through the Jewish population. The constant degradation left them feeling dehumanized; they were systematically robbed of the self-confidence to fight back.

In January 1940, the Seuchensperrgebiet – or 'area

threatened by typhus' was established, and was to be designated a Jewish area. The Germans decided that the world had to know that they were not the only ones who hated Jews. Over Easter 1940, a number of pogroms were arranged. In Warsaw, the German Air Corps paid Polish hoods four zloty a day to beat up and murder Jews. For the first three days, the hoodlums ran amok, unopposed; but on the fourth day the Jews fought back. This resulted in running battles. The Jews published a mimeographed newspaper called *The Bulletin* to celebrate the event – the triumph was brief.

In November 1940, the Germans established the Warsaw Ghetto. Jews living outside the Seuchensperrgebiet were forced to move into it. Houses vacated by Jews were locked and their contents given to Polish merchants and pedlars. Poles living within the boundaries of the ghetto were ordered out, as the walls and barbed wire surrounding it grew higher day by day. By 15 November, it was sealed completely. Two weeks later, shops and small factories inside the ghetto were closed, meaning that Jews no longer had any way of making a living and were cut off from any contact with Jewish communities elsewhere.

The ghetto population was swelled by thousands of Jews being moved in from neighbouring towns. They were allowed to bring nothing with them. Many who knew no one in Warsaw died of malnutrition on the streets. The place became impossibly overcrowded. In spring 1941, the population peaked at 450,000 in just 307 hectares. Hunger and overcrowding brought with it disease and people wrapped in filthy rags, their bodies impossibly swollen or covered with open wounds, could be seen on the streets.

No newspapers were allowed in the ghetto, so the inmates knew nothing of the outside world. Only life inside the ghetto existed. For most, this meant somehow trying to get by on the meagre rations of soup and bread doled out by public kitchens. Some lived on potatoes recovered from garbage pits and begged pieces of bread; but those who still had a little money lost themselves in the chitchat of pavement cafés and the dance music of the nightclubs. This contrast between the poor and the rich, who grew fat on 'food smuggled in from "Aryan" sections', was exploited by the Germans, who used photographs from the ghetto in their propaganda.

Every day the situation deteriorated. Children and the elderly begged on the streets. Some six-year-old boys crawled though the barbed wire to beg for food on the outside – this supported entire families. Often a single shot rang out, indicating the death of another under-aged foodsmuggler.

Starving shadows of boys became known as 'catchers'. They would snatch parcels from passers-by and devour their contents while they were running away. In their haste, they sometimes stuffed themselves with soap or uncooked peas, with disastrous results.

The Germans had organized the Jewish Community Council to try to give some semblance of order to this chaos. This comprised well-respected figures of the Jewish community, who had been forced to join on pain of death. The Germans also instituted a Jewish Police Force to maintain law and order, increasing the risks for the food smugglers and the catchers.

Deaths rose from 898 in January 1941 to 5,560 in January 1939. In all, 100,000 Jews died inside the ghetto, largely from starvation and disease. Some simply fell down in the street and stayed there. Those who died at home fared little better: they were stripped so that their clothes could be sold and their bodies left outside the house. Every morning, between 4 and 5am, the Jewish Community Council sent round carts to pick up the bodies. They could be seen stacked high with naked corpses, heads and limbs bobbing up and down as the carts rumbled down the uneven streets.

Those who died were soon replaced by Jews who had been rounded up in other parts of Poland. The ghetto was so overcrowded that newcomers had to camp on the streets, or would have to go to the 'points'. These were the large unheated rooms of synagogues or disused factories. Hundreds of people would be living in each room with no washing facilities. Whole families were given enough room for one person to sleep in – usually a straw mattress on the ground. Some did not have the strength to rise. The Jewish Community Council provided only one slop of 'water soup' a day. The walls were filthy and mildewed.

Not surprisingly, typhus raged in the ghetto. The hospitals were full to bursting point: 150 people a day were being admitted to a single ward. The sick and dying were two or three to a bed, with others on the floor. Doctors could not keep up; those who were dying were urged to get on with it to make room for the next patient. The gravediggers could not dig fast enough. Even though hundreds of corpses were buried in every grave, hundreds more had to lie around, filling the area with a sweet, sickly odour. The epidemic grew out of all control, at one point as many as 2 per cent of the population were dying every month.

Then came the news that, during November and December 1940, some 40,000 Jews of Lodz, another 40,000 from Pomerania and other areas that were going to be incorporated into Germany, along with several hundred gypsies, had been gassed in Chelmno. The victims had been told that they were being taken there to work. When they arrived in Chelmno, they were ordered to strip and given a towel and soap, having been told they were going to have a shower. It was a cruel hoax. As the Jews were transported in trucks towards mass graves in the woods near Chelmno, exhaust gas was pumped into the sealed vehicles. At the woods, Jewish gravediggers – under the watchful eyes of SS guards – unloaded the bodies and buried them, knowing they would be next.

Three people who had, miraculously, escaped brought the news to the Warsaw Ghetto. Most people did not believe them – the inhabitants of the ghetto were clinging to life so tenaciously that they could not comprehend how people could have died in such a fashion. Some of the youth groups, particularly the young communists, believed the stories, though. They noticed that German terror was increasing and decided they would not go meekly to their deaths like the people at Chelmno. They began to organize propaganda to alert the other inmates of the ghetto to the danger, and they smuggled the news abroad, along with a demand that retaliation be taken against the Germans. The communist delegate to the Polish Government in exile in London broadcast the news to the world, but few people believed it.

When Germany attacked the Soviet Union in the summer of 1941, the Jews of the ghetto began to hear of mass shootings of Jews in Wilno, Slonim, Bialystok and Baranowicze. Tens of thousands of Jews were being slaughtered. Again, most of those inside the ghetto refused to believe it, or put it down to the antics of drunken soldiers rather than an organized policy of extermination.

At this point, the youth groups decided that they must organize resistance. They sent messages to the Polish Underground to ask for arms and, in the mean time, they began training. Several thousand were involved in the resistance movement, though they were organized into cells of between five and seven. They established a co-operative barber's, a tailor's shop and a cobbler's as a front. Youth groups organized a choir and educational courses and put on plays to try to keep the cultural life of the ghetto going. They also produced one weekly and six monthly magazines in an effort to maintain morale.

On one occasion, the girl who was smuggling 40 mimeographed copies of *The Bulletin* was stopped by the Polish police. She pretended to be an ordinary smuggler and offered them a bribe of 500 zloty. This was an unusually high offer and therefore made them suspicious. They asked to see the 'merchandise' and from under the girl's skirt fell not food nor stockings but printed sheets. They were just about to take her to the Gestapo when a colleague, seeing she was in trouble, started a scuffle. The police ran off to stop it, leaving the girl to drop the 500 zloty and run for her life.

The Germans grew angry with the number of Jews managing to slip out of the ghetto to get a little bread or a few pennies. They established special courts to try any one caught on the 'Aryan side'. On 12 February 1941, 17 people, including three women and four children, were executed for leaving the ghetto. Cries were heard from the Jewish jail on Geisha Street from the 700 other prisoners waiting to be tried for the same offence.

Just in case the message had not got through, the German Commissar of the ghetto, Dr Auerswald, filled the ghetto with posters announcing the executions. The ghetto was so intimidated that no protest was made, but things still got worse. The Germans began shooting passers-by in the street for no reason. Between ten and 15 a day were slaughtered randomly. One particularly sadistic policeman claimed to have killed over 300 people in a month. More than half of them were children.

The Jewish police were used to rounding up people for forced labour. The Germans maintained that the people being sent to labour camps were lucky. Although the conditions were harsh, it did give them the opportunity to survive the war. Forced labourers were even allowed to write to their families. However, when the letters arrived, they were full of stories of the mass killing of Jews. Again, the people remaining in the ghetto could not believe what they were being told. Even when they heard of the liquidation of the ghetto in Lublin, the people in Warsaw refused to believe it was going to happen to them.

People tried to convince one another that not even the Nazis would murder 300,000 people when there was a labour shortage – that the Germans were taking people from the Warsaw Ghetto for forced labour showed that they needed manpower.

They did not know about the change of policy in Berlin. Although the Germans had shot tens of thousands of people at Babi Yar and other places throughout the occupied areas of the Soviet Union. and the Baltic states, it was not a very efficient method of slaughter. On 20 January 1942, SS Obergruppenführer Reinhard Heydrich, Adolf Eichmann and others met in the Berlin suburb of Grossen-Wannseee, where they came up with what they called the 'final solution' to the 'Jewish question'. They planned to round up all Jews in occupied Europe and ship them to camps in the east where they would be systematically exterminated.

In the Warsaw Ghetto, the terror tactics continued. On the night of 17 April 1942, over 50 of the Jewish Community Council's workers were dragged from their beds by German officers and shot in the streets. The ghetto was shocked, hysterical, but the inhabitants concluded that this brutal action was aimed at the political leaders who urged resistance. On 19 April, a special edition of the resistance paper *Der Weker* was published, explaining that this was part of the German policy of systematic extermination of the Jews. It urged the people of the Warsaw Ghetto not to go to their deaths as 'meekly as those in Lublin or Chelmno had'. However, the activists still had not managed to get any guns and their words fell on deaf ears.

Guns were promised, though. The Polish socialists said

that a shipment of 100 pistols, a few dozen rifles and some grenades would arrive shortly. The communists in the ghetto organized more military training and tried to work out a plan of action in case the Germans stormed the ghetto.

Their task was not made any the easier by the fact that they were always losing members. Between 18 April and 22 July, the Germans entered the ghetto every night and killed ten or 15 people. None of the activists slept in their own beds. The whole ghetto was unsettled by the Germans' habit of shooting people from one group one night and another the next – smugglers, merchants, workers and professional people.

Other random acts of violence terrorized the people into absolute subordination. A Polish policeman saw three children sitting one in front of another in front of the hospital and killed all three with a single shot. A German watched as a pregnant woman tripped and fell as she crossed the road. Instead of helping her up, he shot her. Every morning a man, shackled, was flung out of an Opel car on Orla Street and shot. It was a Jew who had been caught on the 'Aryan side'.

The Germans adopted a new tactic to stop smuggling. They would dress up as Jews with Star of David armbands and hide machine-guns in burlap bags. Thinking they were safe, smugglers would scale the ghetto walls, only to be gunned down.

In mid-May 1942, 110 people arrested for being on the 'Aryan side' were executed. The prisoners were led out of the central jail into special trucks to be gassed. Only one of the accused protested. A woman stopped on the steps of the trucks and shouted: 'I will die, but your death will be much worse.' Again, Dr Auerswald put up posters announcing the 'just punishment' of these 110 'criminals'.

In mid-July, the rumour circulated that the Deportation Board had arrived and that between 20,000 and 60,000 inmates of the ghetto were to be taken to build fortifications. Supposedly, the Germans planned to take all the ghetto's unemployed, leaving only those who had jobs. Those who had had enough money to sit in cafés all day quickly became clerks and mechanics. The women became seamstresses and the price of sewing machines went through the roof. Many paid what little they had to get work, but it did them no good.

On 20 July 1942, the doctors were rounded up, along with the managers of the Jewish Mutual Aid Committee and a number of the Jewish Community Council. They were locked up.

On 22 July, the Deportation Board arrived at the headquarters of the Jewish Community Council. They brought news – it was a small matter really: all unproductive Jews were going to be deported somewhere to the east. Oberscharführer Hoefle dictated a proclamation that appeared under the Jewish Community Council's name on white posters the following morning. It said that all Jews, except those who worked for the Germans, the Jewish Community Council or the Jewish Mutual Aid Committee, would be deported. The Jewish police would be the agency responsible for organizing this and they would report directly to the Deportation Board.

On the first day, 2,000 prisoners from the central jail, along with beggars and starving people picked up on the streets, were taken. From then on, the quota was to be 6,000 a day.

The following afternoon the activists met. Without guns, they decided, resistance was impossible. Their clear duty was to save as many people as they could. They thought they might be able to get help from their contacts inside the Jewish police, but it was too late. Germans and Ukrainians had moved in and surrounded a block on Muranowska Street. They took over 2,000, enough to fill the shortfall in the daily quota. Even those with papers saying they were working for the Germans were taken. From then on, the Germans said they would look after the 'technical details' of the deportations themselves.

In a meeting on 23 July, the communists began urging resistance. But the majority feared that any actions might be provocative. If they handed over the required quota of Jews every day, the Germans might leave the rest of them alone, they argued. Still, the inhabitants of the ghetto did not believe that they were all going to be killed and those who thought that there might be some possibility of saving themselves willingly condemned others.

However, Adam Czerniaków, chairman of the Jewish Community Council, committed suicide. He knew that deportation meant that hundreds of thousands of Jews from the ghetto were heading for the gas chambers and he refused to take responsibility for it. Activists condemned him. He was a voice of considerable authority in the ghetto, they said; he should have made it his business to inform everyone, particularly the Jewish police, of the fate awaiting deportees. Instead, the communists rushed out an issue of their paper *On Guard*, warning people of the fate that awaited them and urging them to resist by any means at their disposal.

By the fifth day, the resistance knew for certain what was happening to those who were deported. A Polish contact had followed one of the transports to Sokolow. There he was told by a local railway worker that it had taken the branch line to Treblinka. Every day freight trains were taken down that branch, full of people from Warsaw: they came back empty. No consignment of food was ever sent down that line and civilians were forbidden to go anywhere near Treblinka railway station. The Pole also met two naked Jews who had somehow escaped. They told him about the mass extermination that was going on at a camp outside Treblinka.

Another edition of *On Guard* was prepared, explaining in full what deportees could expect; no one believed it. At the same time, the Germans began giving 3kg of bread and 1kg of marmalade to anyone who voluntarily registered for 'deportation'. It was a brilliant ruse. Ghetto inmates said, 'Why would they feed people they intend to murder?' Their hungry stomachs got the better of their reason. Thousands took the short walk down to the Umschlagplatz of their own volition. They waited in line in their hundreds; the transports had to be doubled to accommodate the demand: 12,000 people were deported daily, but still the trains could not accommodate them all.

Once all the volunteers had gone and the children's homes and refugee shelters had been emptied, the ghetto was emptied block by block. People with knapsacks would move from street to street, trying to guess which block was going to be cleared next.

The clearance was done by the Polish police, the Ukrainians and the Jewish police. The Polish police isolated the block; the Ukrainians surrounded the house; and the Jewish police would walk into the courtyards and summon the inhabitants.

'All Jews must come down. Only 30 kilograms of baggage is allowed,' they would say. 'Those remaining behind will be shot.'

People would come running, pulling on their clothes and carrying everything they could grab. They would assemble, trembling, in front of the houses. No talking was allowed. Then the Ukrainians would go in and search the apartments. According to regulations, the doors of the apartments had to be left open. If not, the Ukrainians would break them down with a boot or a rifle butt. There would be shots as anyone left inside was killed. Then they would move on to the next house.

The people in the street would be formed into columns.

Any passer-by who had mistakenly walked down the wrong street would be taken too. The column would be marched off, with old people and children who had to be carried bringing up the rear. Outside the area cordoned off by the Polish police, relatives would desperately try to find their loved ones.

The column would be marched to the Umschlag or deportation point. The tall wall surrounding it had one narrow entrance, guarded by the Polish police. The deportees would hold out their identification papers and be told *rechts* (right) – meaning life – or *links* (left) – meaning death. Although argument was futile, people held out other papers, trying to prove how useful they would be to German industry. It made no difference. The gendarme's decision was quite arbitrary. Sometimes he ordered people to show him their hands and let all those with small hands live. Other days, he picked all the people with fair hair to die. In the morning, short people might live; in the afternoon only the tall survived.

The Umschlagplatz was filled with more than enough people for four days' transports. They were left to camp out in the square or in the surrounding derelict buildings for four or five days before they were loaded into cattle trucks. Some people wore merely a housecoat or nightgown. Every inch of free space was filled. There were no toilet facilities – everything was covered in urine and excrement.

The people were given no food; on the second day, the hunger pains became unbearable. There was no water either; people's lips cracked. While waiting, children sickened and people became smaller and greyer. By now, they had no doubt as to what their fate would be.

The Germans were clever enough to tantalize those they had condemned to die with a glimmer of hope. They set up a children's hospital and an emergency aid station. The staff were clad in white coats and given working

161

certificates. The personnel were changed twice a day, so it appeared that, if you had a white coat, you could walk in and out. White coats were soon fetching fabulous prices in the ghetto. Some nurses took strange children in their arms and walked out with them. If they were sick, older people could be sent to hospital or direct to the cemetery. Healthy people were also sometimes smuggled out in ambulances. But the Germans got wise and checked the condition of the sick. Those found fit had their legs broken without an anaesthetic.

It was possible to get the Jewish police to smuggle one out, if they were bribed enough. But those who escaped usually appeared in the Umschlagplatz two, or possibly three, times before they ran out of money and had to board the train like everybody else.

Some people, who did escape from the Umschlagplatz, survived. Others who were brave enough to come to the Umschlagplatz to try to help get someone else out were swept onto the trains themselves.

The transports left every morning and evening, so twice a day the crowd was rounded up and forced into the cattle trucks. To survive this, you had to be as far from the trucks as possible. The Ukrainians would encircle the square and force the people towards the train; thousands of people would be crushed together. Resist and the Ukrainians shot you. They could not miss at that range and, with thousands of people huddled together, they would probably kill another one or two besides.

People would squeeze into the doorway of the hospital or take to the upper floors of the surrounding buildings; but the Ukrainians would run about, chasing them out like wild beasts. Some hid in the attics; three girls who hid up there for five days were eventually smuggled out by nurses.

The Ukrainians did not have to exert themselves too much, though. No matter how many escaped, there were always enough to pack the cattle trucks. Indeed, the people had to be beaten with rifle butts before the doors could be closed. Those who escaped that shipment would simply wait in the Umschlagplatz. They would either go on the next shipment or the one after that . . . or starve.

The resistance groups were losing a lot of their men. Still, they started to fight back. They set a few fires and beat up the commander of the Jewish police. They also tried to place their people with German firms in a vain effort to save them.

By the middle of August 1942, there were only 120,000 left in the ghetto; 300,000 had been taken to Treblinka to be gassed. There came a short pause in the deportations, while the Germans started liquidating what remained of the Jewish settlements in nearby towns.

Then the deportations from the ghetto started again. This time they were hard to avoid as cleared areas had been sealed off and the ghetto was now much smaller. The people left had become more skilled at hiding, so the Germans gave every Jewish policeman a quota. They each had to prove seven 'heads' a day, so whereas before the Jewish police had sometimes been helpful they were now inflexible. They would grab women with babies in their arms, snatch stray children or tear the white coat off a 'doctor'. If they did not come up with their quota, they would be on the train to Treblinka themselves.

On 6 September 1942, the remaining inhabitants of the ghetto were ordered to move into the area bounded by just four streets. There the final registration would take place. The people remained in the small rectangular block for two days. Yet, even now, the Germans did not leave them completely without hope. Some would go to German firms; along with members of the Jewish Community Council, they were issued with numbered slips that guaranteed them – for the moment – life. Instead of offering any last-minute resistance, everyone without a slip thought of only one thing – how to get one.

Finally, those with slips were marched away to the firms where they would be billeted. The rest were taken to the Umschlagplatz. The last to be taken there were the families of the Jewish police.

There was no escape from the Umschlagplatz now. Sick adults and children moved from the hospitals were left lying in empty halls. They relieved themselves where they lay as there was no one to help. Nurses sought out their parents and gave them an overdose of morphine. One doctor poured cyanide into the mouths of sick children, saving them the horrors of a train ride to Treblinka. In two days, 60,000 people were deported to certain death. On 12 September 1942, the liquidation of the Polish ghetto was over.

Those left alive were some 33,400 Jews working in German factories and 3,000 employees of the Jewish Community Council. However, there were more hidden in cellars, attics and in any other corner where the Ukrainians had not bothered to look. Building work began: new walls were put up to divide the ghetto into three. Jewish workers from nearby factories were billeted there. They were forbidden to communicate with one another and were forced to work at least 12 hours a day without a break. The food was minimal and soon there was another outbreak of typhus.

The garbage carriers and gravediggers became rich, smuggling out what valuables remained to sell on the 'Aryan side' under piles of garbage or in coffins. What was left of the resistance groups in the ghetto joined forces in the Jewish Fighting Organization or, in Polish, ZOB. They organized themselves this time according to the sector they were billeted to, rather than along political lines. They heard that Polish resistance groups were now forming in the forests and they even managed to get some pistols from Polish communists. These they used to attack senior figures in the Jewish police.

ZOB also attacked Jewish foremen who had been harsh with the slave labourers under their care. During one attack, three ZOB men were arrested, but others disarmed the German guards and freed them.

In mid-November several hundred more Jews were deported, ostensibly to the concentration camp at Lublin. During the train journey, a ZOB man broke the bars on the carriage window, pushed six women out and jumped out himself. Before, such an escape had been impossible – the escapees were held back by others, fearful of the vengeance the Germans might wreak. Now everyone knew the deportation meant death and it was better to die honourably.

In December 1942, ZOB received ten pistols from the Polish Home Army, which had recently formed. They planned to take revenge on the Jewish police, but on 18 January they found the ghetto surrounded again as the Germans started a second liquidation. This time, however, they were not unopposed. ZOB put up barricades and, for the first time in the ghetto, offered armed resistance. There was a full-scale battle on the streets and many ZOB men were killed. Realizing that they were not ready to take on the Germans in this way – they did not have the weapons for it – they resorted to guerrilla tactics. Four guerrilla actions were organized, one of which attacked the SS. Again, it cost ZOB lives.

One ZOB battle group was caught unarmed by the Germans. They were taken to the Umschlagplatz, where their leader addressed them. When they were ordered to get onto the train, not a single man moved. Van Oeppen, the chief of Treblinka, shot all 60 himself, on the spot. Tragic though this was, it was an inspiration to others.

Both Polish and Jewish public opinion were altered by these ghetto battles. The halo of omnipotence had been ripped from the heads of the Germans and they were frustrated by these actions. At last, people realized that it was possible to oppose the Germans' will and might.

Although the resistance was puny, rumours began to circulate outside the ghetto that there were hundreds of dead Germans inside. Word spread throughout Warsaw that ZOB was invincible. The Polish Underground was so impressed that they sent 50 pistols and 50 hand grenades. ZOB organized itself into a tight military outfit with sentries and guard posts manned 24 hours a day – they did not intend to get caught napping by the Germans again.

Once more, the German propaganda machine got to work. Two of the Warsaw factories were to be moved to Jewish 'reservations where productive Jews devotedly working for the Germans would be able to live through the war in peace'. In February 1943, 12 Jewish foremen arrived from the concentration camp in Lublin and tried to persuade the Jews of the Warsaw Ghetto to volunteer. The working conditions in Lublin were 'excellent', they said. That night ZOB surrounded the Lublin men's quarters and forced them out of the ghetto.

ZOB began putting its own proclamations on the ghetto walls. When the Germans tried to counter this, ZOB seized their posters from the printing shop and destroyed them: ZOB was now in control of the ghetto. Again, plans were announced, saying that German factories were being evacuated to 'Jewish reservations'. At one joinery shop, only 25 out of the 1,000 Jewish workers volunteered to go. ZOB burned down the joinery shop, causing one million zlotys worth of damage. The Germans issued a statement saying the fire had been started by a parachutist, but no one in the ghetto had any doubt about who was really behind it.

The next factory, a brushmaker's, was to be moved in March. Out of its 3,500 Jewish workers, not one registered to go. When the machinery was being moved, ZOB planted incendiary bombs with delayed-action fuses so the machines burned up on their way.

ZOB now had the backing of the whole ghetto, which supplied them with food. Money was donated to buy arms and ammunition, and they taxed those who would not pay voluntarily. Even the Jewish Community Council was taxed. The money was then smuggled over to the 'Aryan side' where weapons and explosives were bought. These were then smuggled back into the ghetto like other contraband – Polish policemen were bribed to look the other way as heavy packages were hurled over the wall. Inside the ghetto, the Jewish police had no say any more.

Petrol was smuggled in to make Molotov cocktails and explosives were used to manufacture hand grenades. Soon every member of ZOB was armed with a pistol with ten to 15 rounds of ammunition, four or five hand grenades, and four or five Molotov cocktails. Each area had two or three rifles and there was one machine-gun for the entire ghetto.

ZOB now decided to rid the ghetto of all those who had collaborated with the Germans. Death sentences were pronounced on all Jewish Gestapo agents; those who were not killed fled. Later, when four Gestapo agents entered the ghetto, three were killed and the fourth badly wounded.

Realizing that those remaining in the ghetto were not going to go to their deaths voluntarily, the Germans began arresting people for minor offences. However, when ZOB heard that the people caught were going to be deported, they raided the jailhouse and freed them.

The Germans then tried arresting people en masse, loading them onto trucks and taking them direct to the Umschlagplatz; ZOB stopped the trucks and freed them. Finally, the Germans got so frustrated that they decided to forcibly liquidate the remainder of the ghetto, no matter what the cost.

At 2am on 19 April 1943, ZOB observation posts reported that the Germans were coming. German and Polish policemen surrounded the ghetto at 30-yard intervals. Within 15 minutes, ZOB had manned its defensive positions. The inhabitants of the ghetto were warned and fled to pre-arranged shelters and hiding places in cellars and attics.

At 4am, German soldiers arrived in threes and fours, hoping not to arouse the suspicion of the population. Once in the middle of the ghetto, they formed in companies and platoons. At 7am, motorized detachments, including a number of tanks and armoured vehicles, entered the ghetto. Field guns were set up around the walls. SS men came marching in, their goose-stepping boots ringing down the silent streets of the ghetto – the mastery of their situation seemed complete.

However, they had chosen to form at exactly the wrong place – the intersection of Mila and Zamenhofa Streets. ZOB had been waiting for just such an opportunity, and they were manning all four corners of the intersection. They rained gunfire and hand grenades down on the SS men. Even the machine-gun opened up on them, sparingly – ammunition had to be conserved. The SS tried to retreat, but found themselves cut off. Those still alive tried to find shelter in doorways, but were fired on from all sides. A tank was called up to cover the retreat; it was hit with a Molotov cocktail and burned out. Not one German left the area alive.

Another group of Germans tried to enter the ghetto, but they were pinned down. After dozens were killed and wounded, they were forced to withdraw.

In Muranoski Square, the partisans were cornered. But they fought so ferociously that they repulsed the attack, capturing two German machine-guns and burning out a second tank. By 2pm, there was not a single German left alive in the ghetto. It was ZOB's first complete victory.

For the next 24 hours the ghetto was bombed and shelled. Then at 2pm on 20 April, the SS turned up again in close formation. As they waited for the gate into the ghetto to be opened, a partisan set off a remote-controlled mine – 100 SS men were killed. The rest withdrew under showers of gunfire.

Two hours later, the Germans attacked again, this time in a loose formation. Although 30 Germans entered the ghetto, only a handful re-emerged; the Germans were forced to withdraw. They tried to attack again in several points around the ghetto but met with ferocious opposition – every house round the perimeter of the ghetto was now a fortress.

At this point the Germans changed tactics. They sent emissaries – three officers with machine-guns lowered and white rosettes in their buttonholes – who suggested a 15-minute truce to remove their dead and wounded. They also offered all the inhabitants of the ghetto safe passage to labour camps in the Jewish reservations. They would even be allowed to take their belongings with them. The response from ZOB was gunfire.

In one area, the Germans were taking such heavy casualties that, by dusk, they resorted to setting the buildings on fire. ZOB partisans were forced to withdraw, but their retreat was blocked by a wall. A gap in it was the only way to the central ghetto, but it was guarded on three sides by German and Polish police, and Ukrainians. Half the group managed to slip through in the darkness before the Germans found a searchlight and trained it on the wall. One well-aimed shot put the light out and the rest of the partisans escaped.

The ordinary inhabitants of the ghetto were not so lucky. Thousands perished in the flames; others ran out into the courtyards where they were seized by the Germans or killed on the spot. Hundreds committed suicide by jumping from the fourth or fifth storeys of apartment houses – some mothers jumped with their children to save them from the flames. The only consolation was that these scenes of horror were witnessed by thousands of Poles who lived in the surrounding area.

The Germans thought that such horrendous loss of life would subdue the ghetto. They announced a deadline for the inhabitants to report to collection points for deportation: no one turned up. The partisans now began to take the battle to the enemy. They tried to disrupt troop movements into the central ghetto; from balconies, windows and rooftops, they showered SS trucks with bombs. One such vehicle saw all but five of the 60 SS men it was carrying killed. ZOB even succeeded in blowing up a military vehicle outside the wall of the ghetto.

When the deadline had passed, the Germans tried to enter the ghetto again, with force. The partisans had planted mines, but the electricity supply had been cut off, so they could not detonate them. As a result, they began fighting house by house. Again, the Germans were forced to resort to arson. ZOB guided the inhabitants of the ghetto to underground shelters, where thousands sheltered for over a week.

When the burning was over, not a single building was left and the water supply was cut off. Still ZOB fought on – the Germans did not dare to enter the ghetto during the day. Ferocious fighting took place at night and there were heavy losses on both sides. Food and water were scarce, as was ammunition. ZOB knew that there were 20 rifles and more ammunition waiting for them on the 'Aryan side', but there was no way they could get them.

The Germans began looking for the shelters using police dogs and sensitive sound-detecting equipment. When they found them, battle raged. Although ultimately they could not resist the might of the Germans, ZOB fulfilled its aim – the Germans did not evacuate a single living person.

On 8 March, Germans and Ukrainians surrounded ZOB's headquarters. After two hours of ferocious fighting, they hurled in a gas bomb. Seeing the position was hopeless, the partisans committed suicide rather than be taken by the Germans alive. Some shot their families, then themselves – 80 per cent of the partisans perished there.

The remnants banded together. Ten days earlier, two partisans had been sent out of the ghetto to contact their liaison men to arrange the withdrawal of the battle groups from the ghetto when it fell. Now the liaison men turned up. Those who remained were taken down into the sewers to make their way out. The Germans had anticipated this, so the sewers were full of obstacles and entanglements that were booby-trapped and would explode at a single touch. In some places the sewers were only 28in high and it was difficult for the escaping partisans to keep their mouths above the level of the sewage. Every so often, the Germans would pump gas into the drains. At one place, where the sewer was not big enough for them to stand, they had to wait for 48 hours. Partisans kept losing consciousness. For some, the lack of water was too much to bear. Driven mad by thirst they drank the foul sewer water.

On 10 May, a manhole cover was lifted in broad daylight. A number of Jewish partisans emerged and escaped in a truck. Others were left in the sewer. Those who got out were taken out to the woods where they fought with the Polish Home Army. Most died eventually. Those who survived took part in the Warsaw Uprising of 1944.

As the Soviet army approached the city in July 1944, the Polish Underground staged an uprising against the Germans. They were members of the Home Army who were run by the Polish Government in exile in London. However, they knew that in east Poland, which had already been liberated by the Red Army, the procommunist Polish Committee of National Liberation was in charge. Hoping to gain control of Warsaw before the Red Army took it, the Home Army followed the suggestion of the Soviets and revolted.

The Home Army's Warsaw Corps numbered about 50,000 men. Against weakened German opposition, they had taken over most of the city by 1 August. However, the Germans counter-attacked, forcing the Polish Home Army into defensive positions which they bombed and shelled for the following 63 days. The Red Army occupied the suburb of Praga, across the Vistula River from the city, and stopped there while the Germans bombed the city flat. The Soviets also prevented the British and Americans from supplying the rebels.

Out of food and ammunition, the beleaguered Poles had to surrender on 1 October. The remnants of the Home Army and the remaining Jews were taken prisoner and deported, and the rest of the city was destroyed. Only then did the Red Army move on.

This was an entirely cynical ploy by the Soviets: allowing the Germans to destroy the Home Army eliminated the main body of the military organization that supported the Polish Government in exile in London. So when the Soviets over-ran the whole of Poland there was little effective resistance to the communist-led puppet government they installed.

For the Jewish resistance fighters who had survived the Warsaw ghetto, this was the ultimate betrayal – many of them had been communists. On May Day 1943, a week before the ghetto was finally liquidated, they had held a communist-inspired celebration. There were speeches and the sound of the Internationale had rung out across the smouldering ruins of the ghetto. Of the 500,000 Jews who had passed through the Warsaw ghetto, only a handful had survived.

Evil is
Big Business

The Mafia:
Network of Evil

The newspapers of the time reported it in typically racy, lurid terms, as befitted the occasion . . . 'Mafia Godfather Carmine Galante was shot dead over a plate of spaghetti in New York's Knickerbocker Avenue last night. The cigar-chewing 'boss of all bosses' was sipping chianti as two black limousines drew up outside Joe and Mary's Italian restaurant. Four neatly dressed men strolled calmly from the cars into the eating house and opened fire.

'Galante, who rubbed out all gangland opposition to become America's most powerful mobster since Lucky Luciano, tried to rise from his chair but was cut down in a hail of bullets. His bodyguard Nino Copolla also died instantly. The restaurant owner and his 17-year-old son were also wounded, and the boy died later in hospital.'

A typical gangland killing of the 1930s? A regular act of savagery from the days of prohibition, bootlegging, tommy guns and Al Capone? No, that report appeared in the London *Daily Express* of 13 July 1979 – a full 50 years after the infamous St Valentine's Day Massacre which first brought the full horrors of mobster rule to the shocked attention of the world.

In those 50 years and more, organized crime has become bigger and bigger business. But, as evidenced by the shooting of Carmine Galante, its face is just as ugly. And, as ever, this sordid sub-culture and black economy is run by the same, sinister, all-encompassing organization . . .

They may call it 'the Mob', 'the Syndicate', or 'the national network of organized crime'. Older and more sentimental members call it 'Cosa Nostra' – literally, 'Our Thing'. Most people, however, know it simply as the Mafia.

Its roots are as shadowy as its present-day operations. Even the derivation of the word Mafia is unknown. It may come from a Sicilian dialect term for bravado or possibly from an Arabic word, *mehia*, which means boastful. All that is certain about the Mafia's origins is that it was formed in the 13th century as a patriotic underground movement to resist Sicily's unwelcome rulers, the French. And, on Easter Monday 1282, these freedom-fighters led a bloody massacre of the foreign invaders as the bells of the capital, Palermo, rang for vespers.

A similar society, the Camorra, was founded later in Naples. Over the centuries both flourished as secret brotherhoods vowed to protect the local populace from the despotic rulers of their regions. But, almost inevitably, both abused their autocratic powers to exploit and subjugate their people rather than protect them.

America's Italian immigrants took both societies across the Atlantic with them in the 19th century – and it was in the city slums of the United States that the two groups emerged. An early boost to the fledgling 'families' in exile came in 1890 when 11 immigrant Mafiosi were lynched in New Orleans. The government paid $30,000 compensation to the widows and families of the hanged men. But the money was expropriated by the criminal brotherhood.

With further massive influxes of southern Italians around the turn of the century, the Mafia took its hold on immigrant ghettoes of the major cities. At first, they were a protection agency – at a price. Then their activities spread to illegal gambling, loan sharking, prostitution and finally drugs.

The introduction of prohibition in 1920 was probably the biggest single factor in the success story of the Mafia. The market in bootleg liquor to help America drown its sorrows through the Depression was seemingly limitless. Every one of the several, fragmented, ill-organized Mafia families spread across the nation worked together to fulfil that demand . . . at enormous profits.

When Prohibition was repealed in 1933, the profits dried up and new forms of investment had to be found. Loan sharking, the numbers games, 'protection' rackets and prostitution kept the money rolling in. But new areas of exploitation were needed.

The growing drugs market was one of the most potentially lucrative and the Mafia built up French and Far Eastern connections. Another was legal gambling, with the golden boom in casino cities like Las Vegas, Reno and more recently Atlantic City. The third was the labour movement.

Trade unions were cynically milked for the funds that could be misappropriated and, more importantly, for the 'muscle' they could lend to any extortion situation where a strike could prove costly.

Early in the 20th century, the trade unions were manipulated by New York Mafia boss Jacob 'Little Augie' Orgen, whose labour rackets earned him a huge fortune until his death at the hands of gunmen in 1927. Such Mafia notables as Albert Anastasia, Vito Genovese, Meyer Lansky and Lucky Luciano all worked for and learned from Orgen in those early days.

If Orgen's operation was the training ground for union corruption, Jimmy Hoffa's was the finishing school. No trade union had been infiltrated to a more infamous degree than the Teamsters Union. And Hoffa, the teamsters' boss, was its notorious leader.

Hoffa appointed a number of aides who had criminal records. Many were chosen for their expertise in terror and extortion. He also poured millions of dollars into his own pockets and then bought a Miami bank to look after the money. When the crusading Robert Kennedy became chairman of the Senate Rackets Committee, Hoffa became his prime and very personal target. He described Hoffa's leadership of the teamsters as a 'conspiracy of evil'.

Because of the shady deals revealed by the committee, Hoffa was jailed in 1967, sentenced to serve 13 years for jury tampering and defrauding the union's pension fund of almost two million dollars. Four years later President Nixon issued a pardon and freed Hoffa on condition that he held no union office until 1980. That was not good enough for the still-ambitious Hoffa, who fought in the appeal court for the lifting of the ban.

Nixon's orders were not Hoffa's only problem. While in jail, he had appointed his long-time ally Frank Fitzsimmons as leader of the union in his stead, on the firm understanding that he was no more than a 'caretaker' until the former boss was freed. But Fitzsimmons came to enjoy his taste of supreme power and had no intention of giving up the job. The union's Detroit headquarters became the battleground for the feud between Fitzsimmons and Hoffa.

Although Hoffa had many allies in the union ranks, observers believed that his outlandish style no longer suited the 'respectable' image required by the shadowy figures who wanted to get their hands on the union's purse strings. Jimmy Hoffa was an embarrassment.

Shortly after midday on 30 July 1975, Hoffa got into his bullet-proof car to drive to a mysterious luncheon meeting. An anonymous telephone caller later told the police where they could find the car. It was empty. Jimmy Hoffa was never seen again.

Hoffa's crime in Mafia eyes was that he had broken the rule of silence. The low-profile approach ordered by the families since the last war was being endangered by the load-mouthed union boss.

The Mafia always had a vow of silence. A new recruit would hold a scrap of burning paper in his hand while he recited the oath: 'This is the way I will burn if I betray the secrets of the family.' But beyond this natural secrecy lay a more productive lesson for the Mafia chiefs – that they could operate more effectively, more profitably and with less interference from law-enforcement agencies if they did not advertise their shadowy organization's existence with public killings and scandals.

Salvatore Maranzano was first to see this. The first man to claim the title Il Capo di Tutti Capi – The Boss of All Bosses – Maranzano called a conference of the major families in 1931 and proposed a constitution that would end the bitter rivalries within their ranks. But he was ahead of his time. Within five months, he and 40 of his men were murdered.

Gang warfare on such an overt scale alerted Americans to the magnitude of the crime problem in their midst. It also alerted the Mafiosi themselves to the dangers of advertising their power in blood.

The man who ordered Maranzano's killing, Meyer Lansky, learned the lesson best of all. He took up his assassinated rival's theme of co-operation. Lansky and his contemporaries, 'Lucky' Luciano and Vito Genovese, made themselves millions by adopting the low-profile approach to organized crime.

If Maranzano first voiced the new Mafia philosophy and Lansky espoused it, then Carlo Gambino perfected it. Gambino was the inspiration for the character featured as Il Capo di Tutti Capi in the novel and film *The Godfather*. Under the iron rule of this frail old man, the Mafia flourished. By 1976, when Carlo Gambino died peacefully in his bed at the age of 73, the Mafia had apparently vanished into the woodwork.

But there was just one more act necessary to make the transformation complete. And that was the removal of ambitious, brutal, old-time Mafioso Carmine Galante, who saw himself as the new Godfather following Carlo Gambino's death.

Galante's life story is almost the story of the American

Mafia itself. His parents were Sicilian immigrants who settled in the tough East Harlem district of New York. He never weighed more than 10 stones 10lb, but his usefulness with a gun quickly won him respect among mobsters as a 'good soldier'.

On Christmas Eve 1930 he was involved in a shoot-out in which a detective and a six-year-old girl were wounded. He was jailed for 15 years but was released after 12 and returned to the Mafia brotherhood.

Galante was a man of contradictions and surprises. He made a subordinate marry his mistress of 22 years so that her children by him would be legitimate. He was responsible for destroying thousands of lives with the drugs he made available. He ordered countless killings. Yet he loved kittens and was a keen gardener. He controlled prostitutes and a pornography empire but was furious if he heard a man use bad language in the presence of a woman.

Galante's specialized business interests were drug peddling to teenagers, organized prostitution, loan sharking and crooked gambling. He was instrumental in setting up the 'French connection' to flood the east coast of the USA with hard drugs from Marseilles.

He had always lived by the gun and it was this loud, loutish and overtly brutal approach that brought about his premature demise at the age of 69.

Believing that no one would dare stand in his way after the death of Carlo Gambino in 1976, Galante began to encroach on the territories of other Mafia families. He was thought to be trying to amass a $50 million personal fortune to pass on to his relatives. To this end, he risked warfare with other families and put his own gang at risk from the police and the FBI.

In January 1979 he was told to give up his leadership, but he refused. The decision meant that he signed his own death warrant.

That was why Galante's assassins, carrying scatter-guns and wearing ski masks, visited Joe and Mary's restaurant on 'unlucky' 13 July 1979 and killed him so quickly that his trademark cigar was still clenched at a jaunty angle in his mouth as he hit the floor. Then a .45 bullet was calmly fired into his left eye – a traditional Mafia calling card.

Less than a mile away from the bloody scene, when the news was brought that Galante was dead, 20 ruthless Mafia bosses raised their glasses in a macabre toast. They had gathered at another New York restaurant to discuss underworld strategy following the removal of their former associate.

A senior detective on the case said: 'It shows you how cold-blooded and businesslike these people are.'

The FBI first got wind of the underworld summit meeting when a Mafia chief from California flew into New York. They saw him rent a car and tailed him to a restaurant in a seedy Brooklyn side-street. To their astonishment, it was lined with gleaming black Cadillacs and Lincoln Continentals.

Among those at the meeting was Frank 'Funzi' Tieri, boss of New York's Genovese family. Galante had been pushing hard to take over the Genovese mob and police believed that Tieri, 74, had a part in the assassination. He certainly reaped the benefits . . . for he was shortly afterwards voted the new Godfather.

Tieri had done similar 'business' in the past. He had taken control of the Genovese family seven years earlier after the shooting of the former boss Tommy Eboli – a killing that police also put down to Tieri.

The style of Frank 'Funzi' Tieri was much suited to the new image of Mafia businessmen. Unlike Galante, he could keep his nose clean, his mouth shut and maintain a low profile. He had learned his trade as a lieutenant of the infamous Vito Genovese in the bloody 1950s gangster battles of control of the lucrative empire of Lucky Luciano after he was deported to Italy. But since then he had turned to the more orthodox range of Mafia rackets – with the exception of drugs, which he declined to touch.

His legitimate businesses included a sportswear firm, a sales corporation and companies operating school bus services.

Shortly after coming to power, Tieri was described by New York Police Department as the biggest loan shark in the country. They said: 'He controls most of the gambling and loan sharks in the Bronx, East Harlem, Brooklyn and Queens. And he controls gambling in New Jersey, Florida, Puerto Rico, California and Las Vegas'.

Tieri's lifestyle suited the mob. He lived in a neat, three-storey house on a tree-lined street in a middle-class suburb. Every morning he would kiss his wife (her first name was, strangely, America) and leave for work wearing a conservative business suit. He would then be driven by his chauffeur 1 mile to the home of his mistress, Rita Perelli, from where he ran his operation.

He was said never to use the telephone and never to commit any note of his activities to paper. And he kept the loyalty of his criminal family not by threats but by a profit-sharing scheme. The Mafia's transformation from a gang of gunfighters to a band of multi-million-dollar businessmen was complete.

By the 1980s the Mafia had infiltrated almost every area of American business life. The US Justice Department named the following industries as having the biggest Mafia involvement: music, video recording, haulage, garbage collection, clothes manufacturing, commercial banking, insurance, meat supply and processing, hotel and casino operation, baking, cheese making, cooking oil wholesaling and pizza retailing.

Today an American may start his life wrapped in a Mafia nappy, listen to rock music from a Mafia record company, dine out on a Mafia steak, drive a car bought with a Mafia bank loan, holiday at a Mafia hotel, buy a house in a Mafia development and finally be buried by a Mafia funeral service.

Ralph Salerno, a leading US authority on organized crime, has said: 'If New York's five Mafia families conspired to paralyse the city, they could halt every car, taxi, bus, truck, train, ship and plane. They could also shut down literally thousands of wholesale and retail businesses. And they could close down services like laundering, dry cleaning, catering, garbage collection and dozens more.'

'It is no exaggeration to say that in New York every morsel of food you eat at home or in a restaurant, every item of clothing you wear and every journey you make is tainted by the Mob.'

The influence of the Mafia is now so all-pervasive that more than 2,000 past and potential witnesses to Mafia crimes are being guarded by the Witness Protection Program of the US Government. The bill for keeping these 'squealers' safe from the Mafia hit-men is currently $20 million a year.

At one time, the Mafia was estimated to have between 3,000 and 5,000 criminals working for it across the country. Nowadays this is a small proportion of the payroll compared with the thousands of 'front men' and perfectly honest employees who look after the Mob's business interests. A *Time* magazine survey put profits from the Mafia's 10,000-plus legitimate firms at $12 billion a year; four times as high are the profits from crime – an estimated $48 billion.

Such fabulous rewards come mainly from extortion. Companies are forced to buy Mafia products or shut down.

The US Justice Department believes that the cost of bribing a government meat inspector in New York is as low as $25 dollars a day. For that, he will say that kangaroo- or horse-meat is '100 per cent beef'. It is then sold, not to pet-food manufacturers for whom it was intended, but to market traders and restaurants. Similarly, Mafia vegetables often seem crisper – but only because they have been treated with a chemical that can cause cancer.

The Mob controls the supply of goods to companies by its union power. Mafia men stand for election as union officials – rival candidates being discouraged with baseball bats, knives or guns. A company which resists Mafia extortion can easily have its supplies cut off by a strike or union blacking. Few can afford to resist. Most, whether they know it or not, are contributing generously to the Mafia's billion-dollar profits.

Jacob Orgen and Jimmy Hoffa may be dead. But their methods are reaping fortunes of which even they never dared to dream.

Meyer Lansky, 'Lucky' Luciano and Vito Genovese

Meyer Lansky, born Maier Suchowjansky, was a respectable 16-year-old Polish immigrant who had settled with his family in New York and taken a job as an engineering apprentice. One day he passed a doorway on the city's lower East Side and saw a girl being assaulted. Lansky rushed to her rescue, fists flying.

In the ensuing fight, police were called and all three men were arrested and kept in prison 48 hours for brawling. They were 48 hours that changed Meyer Lansky's life.

The girl's two attackers were young thugs named Salvatore Luciano and Benjamin Siegel . . . who later preferred to be known as 'Lucky' Luciano and 'Bugsy'

Siegel. Despite his attack on them, they took Lansky under their wings and Luciano, in particular, tutored him in a life of crime.

Luciano was five years older than Lansky. A Sicilian immigrant, he had been in and out of trouble ever since his arrival in New York at the age of ten. He was first arrested within hours of disembarking from his migrant ship – for stealing fruit from a handcart. His life of petty crime led him to jail for the first time in 1915 for drug peddling, and shortly after his release he met and teamed up with Meyer Lansky.

Luciano was at first Lansky's mentor and later his associate. They controlled a number of New York gangs, mainly Italian and Irish, involved in robbing homes, shops and warehouses.

But there was an area of crime in which Luciano specialized and which Lansky abhorred – prostitution. The Jew would have no part in the vice trade because, when a teenager, he had fallen desperately in love with a young prostitute – then found her one night in an alley with her throat cut, probably by her pimp.

Between 1918 and 1932 Lansky was arrested seven times on charges ranging from disorderly conduct to murder. But he had to be released on every one because of lack of witnesses.

Luciano was more successful in keeping out of police custody. He and Lansky had both become members of the gang of Jacob 'Little Augie' Orgen, who made a fortune from union and organized labour rackets. While Lansky concentrated in less violent crimes, Luciano became New York's most feared hit-man, whose favoured weapon was an ice pick. His reward was a string of Manhattan brothels which, by the mid-1920s, were estimated to be earning him more than $1 million a year.

In 1920 came the ill-judged turn of events that was to turn Luciano, Lansky and others into multi-millionaires . . .

Prohibition.

The soft-spoken Lansky paved the way for a new breed of tommy-gun-wielding thugs to take over the illegal liquor business in the north and ensure the supply of whisky to New York. Principal among these was Alfonso 'Al' Capone, who was fiercely loyal to Lansky and Luciano.

In 1927, Luciano and Lansky were joined by a third ruthless killer and future crime czar, Vito Genovese. Born in Naples in 1897, Genovese had been a friend and neighbour of Luciano since the former's arrival in New York at the age of 16. A petty thief with only one arrest, for carrying a revolver, he too had graduated to organized crime while working 'under contract' to Jacob Orgen.

Despite the combined reputations of Lansky, Luciano and Genovese, the gang of three were still not the most powerful mobsters in New York. That accolade was being fought for between two old-style Mafia leaders, Salvatore Maranzano and Giuseppe Masseria, bitter rivals whose territorial battles had left as many as 60 of their 'soldiers' shot dead in a single year.

Both gang bosses tried to woo Luciano, Lansky and Genovese to their side, probably fearful of the trio's growing power. They refused. By way of persuasion, Maranzano lured Luciano to an empty garage where a dozen masked men lay in wait. Maranzano had him strung up by his thumbs from the rafters and punched and kicked until he lost consciousness. Luciano was repeatedly revived so that the torture could continue anew. Finally, Maranzano slashed him across the face with a knife. The wound required 55 stitches.

Not surprisingly, Luciano told his tormentor that he had changed his mind and was now happy to join the Maranzano mob. He was offered the Number Two job if he would first wipe out the Mafia rival, Masseria.

Luciano invited Masseria for a meal, pretending that he

was now keen to join forces with him. They sealed the deal and toasted one another across the table at Scarpato's Restaurant, Coney Island. But, when Luciano retired to the lavatory, four gunmen burst into the dining-room. Masseria must have known his fate the moment he saw them. They were Vito Genovese, Bugsy Siegel and two other Lansky men, Albert Anastasia and Joe Adonis. Masseria tried to flee but was cut down in a hail of 20 bullets.

Which now left only Maranzano between the Lansky gang and the pinnacle of power in the US underworld.

Maranzano, aged 63, could have claimed to have been the first true Capo di Tutti Capi. After Masseria's death, this elegantly dressed Sicilian, who had once trained to be a priest, called a meeting of the New York families in a hall where the walls were hung with crucifixes and other religious emblems. He drew up a constitution of what he termed La Cosa Nostra and proclaimed himself its effective Godfather. Lansky and his associates had other ideas and in September 1931 he helped Luciano settle his old score with Maranzano.

One morning four 'taxmen' called at Maranzano's real-estate agency on park Avenue. His bodyguards kept their guns hidden as the four identified themselves as Internal Revenue Service investigators and demanded to see the books and the boss. Ushered into his private office, the four revealed themselves as Bugsy Siegel, Albert Anastasia, Red Lavine and Thomas 'Three Fingers' Lucchese. All four drew knives.

Just five months after pronouncing himself Godfather, Maranzano was killed – stabbed several times and then shot for good measure. Over the next few days about 40 more of Maranzano's team and their associates were systematically eliminated.

The mob magnates – Lansky, Luciano and Genovese – were now firmly in power. Gone were the old-style trigger-happy Mafioso leaders derisively termed 'Moustache Petes'. In came the accountants and corporate executives, still backed of course by the ultimate persuaders, the hire killers. One arm of the operation was labelled the National Crime Syndicate; the other was called Murder Incorporated.

Helping set up this mercenary death squad was Albert Anastasia, one of the killers of both Giuseppe Masseria and Salvatore Maranzano. Known as New York's 'Lord High Executioner', he meted out murder on contract for a quarter of a century, becoming head of one of the city's five Mafia clans, the Mangano family.

His growing power finally became too much of a threat to his principal New York rivals, including Genovese, two of whose henchmen followed Anastasia to his barber's shop one morning in 1957. As a warm towel was draped over his face, he did not see the two gunmen position themselves behind the barber's chair. Then they calmly blew his head off.

It was a scene of which Meyer Lansky probably disapproved. He was the man, who, more than any other, welded previously fiery-tempered Mafia families scattered around the nation into a 'federal' unit. Autonomous in their own area, they nevertheless came together to seek agreement on major policy issues. Above all, they maintained a low profile; the days of street warfare were over for good.

In their book *Meyer Lansky: Mogul of The Mob*, authors Dennis Elsenburg, Uri Dan and Ell Landau quote their subject as saying: 'Crime moved out of the small ghettoes and became nationwide.'

An associate, Joseph Doc Stacher, says of Lansky and Luciano: 'They were an unbeatable team. If they had become President and Vice-President of the United States, they would have run the place far better than the idiot politicians.'

Lansky was certainly a wily politician within the crime syndicate. Despite being a Jew in a predominantly Italian society, he became trusted as an 'independent' Mafia mogul, more concerned with money-making than internal power struggles. His value to his associates was his ability secretly to invest the mob's ill-gotten gains in respectable industries and in the gambling casinos of Las Vegas, Cuba and the Bahamas.

Lansky made millions for the Mafia and an estimated personal fortune of $300 million. Seemingly safe from criminal charges, his main concern in his old age was the taxman. He even left the United States on one occasion – to live in a hotel he owned in Israel, much to the displeasure of the Israeli government. But he returned to America to spend his last years in the land that had made his organization fabulously rich. As he himself described it: 'We're bigger than US Steel.'

Like Lansky, his old friend Vito Genovese also seemed to lead a charmed life. Before World War II he salted an estimated $2 million into secret Swiss bank accounts and fled to Naples. A vociferous supporter of Mussolini (he contributed generously to Fascist funds), he switched sides hurriedly when the tide of war changed and offered his services to the occupying American forces.

Genovese pinpointed black-market operations in post-war Italy and helped close them down. He then resurrected them with one of his own 'front men' in charge. His Italian connection came to an end when he was extradited back to the USA to face an old murder charge. It failed to stick after the principal witness was shot dead, and Genovese returned to his New York stamping ground.

His former lieutenant, Albert Anastasia, having been eliminated along with other rivals, Genovese savoured the fruits of power for only a year before being jailed in 1959 for drug smuggling. He had served ten years of a 15-year sentence when he was found dead from a heart attack.

The third of the triumvirate, 'Lucky' Luciano, did not always live up to his name. He must have thought his luck had finally run out when he was sent to jail to serve a 30- to 50-year sentence for 90 vice offences. Then, in November 1942, he got a visit from his old friend Lansky.

Lansky told him that he had just done a deal with US naval intelligence who were concerned that information about Allied convoys was being leaked by pro-Mussolini Italian immigrants working on the New York waterfront. The fears seemed to have been confirmed by the burning of the French liner *Normandie* at its moorings in New York. So many fires had broken out at the same time that the US navy, which was due to use the ship to carry troops and supplies to Europe, was certain Italian saboteurs were to blame.

The deal Lansky had struck was that the Mafia, under Luciano's direction from his prison cell, would work in conjunction with a special unit of naval intelligence to flush out Italian spies and saboteurs. In return, Luciano would win his freedom after the war. He readily agreed.

At least one other Mafia man was immediately freed from jail at Luciano's request. He was Johnny 'Cockeye' Dunn who was responsible for the no-questions-asked removal of two suspected German spies. Apart from keeping peace on the waterfront, the team was also credited with pinpointing an enemy submarine off Long Island. Four German spies were captured as they came ashore from it and, under interrogation, revealed a North American network of Nazi agents.

Before the Allies invaded Sicily, Luciano sent word to local Mafia leaders that all help should be given to the Americans. Four Italian-speaking US naval intelligence officers joined up with the Sicilian Mafia and successfully raided German and Italian bases for secret defence blueprints. Later, in Rome, the Mafia foiled an assassination attempt against Britain's General Sir Harold Alexander and, as a footnote to history, seized Mussolini's entire personal archives.

The American authorities kept their part of the bargain and, in 1945, within a few months of the war in Europe ending, Luciano was freed from jail but was told he was to be deported to Italy.

His comrade in crime, Lansky, was there to bid him farewell – after first giving him $500,000 to help him start his new life. He lived in Rome for a while but grew restless for the 'big time' and shortly afterwards turned up in Cuba. Luciano issued an invitation to leaders of US organized crime to meet him in Havana. But, before his empire-building in exile could begin, US pressure on Cuba's President Batista forced his dispatch back to Italy.

On 26 January 1962, Luciano went to Naples airport to await the arrival of an American producer who was considering filming the Mafia chief's life. But Luciano's luck had at last run out. He dropped dead of a heart attack in the airport lounge.

Extraordinarily, after a lifetime of corruption, torture and violent death, America's three moguls of organized crime – Meyer Lansky, Vito Genovese and 'Lucky' Luciano – all died of natural causes.

Al Capone and the Chicago Mob

Al Capone, 'Legs' Diamond, 'Machine Gun' McGurn, 'Bugs' Morgan, 'Dutch' Schultz . . . they are names that have gone down in America's violent folklore. In books, films and TV series, they have been dramatized, often glamorized and sometimes turned into heroes.

But the stark truth about these gangsters of the 1920s is

far from glamorous. They lived tawdry lives and, in the main, died violently. A principal exception to that rule was the most infamous gangster of the age, Al Capone himself. He died peacefully but deranged, from syphilis.

Alphonse Capone, born in New York in 1899, was one of nine children of Italian immigrants. A street-fighting thug, he gained his lifelong nickname, Scarface, while working as a bouncer for a Brooklyn brothel.

This small-time hoodlum could have faded into criminal obscurity but for a strange quirk of fate. Capone urgently needed to get out of New York where he was wanted for questioning over the death of a policeman. He contacted Chicago gangster Johnny Torrio, who remembered the young thug from his own street-fighting days in New York and immediately invited him to join his team.

Capone arrived in Chicago in 1919 to find Torrio working for old-time Mafioso tycoon 'Diamond' Jim Colosimo. This strange character, so called because of his penchant for jewellery, ran just about every brothel in the city, as well as various labour rackets. Torrio, a cousin of Colosimo's wife, was his principal lieutenant, sworn to guard his boss with his life. It was no informal oath of allegiance: Torrio, like the rest of Colosimo's hired army, had to swear fidelity to their leader on his family Bible.

Colosimo, with his second wife, singer Dale Winter, held court nightly at his restaurant on South Wabash Avenue, surrounded by unsavoury 'heavies' as well as by politicians and entertainers. With the introduction of Prohibition, Torrio tried to persuade Colosimo to expand his business to take advantage of the new market in illicit liquor. The older man refused.

On 11 May 1920 Torrio asked Colosimo if he would be at his restaurant at a particular time to sign for a delivery of whisky. As Colosimo waited in the empty restaurant, Al Capone stepped out of a phone booth and, acting on

Torrio's orders, shot Colosimo dead then took his wallet to make the killing look like a robbery. An hour later he was back at Torrio's side ready to shed tears and swear vengeance upon receiving the news of their boss's death. Torrio and Capone took over the Colosimo crime empire, added bootleg liquor to it and began to amass a fortune.

In the early 1920s, Chicago's underworld was split between the Torrio-Capone Mafia axis and the mainly Irish gang of Charles Dion 'Deanie' O'Bannion.

O'Bannion was perhaps the most remarkable of all hoodlums of his day. Angelically baby-faced, an ex-choirboy once destined for the priesthood, O'Bannion fell into crime almost by accident. He worked for William Randolph Hearst's newspaper the *Herald Examiner* while moonlighting at night as a singing waiter in a club which was the haunt of criminals. It was these villains who introduced O'Bannion to the richer pickings on the wrong side of the law.

'Deanie' O'Bannion was a criminal with a great sense of humour and a considerable style. Unlike his Italian rivals in neighbouring parts of Chicago, the Irishman would not allow brothels in his area, refused to sell any but the finest liquor from his chain of breweries and distilleries and ran his business from the grandest flower shop in Chicago, catering for the city's high-society weddings and funerals.

O'Bannion laughed at the crudities of the Italian overlords. But in 1924 he cracked his most costly joke at their expense – he sold Johnny Torrio a half-share in a brewery for half a million dollars. He did not tell Torrio that he had received a tip-off that the brewery was about to be raided. The police swoop left O'Bannion in the clear. But Torrio, who had been meticulous in his efforts to avoid any police record, was booked. Furious, he sought instant revenge.

On 10 November 1924 three men called at O'Bannion's flower shop to buy a wreath. The baby-faced proprietor did not realize who the wreath was for. The men, Alberto Anselmi, John Scalise and Frank Yale, were killers hired by Torrio and Capone. Yale held O'Bannion down while the others shot him dead.

O'Bannion's funeral was the grandest Chicago had seen. The rich and the famous mingled with murderers, thieves and bootleggers to pay their respects to the supplier of the best booze in town. 'Deanie' would have been proud of the floral tributes. The wreaths alone were worth $50,000.

O'Bannion's funeral was the first of many over the next few years. Torrio and Capone had started a gangland war that they could not finish. Before the 1920s were out, more than 1,000 bodies were to end up on the streets of Chicago in a string of bloody reprisal raids. And the first raid was against Torrio himself.

O'Bannion's loyal henchmen, Hymie Weiss and George 'Bugs' Moran, ambushed Torrio as he left home. They gunned him down and left him for dead. But he survived, was himself arrested over the illicit brewery raid and was jailed for nine months.

The following year, shaken by events in Chicago and doubtless concerned that Capone's own ambitions may not have included him in future plans, Torrio 'retired' at the age of 43. Pursued first out of Chicago and then Florida with Weiss and Moran on his tail, he settled in Naples until he felt safe enough to return to New York in 1928. He worked behind the scenes for Mayer Lansky until 1939 when he was jailed for two years for non-payment of taxes. He died of a heart attack in 1967.

Torrio's flight from Chicago in 1925 meant that Capone was now lord of the richest territory in the underworld. Torrio had taken with him a 'golden handshake' estimated at more than $50 million but that still left him a thriving empire in prostitution, bootlegging, gambling and extortion which Capone ran in a grandiose manner.

But Capone's showmanship almost cost him his life. He controlled his $5 million-a-year business from the Hawthorn Hotel in the wholly corrupt Chicago suburb of Cicero. In September 1926, 'Bugs' Moran and Hymie Wiess, having failed to settle their score with Johnny Terrio, attempted to wipe out his successor. They drove in a motorcade past the Hawthorn Hotel and sprayed it with hundreds of rounds of submachine-gun fire.

Astonishingly, Capone was unhurt. But his pride was ruffled. He had Weiss gunned down in the street at the first opportunity. Moran, however, proved more elusive. Capone had to wait another two years to attempt revenge on him in the infamous St Valentine's Day Massacre.

But first there were other items of business Al Capone had to clear up. The Genna family, a gang led by four Sicilian brothers, were Capone's main suppliers of rot-gut whisky and gin. The liquor was cheap, foul and dangerous. Produced at 40 cents a gallon, it was sold to Capone at two dollars and passed on to drinking dens at six dollars. Many of the customers who drank it were blinded and some even died.

Capone fell out with the influential Gennas, not over the quality of their whisky but because they were vying with him for power and influence among the Italian criminal fraternity. One by one, the Gennas and their gang were gunned down until the remaining members of the family fled, some to Sicily, some to other parts of the United States.

Another victim of the war was a crook-turned-politician called Joseph Esposito. Nicknamed 'Diamond Joe' because of the $50,000 worth of gems studded into his belt, Esposito was a Committee man for Chicago's notorious 19th Ward where he controlled police, politicians and union leaders – as well as running a string of distilleries for Capone. Caught up in the Capone-Genna war, he was gunned down in the street by unknown assailants in 1928.

Another supplier of bootleg liquor to Capone was policeman's son Roger Touhy. Capone wanted him out of the way so that he could take over his business. First he kidnapped Touhy's partner Matt Kilb, held him to ransom and, when Touhy paid the $50,000 asked, shot him anyway. When Touhy still held out against Capone's demands, he was framed for a kidnapping and sentenced to 199 years imprisonment. He served nine years before escaping and proving his innocence. Within days of finally winning his freedom, he was shot dead in a Chicago street.

Capone's blood-letting stretched to New York where Frank Yale, one of the men who had been hired to assassinate Dion O'Bannion, was thought by Capone to have cheated him on liquor deals. In 1927 Yale was lured to a fake appointment in Brooklyn where he was machine-gunned to death from a passing car.

But Capone's most longed-for victim was still 'Bugs' Moran, the O'Bannion aide who had tried to kill Johnny Torrio in that first round of revenge shootings back in 1924. For the task, Capone employed the most deadly hit-man of them all, 'Machine Gun' Jack McGurn.

McGurn's real name was James Vicenzo de Mora, born in Chicago's Little Italy in 1904. A professional boxer, his connection with Capone was through his father who worked in one of the Genna family's distilleries. When his father was killed by Genna lieutenants, McGurn joined Capone as a hired gunman. His reputation was fearsome. His trademark was a nickel coin pressed into the palm of the victim's hand. By 1929 at least 15 bodies had been found with McGurn's 'calling card'. His fees for such contract killings were high and allowed him to buy shares in a number of Chicago clubs. He married one of his club's showgirls. In 1927 when a comedian, Joe E. Lewis, refused to work at one of the clubs, he was beaten up by McGurn and had his vocal cords cut.

On 14 February, St Valentine's Day, 1929, Jack McGurn was ordered by Capone to rid him finally of his arch enemy Moran, who had recently been publicly bad-mouthing 'Alphonse The Beast'.

Moran's gang were expecting a liquor delivery that day at a garage at 2122 North Clark Street. Seven of Moran's men were inside the garage when three 'policemen' burst in carrying machine-guns. They ordered the bootleggers to line up with their faces against a wall and mowed them down in a hail of bullets. The 'policemen' were Capone's men – one of them McGurn.

'Bugs' Moran was not among the victims, however. He turned up late for the liquor delivery and fled when he witnessed the supposed police raid.

The St Valentine's Day Massacre, as the newspapers labelled it, at last brought the measure of public outrage that forced politicians and police – even the crooked ones – to act to curb the violence on Chicago's streets. 'Machine Gun' McGurn, whose role in the slaughter was well known, was no longer wanted as a hired gun by Capone. He was simply not good news to have around.

McGurn believed he could hang up his gun and make a good enough living out of his clubs. But the Depression put paid to that. Hard up, but still flashily dressed in three-piece suit, white spats and highly polished shoes, McGurn was walking down a quiet street on 14 February 1936, seven years to the day after the St Valentine's Day Massacre, when two gunmen approached and blasted him. When police arrived at the scene they found a nickel pressed into his palm and a cut-out Valentine heart by his side.

McGurn's killers were never traced but it is believed that one of them was 'Bugs' Moran. O'Bannion's loyal Irish lieutenant had disappeared from public view after his men were massacred in the garage on North Clark

Street. After the war he turned up again in Ohio where he was arrested for bank robbery. He died in Leavenworth Jail in 1957.

'Bugs' Moran had survived almost every other member of the Chicago gangs of the bloody 1920s. And he had outlived by ten years the most notorious of them all, Al Capone.

After forcing Moran to flee for his life following the 1929 massacre, Capone had taken over control of the entire criminal network of the city of Chicago. But his victory was short-lived . . .

In 1931, what the police failed to achieve in a decade the taxman achieved in a few weeks. On 24 October after a speedy trial, Al Capone was found guilty of tax evasion. He was fined $50,000 and ordered to pay $30,000 costs – chickenfeed to him. But he was also sentenced to a jail term of 11 years. It broke him.

When he was released in 1939, he was already sliding into insanity from syphilis. He hid himself away on his Florida estate, shunned by his neighbours and by the new breed of Mafia leaders who wanted nothing to do with the loud-mouthed, brutish, scarfaced relic of a bloody past best forgotten. Al Capone died alone in 1947.

'Bugsy' Siegel: the Hollywood Gangster

It wasn't a pretty sight when they found the bullet-riddled body of 'Bugsy' Siegel. And that wouldn't have pleased the man who had the reputation of being the Casanova of the Mafia.

Siegel was gunned down as he sat on a sofa in his girlfriend's house. A final bullet was fired into his left eye – the coup de grâce that was the Mafia's 'calling card'. Tall, good-looking, well-groomed and smartly dressed, 'Bugsy' would have abhorred such messy methods. He would have preferred a more dignified death.

Benjamin Siegel, born in Brooklyn in 1906, had always been convinced that he was headed for the big time. But he started small – stealing cars, driving trucks of illicit liquor and guarding illegal gambling houses.

It was when, in his teens, he teamed up with the much lighter, more calculating Meyer Lansky that his fortunes changed. He called his group of small-time criminals the Bug and Meyer Gang and, by the mid-1930s, through his loyalty to Lansky, became a trusted associate of the top racketeers on America's east coast.

In 1935 Siegel was indicted in New York for shooting a rival gang member, one of 'Dutch' Schultz's men. Lansky decided his friend must leave town, so he set him up with a £500,000 investment and sent him to California to team up with local mobster Jack Dragna.

Life in the Californian sunshine was paradise to the impetuous Siegel. Soon after his arrival, he was seducing one starlet after another. A millionairess divorcée, Countess Dorothy Di Frasso, took him under her wing. She travelled with him to Italy, where they met Mussolini. Siegel and the Countess launched an expedition to seek Spanish treasure on the Cocos Islands – but after blasting an island with dynamite they returned empty-handed.

In Hollywood, Siegel was on first-name terms with stars like Jean Harlow, Gary Cooper and Clark Gable. But his greatest friend was actor George Raft, famous for his film gangster roles. He and Raft went on a gambling spree on the French Riviera – until Siegel got a cable from Lansky ordering him to 'stop acting like a movie star' and get back to work.

But it was not all play for Siegel. He and Dragna operated a string of illegal Los Angeles gambling houses and offshore casino ships, as well as drug-smuggling operations and even a wire service. The money rolled in throughout World War II, and in 1945 Lansky helped organize for him a $3 million loan emporium that made the desert town into a mobster's Mecca.

Siegel matched $3 million of his own money with the crime syndicate's stake and started building the Flamingo Hotel, a name chosen by his girlfriend of the moment, Virginia Hill. But, during construction, large sums of money were salted away to Swiss bank accounts, some of them said to be in the name of Miss Hill.

In late 1946 many of America's leading gangsters, including Siegel's east-coast associates Lansky, 'Lucky' Luciano and Vito Genovese, met at a hotel in Havana to spend a holiday, to attend a Frank Sinatra concert and to discuss the problem of the errant 'Bugsy'. Lansky, who considered Siegel a blood-brother, argued the case for his friend. But he was over-ruled. It was decided that Siegel be asked to repay with interest all of the syndicate investment as soon as the hotel was open. If he failed, then . . .

'Bugsy' Siegel's luck was out. He opened the Flamingo Hotel on 26 December 1946 with Virginia Hill at his side. The event was a disaster. Bad weather grounded planes in Los Angeles and few of the invited famous faces turned up. The razzmatazz of the grand opening fell flat, publicity was scant, interest dimmed and the punters stayed away. For two weeks Siegel struggled on. The casino alone lost more than $100,000 before he closed it.

The demands for repayment of the Mob's loan became more and more insistent. But Siegel's money was largely tied up in the hotel, and the sums siphoned off to Switzerland did not add up to what the syndicate demanded. Siegel thought he could bluff his way out of the crisis, under the protection of his old friend Lansky.

Lansky, however, had reluctantly washed his hands of him. 'Lucky' Luciano, who had known 'Bugsy' even longer than Lansky, accepted the task of arranging his execution. He asked for the money one last time. Siegel refused.

On the night of 20 June 1947 Siegel was sitting on the sofa in the living room of Virginia Hill's rented house in North Linden Drive, Los Angeles, when an unknown killer or killers fired five bullets at him.

His rich and famous friends steered well clear of Benjamin 'Bugsy' Siegel once his fame had turned to notoriety. There were only five mourners at his funeral.

'Legs' Diamond and 'Dutch' Schultz: the New York Bootleggers

Jack 'Legs' Diamond and 'Dutch' Schultz were two hoodlums who brought an unwelcome taste of Chicago-style gang warfare to the heart of New York. Both thought themselves smart, stylish, wise guys. Both changed their names to glamorize their image. Both died by the gun – cold-bloodedly executed by their own kind.

Jack 'Legs' Diamond was born John Noland in 1896 in Philadelphia. Moving to New York in his teens, he followed the classic criminal pattern of street-fighting, theft and 'protection'. In the early 1920s he worked for racketeer Jacob 'Little Augie' Orgen, carrying out inter-gang killings at his behest.

The money he earned from Orgen was spent on a lavish lifestyle. Although married, he supported a string of mistresses and earned the nickname 'Legs' from a brief spell as a professional dancer. He bought shares in a number of nightclubs and eventually purchased a top nightspot of his own.

Everything had come easily to Diamond. But in 1927

'Little Augie' Orgen was assassinated and Diamond wounded. He backed out of the impending inter-gang warfare and instead set himself up in the bootlegging business. He went into partnership with an already established bootlegger calling himself 'Dutch' Schultz.

Schultz's real name was Arthur Fliegenheimer, born in New York in 1902 and following the same criminal path as 'Legs' Diamond. Perhaps they were too much alike – for, as partners, Diamond and Schultz made great adversaries. They seemed incapable of keeping their bargains with one another.

When Diamond fled the scene after killing a drunk at his club, Schultz took over much of his business. Diamond retaliated by hijacking Schultz's liquor trucks.

Diamond had felt safe in his activities as long as he had the patronage of his new gangland protector, New York gaming club and brothel owner Arnold Rothstein. But, just as he had lost a friend in the assassinated Orgen, so he did again in 1928 when Rothstein was found dying in a gambling club after refusing to pay a $320,000 debt due from a single poker game.

Schultz deemed it a safe time to get rid of Diamond. A hit squad dispatched to kill him found Diamond in bed with his mistress and sprayed the room with gunfire. Five bullets entered his body but he survived. Two further attempts on his life failed. But on 17 December 1931 Schultz's gangsters finally got their man.

Diamond had been celebrating his acquittal from charges that he had beaten up two rival bootleggers, and in the early hours visited a girlfriend's apartment. From there, he went home. As he lay in bed, the door was shattered from its hinges and 'Legs' Diamond was finally shot dead.

'Dutch' Schultz now had a free hand to run his liquor, gambling and protection rackets which together brought in an estimated $20 million a year. But his gun-slinging style of business was inimical to the new, rising breed of Mafia leader such as 'Lucky' Luciano, Vito Genovese and Meyer Lansky.

After a sensational tax-evasion case, in which Schultz was acquitted after having the trial moved to a small and 'manageable' upstate courthouse, Luciano and his associates decided to spare the Mafia further embarrassment. On 23 October 1935 'Dutch' Schultz was dining with three friends at a Neward, New Jersey, restaurant when a man with a machine-gun entered and shot them all.

The last of New York's old-style gun-slinging gangsters was out of action for good.

Death of a President

The Mafia organization is America's 'Public Enemy Number One'. But for a long time the Mafia itself also had its own very public enemy . . . the Kennedy clan.

The feud went back half a century to the days when, according to mobsters' stories, the Kennedy patriarch, Joseph, made a fortune from the profits of Prohibition whisky illegally imported from Ireland to Boston.

In 1927 one of the Irish cargoes was hijacked by the Mob and 11 smugglers were killed in the shoot-out. It was, believe the Mafia, the start of a long campaign, instigated by Joseph Kennedy and continued by his children – principally John, who became President of the United States, and Robert, who became Attorney-General.

Robert Kennedy was responsible for pursuing Teamsters Union boss Jimmy Hoffa to jail in the US Justice Department's relentless drive to crush Mafia influence within the organized labour movement. It was elder brother John who, as President, failed to give full backing to the disastrous Bay of Pigs invasion attempt of Cuba, planned by the CIA with Mafia assistance.

Many years later, after the assassination of both men, the question was being asked: was the Mafia linked with the killing of the US President in 1963? At one time, such a question would have been unthinkable. But, when dealing with organized crime in the USA, the unthinkable often becomes the perfectly feasible.

That was what happened in 1979 when a committee set up by the US House of Representatives suggested it was likely that a contract killer was involved in the assassination that shocked the world, in Dallas, Texas, on 22 November 1963. After a $3 million investigation lasting two years, the committee's experts reported: 'An individual crime leader or a small combination of leaders might have participated in a conspiracy to assassinate President Kennedy.'

The report went on to name the 'most likely family bosses of organized crime to have participated in such a unilateral assassination plan' – Carlos Marcello of New Orleans and Santos Trafficante of Miami. Both men immediately issued the strongest denials of any involvement with Kennedy's death.

The circumstantial evidence to back a conspiracy theory was that Lee Harvey Oswald, who is presumed to have fired shots that killed the President, had some links with underworld figures. So had Jack Ruby, the man who gunned down Oswald before the latter could be brought to court.

Oswald's connection was through his uncle, Charles Murret, and an acquaintance, David Ferrie – both of whom worked for Carlos Marcello.

Murret took Oswald under his wing when his favourite nephew moved from Dallas to New Orleans in 1963. He gave him a home and a job in his bookmaking business, and treated him like a son. The investigative committee described Murret as 'a top deputy of a top man in Carlos

Marcello's gambling apparatus.' Murret died in 1964.

David Ferrie also worked for Marcello, as a pilot. He had flown him back to the USA after he was deported to Guatemala in 1961 by Robert Kennedy. Ferrie had also had secret connections with the CIA and had trained pilots who later took part in the Bay of Pigs invasion. Oswald's New Orleans work address in 1963 was the same as Ferrie's, and Oswald was in the same air club in which Ferrie was a pilot.

Such evidence, quoted in the House of Representatives committee's report, is circumstantial in the extreme. But, judged alongside the evidence linking Oswald's executioner, Jack Ruby, to the Mafia, the conspiracy theory becomes stronger.

Club-owner Ruby's connections with underworld figures were well established. His telephone records showed that he had been in contact with Mob personalities in Miami, New Orleans and Chicago. He had visited Santos Trafficante. And on 21 November, the day before Kennedy's death, Ruby was seen drinking with a friend of pilot David Ferrie.

Whoever may have been pulling the strings, the evidence points to Ruby's public execution of Oswald being a certain way of keeping him quiet and preventing him naming accomplices during his trial. Ruby's own life would not have been of high account . . . he died in prison shortly afterwards of cancer.

Ruby's connection with Santos Trafficante brings the amazing web full circle.

When Meyer Lansky, 'Lucky' Luciano and their associates ran the Havana hotel and casino business under corrupt Cuban dictator Fulgencio Batista, Trafficante was a small cog in the business. Fidel Castro overthrew the Batista regime in 1959 and threw the Mob's men either into jail or out of the country. Among them was Trafficante.

The fact that Trafficante's pilot, David Ferrie, worked for the CIA may not have been known to his boss. If he did know, he might not have been concerned. He may even have approved of the connection. For the CIA, the Mafia and big business interests had all been involved in various plots to overthrow Castro and return Cuba to 'democratic' – and capitalist – rule. The CIA, with the unpublicized but tacit agreement of the US Government, wanted to remove the communist threat from the Caribbean. The Mafia and big business wanted to restore Cuba's profitable tourist industry, complete with acquiescent officials, politicians susceptible to bribes and gambling and vice interests.

The CIA and the Mafia had previously worked together successfully, even launching joint military operations before and during the Allied invasion of Sicily. A similar link-up made sound sense in the organizing of the Bay of Pigs invasion.

Even the world's richest businessman was involved. The eccentric Howard Hughes was said to have volunteered to fund one particular part of the Cuban invasion – the assassination of Fidel Castro. The plan was discussed by the CIA. Through their connections in Las Vegas, where Hughes had interests in 17 casinos, his aides recruited two Mafia hoodlums. But the invasion was a debacle, the assassination never took place – and the hoodlums died under mysterious circumstances in the 1970s.

Another sensational case in which politics and crime are sinisterly intertwined is the death of Marilyn Monroe. Again, the central characters are John and Robert Kennedy, both of whom were rumoured to have had affairs with the world's leading sex symbol. But this time the government agency suspected of being involved was not the CIA but the FBI.

J. Edgar Hoover, chief of the FBI, had long been hampered by the Kennedys in his autocratic handling of the agency's affairs. Attorney-General Robert, with his brother's White House backing, clipped the wings of the all-powerful Hoover – and earned himself an unforgiving enemy.

Hoover's agents collected every scrap of information about the private lives of every leading politician in the country. It was one of the reasons that Hoover's eccentric handling of the FBI had previously gone unchallenged. In the Kennedys' case, the FBI's personal files bulged with scandal.

Neither John nor his younger brother had been suitably secretive in their extra-marital activities. They had both known Marilyn Monroe and, in her developing state of depression and nervous disorder, it was thought that she might make public some of their indiscretions.

Such stories, which were no more than rumours at the time of Monroe's death, have since become common currency. And in 1981 a reformed criminal, Ronald 'Sonny' Gibson, wrote a book adding some startling new allegations.

In the book, *Mafia Kingpin*, Gibson said that, while working for the Mob, he had been told that Marilyn had been murdered by a Mafia hit-man. J. Edgar Hoover, he said, had been furious about the actress's affairs with top politicians. So the Mafia had taken upon themselves the task of silencing her as a means of repaying favours done for them by the FBI.

Gibson is not alone in his assertion that Marilyn died not because she had swallowed an overdose of barbiturates but because drugs had been injected into her. Even top pathologists who investigated the case have since gone into print to say the same.

Was Marilyn Monroe murdered by the Mafia? Was John F. Kennedy assassinated with the help of the Mob? The theories sound preposterous . . . Almost as preposterous an idea as that the US Government and the Mafia would collaborate in a Caribbean invasion. But it happened . . .

The Kray Twins: the 'Mafia' of London's East End

When London gangsters the Kray twins were sentenced in 1969, the judge Mr Justice Melford Stevenson told them with scornful understatement: 'In my view society had earned a rest from your activities'. These activities included theft, extortion and finally murder, in a reign of terror that marred the memory of Britain's 'swinging sixties'.

The Krays held London's underworld in a Mafia-like grip. In their heyday, they were fêted by showbusiness personalities. They were photographed with the famous. They were generous in their support of charities. And they were feared like no other criminals. In every way, they were a British version of America's 1930s gangsters, whose exploits they studied avidly and emulated slavishly.

Even after the full extent of their crimes was revealed in court and the pair were jailed for life, many people in the East End of London still spoke affectionately of the Krays. Some regarded them as 'Robin Hood' characters. Others, more realistically, saw them as people who maintained gangland peace and kept the seedy streets safe. Few at the time asked any questions as to how such a peace was being maintained and by what sort of men.

The Kray twins were born on 17 October 1933 at Hoxton in the East End. Ronnie was the elder. Reggie arrived 45 minutes later. They also had an older brother, Charles.

The boys had Jewish, Irish and Romany blood in their veins. Their father Charles, who was 25 at the time of the twins' birth, was a dealer in old clothes, silver and gold.

Their mother Violet was just 21.

Just before the war, the family moved to one of the toughest, most run-down areas of Bethnal Green, shortly to become even more decrepit thanks to visits from the Luftwaffe. Ronnie and Reggie became known as the Terrible Twins because of their love of fighting – at first with fists and later with bicycle chains and flick-knives.

By the age of 16, they were carrying guns. A year later, they made their first appearance in court. They were accused of seriously beating up a 16-year-old rival, but the case was dismissed for lack of evidence.

The twins were fighters in every sense. At 17, they became professional boxers. A year later they were called up for their National Service and punched the recruiting corporal on the nose. Much of their subsequent military service was spent in jails.

After their dishonourable discharge in 1954, they went into the protection business. If a bookmaker, store or club owner wanted to ensure 'no trouble', a weekly payment to Ronnie and Reggie would do the trick. As the easy money rolled in, so their gang of collectors grew. Their territory covered the East End and much of North London.

They founded their own clubs – at first in the East End, where a sports hall provided a front for their rackets, and later in fashionable Knightsbridge where the West End found the pair a rough and ready attraction.

By now, Ronnie was known as 'the Colonel', Reggie was 'the Quiet One' and their home in Vallance Road termed 'Fort Vallance'.

The Krays could be magnanimous, loyal and charming. They could also be frighteningly, unpredictably brutal. But mainly it was Ronnie who took the lead, egging his brother on to prove himself by being tough enough to follow his lead.

In 1965 Ronnie shot a man in the leg. When picked out at an identity parade, he avoided being charged by claiming he was Reggie – thus making nonsense of the evidence. Later that year Ronnie was caught and convicted. He received a three-year sentence for stabbing a man with a bayonet in a raid on a rival gang's territory.

It was at this time that Ronnie Kray's dangerous instability became apparent. He went berserk in jail. He became obsessively fearful that someone was trying to have him 'put away'. He even had to be shown his reflection in a mirror to prove he was still in one piece. Finally, he was sent from prison to a mental hospital where he was certified insane.

In true flamboyant Kray style, the family moved in to help – and Ronnie moved out. Reggie paid a visit to the mental hospital and swapped clothes with his brother. When Ronnie was safely away, Reggie owned up to his little trick.

Ronnie remained free for some weeks, during which time his sense of bravado induced him to make surprise calls on East End pubs to taunt the police. But his strange state of mind worried his family and, after a suicide attempt, they allowed the police to recapture him. After further treatment, he was deemed fit to be released, in 1958.

But Ronnie Kray was far from cured – and no one knew it better than his brother. Reggie had a good business brain, and the family's commercial enterprises had flourished during Ronnie's spell in jail. There was the original 'Double R Club' in Bow, a new club in Stratford, a car sales business and even an illegal gambling club a stone's throw away from Bow police station. But Ronnie's return from prison also meant a return of the heavy-handed gangsterism that put such business in peril.

The brothers argued about their 'firm'. But, when in 1960 Reggie was jailed for 18 months for demanding money with menaces, it was his brother's turn to have a free hand at running the business.

Ronnie took a contract from the notorious slum landlord, Peter Rachman. The Krays' hoodlums would guard Rachman's rent collectors in return for a healthy commission. The result was not only added riches for Ronnie but his introduction to a more sophisticated society. His new Knightsbridge club, 'Esmerelda's Barn', became a favourite rendezvous for entertainers and sports people. It also became a haven for penniless young men on the make . . . for Ronnie was now openly homosexual.

Reggie was otherwise inclined. When released from prison in 1961, he fell hopelessly in love with a 16-year-old East End girl. For the first time in their lives, the brothers' lifestyles were now widely different – Ronnie veered towards his swinging friends 'up West' while Reggie returned to his roots on the East side of town. Largely thanks to Reggie's business acumen, the Krays added a restaurant and several other clubs to their empire. And Reggie got married – tragically for his teenage bride who could not cope with the gangster's crazy world and eventually committed suicide in 1967.

It may have been due to the strain of Reggie's failing marriage or it may have been due to the Al Capone fantasy world of brother Ronnie, but the regime of the Krays took an even more violent turn in the second half of the 1960s.

There were beatings, brandings and knifings. One former friend who drunkenly insulted Ronnie needed 70 stitches to face wounds. There were also at least three unsuccessful attempts on the Krays' lives, and Ronnie took to sleeping with a gun under his pillow.

Warfare flared between the Krays and Charles Richardson's gang, based in south London but intent on muscling in on West End protection rackets.

In March 1966, a small-time 'heavy' working for Richardson strayed into Kray territory. The brothers were told that George Cornell had been announcing to East

Enders that: 'Ronnie Kray is a big, fat poof and don't take any notice of him . . . He can't protect you from anything.'

Ronnie was tipped off that Cornell was in a well-known Whitechapel pub called the Blind Beggar. Ronnie walked calmly into the bar and, as he later described in his own words, 'put a gun at his head, looked him in the eyes and pulled the trigger. Then I put the gun in my pocket. His body fell off the stool and I walked out.'

Later he justified the murder by saying: 'Cornell was vermin. He was a drunkard and a bully. He was simply nothing. I done the Earth a favour ridding it of him.'

The following year, Reggie made his own violent contribution to the murder statistics.

By now, the brothers' business had expanded to drugs and pornography, areas that did not endear them to their traditional East End friends. Ronnie's homosexual proclivities were the talk of their 'manor' – quite apart from his by now obvious paranoia. And Reggie, 'the Quiet One', following his wife's suicide, had taken to drink and to shooting at the legs of people who gave him offence.

The Krays were becoming bad news. They were being shunned by the rich and famous as well as by the poor and infamous. They were trouble. The twins became concerned about their 'image' and decided to hold a test of their 150-strong gang's loyalty – a meaningless murder.

The victim was to be Jack 'The Hat' McVitie, so called because of the hat he wore to hide his baldness. McVitie's crime was to owe the brothers £500 and to have insulted them in their absence during a drunken binge.

Four of the Krays' men lured McVitie to a 'party' in a borrowed house in Stoke Newington where Ronnie, Reggie and two henchmen lay in wait. As their victim entered he realized his impending fate and turned to flee. Ronnie pinned him against a wall and told him: 'Come on, Jack, be a man.' McVitie said: 'I will be a man but I don't want to die like one.'

Ronnie led him into a basement room where the killing became near-farcical. As McVitie walked through the door, Reggie pointed a gun at his head and pulled the trigger . . . nothing happened. Ronnie then picked up a carving knife and thrust it at McVitie's back. But it failed to pierce his thick coat.

McVitie made a dash for the window. He dived through it, only to be grabbed by his feet and hauled back in. Ronnie pinioned his arms from behind and screamed at his brother: 'Kill him, Reg. Do it. Don't stop now.' Reggie picked up the knife and stabbed his pleading victim in the face and then through the throat. The knife passed through his gullet and pinned him to the floor.

McVitie's body was never found.

Flushed with their success, the twins decided to form a Murder Incorporated organization along the lines of the American model. But, by now, every move they made was being monitored by a Scotland Yard team led by Detective Superintendent Leonard 'Nipper' Read.

Plans were laid to kill a minor crook who was appearing as a witness at an Old Bailey trial. The murder weapons were a crossbow and a briefcase with a hidden hypodermic syringe filled with cyanide. Another plan was for the contract killing of a gambler who owed an unspecified debt to the Krays' prospective paymasters in Las Vegas. A third plot was the murder of a Maltese club-owner by blowing up his car with dynamite.

Detective Superintendent 'Nipper' Read's case against the Krays was now strong. But he knew that, unless the twins were safely behind bars, prospective witnesses would suffer 'memory loss' or simply vanish.

Then the police got lucky. A Kray associate was stopped while about to board a plane from Glasgow to London. He was carrying four sticks of dynamite, presumably destined for the Maltese club-owner's car. Detectives raided his home and found the crossbow and briefcase complete with poisonous syringe.

On the night of 8 May 1968 Ronnie and Reggie went drinking at the Old Horn pub in Bethnal Green. They went on to the Astor Club in fashionable Berkeley Square, returning to their mother's new council flat in Shoreditch at four in the morning. Reggie went to bed with a girlfriend, Ronnie with a boyfriend. At dawn 'Nipper' Read's men swooped on the flat and arrested them.

The Kray twins were charged with the murders of George Cornwell and Jack McVitie. Eight other members of their 'firm', including their brother Charles, were charged with various lesser crimes.

The twins pleaded not guilty but, after a sensational 39-day trial at the Old Bailey, they were jailed for life with a recommendation that they should serve no less than 30 years. They were 35 years of age when the trial ended on 8 March 1969, which meant that they would be pensioners before they were released.

Ronnie and Reggie were sent to separate top-security prisons. In 1972 they were briefly reunited at Parkhurst jail on the Isle of Wight. But in 1979 Ronnie was again certified and sent to Broadmoor Hospital for the criminally insane.

Reggie found his sentence harder to take than his brother. He was classified as a Category A prisoner – highly dangerous and liable to escape. Shadowed at all times by two prison officers, his movements were logged and monitored while his visits were screened and limited. While of Category A status, no parole board could consider his case. All his appeals fell on deaf ears. In 1982, he unsuccessfully attempted suicide by cutting his wrists.

Ronnie was luckier in his time behind bars. Being an inmate of Broadmoor, he was allowed more privileges than his brother. He received visits from old East End associates and from showbusiness and sporting friends. They bought him parcels of food from Harrods – smoked salmon and game pie – and classical records for the hi-fi in his cell. He also had a colour television set.

Ronnie Kray would regale visitors with details of his exploits in the days when he and his brother wrote headlines in blood. In 1983 he told a visiting journalist, long-time friend Brian Hitchen: 'We never hurt ordinary members of the public. We only took money off other villains and gave a bundle of that away to decent people who were on hard times.'

'I look back on those days and naturally remember the good times. Then, people could take ladies into pubs with them without the risk of their being insulted. Old people didn't get mugged either. It couldn't have happened when we were looking after the East End.'

About life in Broadmoor he said: 'There are some really bad ones in here, Brian, some really bad ones. But they are all some mother's sons – and that's where the heartbreak is. Because no matter what they've done or how bad they've been, the mothers don't stop coming and don't stop loving them. When I see these mums, I feel really sorry for them having to come here.'

In 1982 the twins' strongest link with the outside world ended. Their most constant visitor, their mother Violet, died one week before her 73rd birthday. Violet Kray had become an East End legend in her own right and was said to have been the only person on earth who had any control over the twins.

Ronnie and Reggie were allowed out for a day to attend her funeral, which was turned into a star-studded East End occasion.

Reggie said after his return to Parkhurst jail: 'It's so lonely without visits from our mum. They were always the best ones. I shall miss her so much. Throughout the funeral, Ronnie and I were handcuffed to police officers who must have been 6ft 3in (1.9m) tall. But they needn't have worried. Violence is not part of my life any more.'

'I get angry when I read about the way things are in the East End nowadays – like all those attacks on old ladies. Years ago, if we saw an old lady we would help her across the road and wish her goodnight. Now they rape 80-year-old women and kill them for their pensions. It makes me sick.'

And, of the hopelessness of life in jail, he said: 'You can so easily give up after all these years. They have passed quickly. But it is only when I see the youngsters come in here that I realize what a terrible waste of life it is.'

The Richardson Gang: Scourge of South London

If the Krays were infamous for meting out instant vengeance, the rival Richardson gang, based on the south side of the Thames, were the masters of the slower punishment. They vied with the Krays for the reputation of being the most monstrous merchants of terror in London. Known as the 'torture gang', their speciality was pinning their enemies to the floor with 6in (15cm) nails and removing their toes with bolt cutters.

The gang's leader was Charles Richardson, born in Camberwell in 1934. He and his younger brother Eddie turned to crime after their father left home – leaving the family without any source of income – while the children were still schoolboys.

From petty theft, the brothers slowly built up a thriving string of businesses – some legitimate, others not – throughout south London. Charles specialized in scrap metal but he also ran furniture and fancy-goods firms. Eddie operated fruit machines and a wholesale chemists' supplier.

On their own, these companies would have made the brothers comfortably well off, although not rich. But largely they were no more than fronts for the other and more profitable sides of their business – fraud, theft and receiving stolen goods.

Eddie's fruit-machine business, for instance, was more successful than most in the same line. The reason was simple – if a pub- or club-owner was offered one of Eddie's machines, he would be wise to accept. If not, he knew his premises would be broken into and vandalized, or quite openly smashed up, by 'heavies' in broad daylight.

The Richardsons' most masterful money-making strokes, however, involved what were known as 'longfirms'. A company would be set up under a Richardson nominee and begin trading perfectly legitimately. Goods would be ordered from suppliers and paid for promptly, so creating good credit ratings. After a few months' operation, massive orders would be placed on credit with all the suppliers. The goods would be quickly sold, the Richardsons would pocket the money, and the company would seemingly evaporate into thin air.

Charles was once arrested for receiving stolen goods, but police had to drop the charge for a lack of evidence. They kept a careful watch on the gang's activities, however, and in 1965 they got an insight into the full horrors of the Richardsons' methods for keeping order and repaying old scores.

In July of that year one of the gang's victims walked into a South London police station and related a horrific story of how he had been tortured by the gang after a kangaroo court had found him guilty of disloyalty. Finally, he had been forced to mop up his own blood from the floor.

The trials and torture sessions were, police discovered, the sadistic speciality of Eddie. Sick with fear, the victims would be hauled in by gang members and tried before

Eddie and the others in a mock court. Then the punishments were meted out – anything from beatings to more fearsome forms of torture. Men were whipped, burned with cigarettes, had their teeth pulled out with pliers, were nailed to the floor, had their toes removed by bolt cutters or leaped in agony from the effects of an electric-shock machine. Afterwards if the victims were too badly injured they would be taken to a struck-off doctor for emergency treatment.

In 1966 the police decided they had enough evidence to act. The clincher was the murder trial of a man accused of killing a South African mining speculator to whom Charles Richardson was said to have entrusted a considerable sum of money which had never been returned. There were also stories about Charles being involved with the South African secret service, BOSS – and even talk of an attempt to bug the telephone of Prime Minister Harold Wilson.

Eddie was by now already inside jail, serving five years for affray. In July 1966 police mopped up the rest of the gang in a series of raids throughout southeast London.

It was not until April 1967 that the Old Bailey trial began, with charges of fraud, extortion, assaults and grievous bodily harm. Despite an attempt to bribe a juror, the Richardsons were found guilty after 46 days of evidence. Eddie had another ten years added to his existing sentence. Charles was jailed for 25 years for grievous bodily harm, demanding money with menaces and robbery with violence.

The judge, Mr Justice Lawton, told him: 'You terrorized those who crossed your path in a way that was vicious, sadistic and a disgrace to society . . . One is ashamed to think one lives in a society that contains men like you. You must be prevented from committing further crime. It must be made clear that all those who set themselves up as gang leaders will be struck down, as you have been struck down.'

Like the Kray brothers, Charles Richardson was later to issue an apologia for his crimes. He said: 'The men I was involved with were professional swindlers. I was only trying to get my own money back. I feel sick about the way I have been portrayed. I'm a scapegoat. I got 25 years for grievous bodily harm and not one of them needed an aspirin.'

He told the London *Sunday Times* in 1983 that his links with South Africa and the shadowy BOSS organization had been an embarrassment to the British Government. I was a pawn,' he said. 'The bigger a criminal the British made me out to be, the more leverage they could apply on the South Africans for having used me. Most business is pressure and blackmail, isn't it?'

'I never tapped Harold Wilson's phone – it could have been done but it wasn't. But people here got very upset about that. They wanted to get rid of me for as long as possible.'

A vociferous campaign for his early release was launched by Charles Richardson's loyal family and friends, backed by parole-board reports stating that he was no longer a danger to society. They fell on deaf ears.

In 1980 he walked out of an open prison and went on the run for nearly a year, supposedly to publicize his claims for freedom. He even dressed up as Father Christmas and handed out presents at a children's party. On his return to prison, he was allowed a day release. Within a year or two, he was allowed home for a long, quiet weekend to prepare himself for life again on the outside.

A preview of the lifestyle befitting one of the biggest ex-crooks in London was revealed when he was collected at the gates of Coldingly Open Prison, Berkshire, by Rolls-Royce. He was driven home for a family reunion, then took his relatives – including his freed brother Eddie – to a champagne lunch.

In the following days the festivities continued at a nightclub and a public house. At the Sidmouth Arms, off the Old Kent Road in the Richardsons' old stamping ground, 350 people thronged the bars and lounges to pay their respects to Charles.

'Look around you,' he told reporters. 'I love these people and they love me. I get 200 Christmas cards a year in jail. That's what a bad man I am.'

Charles Richardson was finally freed from prison in July 1984.

Bloodlust

Caligula

There was relief and rejoicing in Rome in AD 37 when 25-year-old Gaius Caesar succeeded to the title of Emperor from the elderly tyrant Tiberius, who had spent brooding years of self-imposed exile on the island of Capri, and had become feared and despised because of the cruel executions of his critics in the Roman army.

But it seemed as if the embittered old Emperor might have done some sort of penance by appointing Gaius Caesar as his successor. The young man was a great-grandson of Augustus and son of the soldier Germanicus, one of the unsullied military heroes of the Roman Empire.

As a baby, Gaius had often been taken by his father on Roman army campaigns and the legionnaires who doted on the child adopted him as a lucky mascot. They dressed him in a tiny uniform complete with hand-crafted boots, called caligae. And they gave him the fond nickname 'Caligula' – little boots. In four brief years that nickname was to strike terror into the hearts of the citizens of Rome and even the old soldiers who helped to rear him.

Caligula had a wild streak of youthful extravagance and an appetite for sexual adventuring. But, if his elders thought he would grow out of such excesses as he adopted the mature responsibilities of Emperor, they were mistaken. His youthful excesses masked a depraved insanity which only surfaced when he began to revel in the full power of his new office.

The first six months of Caligula's reign were a spectacular 'honeymoon' period for the citizens of Rome. He quickly won their affection by giving away most of the treasury of Tiberius in generous tax rebates and cash bonuses for the soldiers of the garrison in Rome. And he paid a small fortune to the soldiers he trusted most – the broad-shouldered German mercenaries who made up his personal bodyguard.

With reckless disregard for the worried senators who warned him he would bankrupt himself and the office of Emperor, he began to lavish unheard-of expense on the blood-letting rituals of the circuses in the Roman amphitheatres.

From all parts of the Empire, a sinister menagerie of lions, panthers, elephants and bears were captured in the forests and deserts to be brought to Rome and bloodily butchered in staged 'hunts' in the arenas, to the delight of the spectators.

Prize money for gladiators and charioteers was doubled and trebled to encourage them to fight each other to the death at the circuses. The shows were breathtaking extravaganzas, wildly acclaimed by their audiences – and they made Caligula an Emperor to be admired and applauded.

The popularity of the circuses also helped his subjects turn a blind eye to the fact that Caligula had made his three sisters leave their husbands and move into his palace in Rome to share his bed. And it helped to stifle any misgivings about reports that the fun-loving young Emperor spent many nights wandering the city with his guards, indulging in orgies with the prostitutes before burning their brothels to the ground.

In AD 38, with his reign only a year old, Caligula was still a popular Emperor when he fell ill with a fever. The circuses suddenly stopped.

Sympathetic Romans gathered in their thousands day and night outside his palace. All traffic of chariots and handcarts, and the noise of music and trade in the street were banned within half a mile of the palace, while the citizens prayed for Caligula's recovery.

For a month he hovered between life and death. Then the fever broke. The Emperor awoke weakened but growing stronger every day. But he had gone stark, raving mad.

Calling his friends and family around him, he confided: 'I wasn't really ill, I was just being reborn as a God!'

And, with just enough money left at his disposal, Caligula celebrated with a programme of circuses which surpassed all his previous spectaculars. He was determined that everyone should enjoy themselves as much as he did. Trade and commerce almost ground to a halt as Caligula declared day after day a public holiday so that none of the citizens might have an excuse for not attending the circuses.

The constant bloody carnival soon took its toll. For the Romans, it was too much of a good thing. And for Caligula's purse it was an expense he could no longer support. With most of his money gone in spendthrift celebration, even the Emperor felt the pinch of the expense of fresh meat to feed the lions being prepared for their daily battle with gladiators – who were themselves deserting the circus because of the falling prize money.

And when one mediocre circus featured mangy, underfed lions and paunchy, middle-aged gladiators lured from retirement it was unacceptable to the crowds, who demanded more and more excitement each time. They rose in the 30,000-seat amphitheatre and actually booed the Emperor.

The mad Caligula reacted swiftly. The ringleaders who had led the jeering were seized by his guards and dragged away to the cellars under the arena. There their tongues were cut out and, choking on their own blood, they were forced into the arena to do battle with the wild animals.

The Roman crowd, used to seeing trained professional 'huntsmen' kill the lions, were stunned into silence by the sight of their fellow citizens being made to face the beasts. But Caligula enjoyed the scene immensely, whooping and clapping until the last of the insolent hecklers had been killed and dragged back to the cages by the emaciated lions.

As he left the arena with a mad glint in his eye, he told

the Captain of the Guard wistfully: 'I only wish all of Rome had just one neck so I could cut off all their heads with one blow.'

Caligula had cowed even the bloodthirsty Romans into shocked submission. Yet he needed more money to stage even more circuses and to keep paying his army for their shaken loyalty. And, mad though he was, he knew that nothing would bring the wrath of his disenchanted subjects down on him quicker than a hefty increase in their taxes.

At least he had solved the problem of the food bill for the lions. From then on, the common criminals of Rome's jails were transported to the amphitheatres at night and fed to the lions. He began to ease his other financial problems with a series of trumped-up treason charges against some of the capital's wealthiest citizens. Their vast estates and fortunes were seized as fines and punishment, and the paid informers who gave perjured evidence against them were rewarded with a few gold coins.

With all of Rome turning against him, the Emperor seemed to see some sense at last and turned to the time-honoured way of raising cash – plundering the captive peoples of France and Spain.

He reserved the last of his Imperial revenues for one bizarre display in the Bay of Naples, where he moored 4,000 boats in a floating causeway – to give the lie to a prediction by a soothsayer who had told him as a boy that he had as much chance of becoming Emperor as crossing the bay and keeping his feet dry.

Caligula galloped across a wooden road of ships still riding at anchor, and Caligula swore he would take revenge on Neptune, the god of the sea. The loss of the ships hadn't dampened his spirits enough to prevent him throwing a party for his favourite horse Incitatus, 'the swift', and presenting the animal with more classical paintings to join the collection already hanging on the walls of its marble bedroom. And Incitatus was 'promoted' from Senator to Consul of the Roman Empire.

Broke and desperate to recoup the cost of his Bay of Naples escapade, Caligula threw all caution to the wind. His guards rounded up ordinary citizens in the street and forced them to contribute every coin in their purses to the Emperor's treasury. Holding back a single coin could mean instant death.

When his loyal guards explained that they had even managed to rob the city's prostitutes of their meagre earnings, Caligula hit on his most obscene idea for raising even more revenue. At a family meeting in his palace, he raged at his sisters Agrippinilla and Lesbia: 'Everyone else in Rome had to work to support me, but I never see any money from you. Now it's your turn to work.'

By imperial decree, Caligula announced that his palace was to be opened as a brothel, with his sisters as prostitutes. Eminent senators were ordered to turn up at the enforced sex orgies and pay an entrance fee of 1,000 gold pieces. To the shame of the most noble men of the Senate, they were then summoned to return to another series of orgies and to bring their wives and daughters as prostitutes to join Caligula's sisters.

When Rome had been bled almost dry, Caligula decided to look further afield and, to the relief of his countrymen, set out to plunder his way through the captured provinces of France and Germany. He sent word ahead to the military garrison commanders and provincial governors in France that he wanted all the richest men in their areas to be assembled in Lyons to meet him. Nervously the Roman administrators complied, fearing that Caligula might rob and kill the French noblemen and provoke another Gallic uprising. But the tortured mind of the Emperor had produced an outrageous compromise. The rich merchants were being offered the bargain of a lifetime, a chance to buy some of the 'treasures' of

Caligula's palace at knock-down prices.

So began the weirdest 'auction' any of them had ever witnessed. Caligula himself did the bidding on behalf of his captive buyers, bidding merchant against merchant until he was satisfied he had taken every piece of gold from them. When his sales assistants, the Imperial Guard, passed out the merchandise to the baffled bidders, the French merchants found they had unwittingly paid thousands of pieces of gold for packages of cloth which contained only old sandals and mouldy pieces of cheese.

With another small fortune in running expenses, Caligula set off for the Rhine, vowing to exterminate his German enemies. In one small skirmish, his legions captured about 1,000 prisoners. Caligula picked out only 300 men from the dishevelled ranks and ordered the remainder to be lined up against a cliff, with a bald man at each end. Satisfied he had enough prisoners for a swaggering triumphal entry to Rome, he ordered his Legions: 'Kill every man from bald head to bald head.'

Then he set off for his last great 'battle'. Camping outside the port of Boulogne, he ordered his dispirited and nervous army to line up on the beaches. Roman archers formed ranks at the water's edge. Huge catapults and slings were dragged on the sand dunes to support the infantrymen; massed troops of cavalry waited on the flanks. All eyes were set on the horizon, watching disbelievingly for the appearance of some distant enemy.

Then Caligula rode with imperial majesty into the shallow water. With blood-curdling oaths, he unsheathed his sword and swore revenge on the sea god Neptune who had wrecked his ships in the Bay of Naples. The soldiers watched in silence as Caligula slashed at the foam with his sword. Then he ordered the catapults to be fired into the sea. The infantry charged, trampling the waves. The archers shot their arrows at the breakers. The shallow waters were pierced with spears and the cavalry rode in and out of the surf, stabbing the seawater with swords.

'Now for the plunder,' shouted an overjoyed Caligula. And each man had to begin looting the sea – gathering piles of sea shells in their helmets.

It was too much. The mighty Roman army had been reduced to clowning for their insane Emperor.

As Caligula began the long march home, the long-overdue conspiracy to rid the Empire of the bestial lunatic quickly gathered strength. When Caligula entered Rome, bringing the straggling German prisoners and a handful of Britons he had captured from a trading boat in Bologne, together with tons of sea shells, the Senate was seething and the army close to revolt.

For the next month they plotted. They let the mad Emperor rant and rave and award himself great honours for his 'victories'. Caligula drew up plans for all the statues of the gods in Rome to be beheaded and replaced with an image of his own head. He danced through his palace in silken women's clothes and carried on blatant love affairs with young man he selected to be his bed partners.

But his days were numbered.

There was no mass uprising to overthrow him, just the sudden anger of one old soldier who had reached the end of his tether.

To Cassius Chaerea, Colonel of the Imperial Guard, was given the most menial task of tax-collecting. As an honourable soldier, he was sworn to give total obedience to his Emperor, no matter what the provocation. But, when Cassius was ordered to torture a young girl falsely accused of treachery, he broke down and wept at the girl's pain and innocent anguish. Word of the veteran soldier's tears reached Caligula and the Emperor began to taunt him with shouts of 'cry-baby'.

To make sure all of the Guard knew of his insults, he teased Cassius mercilessly each day when he issued the new password for the Guard. Cassius was given the password personally by Caligula and had to repeat it in turn to each of his junior officers. The passwords had always been stern military slogans like 'victory' and 'no surrender'. Cassius had to repeat a new series given to him by the mocking Emperor, slogans like 'perfume and powder' and 'kiss me soldier'.

Cassius's sense of honour finally outweighed loyalty to a madman. In January AD 41, he waited in the covered walkway which separated Caligula's palace from his private theatre and sent in word to the Emperor who was watching rehearsals for a new play a troupe of young Greek dancing boys had arrived to perform for him. The perverted Emperor couldn't wait to meet the youngsters. He abandoned the audience and, as he hurried along the passageway, the old soldier Cassius stepped forward.

'I need the password for today, Emperor,' he told Caligula.

'Oh yes,' said the leering Emperor. 'Let me see now. I think the password for today should be "old man's petticoat".'

It was to be his last insult. Cassius drew his sword and smashed Caligula to the ground.

With ten thrusts of the sword, from the skull to the groin, he ended the rule of the Divine Emperor Caligula. Seconds later he strode into the theatre and told the audience: 'The show is over, the Emperor is dead.'

There was a stunned silence. Then a roar of applause louder and more joyous than any heard during the four years of depraved circuses and orgies of the wicked reign of Emperor Caligula.

Vlad the Impaler

If Dracula ever walked the earth as a creature of flesh and blood rather than being just a figure of fiction, then the person who most deserved that terrible title was Vlad Tepes – otherwise known as Vlad the Impaler.

Vlad Tepes ruled over Walachia, now part of Romania, between 1456 and 1476. His father had been given the title 'Dracul' (meaning dragon) because that creature was the emblem on his shield. His son, Vlad the Fifth, gave the title a new meaning by his habit of drinking the blood of his victims, of whom there was no shortage of supply. And his ingenuity in devising ever more horrible forms of death for his enemies was awesome.

On one occasion, he sat down to dinner surrounded by a large number of slowly dying victims. When one of his guests, sickened by the stench and the screams, made the mistake of complaining, Vlad had him impaled 'so that he could be above the smell'.

Twelve years of his reign were spent imprisoned in Hungary where, denied the pleasure of human victims, he pursued his solitary hours in the torture of animals.

Yet Vlad the Fifth was a hero in his own country, a brilliant general who ferociously set about putting an end to decades of internal strife and who then turned his attentions towards the Turks whose territorial ambitions were a perpetual threat to his borders. When the Turks sued for peace, Vlad summoned their envoys before him and had their hats and coats nailed to their bodies, using short nails to prolong their agonies.

Impaling his victims on stakes was Vlad's favoured method of execution. He once triumphantly impaled 20,000 of his enemies. On another occasion, he partook of a hearty breakfast in a field of impaled peasants. He generally insisted that the stakes were not made too sharp

– so that his victims would suffer more.

But there were other ways of avenging himself on those who offended him. A group of protesting peasants were invited to feast at one of his homes, which was then locked and set on fire. He put down one rebellion by making it known that the bodies of plotters would be fed to crabs, then force-fed to their families – a threat he gleefully carried out. He also forced wives to eat the roasted bodies of their husbands and made parents cannibalize their children.

Vlad's excesses were not simply due to a cruel nature. He was a sadist who gained a perverted pleasure from his deeds and whose habit of drinking his victims' blood made him the model for the Dracula myth.

Vlad the Impaler's terrible rule came to an end in 1476 when he was killed in battle against the Turks – although it is believed that the blow that felled him came from one of his own lieutenants.

Gilles de Rais

While Vlad the Fifth was gaining infamy for his barbarity, a noble contemporary of his was gaining glory at the other end of Europe. Gilles de Rais (or de Retz) was a Marshal of France, one of the richest and bravest noblemen in the land, cultured, sophisticated and pious. His main claim to fame was that he fought alongside Joan of Arc. But his claim to infamy is in many ways more horrific than even Vlad's . . . for de Rais secretly tortured and killed hundreds of children to satisfy his craving for the shedding of blood.

Born in 1404, de Rais married into an equally noble family at the age of 16. He owned five vast estates, had a private chapel that required the attendance of 30 canons and was so esteemed in the eyes of the court that he was appointed to the post of Marshal so that he could personally crown King Charles VII of France. Of proud and muscular bearing, he was a brilliant warrior, being instrumental in securing Charles's victories over the English. He rode alongside Joan of Arc and was followed by a personal retinue of 200 knights.

Yet, for all those glittering prizes, de Rais maintained a sick and savage secret. He was guilty of what a contemporary described as 'that which the most monstrously depraved imagination could never have conceived'.

He is said to have sadistically tortured and murdered between 140 and 800 children. Obsessed with the letting of blood, he would order his servants to stab his young victims in their jugular vein so that the blood would spurt over him. He was alleged to have sat on one dying boy while drinking his blood.

Ten years after Joan of Arc's trial for heresy, de Rais was charged with the same offence after he attacked a priest. Haughtily refuting that accusation, he was then charged with murder. In the words of his ecclesiastical accusers, he was a 'heretic, sorcerer, sodomite, invocator of evil spirits, diviner, killer of innocents, apostate from the faith, idolator'.

There was good reason for the Church to have fabricated the case against de Rais. He was a secular challenge to their power over the King and his court, and if found guilty the Church stood to seize his lands. No effort was spared in preparing the most damning case: de Rais's servants were tortured until adequate evidence was given against their master.

De Rais himself was probably not tortured. Yet he made a full and ready confession – not only to the murder of 140 children, of which he was charged, but to the murder of 'at least 800'.

Two rational reasons were given for this slaughter. The

first was the influence on him of a book, an illustrated copy of *Lives of the Caesars* by Suetonius, which included graphic descriptions of the mad Emperor Caligula's sadistic excesses. The second was the approach of an Italian alchemist, Francisco Prelati, who promised the secret of turning iron into gold by black-magic rites and sacrifices. But the real reason for the mass killings de Rais perpetrated could only have been what we now know as paedophilia and sadism – both carried out on a scale probably unequalled before or since.

Predictably, de Rais was found guilty and in a show of public contrition and humility begged forgiveness from the parents of the children he admitted slaughtering. Like Joan of Arc before him, he was sentenced to death by fire. But, as an act of 'mercy' for not recanting his confession, he was first garrotted to death before being thrown on the flames on 26 October 1440.

The Beane Family:
the Ghouls of Galloway

Human monsters who practice vampirism or cannibalism are a vile but fortunately rare breed. Yet there is one case where such beings have worked not only as a team but as an entire clan. They were the notorious Beane family of Galloway, Scotland, made up of Sawney Beane and his wife, their eight sons, six daughters, 18 grandsons and 14 granddaughters.

Sawney (known as 'Sandy') Beane was the vagabond son of a road-mender and ditch-digger who lived near Edinburgh in the late 14th century. Driven out of town because of his ne'er-do-well ways, Sawney fled with his young mistress to the rugged west coast of Scotland, where he settled in a cave and began to raise a family on the proceeds of sheep stealing and robbing travellers.

Their home provided a safe haven for their nefarious activities since its precise location was not known outside the family and because its entrance was blocked by the tide most of the time. But by 1435, at which time the Beane clan had increased by incestuous union to 48 members, the authorities were forced to act.

An entire tract of Galloway was prey to the ravages of the Beanes. And it was not just money, animals or property that travellers risked losing . . . it was their lives and bodies. For the evil clan had turned to cannibalism as the easiest and most satisfying way of both disposing of their victims and feeding their family.

James I of Scotland issued orders that the scourge of Galloway be ended and personally took charge of the force he assembled to clean up the coast. On the first foray of this policing operation, Beane's gang was caught in the act. They were surprised while attacking a man and his wife and fled, leaving the woman's disembowelled body on the roadside.

With the help of dogs, the King's men tracked the Beanes to their lair. Inside the cave they found a charnel-house far exceeding in horror their worst nightmares. There were bundles of stolen clothes, saddles, food and valuables. There were animal carcasses. But in addition there were human corpses, both male and female, some dried, some smoked, some pickled and some salted. They hung, dismembered or still whole, from the damp roof of the cave.

All 48 Beanes were captured and taken to Leith where, after a show trial, the men had their hands, feet and private parts severed. As they bled to death, the women were burned alive – savage justice for the murder of dozens, and possibly hundreds, of innocent victims who ended up as dinner for Sandy Beane's bestial family.

Kürten and Haarmann: the German 'Vampire' Killers

The label 'vampire' conjures up visions of dark, misty forests and bleak castles. But one of the most famous vampires in history was no part of this ancient mythology. The scenes of his appalling crimes were in 20th-century urban Germany. His name was Peter Kürten and because of his vile deeds he became known as 'the Vampire of Düsseldorf'.

Kürten was a brutal sadist who first practised his perversions as a child of nine while working for the local dog-catcher near his home town of Cologne-Mulheim. The youngster loved to torture the animals he rounded up, eventually progressing from dogs to pigs, sheep and goats. He was drawn hypnotically to the sight of blood and loved nothing better than to chop the head off a goose or swan and gorge himself on the blood that spurted out. Gradually Kürten switched from animals to human victims.

As a boy, he drowned two playmates swimming in the Rhine, but their deaths were clean, easy, almost mundane. As an adult, he sought excitement through theft, fraud, arson and the beating of prostitutes. But the thrills he experienced were not enough and he coolly planned the ultimate crime, premeditated murder.

Strangely for such a calculating fiend, his first attempt failed. He attacked a girl in a wooded park, leaving her for dead. The victim, however, recovered and crawled away, too ashamed ever to report the incident.

His next attempt was tragically successful. The victim was an eight-year-old girl whom he strangled and raped before cutting her throat. The murder took place in 1913 but it was 17 years before the full story was known . . .

related by Kürten himself at his trial.

Without emotion, he told the court: 'I had been stealing, especially from bars and inns where the owners lived on the floors above. In a room above an inn at Cologne-Mulheim I discovered a child asleep. I seized her head and strangled her for about a minute and a half. She woke up and struggled but lost consciousness.'

'I had a small, sharp penknife with me and I held the child's head and cut her throat. I heard the blood spurt and drip on the floor. The whole thing lasted about three minutes, then I locked the door and went home to Düsseldorf.'

The following day, Kürten returned to the scene of the crime, sitting at a café opposite the bar where the girl had been murdered. 'People were talking about it all around me,' he said. 'It did me good.'

There was a tragic sequel to this murder, of which Kürten must have been fully aware. The butchered girl's uncle became a prime suspect in the case. He was arrested and tried for murder. After a shameful trial, the poor man was acquitted but the stigma of the accusation haunted him until his premature death two or three years later.

Meanwhile, Peter Kürten, who had been called up for service in 1914, deserted within days and spent most of World War I in jail. Even when freed, he turned again to crime and was imprisoned for fraud. Finally released in 1921, he seemed to make a concerted effort to attain respectability. He got married, albeit to an ex-prostitute, gave up crime and took a job in a factory. He dressed smartly, spoke courteously and was well liked by his neighbours.

In 1925 the monster reverted to form. He employed prostitutes and beat them within an inch of their lives. Then he began attacking complete strangers in the street, mesmerized by the sight of their blood.

Kürten's savagery became uncontrollable in 1929. He

accosted two sisters, aged 14 and five, as they walked home from a fair, strangled both and cut their throats. Within 24 hours, he pounced on a housemaid and stabbed her repeatedly in an uncontrollable frenzy until the blade of his knife broke off in her back. The girl's screams alerted passers-by who arrived in time to save her life but not to catch her attacker.

The city of Düsseldorf was by now in a state of panic. Police had a file of more than 50 attacks they believed had been committed by the man referred to as 'the Vampire'. But there was no suspect, no evidence, no link between the horrified victims and the quiet, self-controlled murderer.

Then, in 1930, the police were led literally to Kürten's door. A young country girl, newly arrived at Düsseldorf's main railway station, was being pestered by a stranger who promised to direct her to a cheap hotel. Just as the man's advances became frighteningly persistent, a second man arrived on the scene and intervened. As the first offender skulked away, the 'rescuer' introduced himself – as Peter Kürten.

The girl was invited to recover from her ordeal with a meal at Kürten's home, after which he walked with her into the city's Grafenburg Woods and viciously assaulted her. Just as she was about to pass out, Kürten did what he had never done before . . . he allowed his victim to go free. He asked her if she could remember where he lived and, after naïvely accepting her assurance that she could not, he escorted her to a public thoroughfare and walked calmly away.

Incredibly, perhaps through a sense of shame, the girl did not go to the police, and the Vampire of Düsseldorf might even then have escaped except for an extraordinary coincidence. The young girl wrote of the incident to a friend but incorrectly addressed the letter. A postal official who opened it to seek the sender's address could not contain his curiosity and read the account of the attack. He immediately called in the police.

Detectives found the girl and made her retrace her steps to Kürten's home. There, they spotted Kürten but he had seen them first and fled through the streets. Under threat of capture, the killer turned to his unsuspecting wife. He met her in a restaurant where she worked and, over a double helping of lunch, he confessed to her, in a matter-of-fact way, his many crimes. His disgusted wife arranged a further secret meeting but instead went to the police, who lay in wait for Kürten at the rendezvous.

In court, 47-year-old Kürten was as cool as ever. He horrified judge and jury by the calm, clinical manner in which he related in sickening detail the long catalogue of his crimes. He told how he had strangled, stabbed or clubbed to death his innocent victims and had then drunk the blood from one person's slashed throat, from another's wounded forehead and from another's half-severed hand.

His own defence counsel called him: 'the king of sexual delinquents; uniting nearly all perversions in one person; killing men, women, children and animals – killing anything he found.' His lawyer was making a plea for a ruling of insanity, but to no avail.

Kürten was sentenced to die by guillotine and on the morning of his death, 1 July 1932, he ate a hearty meal twice over, then told a prison doctor of his last hope . . . to experience what he described as 'the pleasure to end all pleasure'. It was, said Kürten, 'that after my head had been chopped off I will still be able to hear, at least for a moment, the sound of my own blood gushing from the stump of my neck'.

It is incredible that two 'vampire' killers could turn up in the same country in the same period. Yet while 'the Düsseldorf Vampire', Peter Kürten, was beginning to gain infamy for his deeds, another brutal monster was coming to the end of his reign of terror. He was Fritz Haarmann, 'the Hanover Vampire'.

At the end of World War I, Haarmann, then aged 39, emerged from a five-year jail sentence for theft and returned to his home town of Hanover to try to scrape together a living in the chaos of post-war Germany. The business he chose was as a purveyor of meats, pies and second-hand clothes in a poor area of the city. He prospered because of the cheap and simple source of his raw materials . . . murdered young men and boys.

Haarmann spent his evenings and nights prowling Hanover's railway stations and back alleys to seek out the human flotsam sleeping rough there. He would offer those who were jobless or homeless the chance of free food, lodging and companionship. In return, they would be sexually abused and often murdered. Their bodies would be butchered, their clothes sold and their flesh put into Haarmann's tasty pies.

The method of murder gave rise to Haarmann's sobriquet as 'the Vampire of Hanover' – he would kill his victims by biting through their throats.

Incredibly, police and voluntary workers, who must certainly have suspected Haarmann, not only turned a blind eye to his nefarious activities but actively encouraged him. He became a police informer, passing on details of suspicious newcomers to town, of planned crimes and of hidden loot. So close was his relationship with the police that, when in 1918 the parents of one 17-year-old boy reported their son missing after being seen in Haarmann's company, the ensuing search of the killer's room was no more than cursory. The murderer was later to boast at his trial: 'When the police examined my room, the head of the boy was lying in newspaper behind the oven.'

The following year Fritz Haarmann met the accomplice who was to speed up the 'production line' at his cooked-meats plant. His name was Hans Gans; he was just 20 but was already a heartless, vicious thug whose job it was to pick out the victims ready for the executioner. Together, they began disposing of boys and young men at a prodigious rate.

Hanover had by now gained an unenviable reputation as the city where people could vanish from the streets without trace while the police were apparently powerless to act. In fact, the police could have acted and saved many lives, but they found Haarmann's information so helpful that they effectively gave him immunity. They even failed to respond to complaints about the one-way traffic of boys into Haarmann's rooms, the buckets of blood carried out and the bloodied clothes and suspect meat (labelled as pork) which he was selling.

Eventually, the discovery of two human skulls, one of a youngster, on the bank of the River Leine forced police to act. They searched the riverside and discovered more human remains. Boys playing nearby found a sack packed with human organs. and the dredging of the river bed raised more than 500 human bones. Haarmann's blood-spattered apartments and workshops were raided.

In December 1924 Haarmann and Gans went on trial. 'How many victims did you kill?' asked the prosecutor. Haarmann replied: 'It might be 30, it might be 40, I can't remember the exact number.' Asked how he had killed his victims, Haarmann replied dispassionately: 'I bit them through their throats.'

While Hans Gans received a life sentence (of which he subsequently served only 12 years) the Vampire of Hanover was predictably sentenced to death, having been found sane and entirely responsible for his bloody deeds. Before being beheaded, he declared: 'I will go to my execution as if it were a wedding.'

Herman Mudgett and the Chicago 'Torture Castle'

If there were a league table of mass killers, the name of Herman Webster Mudgett would be high on the list. He is reckoned to have murdered at least 200 victims – mainly young women – for the sheer pleasure of cutting up their bodies.

Mudgett researched his dreadful pastime at America's Ann Arbor medical school. An expert in acid burns, he boosted his student allowance by body-snatching. He would steal corpses, render them unrecognizable, then claim on life-insurance policies he had previously taken out under fictitious names. He got away with several of these frauds before a nightwatchman caught him removing a female corpse and the errant student fled.

Mudgett next turned up in Chicago where, under the alias 'Dr H.H. Holmes', he ran a respectable pharmacy without a hint of scandal. So successful was he that in 1890 he bought a vacant lot and set about building a grand house.

But this was no ordinary home. It contained a maze of secret passages, trapdoors, chutes, dungeons and shafts. Suspicion was averted during the construction of what later became known as the 'Torture Castle' by the expedient of hiring a different builder for each small section of the house.

The house was finished in time for the great Chicago Exposition of 1893 when the city filled with visitors, many of whom were to be Mudgett's prey. He lured girls and young women to his 'castle' where he attempted to seduce them before drugging them. They were then popped into one of the empty shafts that ran through the building. The hapless girls would come round only to find themselves trapped behind a glass panel in an airtight death chamber into which would be pumped lethal gas.

The bodies would be sent down a chute to the basement which contained vast vats of acid and lime and, in the centre of the room, a dissecting table. Here Mudgett would cut up the corpses, removing particular organs which took his fancy and disposing of the rest in the vats.

Mudgett later admitted to having murdered 200 girls during the Exposition alone, and the orgy of blood-letting might have continued for much longer but for the phoney doctor's greed. He had murdered two visiting Texan sisters and, rather than quietly dispose of their remains, he set fire to the house in an attempt to gain the insurance money and make good his escape from Chicago.

The insurance company refused to pay and the police began an investigation into the blaze. Strangely, the police work was not pursued vigorously enough to produce any evidence of Mudgett's bloody activities – but the killer did not know this, and he fled.

This time he went south to Texas, where he traced relatives of the sisters he had so clumsily murdered. Having ingratiated himself with them, he tried to swindle them out of a $60,000 fortune. They were suspicious, so Mudgett again took to the road, this time on a stolen horse. Police caught up with him in Missouri, where, using the name H.M. Howard, he was charged with a further fraud attempt. With the help of a crooked lawyer, he was granted bail – and promptly absconded.

Mudgett next turned up in Philadelphia where an associate in crime had been operating insurance frauds at the mass killer's behest. In an apparent accident one day in 1894, this co-conspirator blew himself up. In fact, he had been murdered by Mudgett who ran off to Toronto with his victim's wife and their three children. Their young bodies were later found in the basements of two rented houses.

It was not any of his many murders that finally brought Mudgett to justice but the jumping of bail in Missouri and the theft of a horse, a capital offence in Texas at that time. Detectives traced Mudgett through his aged mother who was happy to give them the whereabouts of the son of whom she was so proud.

The mass killer was arrested with his mistress in Boston and was charged with horse-stealing and fraud. It was only at this stage that police searched the burned-out Chicago Torture Castle. They pieced together the remains of 200 corpses. Mudgett confessed to the murders of all of them. He was hanged on 7 May 1896.

The Marquis de Sade

When police raided the house of 'Moors Murderers' Ian Brady and Myra Hindley in 1965, they found, along with the remains of one their victims, the collected works of the Marquis de Sade. De Sade and Adolf Hitler's *Mein Kampf* were read as 'Bibles' in the killers' household. Although Hitler's philosophy is political and de Sade's sexual, both are in their own way equally dangerous. Both are able to snare the weak-minded. Both can turn mild men and women into monsters.

De Sade's distorted view of life, morality and sexual fulfilment is flaunted in books like *Justine*, *Juliette*, *Philosophy in the Bedroom* and *120 Days of Sodom*. Stories of sexual deviation are told with relish. The extent of the perversions are limited only by de Sade's imagination – and that is considerable.

The man who gave his name to sadism was born Donatien Alphonse François De Sade on 2 June, 1740 in pre-Revolutionary Paris, which was a hotbed of vice and corruption. Related to the royal house of Condé, his father was a court diplomat and his mother a lady-in-waiting to the Princess de Condé. Educated by his uncle, the Abbé de Sade of Ebreuil, he grew up good-looking, wealthy and spoilt. By the age of 18 he had experimented in every form of sexual adventure he could devise. But it was not enough. His over-fertile imagination began to invent new and terrible perversions to fuel his fantasies. The principal tenet of his philosophy was that the finest form of sexual pleasure is achieved through cruelty and pain.

De Sade served in the army during the Seven Years' War, leaving in 1763 and marrying the daughter of a judge. But within a month he was having an affair with an actress known as La Beauvoisin and was inviting prostitutes into the marital home at Arceuil. There he put his sadistic theories into practice with numerous victims, many of them strangely willing to subject themselves to his cruel whims. But some complained about their sexual abuse and de Sade was ordered to be detained in jail at Vincennes.

Within weeks he was freed and, despite having fathered two sons and a daughter by his long-suffering wife, he returned to his old ways. This time, his activities created a national scandal. In 1768 he hired a Paris prostitute called Rose Keller whom he locked up and tortured to such a degree that she complained to the authorities. De Sade was sent to jail in Lyons.

Possibly because of his family connections, he again secured an early release and in 1772 moved to Marseilles where in the busy port his pockmarked valet, Latour, found for him a ready supply of prostitutes. But, as ever, his sensual experimentation was his undoing. De Sade fed the girls sweetmeats laced with various aphrodisiacs. The girls were sick, believed they had been poisoned and complained to the police. The Marquis and Latour fled.

At Aix, master and servant were sentenced to death in their absence and were executed 'in effigy'. The fugitives were finally captured and thrown into the fortress of

Miolans. But de Sade still seemed to have the ability to get out of prison as easily as he had got himself in. He escaped and hid away with his wife at their château. By now she too was debauched, both were in debt and further trouble with the authorities was inevitable. His wife became an enthusiastic partner in his perversions and, when a new scandal broke involving young boys, both husband and wife fled.

The Marquise de Sade sought refuge in a convent while her husband bolted to Italy with his latest mistress – his wife's own sister, the Canoness de Launey. A year later, in 1777, they foolishly risked returning to France and de Sade was arrested in Paris. Thrown into the dungeons at Vincennes and then into the notorious Bastille, he suffered at the hands of harsh wardens and fellow prisoners. The cruelty he had always been ready to mete out to others was now his lot.

His enforced isolation did, however, allow him to develop his blasphemous philosophy through his writing. In de Sade's eyes, there was no god but nature – and nature was not only the creator of beauty but also of destruction, through earthquake, flood, fire and tempest. Man's destiny, he believed, ran parallel with nature, and man's destructive impulses had to be obeyed in the same way as his more gentle ones were. So a truly 'complete' man should fulfil himself by becoming a monster.

De Sade propounded such lofty thinking as a camouflage for his real designs which are clear to see in books like his elegantly titled *120 Days of Sodom* which was written in the Bastille on a single roll of paper about 12m (39ft) long.

He would probably have spent the rest of his days in prison but for a strange quirk of fate. In the chaos of the French Revolution – the Bastille itself was stormed on 14 July 1789 – De Sade was freed.

Despite his aristocratic background, he became 'Citizen

Sade', head of one of Paris's ruling revolutionary committees. As such, he managed to save his father-in-law from the guillotine – but only just escaped it himself. Strange as it may seem, 'Citizen Sade' began to deplore the unbridled brutality of France's new rulers and was accused of being 'moderate'. He was sentenced to be guillotined but was overlooked in the prison line-up on his day of execution. The following day, Robespierre, hard-line leader of the Revolutionary Convention, was overthrown and de Sade was safe once more.

In desperate poverty, he set up home with a young, widowed actress, Marie-Constance Quesnet, and wrote, among other books, *Justine* and *Juliette*. But it was these works that finally ended his freedom for ever. In 1801, on the basis of his writings, he was judged insane and locked up in Charenton asylum. Napoleon Bonaparte himself ordered that he should never be released.

Visited by his actress mistress, he continued writing books and plays, which were performed by the asylum inmates. On 2 December 1814 he died. His son visited Charenton, collected 13 years of his work and burned the lot.

A will was discovered. Written nine years previously, it instructed that his body was to be buried in the midst of a particular thicket on his old estate and the grave sown with acorns so that over the years it would be obliterated. He wrote: 'The traces of my grave must disappear from the face of the earth as I flatter myself that my memory will be effaced from the minds of men.' His wishes were ignored and de Sade the atheist was given a Christian burial, a stone cross being erected above his grave. Shortly afterwards the grave was broken into and the body stolen. The skull later came into the possession of a leading phrenologist who read de Sade's bumps and declared that he was a man of 'tender character and love of children'.

The contribution de Sade left to the world of literature

is slight – but his contribution to criminality is considerable. The sickening philosophies he propounded have taken seed in the minds of the bad and the mad, the weak and the willing, murderers and mutilators from the beginning of the 19th century to the present day. Because he could so well express the fantasies of his own evil mind, others who followed him have been encouraged to act out their own. Indirectly, he may have been responsible for more murders than any other individual in peacetime history. The name of the Marquis de Sade is synonymous with evil.

Judgement on the Ripper

A notice, handwritten by Bradford lorry-driver Peter Sutcliffe, was displayed in the cab of his vehicle. It read:

IN THIS TRUCK IS A MAN WHOSE LATENT GENIUS IF UNLEASHED WOULD ROCK THE NATION, WHOSE DYNAMIC ENERGY WOULD OVERPOWER THOSE AROUND HIM.
BETTER LET HIM SLEEP?

The humour sours when you remember that Sutcliffe turned out to be the Yorkshire Ripper – a man who killed and horribly mutilated 13 women in his five-year reign of terror.

The murders began in October 1975 and the killing of Wilma McCann, a 28-year-old prostitute whose corpse, battered by hammer blows to the skull and pierced by screwdriver stab wounds, was discovered on a Leeds playing field. The Ripper's next three victims had all plied the same trade in the red-light districts of Leeds and Bradford. But the pattern of murder changed in June 1977 when a perfectly respectable 16-year-old girl fell victim to the killer's brutal impulse. Other non-prostitutes were to succumb later; the case brought stark terror to the women of West Yorkshire, and indeed all over Britain.

It also prompted the biggest murder hunt of the century. But in January 1981, when the Ripper was finally caught, it happened almost by chance. The bearded Sutcliffe was discovered by Sheffield police in his Rover V8 with a coloured prostitute named Ava Rivers. The car carried false number plates, and contained the grim tools of the Ripper's trade: a hammer, garotte and sharpened Phillips-type screwdriver. Ava Rivers could count herself the luckiest woman in Britain that night – she would have been the next victim.

Back at the police station, the police knew that they had found the Ripper at last. He turned out to be a married man, born in 1946 at Bingley near Bradford and now living in a respectable middle-class district of that city. In his time he had held down a variety of jobs – including that of gravedigger at Bingley Cemetery. Ironically, he had been interviewed routinely no fewer than nine times before in the police trawl for the mystery killer.

What had motivated him? In August 1974, Sutcliffe had married a demure schoolteacher named Sonia Szurma; the murders started little more than a year later and many people speculated that, in killing his victims, Sutcliffe was really trying to destroy his wife. Though the couple seemed loving and were well liked, there were known to be rows. It was Sonia who did the shouting; the slightly built Sutcliffe would meekly ask only that she keep her voice down so as not to disturb the neighbours. Sonia had, moreover, suffered a period of mental illness in which she believed, among other things, that she was the Second Coming of Christ. In short, there were tensions in the household – tensions which hardly explain the Ripper's acts, but help to fill in their background.

The three-week trial took place at the Old Bailey in May

1981. Fascination with the case was international, and illegally taken photographs of Sutcliffe in the dock were published in foreign magazines. The trial also raised important questions about the way in which the Ripper case had been handled by police: the £4 million manhunt had been badly misled by a hoax tape sent by a man with a Geordie accent who had posed as the Ripper. But the over-riding issue, on which Sutcliffe's fate depended, was whether he was mad or not.

Peter William Sutcliffe was charged with the murder of 13 women and attempts to kill another seven. He denied the murder charges – but admitted manslaughter on the grounds of diminished responsibility.

Under the 1957 Homicide Act, a prisoner may plead for a reduced charge of manslaughter on the grounds that he or she suffered some 'abnormality of mind' which impaired his or her mental responsibility. In the Ripper case, the Attorney-General was prepared to accept such a plea. But the judge was unhappy that the murder charges should be so easily disposed of; he insisted that the case go before a jury. And so it was left to 12 ordinary people – six men, six women – to judge the killer's state of mind.

From a certain point of view, anyone who did what Sutcliffe did must be mad. But the law cannot accept such a proposition, for it would result in a legal absurdity. Every crime is an abnormal act, so anyone who committed one might claim 'abnormality of mind' in expectation of lenient treatment. Sutcliffe's defence was more specific: he alleged that he had heard voices ordering him to kill prostitutes; his had been a 'divine mission'. In prison, he had been examined by three psychiatrists who unanimously declared him to be a paranoid schizophrenic.

Impassive in the dock, Sutcliffe gave no clue as to his mental health condition. But against the experts' testimony was the possibility that the prisoner had simply faked his symptoms. For example, he had not mentioned hearing voices until several interviews after his capture. In custody he was alleged to have remarked that if found to be 'loony' he would serve only ten years instead of 30. From Sonia's bout of mental disturbance he could have recalled convincing symptoms such as tactile hallucinations (he claimed that he had experienced a hand tightening around his heart).

But perhaps the most damning flaw in his story was the simple fact that many of his victims were not prostitutes at all. There were teenage Jayne Macdonald, Josephine Whitaker, clerk in a building society, Barbara Leach and Jacqueline Hill, students, and Margo Walls, a 47-year-old civil servant.

On 22 May 1981, the jury retired, deliberating for five hours and 55 minutes. On return, they found Peter William Sutcliffe guilty of murder. He was sentenced to life imprisonment, the judge recommending that a minimum of 30 years be served. In the streets outside the Old Bailey, when news of the verdict arrived, a large crowd gave three cheers for the jury. It was reported that, even in the psychiatric community, relief was immense that the experts' testimony had been rejected.

Mystery, though, still surrounds the Ripper's mind. In prison at Parkhurst he continued to claim that he heard voices, and in March 1984 the Home Secretary ordered his removal to Broadmoor. Peter Sutcliffe, he disclosed, was in a condition of grave mental illness, doctors both at Parkhurst and Broadmoor diagnosing paranoid schizophrenia. His state of mind had seriously deteriorated since admission to prison, and he could now be a threat to prison staff and others.

Was he mad all along? Or did he go mad faking madness?

Caught by a New Invention:
Dr Crippen

No name in the annals of murder is more notorious than that of Dr Hawley Harvey Crippen. Yet Crippen killed only once and, but for three fatal errors, might have got away with it. He was a quiet, inoffensive little man, intelligent, courteous and kind with a touch of nobility about his actions. Perhaps that only served to enhance the horror of his ghastly crime.

Born in Coldwater, Michigan, in 1862, he studied long and hard for his medical degrees in Cleveland, Ohio, London and New York. He practised in several big American cities, and was already a widower when, at 31, he became assistant to a doctor in Brooklyn, New York. Among the patients there was a 17-year-old girl who called herself Cora Turner. Attractive and lively, she was the mistress of a stove manufacturer by whom she was pregnant. She miscarried.

Despite her circumstances, Crippen fell in love with her, and began trying to win her affections. He found that her real name was Kunigunde Mackamotzki, that her father was a Russian Pole and her mother a German, and that the girl wanted to be an opera singer. Crippen paid for singing lessons, though he must have known her dreams were bigger than her talent. They married in 1893.

In 1900, Crippen, now consultant physician to Munyon's, a company selling mail-order medicines, was transferred to England as manager of the head office in London. Later that year Cora joined him, and decided to switch her singing aspirations to music-hall performances. She changed her name to Belle Elmore, and Crippen too took a new name. He dropped Hawley Harvey and called himself Peter.

Cora cultivated a large circle of Bohemian friends, dressing gaudily, bleaching her hair, and acquiring false blonde curls. She was extrovert and popular, particularly with men, and for a time her insignificant husband, small, slight and with an over-sized sandy moustache, was happy to observe her gay social whirl through his gold-rimmed spectacles, occasionally buying her furs or jewellery which he loved to present in front of her friends. The finery contrasted with the squalor of their home – neither had much inclination for household chores, and both were content to live in a dingy back kitchen, surrounded by dirty crockery, piles of clothes, and two cats that were never let out.

Any bliss that there had been in this marriage of apparent opposites vanished while Crippen was away on the company's business in Philadelphia. He returned after several months to be told by Cora that she had been seeing an American music-hall singer called Bruce Miller, and that they were fond of each other.

In September 1905, the Crippens moved to 39 Hilldrop Crescent, off Camden Road, in north London. It was a leafy street of large Victorian houses, enjoying its heyday as a good address, and cost £52 10s (£52.50) rent a year – a large slice out of Crippen's £3 a week salary. But the new home did nothing to heal the growing rift between husband and wife. Crippen was to recall: 'Although we apparently lived very happily together, there were very frequent occasions when she got into the most violent tempers and often threatened she would leave me, saying she had a man she would go to and she would end it all. She went in and out just as she liked and did as she liked. I was rather a lonely man and rather miserable.' Soon they were sleeping in separate rooms.

Cora threw herself into working for the Music Hall Ladies Guild, pretending to be a big star helping the less lucky members of her profession via the charity organization. She also took a succession of lovers, some of whom gave her gifts and money. Crippen found consolation too, in the form of Ethel Le Neve, a secretary at Munyon's offices in New Oxford Street. She could not have been less like Cora. Quiet, ladylike, she craved respectability, and the doctor had to use all his powers of persuasion before she at last agreed to accompany him to a discreet hotel room for the first time. Thoughts of her kept Crippen's spirits up as life at home became even worse. His wife began taking in 'paying guests', and when he returned from work he was expected to clean their boots, bring in their coal, and help with cleaning.

By 1909, Crippen was also a paying partner in a dental clinic, and his expenses, with two women to support, were strained. That November, he lost his job as Munyon's manager, and was paid only a commission for sales. The following month, Cora gave their bank 12 months' notice that she was withdrawing the £600 in their joint deposit account. She did not need her husband's consent for that. Cora had also learnt of Crippen's affair with Ethel, and told friends she would leave him if he did not give the girl up.

On 17 January 1910, Crippen ordered five grains of hyoscine from a chemist's shop near his office. The drug, a powerful narcotic used as a depressant in cases of mental or physical suffering, was then virtually unknown in Britain, and the chemist had none in stock. He delivered it to the doctor two days later.

On 31 January, the Crippens entertained two retired music-hall friends to dinner and whist. It was, according to one of the guests, Clara Martinetti, 'quite a nice evening and Belle was very jolly'. Clara and her husband Paul left at 01.30. Then, according to Crippen's later statements, Cora exploded with fury, threatening to leave home next day because he, Crippen, had failed to accompany elderly Mr Martinetti to the upstairs lavatory.

Cora Crippen was never seen alive again. On 2 February her husband pawned some of her rings for £80 and had Ethel Le Neve deliver a letter to the Music Hall Ladies Guild, saying that Cora, by now treasurer, would miss their next few meetings. She had rushed to America because a relative was seriously ill. On 9 February Crippen pawned more of his wife's gems, receiving £115. And soon her friends noticed still more of her jewels and clothes – being worn by Ethel Le Neve. She even went to the Guild's benevolent ball with Crippen, and wore one of Cora's brooches.

Inquiring friends started to get increasingly bad news about Belle Elmore from her husband. First she was uncontactable, 'right up in the wilds of the mountains of California'. Then she was seriously ill with pneumonia. And on 24 March Crippen sent Mrs Martinetti a telegram just before he and Ethel left for a five-day Easter trip to Dieppe. It read: 'Belle died yesterday at six o'clock.' Two days later, notice of the death appeared in *The Era* magazine. Her body, according to Crippen, had been cremated in America.

Meanwhile, Ethel Le Neve had moved into 39 Hilldrop Crescent as housekeeper, bringing a French maid with her. She told her own landlady that Crippen's wife had gone to America. Clearly she was not likely to come back – Ethel left her wardrobe behind, expecting to use Cora's clothes.

Crippen had given his own landlord notice of quitting, but he grew more confident as the constant questions about Cora tailed off, and so extended his lease until September. Then, on 28 June, came the first of what would prove fatal blows. A couple called Nash arrived back from touring American theatres, and told Crippen they had heard nothing of Cora's death while in California. Unhappy with his answers, they spoke to a highly placed friend of theirs in Scotland Yard.

On Friday 8 July, Chief Inspector Walter Dew and a sergeant called at Crippen's office, and asked to know more about Cora. Did her husband have a death certificate? Crippen admitted that the story of her death was a lie, designed to protect her reputation. She had, in fact, run off to America to join another man, probably her old flame Bruce Miller. The doctor dictated a long statement over five hours, broken only for amicable lunch with the policemen at a nearby restaurant. He readily agreed to accompany the officers back to Hilldrop Crescent for a search of the house. Dew was mildly puzzled that Mrs Crippen had left behind all her finest dresses, but he left satisfied nothing was amiss.

Crippen did not know that, however. He panicked, and made what would prove to be his biggest mistake. Overnight, he persuaded Ethel to leave with him for a new life in America. Early next morning, he asked his dental assistant to clear up his business and domestic affairs, then sent him out to buy some boy's clothes. That afternoon Crippen and Ethel left for Europe.

On the following Monday, Chief Inspector Dew returned to ask Crippen to clarify a few minor points in the statement, and discovered what had happened. Alarmed, he instantly ordered a more thorough search of Crippen's house and garden. At the end of the second day, Dew himself discovered a loose stone in the floor of the coal-cellar. Under it he found rotting human flesh, skin and hair, but no bones.

A team of top pathologists from St Mary's hospital, Paddington, painstakingly examined the remains, and decided they were of a plump female who bleached her hair. Part of the skin came from the lower abdomen, and included an old surgical scar in a position where Mrs Crippen was known to have one. The remains also contained huge traces of hyoscine, which kills within 12 hours if taken in excess. On 16 July, warrants for the arrest of Crippen and Ethel were issued. They were wanted for murder and mutilation.

Crippen had made two errors. He had carved out the bones of the body, and presumably burned them in the kitchen stove. But he had treated the fleshy remains with wet quicklime, a corrosive substance only effective when dry. And he had wrapped them before burial in a pyjama jacket with the label 'Shirtmakers, Jones Brothers, Holloway'. All might still have been well but for his third error, fleeing.

The discovery of the body aroused horrified indignation in the British press, but the two runaways, staying in Rotterdam and Brussels, did not realize the storm had broken. On 20 July, they left Antwerp in the liner SS *Montrose*, bound for Quebec. Crippen had shaved off his moustache and discarded his glasses, and was posing as John Philo Robinson, while Ethel, dressed in the boy's clothes Crippen's assistant had bought, pretended to be his 16-year-old son, John. But if they thought they were safe they were wrong.

The ship's commander, Captain Kendall, had read all about the gruesome findings at Hilldrop Crescent, and was aware that the *Daily Mail* had offered £100 for information about the couple the police were hunting. Kendall noticed an inordinate amount of hand-touching between Mr Robinson and his son. The boy's suit fitted badly, and he seemed almost ladylike when eating meals, when his father would crack nuts for him or offer him half his salad.

Kendall surreptitiously collected up all the English-language papers on board so as not to alarm the couple. He checked Crippen's reaction when he called him Robinson, and invited the couple to dine at his table. After two days at sea, he sent a message to the ship's owners over the newly installed wireless telegraph, reporting his suspicions. On 23 July, Chief Inspector Dew and his sergeant set sail from Liverpool in the *Laurentic*, a faster transatlantic liner, which would overtake the *Montrose* just before it reached Quebec.

Then followed eight bizarre days. Crippen sat on deck, admiring the 'wonderful invention' of the wireless telegraph, not realizing that he was the subject of the crackling messages. Kendall's daily reports were avidly printed by the *Daily Mail*, whose readers relished every word as the net closed in on the unsuspecting doctor.

It was 08.30 on 31 July when Dew, accompanied by a Canadian policeman, boarded the *Montrose* disguised as a pilot. The ship was in the St Lawrence, and only 16 hours from Quebec. After reporting to Captain Kendall, Dew walked down to the deck and approached his suspect. 'Good morning, Mr Crippen,' he said. 'I am Chief Inspector Dew.' Crippen said only: 'Good morning, Mr Dew.' Ethel, reading in her cabin, screamed, then fainted, when a similar introduction was made. Crippen said later: 'I am not sorry, the anxiety has been too much. It is only fair to say that she knows nothing about it. I never told her anything.' He described Ethel as 'my only comfort for these three years'.

Extradition formalities took less than three weeks, and on 20 August Dew set sail for England with his celebrated prisoners aboard the liner SS *Megantic*. Dew, who was travelling as Mr Doyle, kept Crippen, now known as Mr Neild, apart from Ethel, though on one evening he did allow the two to gaze silently at each other from their cabin doors, after a request from Crippen. Huge, angry crowds greeted the two at every stage of their rail journey from Liverpool to London. And public feeling was still at fever pitch when their trials began. Crippen was charged with murder, Ethel being an accessory, and wisely they elected to be tried separately.

The doctor refused to plead guilty, even though he knew he had no credible defence. Seven days before his hearing began, at the Old Bailey on 10 October, the remains found at Hilldrop Crescent were buried at Finchley as those of Cora Crippen. Yet her husband claimed in court that they could have been there when he bought the house in 1905. That argument fell when a buyer for Jones Brothers swore that the pyjama material in which the remains were wrapped was not available until 1908. Two suits in it had been delivered to Crippen in January 1909.

Crippen had no answer to questions about why he had made no effort to search for his wife after she vanished on 1 February, why no one had seen her leave the house, why he had then pawned her possessions or given them to Ethel. Bruce Miller, now married and an estate agent in Chicago, said he last saw Cora in 1904, and denied ever having an affair with her.

On the fifth day of the trial, the jury found Crippen guilty after a 27-minute retirement, and Lord Chief Justice Alverstone, who had been scrupulously fair throughout the proceedings, sentenced him to death. Crippen, who had stood up remarkably well to cross-examination, declared: 'I still protest my innocence.'

A curious story, that Crippen had rejected a suggested defence because it would compromise Ethel, began circulating. The line, allegedly suggested by eminent barrister Edward Marshall Hall, was that the doctor had given his nymphomaniac wife hyoscine to calm her demands on him, because he was also making love to Ethel, and that Cora had died through an accidental overdose. Crippen was wise to reject the story, if he did so. For, if death was accidental, why go to so much trouble to chop up the body, remove the bones, and hide the flesh?

All along, he had been anxious to clear Ethel Le Neve's name, and on 25 October the Old Bailey did so after a one-day trial dominated by a brilliant speech by her defence lawyer, F.E. Smith, later Lord Birkenhead. He asked the jury if they could really believe that Crippen would take such care to hide all the traces of the murder, then risk the 'aversion, revulsion and disgust' of a young, nervous woman by telling her. 'This is how I treated the woman who last shared my home, and I invite you to come and share it with me now.' Ethel was found not guilty and discharged.

But she did not desert her lover, and as he waited for execution he thought only of her, continually proclaiming her innocence, kissing her photograph, and writing touching love letters to her. He also wrote in a statement: 'As I face eternity, I say that Ethel Le Neve had loved me as few women love men . . . surely such love as hers for me will be rewarded.'

The man whose name has become synonymous with murder was hanged in Pentonville Prison on 23 November 1910, still protesting that he had murdered no one. His last request was that Ethel's letters and photograph be buried with him. They were. A curious kind of sympathy had grown for the quiet, considerate little man, both among prison staff and those who came into contact with him. F.E. Smith called him 'a brave man and a true lover'. And there were many who agreed with Max Beerbohm Tree's verdict on the day of execution: 'Poor old Crippen.'

Ethel Le Neve slipped quickly into obscurity. Some say she emigrated to Australia, and died there in 1950, others that she went to Canada or America. Another report was that, for 45 years, she ran a tea-room near Bournemouth under an assumed name. And there have been rumours that she wrote her version of the Crippen affair, to be published after her death. But all the theories could be as wide of the mark as the wild legends that have turned her mild-mannered lover into the most monstrous murderer the world has even seen.

The Killer Clown:
John Wayne Gacy

When they christened him with the name of their favourite film star, John Wayne Gacy's parents had high hopes that their little boy would one day become famous. In a way they saw their dreams realized – although not quite as wished.

John Wayne Gacy today is a name that conjures up revulsion among millions of Americans. He is one of the country's most sadistic and prolific mass murderers, and known as the Killer Clown. When he was finally tracked down and tackled by the Chicago police in 1978, Gacy readily admitted to murdering no fewer than 33 young men and boys. Before strangling and stabbing them to death, he had brutally raped them.

Gacy was a fat, lonely homosexual with an insatiable sexual appetite. He longed to be loved by the neighbours who regarded him as 'a weirdo'. And he had aspirations of becoming somebody in local politics. To that end, he began a deliberate campaign to win over the local populace in the Chicago suburb of Norwood Park Township. A friend with connections in the Democratic Party showed him how: he would have to become a local benefactor with particular emphasis on the neighbourhood children.

Gacy set about this task with gusto. He designed three clown outfits himself, then set about creating a character. Very soon he was a local celebrity as Pogo the Clown, performing in the streets, at children's parties and other functions. He was so successful that President Carter's wife Rosalynn posed with him for a photograph, then sent him an autographed copy. He treasured that.

But, while 38-year-old Gacy clowned for the kids and

posed for posterity, the Chicago police were baffled by the mysterious disappearance of a number of local youths. On their files were also several missing persons from other states.

It took the police six years to nail Gacy. When they did, they met with a torrent of abuse from residents of Northwood Park for the appalling record of overlooked clues and bungled detective work. Had they been more efficient, people argued, at least some of the Killer Clown's victims might have lived. In fact, on four occasions between 1972 and 1978, Gacy's name had appeared on police files as a suspect in the missing-persons cases. He had also been convicted twice for sex assaults on young men.

Interviewed at police headquarters, Gacy drew a detailed map of his property, pinpointing the location of 28 of the bodies. After raping and killing his victims, he had methodically buried them in the extensive, landscaped garden of his neat and modern ranch house. The bodies of five other boys had been thrown into the Des Plaines River, near his home.

Gacy had been heavily influenced by his mother since childhood. His older sister also seemed to dominate him. He was a weak-willed man who carried his resentment towards women with him through later life. Nevertheless, he was determined to succeed in business. And that much he did. From humble beginnings, he built up a construction business that flourished.

Gacy took advantage of the rising unemployment in Chicago and offered jobs to young unskilled men who stood the least chance of finding employment. His local lads were all under 20 and receiving unemployment benefit. Others he picked up from the Greyhound Bus station in Chicago: these were often drifters heading for California hoping to find their pot of gold. Instead they found death.

'I wanted to give these young people a chance,' he told police during questioning. 'Young people always get a raw deal. But if you give them responsibility they rise to the occasion. They're hard workers and proud of their work.'

Gacy's teenage workforce were well paid and happy. As the contracts continued to pour in, he needed more labourers. At the end of a hard day – for he put in many hours himself – Gacy would get into his Oldsmobile and head for the Greyhound station, looking for more employees among the itinerants. He always found somebody.

He had been married in 1967 and again five years after that. His first wife, who divorced him in 1969, bore him two children. She said of him: 'He was a likeable salesman who could charm anything right out of you.' Wife number two, Carole Hoff, said her husband 'started bringing home a lot of pictures of naked men' just before they separated. They were divorced in 1976. Both his wives described him as 'mysterious' and said he had been a normal husband for the first few months of marriage, but then began staying out at night in his car. He beat his wives.

Where did Gacy go? Later it emerged that he would frequent 'Bughouse Square', a notorious corner of Chicago populated at night by legions of young homosexuals and male prostitutes. He picked up young men and they, like the itinerants and the local boys who worked for his building company, were among the dead found later by police. All this time, Gacy was winning friends and influencing people with his Pogo the Clown antics. He made hefty contributions to the Democratic Party, which he supported wholeheartedly. In the three years before his capture, Gacy funded and organized an annual political summer fête with beer, hamburgers and music and attended by 500 local dignitaries and business bigwigs.

The proceeds went to President Carter's re-election fund, and for his efforts he was lauded by the White House.

A pure coincidence led to his arrest. One of Gacy's political contacts during this time had known one of the victims, and harried police into mounting an extraordinarily intensive search for the missing youngster. Once again, as had happened on several occasions years before, the trail seemed to lead to Gacy. Police raided his luxury ranch house in December 1978. They placed Gacy under arrest and a team of forensic experts moved in, combing the place for clues.

As the horrified neighbours watched, police systematically dug up the garden. By the third day, the remains of 28 different bodies had been unearthed. Gacy had at first denied murdering anyone, but gradually admitted the first few, then finally drew a detailed map of his garden for police. The five remaining corpses were fished out of the Des Plaines River by police frogmen in a massive dredging operation.

Details of Gacy's *modus operandi* emerged over the ensuing months. Since boyhood, he had had a fixation for police matters. He loved to play policeman, and owned guns and other paraphernalia, including handcuffs. When he got a young man back to his house he would show the unsuspecting fellow the 'handcuff trick', assuring him that he would be released after only a few seconds.

Instead, of course, once the victim was in Gacy's power, he would become the subject of a wild homosexual rape. Instead of learning, as Gacy had promised, how to get free from the handcuffs, the victim would hear Gacy say: 'The way to get out of these handcuffs is to have the key. That's the real trick.'

The handcuff trick was quickly followed by the 'rope trick' and this always spelled the end for the victim. Gacy would throw a piece of cord around the victim's neck, and tie two knots in it. Then he would push a piece of wood through the loop and slowly turn. Within seconds the victim was unconscious; a few seconds more and he was dead.

At his trial in 1979, Chicago District Attorney William Kunkle described him as a sick man who methodically planned and executed his many murders. Kunkle asked for the death penalty; the State of Illinois was then debating whether to reintroduce execution for certain types of murder.

Defence attorney Sam Amirante pleaded that Gacy was insane at the time he committed the murders. But there had been so many, and over such a long period of time, that Gacy was convicted and given life imprisonment.

The Sadistic Romeo: Neville Heath

Neville George Clevely Heath had the looks that boys' comic heroes are made of. His wide, blue eyes and fair, wavy hair set off a fresh-complexioned face which had women swooning. And his suave charm around the clubs and restaurants of London ensured that he was never short of a pretty companion when the evening ended. Girls fell for his impeccable manners, and his tales of derring-do in the war that had just finished. But Heath's handsome face hid a terrible secret. Possibly bored with the conventional sex that was so readily available to him, he began pandering to a sadistic streak. And, in the summer of 1946, that perversion turned him into a ladykiller in every sense of the word.

Heath was then 29, and well known to both the police and the armed forces. He had served time in civilian jails for theft, fraud and false pretences. He had been courtmartialled by the British RAF in 1937 (absent without leave, escaping while under arrest and stealing a car), the British army in 1941 (issuing dishonoured cheques and going absent without leave) and the South African Air Force in 1945 (undisciplined conduct and wearing unauthorized decorations). In April 1946, he was fined £10 by magistrates in Wimbledon, London, for wearing medals and a uniform to which he was not entitled. By then, unknown to the authorities, he was also indulging in much more sinister fantasies.

A month earlier, the house detective at a hotel in London's Strand burst into a locked room after other guests reported hearing screams. He found Heath standing over a naked girl who was bound hand and foot, and being savagely whipped. Neither she nor the hotel wanted any publicity, and Heath was allowed to slink away, but in May he was at it again. This time he had a more willing victim, a 32-year-old masochist called Ocelot Margie to doormen at the clubs where she turned up in an ocelot fur coat, looking for men prepared to satisfy her craving for bondage and flagellation. Heath was more than ready to oblige, but when he took her to the Pembridge Court Hotel in Notting Hill Gate the hotel detective again intervened after hearing the sound of flesh being thrashed.

Ocelot Margie did not learn from her escape. When Heath phoned her a few weeks later, she agreed to meet him on Thursday 20 June. After drinks at one of Heath's favourite haunts, the Panama Club in South Kensington, they took a taxi back to the Pembridge Court, where Heath had booked in four days earlier with another girl who had since left. It was after midnight when they arrived. Guests in adjoining rooms heard nothing to disturb their slumbers that night.

At 2pm next day, a chambermaid entered Room 4 on the first floor of the 19-bedroom hotel and recoiled with horror when she drew back the curtains. The two single beds were bloodied and disordered. And in one of them lay the lifeless body of Ocelot Margie. She was naked, her ankles bound tightly together with a handkerchief. Her face and chin were bruised, as if someone had used intense force to hold her mouth closed. There were 17 criss-cross slash marks on her face, front and back. Her breasts had been badly bitten. And she had been bleeding profusely from the vagina.

Police forensic experts quickly built up a grisly picture of the indignities inflicted on the woman before her death from suffocation. Her wrists also showed signs of being tied together, though the bond had been removed and was missing. The killer had washed the face of the corpse, but left dried blood in the nostrils and eyelashes.

On Saturday, Heath was in Worthing, Sussex, wining and dining the girl with whom he had first occupied the room in Notting Hill. She was Yvonne Symonds, a 19-year-old who had met the chilling charmer at a dance in Chelsea seven days earlier, and only consented to spend the following night with him after accepting his whirlwind proposal of marriage. Now she was back at her parents' home. Heath booked into the nearby Ocean Hotel, and took her for dinner at a club at Angmering.

There he told her his version of the murder in the room they had shared. He said he met the victim on the evening of 20 June, and she asked to borrow his room to entertain another man, since they had nowhere else to go. Heath claimed he slept elsewhere, and was taken to the room by an Inspector Barratt next day and shown the body. It was, he told Yvonne, 'a very gruesome sight'. He added that the killer must be 'a sexual maniac'.

Both Yvonne and her parents were puzzled next morning to read in the Sunday papers that police were looking for Neville George Clevely Heath. Surely they had already seen him? Yvonne rang Heath at the Ocean Hotel, and he told her he was going back to London to clear up what must be a misunderstanding. He did indeed leave Worthing – but not for London. He went further down the south coast, to Bournemouth, where he booked in at the Tollard Royal Hotel as Group Captain Rupert Brooke.

Before he left Worthing, he posted a letter to Inspector Barratt at Scotland Yard. The two had never met, but Heath, who signed the letter with his real name, said he felt duty-bound to report what he knew of the murder in his room. He again said Margery Gardner asked for his keys, but said she was obliged to sleep with the other man for mainly financial reasons. She hinted that, if Heath arrived back at 2am she would spend the rest of the night with him. He arrived at the appointed time, found her 'in the condition of which you are aware', then panicked and fled because of his 'invidious position'.

Heath gave a fictitious description of the other man – a slim, dark-haired character called Jack – and curiously added: 'I have the instrument with which Mrs Gardner was beaten and am forwarding this to you today. You will find my fingerprints on it, but you should also find others as well.'

The instrument never arrived, though Inspector Barratt was not surprised by that. Yet despite his suspicions, increased by the letter, Scotland Yard did not issue a photograph of the wanted man. Heath was thus able to enjoy himself in Bournemouth for 13 days, drinking freely, going to shows, and chatting up holiday-making girls at dances. On 3 July, he invited the friend of one of his dancing partners to tea, and they got on so well that a dinner date was fixed for that night at his hotel. Just after midnight, Heath left to walk her home along the promenade. He was asleep in his own bed at 4.30am when the night porter checked, not having seen him return.

Two days later, the manager of the nearby Norfolk Hotel reported one of his guests missing. Miss Doreen

Marshall, a 21-year-old from Pinner, Middlesex, had last been seen leaving for dinner at the Tollard Royal. The manager there asked 'Group Captain Brooke' about his guest, and suggested he contact the police. Heath duly called at the station, identified the girl from photographs, and consoled her anguished father and sister.

But an alert Detective Constable thought the handsome six-footer fitted a description Scotland Yard had sent them. Heath was asked if he was the man wanted for questioning about a murder in London. He denied it, but was delayed long enough for other officers to take a good look at him. When he complained of feeling cold as the evening drew in, an inspector went to the Tollard Royal to collect Heath's jacket. And in the pockets was all the evidence the police needed.

As well as a single artificial pearl and the return half of a first-class rail ticket from London to Bournemouth, there was a left-luggage ticket issued at Bournemouth West station on 23 June. It was for a suitcase which contained clothes labelled Heath, a bloodstained neckerchief, a scarf with human female hairs stuck to it, and a vicious-looking leather-bound riding crop, with a criss-cross weave. The end had worn away, and there was blood on the exposed wires.

Heath was taken to London and charged with the murder of Margery Gardner. On the same evening, 8 July, the body of his second victim was discovered. A woman walking her dog in a deep, wooded valley called Branksome Chine, a mile west of the Tollard Royal, noticed swarms of flies around a rhododendron bush. She called the police, having read of the missing girl. And officers found a sickening sight.

Doreen Marshall was naked except for one shoe. Her battered body had been covered with her underwear, her inside-out black dress and yellow jacket. Her ripped stockings, broken pearl necklace and powder compact were discarded close by. Her wrists were tied and the inside of her hands ripped, as if she had been trying to avert the blade of a knife. One of her ribs was broken and sticking into her lung, as if someone had knelt on her. And her flesh had been mutilated – mercifully, as forensic experts later proved, after she had been killed with two deep cuts to the throat.

Heath told the police that he left Doreen near Bournemouth pier, and watched her walk towards her hotel through some public gardens. He then returned to his own hotel at around 12.30am, and, because he knew the night porter would be waiting for him, decided to play a practical joke on him, climbing to his room via a builder's ladder left outside. He described it as a 'small deception'. The police dismissed the whole statement as a great deception. And on Thursday 24 September Heath was charged at the Old Bailey, London, with the murder of Margery Gardner.

His guilt was easily proved. And, because he had subsequently killed again, Heath was unable to use what might have been a plausible defence – that Ocelot Margie willingly submitted to whipping and beating, and died accidentally when things got out of hand. Heath knew the game was up, and wanted to plead guilty and accept his punishment coolly and calmly. But his defence counsel persuaded him, against his better judgement, to plead insanity. The attempts of a psychiatrist called on his behalf to try to prove that insanity provided the only memorable moments of the two-day trial.

Dr William Henry de Bargue Hubert, a former psychotherapist at Wormwood Scrubs jail, and one of the leading practising psychiatrists of the day, was utterly discredited by the prosecution cross-examination. A year later, he committed suicide.

Under close questionning from Mr Anthony Hawke for the prosecution, Dr Hubert claimed Heath knew what he was doing when he tied up and lashed Mrs Gardner, but did not consider or know it to be wrong. Did he then think it was right, Dr Hubert was asked. 'Yes,' came the reply. 'Are you saying, with your responsibility, that a person in that frame of mind is free from criminal responsibility if what he does causes grievous bodily harm or death?' asked the astounded Hawke. Hubert said he was, because sexual perverts often showed no regret or remorse.

Hawke then asked: 'Would it be your view that a person who finds it convenient at the moment to forge a cheque in order to free himself from financial responsibility is entitled to say that he thought it was right, and therefore he is free from the responsibility of what he does?' Hubert: 'He may think so, yes.'

Hawke: 'With great respect, I did not ask you what he thought. I asked whether you thought he was entitled to claim exemption from responsibility on the grounds of insanity.' Hubert: 'Yes, I do.'

Hawke: 'You are saying that a person who does a thing he wants to do, because it suits him at the moment to do it, is entitled, if that thing is a crime, to claim that he is insane and therefore free from responsibility?' Hubert: 'If the crime and the circumstances are so abnormal to the ordinary people, I do.'

It was an extraordinary thing to claim, and even Heath knew the doctor was harming, not helping, his case. He passed anguished notes to his own counsel, urging him to drop the insanity ploy.

In 1946 the dividing line between the noose and being confined in a mental hospital was the difference between psychopath and psychotic. Psychopaths were considered able to control their evil urges, psychotics were not. In Heath's case, two Home Office prison doctors said he was certainly abnormal, a sadistic sex pervert, but as a psychopath he was not insane.

The jury of 11 men and one woman found him guilty

after only an hour's consideration, and Heath was sentenced to death. He did not bother to appeal, expressed no remorse or sympathy for the families of his victims, and refused to discuss his life or beliefs with any of the experts sent to examine him. He spent most of his last days writing letters, one of which was to his parents: 'My only regret at leaving the world is that I have been damned unworthy of you both.'

He was hanged at Pentonville Prison in London on 26 October 1946.

Crooks and Conmen

The Politician Who Faked His Own Death

Sixty-five-year-old Mrs Helen Fleming was happy to help the pale Englishman who approached her on Miami Beach on a grey, blustery day in November 1973.

Mrs Fleming, who ran the Fontainebleau Hotel beach office, had already talked to him some ten days before. He had then told her that he was in Florida on business and that on a previous trip all his possessions had been stolen from the beach. That was why he now asked Mrs Fleming to be good enough to look after his clothes while he went for a swim. The old lady was glad to oblige such a polite, well-spoken gentleman.

The Englishman also impressed on Mrs Fleming his name. He mentioned it several times, and she had no trouble in recalling it later. The name was . . . John Stonehouse.

Stonehouse, 48-year-old Member of Parliament, strolled down the beach to the choppy sea – and vanished. He left behind him a wife, two children, a mistress, a constituency, several ailing companies and debts of about £800,000.

Next morning, James Charlton, a director of one of Stonehouse's companies, who had travelled to Miami with him, reported to the police that his partner had not been seen all night. A search was organized but no body could be found. It was assumed by everyone that he had drowned.

But John Stonehouse had not drowned. His 'death' was simply the final step in an amazingly devious plot.

At the time of his supposed death, Stonehouse was in fact strolling along Miami Beach to a derelict building near the Fontainebleau. There he retrieved a hidden suitcase containing clothes, money, travellers' cheques, credit cards and a passport – all in the name of Joseph Markham. He took a cab to Miami International Airport, boarded a plane to San Francisco and booked into a hotel there under his assumed name.

Over the next week he made his leisurely way by air to Australia. From room 1706 of the Sheraton Hotel, Honolulu, he made two phone calls to his beautiful mistress, Sheila Buckley, at a London hotel. He went night-clubbing in Honolulu, sight-seeing in Singapore, and on 27 November flew into Melbourne.

There, in the heat of a southern summer, 'Joseph Markham' lazily acquired a suntan, planned a reunion with his young mistress, and congratulated himself on the success of the most brilliantly executed and foolproof deception of the decade . . . or so he thought.

John Thomson Stonehouse had always been an arrogant man. His conceit made him few friends as he carved a career in politics and business. He wanted to be a millionaire but he ended up in debt. He aimed to be Prime Minister but he ended up in jail.

Stonehouse first entered the House of Commons as a Labour MP in 1957, and subsequently held various ministerial posts, including Postmaster General. But when Labour lost power in 1970 he was offered only a minor post in the shadow cabinet. He turned it down and decided to use his political contacts to enter the business world and 'make a million'.

Financial independence, he told his beautiful wife Barbara, would allow him to return full-time to politics and make an attempt at the Labour leadership. But again his ambitions outstripped his ability.

Stonehouse formed 20 companies in five years, including a merchant bank. One by one they ran into trouble. His little empire only lasted as long as it did because of the way he manipulated funds between one company and another. Whenever the accountants were due to inspect the books of one company, cash would be pumped into it from another so that trading figures looked good.

It was a survival system that could not last. Finally, Stonehouse owed more than £1 million. Banks and credit-card companies were demanding £375,000 and he had signed personal guarantees, that he had no chance of honouring, to the tune of £729,000.

By 1974 Stonehouse knew that a Department of Trade investigation was imminent. It would expose him as a liar and a cheat, signal the collapse of his companies, and lead to personal ruin and disgrace and possibly prosecution for fraud. So he turned to the only ally he could fully trust – his mistress.

Mrs Buckley, 20 years younger than her lover, first worked for Stonehouse as his secretary when he was Minister of State for Technology. With her long black hair, full lips and flashing eyes, the 22-year-old beauty was a popular figure in the Commons. But she had eyes only for her boss. Separated from her husband, in 1973 she moved into a nearby apartment and became Stonehouse's mistress. Her pet name for him was 'Dum Dum'.

After her divorce in 1973, on the grounds of her husband's adultery, Sheila Buckley and her 'Dum Dum' set in motion a plan to salvage as much as possible from what remained of Stonehouse's companies. His eventual aim was to tuck away a nest-egg of more than £100,000 in banks in Switzerland and Australia and use the money to establish himself and his mistress in a new life together with fresh identities in New Zealand.

But first John Stonehouse had to 'die' . . .

The initial step was to find someone else, someone who was *really* dead, so that he could assume that man's identity. As MP for Walsall, Staffordshire, Stonehouse tricked a local hospital into giving him details of men of his age who had died in the wards. He told them he had money to distribute to widows and that he was carrying out a survey. They gave him two names.

He used the same cover story when he called on Mrs Jean Markham and told her how sorry he was that her 41-year-old husband Joseph had died some weeks earlier of a heart attack.

He extracted from Mrs Markham all the information he needed for his plot to steal her dead husband's identity – particularly the fact that since Mr Markham had never travelled abroad he had not needed a passport.

Then Stonehouse repeated his act with Mrs Elsie Mildoon, whose husband Donald had also died in the same hospital.

Everything was now ready. Stonehouse obtained copies of the two men's death certificates. Then he applied for a passport in Markham's name. He had himself photographed in an open-necked shirt with hair brushed straight back, large spectacles, and a wide grin to distort his features.

He signed copies of the photograph, certifying it to be a true likeness of Joseph Markham, in the name of Neil McBride MP. Stonehouse knew that McBride was fatally ill with cancer. He died two months later.

On 2 August 1974, the Passport Office issued British Passport Number 785965 in the name of Joseph Arthur Markham. Stonehouse had his new identity.

In order to establish Markham as a real person, he got him a private address in a cheap London hotel and a business accommodation address as J.A. Markham, export-import consultant. He opened a bank account as Markham, deposited sums of money in it, then transferred the money to another Markham account with the Bank of New South Wales in London. He flew to Switzerland and put large sums in special Markham accounts there; and he obtained an American Express credit card in the dead man's name.

By November 1973 Stonehouse had no fewer than 27 different accounts in his own name in 17 banks, as well as nine accounts in the names of Markham or Mildoon. The ground plans had been well laid for his disappearance. But there was still one more major test to make.

On 6 November Stonehouse flew to Miami, supposedly to try to raise a big investment to save his ailing merchant bank. On the beach he chatted with Mrs Fleming. He travelled out under the name of Markham, even buying his plane ticket with a Markham credit card. No one was suspicious. The dummy run was a success.

Ten days later he was back in Miami on his final business trip – this time travelling on his own passport – and it was then that he performed his vanishing trick on Miami Beach. A day later the Miami Beach Police Department contacted London with the message: *John Stonehouse presumed dead*.

And 'dead' John Stonehouse might have stayed but for the most astonishing stroke of bad luck.

The day after his arrival in Australia, Stonehouse called at the Bank of New South Wales in Collins Street, Melbourne. There he checked that Aust. $24,000 had been transferred from London in the name of Markham. He withdrew $21,500 in cash and walked down the road to the Bank of New Zealand, where he introduced himself as Donald Mildoon. He said he was planning to emigrate to New Zealand and wished to deposit $21,500 in cash.

The teller to whom he handed the money was 22-year-old Bryan King. Later, returning from lunch, Mr King spotted Mr Mildoon emerging from the Bank of New South Wales. Mildoon strolled down the street to the Bank of New Zealand. There he deposited another $2,200 in cash.

The young man was suspicious. He told his boss, who telephoned the Bank of New South Wales. 'No,' he was told: 'We have no customer by the name of Mildoon. But we do have a newly arrived British immigrant named Markham who has been drawing out large sums of money in cash.'

The bank notified Victoria State Police and from that moment Stonehouse, alias Markham, alias Mildoon, was watched. The police did not have to wait long for his next move. For the following day Stonehouse boarded a plane at Melbourne Airport and flew to Copenhagen for a secret meeting with Sheila Buckley.

On 10 December he was back in Melbourne. While he was paying a call on his bank, Stonehouse's apartment was visited by Detective Sergeant John Coffey of the Melbourne Fraud Squad. He found nothing incriminating – but a book of matches caught his eye. They came from a hotel which Coffey had once photographed while serving as a steward on a cruise liner almost 20 years earlier. The hotel was the Fontainebleau, Miami Beach.

Coffey had Stonehouse closely tailed 24 hours a day. His actions were entirely unsuspicious. The only regular event in his life was his daily walk to buy *The Times*: but he could never wait until he was home to begin reading it. He always searched through it intently as he stood on a street corner.

Coffey bought copies of the newspaper, trying to discover what the Englishman was looking for. All that he found were reports about the disappearance of another Briton, Lord Lucan, wanted for the murder of his family's nanny.

Coffey naturally assumed that Mr Markham and Lord Lucan were one and the same man. But three days later he read about inquiries into the affairs of another missing Englishman, John Stonehouse MP, who had vanished from the Fontainebleau Hotel, Miami Beach. Coffey remembered the book of matches.

Victoria police called Scotland Yard and asked them

urgently to airmail photographs of both Lucan and Stonehouse. The Yard also supplied the information that Stonehouse had a long scar on his right leg.

Early in the morning of Christmas Eve, Coffey and other detectives, armed with revolvers, arrested 'Mr Markham'. At first Stonehouse refused to answer questions. But, when his right trouser leg was raised to reveal a scar just as described by Scotland Yard, he admitted his real identity.

In the fugitive's pocket was a letter addressed to Donald Mildoon. It read: 'Dear Dums, do miss you. So lonely. Shall wait forever for you.' It was from Sheila Buckley – one of many she wrote to Stonehouse while he was on the run.

On the day of his arrest in Melbourne, Stonehouse telephoned his wife Barbara. Unknown to either of them, the call was recorded. Stonehouse apologized to her, describing what had happened as a 'brainstorm' and explaining that by adopting another identity he hoped to set up a new life.

He concluded with an amazing request. He asked his deserted wife to fly out to Melbourne and to bring his mistress as well. 'Bring Sheila, ' he said, 'and we'll link up. If the Australian authorities will allow it, I will remain here and start a new life . . .'

Stonehouse then spoke to his 14-year-old son, Matthew, telling him that he would understand it all one day and urging him to be brave.

He ended the call with a final plea to his wife to fly to his side with Sheila Buckley in tow: 'Please tell her . . . and try to persuade her. I know she'll need enormous support. The poor girl's been going through hell like you have. I feel for you both.'

Incredibly, wife and mistress flew out separately to join Stonehouse who was now out on bail. But, after an emotional scene, with Stonehouse threatening to commit suicide, Barbara returned home. Sheila Buckley stayed on in Australia with her lover – a sort of phoney honeymoon for them both – until in April 1975 an extradition order was signed. Three months later the couple were flown back to Britain. Finally, in April 1976, their trial began at the Old Bailey. It cost the British taxpayer an estimated £750,000 to bring John Stonehouse to justice. There was a six-week preliminary court hearing, six barristers were involved in the 68-day trial, and a subsequent civil inquiry cost £100,000.

For almost two years an eight-man Scotland Yard fraud team had been tied up sifting through mountains of documents. They had visited America, Australia, Switzerland, Holland, Hawaii and Liechtenstein. Witnesses were brought from Australia and Hong Kong; altogether more than 100 people gave evidence in court.

On 6 August 1976, guilty verdicts to 14 charges involving theft, forgery and fraud rang out in the Old Bailey's historic Number One Court.

Jailing Stonehouse for seven years, the judge, Mr Justice Eveleigh, said: 'You are no ill-fated idealist. In your evidence, you falsely accused people of cant, hypocrisy and humbug – when your defence was all these things.'

Sheila Buckley collapsed in tears as she was given a two-year suspended sentence for helping her lover spin his web of fraud. Throughout his years in prison, she stood by him. He suffered two heart attacks and for several days seemed close to death in a prison hospital. Sheila Buckley visited him regularly.

Stonehouse served only three years of the seven-year sentence. And when he left jail, sick, bankrupt and broken, Sheila and he moved into a small £13-a-week love-nest in an unfashionable area of London.

In February 1981 the couple married at a secret ceremony in the small Hampshire town of Bishop's Waltham. Perhaps at that ceremony the new Mrs Stonehouse recollected the words she spoke to reporters after her lover's arrest in Australia in 1974 . . . 'If I had the same decisions to make all over again tomorrow, I feel certain that those decisions would remain the same.'

Going Cheap – Some of the World's Best-loved Landmarks

In 1925, within the space of a few weeks, a plausible Scottish rogue named Arthur Furguson sold off three of London's best-known landmarks to gullible American tourists. Buckingham Palace went for £2,000, Big Ben fetched £1,000 and Nelson's Column was sold for £6,000.

That anyone could fall for such an obvious confidence trick seems beyond belief. Yet Furguson was a past master at the art of gentle persuasion, thanks to his training as an actor. He appeared in repertory company melodramas throughout Scotland and northern England, once acting the role of an American conned by a trickster. Perhaps it was this part which inspired him to move south to London to try his hand in earnest at the con game.

The ex-actor would take up his position near a London monument, studying it with an air of rapt concentration. Soon a tourist would make an inquiry about the history of the monument and Furguson would engage him in conversation.

Once, while pacing around Trafalgar Square, he was approached by an American tourist from Iowa. Yes, said Furguson, the tower in the centre of the square was Nelson's Column, erected in honour of the great admiral. But sadly, he said, it would be not be there for long. It was to be sold and dismantled along with several other landmarks to help repay Britain's vast war loan from the United States. And it was he, Furguson, who as a ministry official had been given the task of arranging the sale.

Yes indeed, Furguson informed the gentleman from Iowa, he was reluctantly authorized to accept a bid for the column even at this late stage. Furthermore, since the tourist was so obviously a lover of great art, he could arrange for him to jump the queue.

A cheque for £6,000 promptly changed hands and the American was left with a receipt and the address of a demolition company. It was only when the demolition company refused to consider carrying out the job of knocking down one of London's most historic sights that the American at last began to suspect that he had been taken for a ride.

Furguson used much the same ploy to dispose of the Big Ben clock tower and the King's royal residence of Buckingham Palace. Then, encouraged by his success in extracting cash from trusting Americans, he emigrated late in 1925 to enjoy this fount of easy money.

Within a few weeks he was back in action. In Washington DC, he met a Texas cattleman admiring the White House. Pretending to be a government agent, Furguson spun a slender yarn about how the administration was looking for ways of cutting costs. Now, if the Texan would care to lease the White House at a knockdown rent of $100,000 a year . . .? Furguson was in business again.

Moving on to New York, the wily Scotsman explained to an Australian visitor that, because of a proposed scheme for widening New York Harbour, the Statue of Liberty would have to be dismantled and sold. A great loss to the US, but would it not look good in Sydney Harbour . . .? The Australian immediately began to raise the $100,000 that the conman asked for the statue. But his bankers advised him to make further inquiries, and the police were tipped off.

This time Furguson had really slipped up. He had

allowed the Australian visitor to take a souvenir snapshot of himself with the Statue of Liberty in the background. Police were immediately able to identify him as a man they had been watching.

Furguson was arrested, and a court sentenced him to five years in jail. When he came out, the master-hoaxer retired from the ancient monuments business and, until his death in 1938, lived in California – languishing in luxury on his ill-gotten gains.

The Bouncing Czech Who Sold the Eiffel Tower at a Knock-down Price!

The idea came to Victor Lustig in a flash. There he was lounging in his Paris hotel room in March 1925 idly perusing the newspapers when he came across an item that made his eyes widen. The Eiffel Tower, said the report, was in need of major renovation. It had been suggested that the city's most famous landmark should be demolished and rebuilt . . .

To an artist, inspiration can come in a flash – and Victor Lustig was nothing if not an artist. The only difference was that his art was outside the law – he was a genius at deception. And the news item in that Paris paper opened up the opportunity for the coolest confidence trick of the present century.

First, Lustig (or 'Count Lustig', as he styled himself) acquired some printed notepaper from the French Ministry of Posts, which was responsible for maintaining the monument, and invited five French businessmen to a secret meeting at the Crillon Hotel, Paris.

When they arrived, they were ushered into a private

suite by Lustig's 'ministerial secretary', a fellow conman named Robert Tourbillon. The five were then sworn to secrecy and told the terrible news: that the Eiffel Tower was in a dangerous condition and would have to be pulled down.

There was sure to be a public outcry over the demolition of such a well-loved national monument, so the French Government had to ensure total security. This was why five highly respectable and trusted members of the business community had been specially chosen for their loyalty and discretion.

The five flattered fools fell for Lustig's ruse completely. They each agreed to submit tenders for the value of the 7,000 tons of scrap metal that would be produced by demolishing the tower. Then they went away to make their calculations.

Lustig, however, had already picked out his candidate, a scrap-metal merchant named André Poisson, one of the provincial nouveaux riches anxious to make a name for himself in the Paris business world. When, within the week, all five bids were in, Lustig accepted Poisson's and invited him back to the hotel to give him the good news.

It was then that the conman played his master stroke. He asked Poisson for a bribe to help the deal go smoothly through official channels. The duped dealer agreed willingly, and gave the back-hander in cash. If he had ever had any suspicions, they were now allayed. After all, a demand for a bribe meant that Count Victor must be from the Ministry!

Poisson handed over a banker's draft. In return, he received an utterly worthless bill of sale.

Lustig and Tourbillon were out of the country within 24 hours. But they stayed abroad only long enough to realize that the outcry they had expected to follow their fraud had not materialized. Poisson was so ashamed at being taken for a ride that he never reported the hoax to the police.

The 'count' and his partner returned to Paris and repeated the trick. They sold the Eiffel Tower all over again to another gullible scrap merchant. This time the man did go to the police, and the conmen fled. They were never brought to justice, and they never revealed just how much money they had got away with.

To a man like Lustig, proud of his art, selling the Eiffel Tower not once but twice was the pinnacle of a long career in confidence trickery. Born in Czechoslovakia in 1890, he had worked his way through Europe, using 22 aliases and being arrested 45 times.

He emigrated to America – but found the pickings so rich among the wealthy passengers on his Atlantic liner that he returned to make the transatlantic trip over and over again!

During the roaring 1920s, when 'making a fast buck' seemed to be all that life was about, Lustig preyed on the avarice of the greedy and gullible.

His cardinal rule when setting up a 'prospect' was to listen. Lustig never sold hard; he always let his victim do the talking, while the conman showed deep interest. He would seek out his victim's political views and religious preferences and concur wholeheartedly to make him feel he had found a kindred spirit. But, at the end of the day, the most crucial common interest would always be money.

Rags-to-riches multi-millionaire Herbert Loller had amassed all the money he could ever need. But he still wanted more, however dubiously it was acquired. Lustig demonstrated to him a machine which duplicated banknotes, and sold it to him for $25,000. Of course, it never worked. But, by the time Loller discovered the fact, Lustig had disappeared to the next town, with another name and a new identity.

In the bootlegging days, Lustig insinuated himself into the company of Al Capone. It took a very brave, or perhaps foolhardy, man to tangle with the Chicago gangster, but Lustig actually tried to swindle him out of $50,000. The conman told him he had a system that would ensure he doubled his money on Wall Street within two months.

Lustig took the money but after a while he got cold feet and returned the $50,000 intact to Capone. The gangster must have taken a liking to the genial fraudster, because he forgave him and even gave him a $5,000 'tip' for his troubles.

Lustig's associations with the Capone gang continued for several years and led the trickster into an area of crime in which he found himself out of his class. That crime was counterfeiting.

By 1934 a special team of federal agents had been assigned to capture Lustig and his old Capone associate William Watts and to stem the flow of forged $100 bills which the pair were producing at the rate of $100,000 a month.

After tapping their phones for several months, the agents thought they had enough evidence. The pair were arrested and, although Lustig offered to reveal the whereabouts of the counterfeit engraving plates if he were freed, he was thrown into New York's dreaded Tombs prison.

He didn't remain there long. One morning wardens found his cell empty and a sheet missing. They discovered it dangling from a window. Lustig had gone to ground again.

The master fraudster may well have learned his lesson by now. After his jailbreak he fled to Pittsburgh and took on identity number 23 – that of quiet, retiring Mr Robert Miller. But luck was against him. A tip-off led police to his apartment and, after arrest number 47, he was put back in jail to await trial.

The outcome was the worst Lustig could have expected.

In December 1945 he was found guilty of distributing a staggering $134,000,000 in counterfeit bills and was sentenced to 20 years' imprisonment – the first part of it to be served on the escape-proof island of Alcatraz.

'Count' Victor Lustig, king of the conmen, served only 11 years of his sentence. He died in Springfield Prison, Missouri, in March 1947.

But what of Lustig's partner, Robert Arthur Tourbillon, the man who acted out the role of his 'secretary' in the greatest confidence trick of the century, the sale of the Eiffel Tower? Tourbillon, or 'Dapper Dan Colins' as the police knew him, had almost as amazing career as Lustig himself.

Born in 1885, Tourbillon's first job was as a lion-tamer in a French circus. His act was called the Circle of Death and it involved him riding a bicycle around a pride of lions. Circus life was too tame, however, and at an early age he turned to crime.

He was 23 when he emigrated to America and was 31 when he when he first went to jail – for, of all things, 'white slavery'. He emerged from a prison four years later determined to stick to the one crime he was best at: fraud. Until then, he had been known among the criminal fraternity as the Rat (after his initials) but he now styled himself 'Dapper Dan Colins', bought himself the smartest clothes in New York and set sail for his homeland, France.

He lived for several years in Paris, mainly off the proceeds of rich, old ladies who fell for the Casanova charm of this suave 'American'. In 1925 he and Victor Lustig pulled off their Eiffel Tower fraud and afterwards both men went to ground.

Further bad luck brought Tourbillon to the end of the road. Two American detectives who were in Paris with an extradition warrant for another crook heard about the suspicious exploits of 'Dapper Dan', sought him out – and recognized 'the Rat'. They arrested him and returned him

to New York aboard the liner *France*. It was an amazing
voyage. Tourbillon was given the freedom of the ship,
and, on his money, the trip turned into one large party for
passengers, crew, criminal and detectives.

Amazingly, when the liner reached New York and
Tourbillon was arraigned before a court, the robbery
charges that had been brought against him failed to stick
and he was freed. But not for long . . .

In 1929, Tourbillon was charged with defrauding a New
Jersey farmer out of $30,000 savings and was jailed for two
years. He served 16 months and left jail vowing to return
to France. Whether he did so or not no one knows – for,
after speaking to reporters outside the jail, Tourbillon was
never heard of again.

The Great Howard Hughes
Rip-off

It was billed as the publishing coup of the decade. But it
proved to be the literary hoax of the century. The project
was the 'autobiography' of the richest eccentric in the
world, the legendary multi-millionaire recluse Howard
Hughes.

The man behind this ambitious venture was an author
named Clifford Irving, a man who, despite never having
met Hughes, planned to write the mystery man's life
story and sell the book to a publisher as being Hughes's
own words.

Hughes was a sick, semi-senile man, possibly drug-
addicted, and a fanatical recluse. He would allow nobody
near him apart from the tight circle of Mormon male
nurses who tended his needs in a succession of hotel
suites around the world.

Clifford Irving was an altogether different character.

Born in New York in 1930, he was an incurable adventurer. Educated at art college and Cornell University, he sailed the Atlantic and lived with California's beatniks and Kashmir's drop-outs. He ended his ramblings when he married a pretty, slim blonde named Edith and settled down to write on the Mediterranean island of Ibiza.

His New York publishers, McGraw-Hill, encouraged him in his work and he obtained moderate success. It was McGraw-Hill to whom Irving turned when he wanted to sell his 'publishing coup of the century'.

Irving's amazing lie was this. He had sent a copy of one of his own books to Howard Hughes for his critical comments. Hughes had replied in the kindest terms. The two had hit it off so well that Irving had boldly suggested 'ghosting' a Howard Hughes autobiography. And, to Irving's surprise, the old recluse had agreed.

McGraw-Hill fell for the bait. They agreed that Hughes would receive a hefty payment for allowing a series of tape-recorded interviews with Irving. And, of course, the author himself was to get large advances on the project. The total sum: one-and-a-half million dollars!

None of this went to Hughes. Roughly half of it was paid out – and all went into Irving's pocket. Not that it stayed there for long. The spendthrift author splashed out on luxury trips around the world. Wherever he went, he claimed to be keeping secret appointments with Hughes or his associates.

McGraw-Hill constantly fired off telegrams to Irving inquiring about the progress of the book. The author would reply from one five-star hotel or another, stressing the extreme difficulties of his task and Hughes's paranoid insistence on secrecy. Craftily, he maintained the publishers' interest by mailing them sample sections of the manuscript and providing letters supposedly sent to him by Hughes.

The sample chapters contained tantalizing quotations

supposedly transcribed from tape-recordings made by Irving with Hughes. Some conversations were said to have taken place over the phone, others in person. The contents of the texts were mainly lies – but lies cleverly intertwined with rumour and half-truth and embroidered with the gleanings of newspaper libraries.

Irving's art-school training came in useful at this stage. For the letters signed by Hughes were in reality written by Irving himself. The forgeries were so perfect that they fully satisfied the more doubtful sceptics at McGraw-Hill. At one stage, when the publishers became worried about the delay in receiving substantial parts of the manuscript, they secretly took the Hughes letters to New York's leading handwriting analysts – who confirmed without doubt that they were indeed written by the old man.

Not all of Irving's work was pure fiction, however. The author had a secret source of hitherto unpublished revelations about the recluse. The source was Hughes's former aide, Noah Dietrich, who made copious notes about his long liaison with the billionaire. Dietrich had been planning to turn this material into a book of his own. But Irving secretly borrowed the aide's notes, copied them and proceeded to lift from them some of the more interesting tit-bits.

McGraw-Hill were well and truly hooked. Tempted by fantastic stories of Hughes's secret World War II missions, of his friendship with novelist Ernest Hemingway and of his glamorous, globe-trotting lifestyle, they kept the money pouring in. It arrived by post in the form of cheques made out to Hughes. They were paid into a Swiss bank account but the money did not remain there for long. The account, in the name of H.R. Hughes, had been opened by Edith Irving, using a passport forged by her husband.

Irving must have known that his amazing confidence trick could not last for ever. But when the crash came it was from the most unexpected direction. By an amazing coincidence, someone else had been plotting a similar scheme to Irving's. A rival publishing house had taken the bait and proudly announced that an authorized biography of Hughes was shortly to be printed.

For a while, panic reigned at McGraw-Hill. The scene of confusion was repeated at the Time-Life organization which had agreed to buy the serialization rights to the Irving book. But the man at the centre of the storm remained as cool as ever. Irving produced a new forged letter from Hughes denouncing the rival book as a fake – and demanding more money for his own.

Raising the price was a master stroke. McGraw-Hill once again fell for Irving's tale. But for the first time they had to show their own hand and announce the existence of the Irving book.

That sealed the conman's fate. Hughes ordered his lawyers to hold a press conference at which reporters who had followed the astonishing saga of the billionaire recluse were allowed to question Hughes by telephone. The Irving 'autobiography' was denounced, yet the trickster continued his protestations of innocence.

The man who finally shattered Irving's story was Robert Dolan Peloquin, a super-sleuth who had won the title 'Sherlock Holmes of the jet age'. This handsome 6ft 1in American lawyer had spent 16 years in the service of the US Government, taking on the conmen of the Mafia and the sophisticated criminals of the computer world. He was one of Bobby Kennedy's closest aides when the assassinated politician was America's Attorney-General.

Peloquin later left government service to become president of Intertel, a private international intelligence agency based in Washington DC, with branches throughout the world. Ex-Scotland Yard head of CID Sir Ranulph Bacon joined him on the staff of what has been called 'the world's most formidable private investigating firm'.

It was at Intertel that Peloquin took a call from Chester Davis, lawyer for legendary recluse Hughes, who was alarmed at impending publication of the 'autobiography', and wanted Peloquin to prove the book was a fraud.

This meant knocking holes in publisher McGraw-Hill's claim that Hughes had collaborated with Irving. They based their claim on cheques made out to and endorsed by H.R. Hughes, and deposited in a numbered Swiss bank account. McGraw-Hill said handwriting experts had verified the signature on each of them as that of Howard Hughes. But they refused to let Intertel see the cheques for themselves.

The controversy over the book was headline news. And that helped Peloquin get the evidence he needed. An executive of McGraw-Hill went on America's early-morning 'Today' TV programme, brandishing three cheques worth a total of $650,000 and cashed by H.R. Hughes. Peloquin immediately obtained a video-tape of the show, froze the frames where the cheques appeared, and had enlargements made of the prints.

It was just possible to see the name of the Zurich bank which had endorsed the payments. Peloquin was on the first available plane.

In Zurich, he was told that H.R. Hughes was a woman. Her description gave him a hunch. He phoned his Washington HQ and asked for a photograph to be wired to him. Four hours later he was back in the bank. The woman in the picture had her hair in a different style, but officials were almost sure she was H.R. Hughes. The picture, of course, was of Irving's wife.

Within minutes, the information had been cabled to Chester Davis, who called in the US Attorney in Manhattan. Irving and his wife were arrested.

Irving denied all until the very end. But his lies were

finally seen for what they were when internationally famous singer Nina, the beautiful blonde half of the Nina and Frederick folk duo, revealed that, at a time when Irving had supposedly been closeted with Howard Hughes, the author had really been with her.

In 1972, Edith Irving, distraught over the stories of her husband's womanizing, was sent to jail for two years in Switzerland. After hearing her sentenced, Irving sobbed: 'I have put my wife in jeopardy. She has suffered terribly. I have heard her cry herself to sleep at night.'

Then he too went down. After cracking and confessing all, Irving was fined $10,000 and sentenced to 30 months' jail in the USA. He was also ordered to pay back some of the $500,000 he owed McGraw-Hill.

Edith Irving served only 14 months of her sentence and her husband 17 months. But they were never reunited. Edith won a divorce and remarried her husband's former tennis partner. Clifford himself moved down to Mexico with a young woman friend.

There he set about writing another book, legitimately this time. It was a detailed, dramatic account of how he pulled off his $1.5 million superhoax. He needed to sell well in order to pay off his huge debts. And, ironically, the book was given a huge and topical sales boost soon after with the death in 1975 of the one man whose fabulous wealth had made the hoax of the century possible – Howard Hughes.

The Underground 'Mole' Behind the World's Biggest Bank Robbery

The 1976 raid on the Nice branch of the Société-Générale was the biggest bank robbery ever. Afterwards, owners of rifled strongboxes put in claims totalling £6 million, but

French police believe the haul could have been nearer £50 million.

Most of the raiders, who tunnelled from a sewer into the bank's vaults, were never caught. The mastermind, Albert Spaggiari, was arrested but escaped from a courtroom and was believed to have headed for South America. To the French, he became something of a cult hero. He even wrote a book about the robbery, which was made into a film.

Spaggiari evidently set his heart on big-time crime in his teens. At 16 he applied in writing to join a group of Sicilian bandits, but received no reply. Two years later he joined the army as a paratrooper in Indo-China, where he had three citations for bravery in action. But after staging a robbery at a nightclub he was courtmartialled, jailed and dishonourably discharged.

He then joined the OAS and went to Algeria. The OAS hated France's President, General de Gaulle, and Spaggiari claimed to have organized an assassination attempt – along the lines of the one featured in Frederick Forsyth's thriller, *Day of the Jackal*. When de Gaulle visited Nice, Spaggiari had him in the sights of a rifle from the upper window of his mother's shop. The reason he did not want to fire was that his OAS chief failed to give the order.

A year later Spaggiari was arrested with four accomplices for printing and distributing right-wing pamphlets. Police searching their print shop and homes discovered an illegal cache of arms and ammunition. Because of his previous record, Spaggiari got four years' imprisonment, while his friends were put on probation.

After his release, he became a photographer, opening a shop and specializing in smart weddings and pictures of the rich and famous who pass through Nice.

His work brought him in contact with the town's top people, and he cultivated a friendship with the mayor,

Jacques Médicin. Later Médicin became France's Minister of Tourism and took Spaggiari with him on a tour of Japan as his official photographer.

Spaggiari used the profits from his photographic business to invest in a chicken farm in the hills. He lived there with his wife Baudi, his collection of German Imperial Army spiked helmets and an armoury of guns, ammunition and explosives. It was at the farm that he and his accomplices plotted the biggest bank raid ever.

Spaggiari, lean and handsome and always smoking a big Dom Miguel cigar, was a popular and respected character in Nice.

The city was considered by many to be the crime capital of southern France, having inherited the dubious honour from Marseilles. Violence and gang warfare were a part of everyday life. At stake were the rich pickings from drugs, vice and robberies.

Much of the illicit profit ended up in safe-deposit boxes in bank vaults. Other boxes in the vaults of the Société-Générale would have held assets undeclared for tax reasons. Many victims of Spaggiari's raid claimed much less than they had lost – for fear of attracting the attention of the tax inspectors or the police.

Some of the boxes broken open by thieves held humble secrets. One was filled with coffee, sugar and biscuits, presumably hoarded in case of the outbreak of World War III. Others held chocolates, toffees, cigarettes and flasks of alcohol, belonging to secret smokers, drinkers and dieters who could not resist the occasional lapse.

Spaggiari is thought to have got hold of a map of the town's sewer system with the help of a highly placed town-hall official. He rented a safe-deposit box at the Société-Générale to note the layout and security system.

To check for electronic sensors, he left a wound-up alarm clock in his box, to see if its ringing set off detectors. It did not. There was no alarm system in the vaults because they were considered impregnable. The walls were 5 ft thick.

Spaggiari decided to tunnel from the nearest sewer to the vaults, then break through the masonry walls with electric drills. After 18 months' planning, the gang entered the sewer system via a small underground river.

They reached the vaults of the Société-Générale by digging a tunnel 24ft long and 4ft high. It took them two months, working by night and laboriously carrying their equipment in and out every evening and morning. They carried the soil away in plastic sacks, to dump in the hills above Nice. The tunnel, supported at the correct intervals by jacks, was constructed so professionally that when police discovered it they first checked on ex-miners.

The gang broke through to the vaults on the evening of Friday 20 July 1976. They brought in an air pump to set up a ventilation system. Then they opened safe-deposit boxes with jemmies, taking notes, gold and jewellery, and scattering share certificates and private documents over the floor.

The gang could have worked undisturbed until the early hours of Monday morning but for one piece of bad luck – rain.

Their getaway sewer was a main storm drain. A heavy downpour threatened to flood it and on Sunday the gang made a hurried escape in rubber dinghies after rifling 317 of the 4,000 deposit boxes in the vaults.

Before leaving, they welded shut the door leading to the bank to give themselves a few more hours before the robbery was discovered. A bank employee who tried the door on Monday morning assumed it was stuck and it was not until lunchtime that a professional was called in to cut through it.

In their haste, Spaggiari and his gang left behind thousands of pounds' worth of equipment. Police found heavy-duty blowtorches, 27 gas cylinders, 11 crowbars, pit-props, sledgehammers, jemmies, bolt-cutters, lamps, hacksaws, rope, pliers, hammers, spanners, drills, cooking stoves, eating utensils, empty wine bottles and the remains of meals. On one wall was scrawled the message 'Without anger, without violence, without hatred'. Above it was the peace symbol.

While bank employees were still trying to free their welded-up vault door, the raiders were counting their loot, a task which took them from Monday morning until Wednesday evening.

Spaggiari was eventually traced through a shop from which he had bought equipment for the raid – and by the Dom Miguel cigar butts found in the vaults.

On 10 March 1977, Spaggiari was being questioned by an examining magistrate about the disposal of the loot, which he steadfastly claimed to have handed over to an underground OAS-style group. The prisoner complained to the magistrate that the room was stuffy and moved towards a window, apparently for some fresh air. He threw the tall casement open and jumped.

Spaggiari fell 20 ft, landed with an expert paratrooper's roll on a parked car, and sprang onto the the pillion of a waiting motorbike. As he sped away, he turned and made a rude gesture to the police. After a 15-minute journey to the airport, he caught the early evening flight to Zurich.

After his escape, sightings were reported in Spain and South America. But it was felt in France that some police were only half-hearted in their efforts to catch the thief whom many regarded as a folk hero.

The Match King
Who Struck It Rich

Ivar Kreugar struck it rich and created one of the biggest financial empires ever seen. The wily Swede, who captured almost three-quarters of the world's supply of safety matches, built his entire empire on a gigantic fraud. He conned millions of pounds from investors and banks in Europe and America before the bubble burst in 1932 and Kreugar – the man the world knew as the Match King – shot himself through the heart in his Paris apartment.

Kreugar was already a rich man when he embarked on his mammoth fraud. Born in Kalmar, Sweden, in 1880, he went to America when he was 19. When he returned to Sweden in 1908, he had amassed a tidy sum from dealing in South African gold and diamond shares.

Once home, he went into partnership with a friend called Toll. Between them they set up a building company which went from strength to strength, using many new techniques Kreugar had picked up while in America.

By 1914 Kreugar and Toll were wealthy. Then, suddenly, Kreugar quit and took over his family's ailing match business. He had taken the first steps on the rocky road of fame, fortune and suicide.

Kreugar was ruthless. By 1917 he had created the Swedish Match Company, of which he was President, by taking over or crushing all his competitors.

From this position of strength, he began to build a succession of companies. Each one was tied to the next by such a complicated web that only Kreugar knew how it all strung together. He wrote his own company reports and declared the profits and dividends.

Kreugar had such tight control of his empire that everyone believed his valuation of its profits. It was almost impossible for anyone to unravel the deliberately complex figures in his reports.

Kreugar wanted desperately to be known as the world's number one wheeler-dealer. He was already leading a frantic life of fast cars and mistresses in many European capitals when he decided to build himself a massive headquarters in Stockholm.

It was a huge commercial palace full of marble columns and fountains. His own office was magnificent with rich carpets, mahogany panels, beautiful decorations and a bank of telephones on his desk to impress even the most important clients.

By 1921 Kreugar had established such a reputation and had such vast reserves of money available to him through investors and bank loans that he could embark on his financial plan – to control the world's match market.

He knew what he wanted and he didn't care how he got it. If a rival company wouldn't sell, Kreugar either cut off their supplies of raw materials or sent in the thugs on his payroll to persuade or blackmail them into submission.

By 1922 the match industries of Sweden, Norway, Denmark, Finland and Belgium were in his hands.

In countries where the match industries were state-owned he simply offered to make loans to the governments in return for the right to total control of the industry. To do this he needed money – many millions, all of which he raised in America by persuading bankers and private investors to sink their cash into yet another of his new companies.

Much of the money went straight into Swiss banks. Not because he wanted to steal it – he just wanted it under his control so that he could use it as and when he wanted.

Over the next two years he loaned more than £150 million to 20 countries, giving him control of 65 per cent of the world's match production.

But the Wall Street stock-market crash of 1929 sealed the

fate of the Match King. As credit began to dry up all over the world, so many of Kreugar's clients who had borrowed money began to miss their repayments.

At the same time Kreugar still had to find the money for the governments to whom he had promised loans. He had to retain the confidence of his investors and creditors or his financial edifice would collapse.

He even resorted to straight trickery to get new loans from banks, using a receipt from one bank to get credit from another.

The final reckoning came in 1931 when he tried to sell one of his companies to the giant American-owned ITT corporation. Their investigation of the company books showed £7 million was missing. They called off the deal.

When the news broke, everyone wanted their money out of the Kreugar companies.

The Match King tried desperately to keep up the price of his shares by buying them with millions of pounds of his own money. But it was to no avail. The following year, when he heard the Swedish Bank were investigating one of his phoney deals involving forged Italian bonds, he went to his Paris flat and shot himself.

It has been said that Kreugar never intended to keep the money he conned for his personal use. If that had been the case, he would simply have disappeared when things started to go wrong instead of spending his personal fortune trying to prop up his empire.

No, say many who knew him, he just wanted to be number one.

How the Great Escaper
Became a Runaway Success

A handsome weatherbeaten man of 52 strode out to greet waiting crowds in Bridgetown, Barbados. His reception was tumultuous. In the carnival atmosphere of cheering and singing, he announced exultantly: 'Champagne for everyone – the drinks are on me!'

Yet the hero of the moment was no popular republican, no victorious sportsman. He was a crook – and not a very good one at that. His name: Ronald Biggs.

In 1963, 18 years earlier, a gang of thieves held up a mail train at a remote spot in the English countryside and got away with £2.5 million in used banknotes. The daring robbery was labelled the crime of the century.

Best-known of the so-called Great Train Robbers was Ronnie Biggs. Not because he was one of the gang leaders – his part in the raid was relatively minor – but because of his amazing ability, after later escaping from jail, to keep one step ahead of the law.

Every night used banknotes were sent from Scotland by rail to London to be destroyed. The money travelled in a special coach which formed part of the regular night train from Glasgow to Euston. The amount varied but always rose dramatically after a Bank Holiday. On 3 August, the gang believed, it might be as much as £4 million.

The gang were a colourful bunch. Principal among them were: Bruce Reynolds, aged 30, fond of the 'good life', who considered himself a cut above London's East End criminal fraternity; Gordon Goody, a 32-year-old tough loner with a sharp taste in clothes and girls; Ronald 'Buster' Edwards, aged 30, club-owner, and devoted family man; Charles Wilson, 32, a resourceful criminal friend of Reynolds; Jimmy White, a quiet 42-year-old ex-paratrooper; Bob Welch, 32, a South London club-owner; Tommy Wiseby, a 32-year-old bookmaker; and Jim Hessey, aged 30, who ran a Soho restaurant.

The gang also bought in three specialists: 'wheels' man Roy James, 23, a silversmith and racing driver; Roger Cordrey, a 38-year-old florist who was an expert at 'adjusting' railway signalling equipment; and a retired train driver.

At the last minute, they also recruited a small-time thief and decorator, with a pretty wife, engaging smile and a yearning for the luxury life he could never afford. His name was Ronald Biggs.

Bridego Bridge in Buckinghamshire was the lonely spot where the gang decided to rob the train. Their base was isolated Leatherslade Farm, 26 miles away.

At around midnight on August 2, these motley 'soldiers' of fortune, dressed in an assortment of commando gear, set out from the farm for Bridego Bridge with two Land Rovers and a lorry.

Cordrey switched on two warning lights – one several hundred yards up the track, another closer to the bridge. The first would cause the train to slow, the second would bring it to a halt. The gang also cut the lines to trackside emergency telephones and to nearby farms and cottages.

Aboard the train at precisely 3am, driver Jack Mills looked out for the usual green trackside light. But tonight it was amber. He put on the brakes and throttled back the mighty diesel. The overhead signal gantry came into sight. It glowed red. Mills stopped the train and asked his fireman, David Whitby, to use the emergency telephone beside the gantry to find out what was going on.

Whitby vanished into the darkness, Mills heard him ask someone: 'What's up, mate?' Then nothing. In fact, Whitby had run into Buster Edwards. Bundled down the embankment, he was pinioned to the ground.

Back in the cab of the train, driver Mills was being

attacked from both sides. He was overpowered from behind and hit twice across the head.

The engine and two front coaches, including the one carrying the money, were separated from the train and were moved the short distance to the bridge by the ex-driver. The gang then smashed the doors and windows of the High Value Packages Coach with an axe and crowbars. Five Post Office guards were made to lie on the floor while the gang unloaded 120 mailbags along a human chain which led down the embankment and into the back of the lorry.

Then, sweating but jubilant, they drove back in their convoy to Leatherslade Farm. All had gone according to plan, but for the blow on the head received by driver Mills. It proved to be a big 'but' – for that moment of violence weighed heavily against the robbers at their trial.

But, for the time being, the future looked rosy. The gang spent the rest of the night counting out the money, setting aside sums for major bribes and back-handers, and sharing out the rest. In all, there was £2.5 million.

Having concocted their alibis and arranged to salt away their shares until the hue and cry was over, they went their separate ways, brimming with confidence. It was short-lived . . .

Damning evidence had been left behind – fingerprints, clothing and vehicles. Although the robbers had arranged for an associate to stay at the farm and clean it from top to bottom, the job was never done. The contract was bungled.

Detectives had no difficulty in identifying the men from fingerprints and palm prints. A Monopoly board was a mine of information to forensic scientists. Soon the faces of the robbers were on wanted posters all over Britain.

Within a year, most were in jail. The sentences meted out for 'a crime against society' shook the thieves – and created public sympathy. Goody, Welch, James, Wiseby and Hessey all got 30 years, although they were eventually released after serving 12. Wilson and Biggs also got a 30-year term. Cordrey was given 14 years and freed after seven. But some of the robbers were to give the police enormous trouble in the years to come.

White evaded arrest for three years before being captured in 1965, and was jailed for 18 years, of which he served nine.

Reynolds and Edwards hid out in London for almost a year, then fled to Mexico City. They spent money at a frightening rate and both eventually returned to Britain.

In 1966 Edwards surrendered. He was given a 15-year sentence and served nine. Reynolds was arrested on 1968 and received 25 years. He was released in 1978.

In prison the train robbers were kept under the closest security because two of them had made sensational escapes . . .

In 1965 Wilson escaped from Winson Green Prison, Birmingham, and joined Reynolds in Mexico City. But he too tired of the place and moved to a smart home near Montreal, where he was caught in 1968. He returned to continue his 30-year sentence and was freed 10 years later.

The second escape was even more sensational – and launched a criminal legend. In July 1965 Ronald Biggs was 'sprung' from London's Wandsworth Prison by a daring group of associates. He scaled the wall and landed on the roof of a waiting furniture van.

After undergoing plastic surgery in France to restyle his nose and cheekbones, Biggs collected some of his share of the loot and flew to Australia. He set up home in a Melbourne suburb, took a job as a carpenter and was joined by his wife Charmaine and their three sons. There they lived under assumed names for several years, with only one event to mar their happiness – the death in a car crash of their eldest son.

Eventually Biggs received a tip-off that Scotland Yard

detectives were on to him and that he was in imminent danger of arrest. This time he fled to Brazil.

Life without his family was difficult. He settled near Rio de Janeiro and sought solace in drugs, alcohol and women.

Early in 1974 a reporter of a London newspaper tracked him down and set about writing his story. But the paper's executives tipped off Scotland Yard about their projected scoop. On 1 February 1974, Chief Superintendent Jack Slipper and another police officer arrived in Rio to arrest Biggs. To their dismay they learned that Brazil had no extradition agreement with Britain. The Rio police refused to hand him over.

Then Biggs's young Brazilian girlfriend, Raimunda, announced that she was pregnant. It was news that left the lucky father-to-be overjoyed – simply because the father of any Brazilian child could not be deported.

So Biggs went free again. And Slipper, after his much-publicized swoop, flew home alone.

It was not till 1981 that the great escaper found himself back in prison, thanks not to Scotland Yard but to a gang of kidnappers.

Masterminding the kidnap plot was 36-year-old ex-British army sergeant John Miller. He and his four-man team arrived in Rio in April and befriended the unsuspecting Biggs, long separated from Raimunda but living with six-year-old son Mike. One night, outside a Copacabana bar, the gang overpowered him, gagged him and stuffed him inside a sack, which they bundled into a waiting van.

Biggs was smuggled out of the country through the northern port of Belem, put aboard a chartered yacht and taken outside Brazilian territorial waters.

The kidnappers and their hostage sailed north to the Caribbean where, in an extraordinary auction, the hapless Biggs was held to ransom.

Ringleader Miller based himself at a Barbados hotel and told the assembled representatives of the press that he would 'sell' Biggs to the highest bidder.

But now the operation went wrong. The yacht on which Biggs was held broke down and, as it drifted into Barbados waters, it was seized by coastguards. The kidnappers quietly dispersed and Biggs was thrown into prison to await extradition to Britain.

As Biggs languished in a cockroach-infested cell in Bridgetown, Barbados, hope must have almost gone. Extradition was surely only a formality. But it proved otherwise.

Biggs's closest friends in Rio were Cockney John Pickston and his Brazilian wife Lia. They hired top lawyer Ezra Alleyne to fight the extradition. After three weeks of legal wrangling, the island's Chief Justice, Sir William Douglas, ruled that the extradition treaty between Barbados and Britain was not valid.

Biggs walked free with £30,000 for the costs of his case.

The crowds outside the court swept him through the streets in an impromptu display of Caribbean dancing. The delighted Biggs shouted: 'Isn't it bloody marvellous? I just don't believe it. Champagne for everyone.'

Even more emotional was Biggs's return to Brazil. At Rio airport the tough train robber was reduced to tears as he was reunited with son Mike.

They clung to one another as Biggs said: 'I didn't know if I would ever see you again.' He gave the boy a table- tennis game he had spent the last of his money on. And little Mike gave his father an Easter egg and 20 pictures he had painted – all inscribed 'Welcome home Daddy'.

Then the ex-train robber was handed a brand-new Brazilian passport, an amazing gesture by the adopted country where he had become a national hero. He waved the passport above his head and vowed: 'This marks a new chapter in my life. I am now able officially to work for a living. I'm going to get a job . . . anything honest!'

The Master-faker Who Even Took Göring for a Ride

How many of the treasures of the world's museums and art galleries are genuine and how many are fakes will probably never be known. The art forgers are just too clever for most experts.

According to ex-forger David Stein: 'I can open an art catalogue anywhere in the world and recognize my own work.' Master-faker Elmyr de Hory said of the experts: 'They know more about fine words than fine art.' And Hans van Meegeren described them as 'arrogant scum'.

Van Meegeren is recognized as the greatest art forger of all time. But his criminal career was revealed only through the most amazing sequence of events . . .

After the fall of Nazi Germany in 1945, Hermann Göring's priceless collection of old masters was uncovered at his Berchtesgaden mansion. Most had been looted from churches, galleries and private collections during the German march through Europe. A few, however, had been honestly purchased, and one of these was a painting entitled *Woman Taken in Adultery*. It was signed by Jan Vermeer, the 17th-century Dutch master.

In those first days after the war's end, the hunt was on throughout newly liberated Europe for collaborators. And when it was discovered that Göring's agents had paid £160,000 for the painting from a dealer in Amsterdam, Dutch police thought they had found someone who had been too generous to the Nazis. That someone was van Meegeren.

At that time van Meegeren was a rich nightclub-owner

309

who had amassed a small fortune by selling previously undiscovered old masters to major art galleries. Apart from the painting purchased by Göring, he had sold six other works signed by Vermeer to Dutch galleries.

Van Meegeren was arrested and thrown into prison to await trial as a collaborator – a charge which could carry the death sentence. He was interrogated daily for three weeks without changing his story. Then, when he was finally brought to court, he came up with the most astonishing defence.

He said that, far from collaborating with the Nazis, he had actually duped them. He had not sold Göring a Vermeer but a van Meegeren – the old master's work was a fake he had painted himself. And he had sold dozens of others for vast sums around the world.

At first the judge did not believe him. But he gave van Meegeren a chance. Placed under guard in his Amsterdam studio, he was told to paint another Vermeer that would fool the experts. He did so – it was titled *Jesus Among the Doctors* – and he was freed.

The master-forger's freedom was, however, short-lived. For as more and more van Meegerens came to light, he was brought to trial again, this time charged with deception. He was jailed for 12 months, but died of a heart attack six weeks later at the age of 57.

What made van Meegeren embark on his career of forgery? Surprisingly, in view of the huge sums his fakes fetched, the motive was not money. Van Meegeren was a relatively successful painter who had his first major exhibition at The Hague when he was 33. It was a sellout, yet the critics slated it.

Foremost among them was a pompous professor, Dr Abraham Bredius, who dismissed van Meegeren's work with contempt. Over the years, the struggling painter's pent-up anger and frustration over Bredius's attacks found an outlet. Van Meegeren began to paint copies of the works of the artist whom Dr Bredius admired most of all: Vermeer.

Throughout 1936 van Meegeren remained in self-imposed exile in a rented villa in France, working on his masterpiece, a perfectly executed 'Vermeer' which he titled *Christ and the Disciples at Emmaus*. He 'aged' the painting 300 years by a process he had painstakingly developed.

In 1937 he put the painting on the market through a Paris lawyer, claiming that it had been in the possession of a Dutch family living in France. The family, so the story went, had fallen on hard times and now needed to sell their heirloom.

Naturally enough, the lawyer first approached Dr Bredius who, as the world's leading authority on Vermeer, could vouch for the painting's authenticity. He had no hesitation in doing so.

But not only did Bredius give his stamp of approval to the painting, he also – to van Meegeren's great delight – claimed the work as his own discovery. Bredius urged that it be bought for £50,000 by Rotterdam's Boyman's Museum. Bredius would often go there to study it – and van Meegeren to gloat over it.

Disgust at the ignorance of art 'experts' and anger at the dishonesty of dealers prompted another artist, Elmyr de Hory, to go into the faking business.

De Hory, a stateless Hungarian, received the greatest accolade of them all when another famous faker, Clifford Irving, the American author later jailed for his forged biography of Howard Hughes, wrote a book about the artist, entitling it simply *Fake*.

It was reported that paintings by the stateless Hungarian artist were among millions of dollars' worth of fakes sold to a Texas millionaire. The ensuing scandal made de Hory famous, although he insisted that he never put a famous signature to one of his paintings – even when that painting was in the precise style of a sought-after artist.

In 1974, at the age of 60, de Hory was taken from his home on the Spanish island of Ibiza and jailed on Majorca. There was no formal charge, and the artist was out again after four months.

Like so many with his talents, he never disguised his contempt for the international art pundits who 'know more about fine words than fine art'. He claimed he could paint a portrait in 45 minutes, draw a 'Modigliani' in 10 and then immediately knock off a 'Matisse'.

'The dealers, the experts and the critics resent my talent,' he said, 'because they don't want it shown how easily they can be fooled. I have tarnished the infallible image they rely upon for their fortunes.'

Almost as quick on the draw as de Hory, but displaying rather more daring, was another brilliant artist, David Stein, who for a brief but mind-boggling four-year reign was undisputed king of the art forgers.

He was a talented painter in his own right, but the high prices paid in the art world were too great a temptation to resist. Working in watercolours or oils, he recreated the styles of some of the world's best-known artists – living and dead.

The dead gave David Stein no trouble, but the living led to his downfall.

Pressed for time one day, he rushed off three watercolours he had promised a dealer. Working furiously in his New York apartment, the whole fateful operation took just seven hours. At six in the morning he was lying in bed dreaming up ideas for the paintings. At one o'clock the same day he was handing a satisfied art dealer the 'genuine' works of French artist Marc Chagall, each with its own certificate of authentication.

In those seven hours he had treated the paper he used with cold tea to give it the impression of aging, executed the watercolours, forged the certificates of authentication and Chagall's signature, and had the pictures professionally framed.

The art dealer was delighted when Stein handed over his 'find'. He examined the three forged Chagalls and, without ever suspecting the truth, began haggling with Stein over the price. Eventually a cheque for $10,000 changed hands.

The dealer was so proud of his new acquisitions that he determined to show them to someone who had newly arrived in New York – Marc Chagall himself. For, while Stein had busied himself with the forgeries, Chagall had been flying into the city to supervise the installation of two huge murals he had painted in the Metropolitan Opera House.

The dealer had already fixed an appointment to see Chagall and, at their meeting, expected that the great artist would be delighted to see three of his earlier works again. Chagall's reaction at first bewildered then horrified him. 'Diabolical!' said the Frenchman. 'They are not mine.'

Had 31-year-old Stein stuck to Cézannes, Renoirs or Manets, he would have got away with it. As it was, the police came to arrest him that evening. The daredevil forger said afterwards: 'As they arrived at my front door, I left through the back with a glass of Scotch in my hand!'

He made his way to California and it was there that his luck ran out. He was arrested and confessed all. 'If only I had stuck to dead men,' he moaned when he was later indicted on 97 counts of grand larceny and counterfeiting.

While in jail, Stein shared his knowledge of faking with the New York Police Department, helping them to create a special art forgery squad. With remission, he served just 16 months and, on his release, he left his three American galleries and half-a-million dollars a year income to return to his native Europe.

This was when the half-French, half-British Stein made

his second mistake. He had not realized that the French police also wanted to ask him a few questions. That error cost him another two-and-a-half years in jail.

In the early 1970, a free man at last, Stein decided to forget the old masters and stick to painting Steins. His fame as a brilliant forger aided his success and he later set up businesses and homes in both London and Paris.

But Stein was still angry at those people he regarded as the real fakers of the art world, the band of ignorant people who claim to be experts.

'A lot of the art world is fake,' he said. 'About two or three hundred of my forgeries are still on the market listed as originals.'

The Faker Famous for his 'Sexton Blakes'

Brilliant faker Tom Keating rocked the art world he despised with his amazing imitations of the works of great masters. In 1979, at the age of 62, he went on trial at the Old Bailey for forgery. But all the charges were dropped when his health deteriorated.

Keating, a big bearded ex-naval stoker, called his fakes, in Cockney rhyming slang, 'Sexton Blakes'. At first he painted them to get even with the dealers who had, he reckoned, exploited him.

As a young man, he had lived in a damp prefab with his wife and two children, and was paid £5 a time to copy other artists. He angrily quit the job when he found his paintings on sale in galleries for £500.

'Those dealers are just East End blokes in West End suits,' he said. 'They don't give a damn about the paintings. All they are after is the profit.'

In the 1950s his marriage broke up and he went to

Scotland to restore murals. While he was there he began imitating the works of other painters and sending them to auction.

He returned to London in 1960 for his most important commission – restoring the pictures in Marlborough House which had been empty since the death of Queen Mary in 1953.

One day he met Queen Elizabeth while carrying out the restoration of a giant painting by Laguerre of the Duke of Marlborough.

In his book, *The Fake's Progress*, Keating recalls: 'The Queen came up the stairs and gazed in astonishment. She turned to me and mentioned that she had run up and down the stairs hundreds of times as a little girl but had not been aware these beautiful pictures were on the wall. "Well, they are, madam," I said. 'And there's a lot more under the black varnish on the other walls." '

Then, according to Keating, the Queen watched him use a solvent to clean a section of the painting.

The work at Marlborough House was an isolated job for hard-up Keating. Most of his time would be spent turning out his 'Sexton Blakes' by the score, giving most of them away but selling others through auction rooms.

In 1963 he read a book on the 19th-century artist Samuel Palmer and became captivated by him. He scoured the art galleries looking for examples of Palmer's work to copy. At the Tate, said Keating, he touched one 'and a strange sensation went through me like an electric shock'.

Keating was a perfectionist. He was always careful about selecting the right paper or canvas. And he claimed that the spirit of Palmer would guide his hand.

'I'd sit in my little sketching room waiting for it to happen,' he explained. 'I have never drawn a sheep from life but then Palmer's sheep would begin to appear on the paper. Then Palmer's *Valley of Vision Watched Over by the Good Shepherd on the Shadows of Shoreham Church*. With

Sam's permission I sometimes signed them with his own name, but they were his, not mine. It was his hand that guided the pen.'

It was also in 1963 that Keating met Jane Kelly, a pretty convent-educated schoolgirl busy studying for her exams. In Bohemian coffee bars, she and her friends would cluster round the painter, treating him almost as a guru.

Jane was 17, Keating 46. Yet, after the death of her boyfriend in a road accident, they fell in love – and the impressionable teenager became the painter's mistress. They moved to historic Wattisfield Hall in Suffolk, where Jane restored pictures and Keating embarked on a prodigious output of fakes.

When, at the Old Bailey in 1979, Keating was shown his most famous fake – a sepia ink-wash of *Sepham Barn* sold for £9,400 as a genuine Palmer – he told the jury: 'I am ashamed of this piece of work.'

He had no recollection of painting it, he said. It had, however, been done using modern materials, the main figure of a shepherd was 'un-Palmerish' and the flock of sheep 'unsheep-like'. It was the sort of painting, he confessed, that he would normally have burned or thrown away.

Looking at another work subsequently sold for £2,550, Keating appeared bemused and said: 'That must have taken me about half an hour. It's just a doodle. It had the ingredients of Palmer but not his technical ability or aesthetic appeal.'

The 'doodle' was of a barn at Shoreham, which had been sold at a country auction for £35. It was later sold by a London gallery to Bedford Museum for £2,550 after restoration work by the National Gallery.

After the sale of *Sepham Barn*, Keating and Jane went to live in Tenerife. There, Jane met a Canadian with whom she fell in love and whom she later married. The nine-year affair between Jane and Keating was over. They met again seven years later – when Jane gave evidence at the Old Bailey about Keating's famous fakes. The scandal, which ruined many reputations in the art world, broke after an expert had written in *The Times* suggesting *Sepham Barn* was not genuine.

By Keating's own rough count, no fewer than 2,500 of his fake pictures are hanging in galleries or on collectors' walls. No one will ever know which are fakes and which are old masters. Not even Tom Keating who, after his trial was stopped, continued turning out his paintings – at a price.

Because of his notoriety, Keating's works became highly prized. 'Suddenly everyone wants to own a Keating,' said one gallery owner. 'Prices have doubled in a month. His paintings are going around the world.'

Keating was offered a £250,000 contract from one London gallery and a £30,000 commission for a single portrait. He turned both down.

'I have enough work to make me rich beyond my wildest dreams,' he said. 'But I've met many millionaires and they have all been miserable. All I have ever wanted to do is paint. I would give all the damn things away if I could afford to. Painting is God's gift, not mine, and it should be used to bring pleasure.'

At the height of his fame, a television film was made about the master-faker's life and work. Director Rex Bloomstein got to know him well. He said of Keating:

'He was a very emotional man. When painting, he would cry and shiver. He said he felt the artist come down and guide his hand. He was the most fascinating, complex person I have ever met.'

The Clerk Who 'Invested'
His Bank's £32 Million

Marc Colombo was a little man with big ideas. As a lowly foreign-exchange dealer working for a British bank in Switzerland, he saw fortunes changing hands daily. Fluctuations in the values of the world's leading currencies opened up enticing opportunities for men shrewd and brave enough to buy when the price was right and sell at a profit.

Colombo, a handsome 28-year-old, was one of only 16 employees at the Lugano branch of Lloyds Bank International. Lugano was the smallest of the organization's 170 branches – yet, after Marco Colombo had finished with it, its name was better known than any other in the world!

The Middle East war of 1973 led to an oil embargo by Arab states. This sent foreign exchange rates crazy and made Colombo believe that the dollar's value would tumble while the Swiss franc remained strong. So he struck what is known as a forward deal with other international money dealers.

In November 1973, he agreed that – at current rates – his bank would buy US $34 million with Swiss francs the following January. He thought that the dollar's value would have fallen by that time and he would be able to use cheap dollars to buy back his francs. But instead the dollar went from strength to strength.

He now realized he had cost Lloyds about £1 million. He wasn't too worried. After all, his bank had just declared half-yearly profits of £78 million.

One person who had to be kept in the dark, however, was the bank manager, Egidio Mombelli. Having worked for Mombelli for a year, Colombo knew that if he kept up a show of confidence his boss would not suspect a thing. But he had to recoup his losses.

Without Lloyds' knowledge, Colombo continued to speculate. After pinning his faith on the dollar falling, which it did not, he changed his tactics, believing it would go on rising. Instead it eventually fell.

Lloyds had a £700,000 daily limit on debts or holdings; Colombo went way above this. The only records he kept were in his diary. The bank and the Swiss banking authorities had no clue as to what was going on.

And neither did his colleagues or the unfortunate Mombelli. To them, Colombo was a hard-working, trustworthy employee.

But everything changed in August 1974. It was then that a Lloyds Bank man in London was told by a top French banker that their Lugano branch had 'reached its limit with us'. Lloyds' offices in Queen Victoria Street were on the alert. Phone calls showed that a German bank had also been doing huge currency deals with Lugano.

A plane from London took Lloyds chiefs to Lugano the next day. They interviewed Colombo, Mombelli and the man in charge of all three of Lloyds' Swiss branches, Karl Senft. A mass of documents and the three Swiss employees accompanied the bankers back to London.

It took a full weekend to sort out the mess. At the end, Lloyds men were shocked to find that there was £235 million still tied up in the dangerous 'forward' deals. Colombo had believed in putting all his golden eggs in one basket. A sum greater than the combined capital and reserves of all three Lloyds banks in Switzerland was staked. The bank records had shown a mere £36,000.

Lloyds had to call in the Bank of England to unscramble things. The Governor himself agreed to allow them to transfer vast quantities of money to Lugano so that the deals set up by Colombo would be honoured.

The bank's international money director, Robert Gras,

also had his work cut out. He had to buy in the dollars Colombo had agreed to sell, without people realizing. It was a tricky operation which could be made vastly more expensive if international money men knew Lloyds were over a barrel.

It took three weeks of quietly feverish activity to settle the debts and, at the end, the world was told that Lloyds in Switzerland had lost a horrific £32 million. Never before – in Switzerland or in Britain – had such a loss been known. Lloyds' London shares immediately lost £20 million when chairman Sir Eric Faulkner broke the news.

By that time, Colombo and Mombelli and their families had gone into hiding away from the eager questioning of the Press.

A year later both appeared in Lugano's court on charges of criminal mismanagement, falsification of documents and violations of the Swiss banking code. Colombo denied that he had accepted illegal commissions or had any criminal intent, but he did admit breaking the dealing limits and conducting unauthorized transactions. He also slammed Lloyds Lugano branch for its lax systems of checking and criticized the 'frustrating' spending limits that had been placed on him. Colombo seemed unmoved when the prosecution described him as the 'mouse that made Lloyds tremble' and accused him of throwing money about like a man at a casino.

'Being a foreign-exchange dealer is always a hazardous operation,' he told them. 'It is a gambler's profession.'

He was unrepentant about the extent of his speculation. 'There was the pride of the foreign-exchange dealer who will not admit failure,' he told the court. 'I was at all times convinced that I could recoup my losses, but it only takes something a little unforeseen to upset the market. I was a prisoner of events.'

Even if Colombo had ended up with a profit he would still have faced the sack for breaking banking rules. But he claimed he would have netted £11 million for Lloyds if they had allowed his currency deals to stand.

Mombelli, 41, admitted that he had never understood what was happening and said he had signed papers without realizing what they were.

'It's a foreign-exchange Mafia,' Mombelli said after the trial. 'For every dealer you need at least four administrators to check what he is doing. They do things no ordinary banker understands.'

The two men walked from the court, much to Lloyds' amazement. Colombo received an 18-month suspended sentence and Mombelli one of six months, with a £300 fine each. The judge accepted that the two had not been out to line their own pockets.

The 'Count' from the Back Streets of Sicily

For seven years, Count Cagliostro dazzled the high society of Europe's most fashionable cities. Royal courts marvelled as his magic elixirs performed apparent miracle cures. Scientists gasped at the gold and gems he could seemingly create from ordinary metal. Religious leaders believed him when he spoke of conversations with Moses and Solomon.

London, Paris and Strasbourg were bewitched by his glittering lifestyle. Tales of his achievements spread like wildfire. A Baltic state offered him its throne. Ministers at the Tsar's Moscow court lined up relatives for him to heal.

Then, in France, he was thrown into the Bastille for a crime of which he was innocent. Shocked princes and priests learned that the count they had fêted was not what he seemed.

He was, in fact, a humble Sicilian named Giuseppe

Balsamo. Born in a poverty-stricken back street of Palermo, in 1743, he had been living on his wits since stealing enough money from the church poor box and his uncle's savings to flee the island. He roamed the Mediterranean, staying for a while in Egypt, before settling to a lucrative life of crime in Rome, peddling home-made beauty creams and aphrodisiacs, copying paintings, forging banknotes and wills.

Here he met and married Lorenza Feliciani, a beautiful 15-year-old slum girl. Lorenza became the bait to lure rich victims into Balsamo's clutches. She was to help him reach the heights of fame and fortune – and send him tumbling to disgrace.

It was 1777 when the couple arrived in London. Rome had become too hot for them after a series of spectacular confidence tricks, and they had wandered for ten years through southern Europe and North Africa, perfecting the art of deception. Now they were ready for the big time.

Overnight, Giuseppe and Lorenza Balsamo became Count Alessandrio di Cagliostro and Countess Serafina. He claimed he had stolen her from an Oriental harem. They lived up to their titles with the richest clothes and jewellery, elegant coaches and hordes of servants in sumptuous livery. When people asked where their money came from, admirers whispered that the count had the power to turn base metals into gold.

The truth was more prosaic. The couple arrived with £3,000, the proceeds of their Mediterranean adventures.

But shortly after arriving in London Balsamo had joined a London lodge of freemasons. Such Orders were spreading quickly throughout the Continent, with the riches, noblest men clamouring to join. Balsamo progressed quickly, being elected Grand Master of his lodge. And that opened many doors to him in Europe when he began travelling.

In Paris, he invented what he called an 'Egyptian Rite'

order of freemasonry, appointing himself as Grand Cophta. This entitled him to collect heavy initiation fees and membership dues. And, whereas freemasonry was for men only, he opened a female lodge, with Lorenza in charge as the new Queen of Sheba.

Gullible Parisians flocked to join, lured by the promise of learning some of the Grand Cophta's secrets. The Queen of Sheba confided to duchesses that though she looked 30 – which she was – she was really 60. Her husband's magic five-drop potion kept her looking young.

Listeners promised to keep her 'secret' – and became even more desperate to pay any price that the cure-all count demanded for his elixirs. His suave charm, irresistible bedside manner and touches of luxury – wrapping pills in gold leaf – all helped him get away with extortionate charges for herbal remedies any doctor could have prescribed.

As the Grand Cophta's fame spread, more and more countries demanded to see this man of magic powers for themselves. The nobles of the independent Baltic state of Courland were so impressed that they proposed crowning the count King. He wisely declined.

In Moscow one of the Tsar's ministers urged Cagliostro to cure his insane brother. The count deigned to inspect the patient, who was brought before him, securely bound. Acting on the count's instructions, the Russians untied the madman, and he charged his would-be benefactor, threatening to kill him. The count knocked him aside, then had him thrown into an icy river. Amazingly, when pulled out, the man was sane and apologetic.

But it was after this that he achieved his greatest fame. By this time, he was claiming to have been born before Noah's flood, to have studied under Socrates, to have talked with Moses, Solomon and Roman emperors, to have drunk wine at a wedding feast in Cana, Galilee. And he was dating his letters 550 BC.

He was also still confidently dispensing potions which cured patients whom ordinary doctors had given up as lost causes. The French Government set up a commission of eminent medical men and scientists to investigate several unorthodox healers, and they pronounced many of Cagliostro's cures genuine, while admitting they could find no scientific explanation.

Soon his achievements came to the attention of the arrogant archbishop of the city, Prince-Cardinal Louis de Rohan. A servant was sent to summon Cagliostro – but returned alone with a message.

'If the prince is ill, let him come to me and I will cure him,' the count had said. 'If he is not ill, he has no need of me and I have no need of him.'

Such impudence was unheard of. But, once de Rohan overcame his initial rage, he was intrigued enough to invent a minor ailment to justify visiting the man everyone was talking about. And so began the patronage that was to establish the count as one of Europe's most powerful men – and drag him down to despair.

When Cagliostro cured the Prince-Cardinal's brother, Prince de Soubise, of scarlatina – something the greatest doctors of Paris had failed to do – adulation knew no bounds. The count's effigy began appearing on snuff boxes, shoe buckles, rings and medallions.

Then de Rohan overstepped himself. Anxious to ingratiate himself with Queen Marie Antoinette, with whom he had fallen out of favour, he hatched a bizarre plot to obtain a diamond necklace she wanted. When King Louis XVI learned he had been forging letters in the queen's name and disguising a woman as the queen, he had the Prince-Cardinal arrested – and his protégés, the Cagliostros, were thrown into the Bastille.

A public trial completely cleared them of involvement in the conspiracy, and nine months later they were escorted home in triumph by thousands of delighted supporters. But the damage had been done. Under intense interrogation. Lorenza had revealed too much about the tricks of Balsamo's trade. Slowly the truth about his money, his elixirs and his lifestyle began to emerge.

The furious Louis kicked the couple out of France, with dire warnings not to return. Again they wandered Europe, growing increasingly poor and shunned. Finally, Lorenza, tiring of her husband now that the glamour, riches and excitement had gone, persuaded him to return with her to Rome.

It was a crazy blunder – any Roman Catholic joining the freemasons was subject to excommunication as a heretic. Yet Balsamo compounded his career by creating a new Egyptian Rite Masonic Lodge to try to revive his fortunes.

The papal police quickly seized him, and on 7 April 1791 he was found guilty of heresy and sentenced to die. Lorenza had denounced him, hoping to save herself. She was locked away in a convent for the rest of her life.

The Pope's mercy saved Balsamo for a while. The death sentence was commuted to life imprisonment in the dungeons of Italy's strongest fortress, San Leo. And there, on 26 August 1795, Count Alessandrio de Cagliostro, the man who had proclaimed himself immortal, died, aged 52.

The 'Professor' with an Academic Act

Thousands of former American college students owe their qualifications to the professor who never was. They were guided to examination success by a man who hoaxed his way into a series of top university posts – and proved he was suited for the job he had no right to hold.

Marvin Hewitt, born the son of a Philadelphia policeman in 1922, was a loner as a child. He discovered advanced mathematics at the age of 10, and was soon so well versed in the subject that neither his family nor his playmates could understand a word of what he was talking about.

He yearned to continue his studies at university, but could not qualify because routine schoolwork bored him. He left secondary school early, at 17, and for six years worked unhappily in factories and freight yards.

Then a newspaper advertisement caught his eye. A military academy needed a senior preparatory school teacher. Hewitt applied, claiming he was a Temple University graduate, and landed the post.

For the first time in his life he felt at home – admired and respected by pupils and fellow teachers alike. When the spring term finished, he decided to further his own education – as an aerodynamicist at an aircraft factory. He picked out a name from a universities' *Who's Who* list and landed a job on the strength of the borrowed qualifications. With his knowledge of advanced mathematics, even the most complex tasks were simple.

That summer, growing in confidence, he chose a fresh name for another post in education. Julius Ashkin was about Hewitt's age, had had a promising career at Columbia University and was about to start work as a teacher at the University of Rochester.

Hewitt usurped his name and his qualifications, and applied to Philadelphia College of Pharmacy and Science for a job as physics teacher. He got it, at £1,750 a year. Students watched with admiration as their new master did complicated calculus in his head. And at the end of the year his classes did as well as any others in departmental examinations.

The only dark cloud on Hewitt's horizon was his salary. He felt Ashkin was entitled to better things. So he began writing to other colleges, enhancing his prospects by introducing the Christie Engineering Company in his list of references. This was a simple matter of getting letterheads printed, hiring a secretarial service to handle mail.

Soon the Minnesota Bemidji State Teachers College sent Christie an inquiry about physicist Ashkin. They received a glowing testimonial – and Hewitt landed a job at £4,000 a year.

On the strength of his new-found means, Hewitt married. His wife Estelle was unperturbed by his bizarre explanation that because he had qualified under an assumed name he had to continue using it. She was even prepared to have all her 'Mrs Hewitt' mail delivered to a post-office box, and to put off her parents when they wanted to visit the couple.

Despite such precautions, Hewitt was running into problems. The President at Bemidji had also attended Columbia University, and was ever-ready to discuss mutual friends and acquaintances with 'Ashkin', a fellow campus old boy.

It was time to move on, and Hewitt decided to return to higher education, where he could mix with minds he considered more his equal.

Out came the Christie notepaper again, and back came an interview offer from the physics department at St Louis University. Hewitt was too scared to go, and wrote excusing himself, saying that he could not get away on the suggested date. To his surprise, he was offered the post anyway, at $4,500 a year.

Now Hewitt was in his element. He was teaching graduate courses in nuclear physics, statistical mechanics and tensor analysis. He was proud of lecturing at PhD level. Students liked him and fellow staff respected him, even if some did comment on inexplicable gaps in his knowledge of basic physics.

But again the close links between colleges and academics put his future in peril. A professor who travelled occasionally to Argonne National Laboratory, Chicago, for research, returned one day to tell Hewitt that he had run into an old friend who had worked with Ashkin at Columbia – and remembered him well.

Hewitt was now living on his nerves every time his colleague went to Chicago. But, amazingly, the conversation at Argonne, faithfully reported on the professor's return, did not give the imposter away.

In the spring of 1948, Hewitt got another shock. An article appeared in the journal *Physical Review* – written by the real Julius Ashkin. Hewitt dashed to see his professor, and explained that he had written the paper, but signed it from Rochester University because that was where he had done the work on which it was based. Although his explanation was accepted, Hewitt wisely decided that there was a limit to how long his luck could last at St Louis.

He applied to the University of Utah at Salt Lake City, and received the red-carpet treatment when he arrived for his interview. Glowing references from St Louis and Columbia backed up the good impression he made. Nobody realized that they were references for two different men. And nobody checked with Rochester University.

A dean at Columbia had even given Hewitt a quite unexpected 'insurance' bonus. He told Utah there had been two Ashkins on his books.

The Utah authorities were so delighted to get their man they appointed him to a $5,800-a-year position as full professor. Hewitt had now overtaken the man whose qualifications he had borrowed. The real Ashkin was still an assistant professor at Rochester. It was the moment he had dreamed of. But his joy was not to last for long.

A month after he began work as a head of department,

a letter arrived addressed to 'Dr Julius Ashkin (?)'. It demanded that the masquerade be ended, but added:

'Let me assume that you are versed in theoretical physics and that you are a fundamentally decent man. I should then be willing to help you relieve yourself of what must have become an almost unbearable burden. It is in these assumptions that I have decided not to take any immediate steps to notify university officials.'

The letter was from the real Julius Ashkin. And, though he kept his word, one of his colleagues at Rochester was less merciful and tipped off the authorities. Hewitt was hauled before the Utah President and had to admit the truth. Generously, the authorities offered him the choice of staying on as a research fellow, or to qualify for the degrees he needed to hold his position legitimately, or of transferring to another college to qualify.

But Hewitt was too shaken by events to take up either offer. He slunk back disgraced to his mother's home in Philadelphia, and for 18 months laid low, supported by his family and in-laws.

Then, in the spring of 1950, he launched a new bid for bogus academic fame. He wrote to a teachers' placement agency, announcing that George Hewitt, DSc, Johns Hopkins University, was available for a posting. Qualifications included work as a research director for the giant RCA communications company.

Hewitt had invented an RCA Vice-president, and given him an address in Camden, New Jersey, where letters could be sent – and answered by Hewitt.

The dead-letter ploy worked again. Hewitt took up an appointment teaching electrical engineering at Arkansas University's college of engineering, and flung himself into work. Apart from lessons, he gave a local engineering society a lecture on 'The Orthogonality Property in Microwave Transmission'. He also presented a paper on 'The Theory of the Electron' at the Arkansas Academy of

Science, and worked on two research programmes.

Then an RCA chief came to the university seeking engineering recruits. 'We have your former research director here,' he was told.

'Oh yes, who's that?'

'George Hewitt.'

'Who?'

It was back to Philadelphia for Hewitt. But by now he had twin baby sons to support as well as a wife. So he became Clifford Berry, PhD, Iowa State College, and took a post at New York State Maritime College.

Bored by teaching undergraduates, he tried to gatecrash technical industry. But this proved a tougher nut to crack than colleges. So he became Kenneth Yates, PhD, Ohio State University. And in January 1953 he began work teaching at the University of New Hampshire.

Again he was unmasked. One of the students in theoretical physics and relativity became suspicious of lapses in his tutor's knowledge. Checking a copy of the American *Men of Science* catalogue, he found the real Yates was working near Chicago for an oil company.

Confronted by the facts, Hewitt again owned up and quietly resigned. 'I always do all I can to straighten things out,' he said. But this time, any hopes he had of reappearing quickly in a new area were dashed. The news leaked to a newspaper, and quickly his career as a bogus boffin was splashed over every front page in the country.

Hewitt had always caused more trouble to himself than to anyone else. He said wistfully: 'If only they'd let me be a professor, I'd never want anything else or lie. I lied only to get those jobs. I was a good teacher, I've never really hurt anyone.'

The Piltdown 'Missing Link'

In 1912 two men made monkeys out of the world's scientific establishment. One of them was a quiet, studious English country lawyer and respected amateur geologist named Charles Dawson. But it is the name of the other that has gone down in history – Piltdown Man.

Piltdown Man was the title given to a prehistoric skull which Dawson claimed to have discovered in a gravel pit near Piltdown Common, Sussex. He had been tipped off about bones in the pit by a workman. Dawson had spent many days searching the pit. First he turned up a few tiny fossilized bone fragments. Then he found flint tools, fossilized teeth – and finally parts of a skull.

The lawyer packaged up his treasures and sent them to an acquaintance, one of the world's leading authorities on the history of man, palaeontologist Dr Arthur Smith Woodward of the British Museum.

Woodward was so excited that, at the first opportunity, he sped down to Sussex to join Dawson at the gravel pit. His enthusiasm knew no bounds, for here at last was the discovery that scientists had anxiously awaited for half a century – the proof of Charles Darwin's controversial Theory of Evolution.

When Darwin published *On the Origin of Species* in 1859, he was denounced as a crank and even a heretic. Even the more level-headed critics demanded to be shown some proof of his theory. Where, they asked, was the Missing Link? Why had no one ever discovered any fossilized remains of the creatures that Darwin claimed linked man with the ape? Here, thought Woodward, was that proof.

He and Dawson carefully sifted through the gravel pit debris in the area where the first bones had been unearthed. More finds were made and other experts called in. They agreed – Piltdown Man was indeed the Missing Link.

They pointed to the thick bone structure of the skull fragments, to the tiny brain area, to the ape-like jaw – and, above all, to the teeth which were ground down, not in the manner of an ape, but as human teeth were worn away.

Woodward painstakingly pieced together the finds until they formed the greater part of a complete skull – and announced that what they had unearthed was a creature, half-man half-ape, which had lived 500,000 years ago. Although the skull was that of a woman, the find was officially named *Eoanthropus dawsoni* – Dawson's Early Man.

The announcement threw scholars worldwide into a dizzy delight. Piltdown was scheduled to be named a National Monument. Dawson became a hero. Woodward wrote a book about this discovery of 'the earliest Englishman'. The British Museum displayed the skull with a pride bordering on rapture.

Even the local public house changed its name to The Piltdown Man. Trippers travelled by the coachload to view the site of the earth-shattering find.

Dawson continued his excavations in the Piltdown area and, over the next few years, pieced together parts of a second skull. The finds only ended when he died in 1916, at the age of 52. Others continued the search but no further evidence was ever found.

The drying-up of the discoveries after Dawson's death was realized later to have been no coincidence. For Piltdown Man was a fake.

The skull was indeed that of a human, but the jaw and teeth were those of an orang-utan. The teeth had been filed down to look like human teeth, then the skull had been skilfully stained and aged before being broken up and buried in the gravel pit.

Right from the start, a few sceptics had raised doubts about the authenticity of Piltdown Man. But the cynics were not allowed access to the relics to make more thorough tests. All requests to have the samples scraped and probed were turned down. It was not until 1949 that one of Woodward's successors at the British Museum, a young geologist, Dr Kenneth Oakley, was allowed to take samples of the skull fragments and subject them to chemical tests. His verdict: the skull was not 500,000 years old but 'only' 50,000 years old.

Oakley, too was wrong. In 1953, using newly developed techniques of age assessment, more extensive tests were made by a committee of palaeontologists. They finally and officially declared Piltdown Man a fake.

Who had perpetrated such an elaborate and outrageous confidence trick at the expense of the scientific world?

Although nobody was ever able to prove it, Hoax Suspect Number One had always been Charles Dawson. He had never sought money on the strength of his 'discovery'. But he was ambitious for academic distinction. And once a visitor had walked into his laboratory uninvited to find Dawson busy over a bubbling crucible – staining bones.

The other prime suspect was Australian-born Sir Grafton Elliot Smith, one of the leading experts then employed by the British Museum. He had the temperament for such a massive practical joke. His possible motive: to liven up the deadly atmosphere pervading the famous mausoleum.

Whoever the culprit was, he took his secret with him to the grave – and left behind some very red scholarly faces.

Cranks and Crackpots

Naturalist with a Difference

'Cooked a viper for luncheon,' surgeon and naturalist Frank Buckland gleefully recorded in his diary. He added that he had also prepared some elephant's trunk soup. Disappointingly, in spite of boiling for several days, the trunk itself proved too tough for eating.

Friends who called one day found him making a huge savoury pie, filled with chunks of rhinoceros. He had to admit it tasted like very ancient, very strong beef.

Lunch with Buckland, gourmet extraordinary and author of the 19th-century best-selling *Curiosities of Natural History*, was an experience of a lifetime. With his ever-inquisitive palate and incredibly strong stomach, he would sample and eat almost anything.

London Zoo provided him with some rare opportunities. Hearing that a prize panther had died he begged the curator to dig it up and send him some panther chops which, he confessed later, 'were not very good'; and after a fire at the giraffe house he was cock-a-hoop at the prospect of several weeks' supply of succulent roast giraffe.

Buckland's Regency house, on a site near Euston Station now occupied by part of the Royal College of Physicians, was a happy chaotic place, not so much a home as a menagerie. By the fire lived his monkeys. They did terrible damage and bit everyone in sight, but he loved them dearly, giving them beer every night and a drop of port on Sundays. A pet mongoose had the run the of the house, pet rats scuttled over his desk and a jackass let out a wild laugh every half hour.

Buckland would stand in the middle of it all, good-humouredly puffing a cigar. Short and powerfully built, he was usually found during working hours wearing an old flannel shirt, trousers hitched under the armpits by short braces, and a bowler hat. Hating boots or shoes, he was normally bare-footed.

He obviously inherited his strange culinary taste from his father, Dr William Buckland, Dean of Westminster and one of the founders of modern geology. Buckland senior was said to have sampled a portion of Louis XIV's embalmed heart. He reckoned that the worst thing that he had ever tasted was a mole, but on reflection confessed to an even more unappetizing dish – stewed bluebottles. Frank's own pet aversion was earwigs. He complained they tasted terribly bitter.

Frank Buckland was born on 17 December 1826 and spent the first 20 years of his life in a splendid house on the great quadrangle of Christ Church, Oxford, where his father was then canon.

There was never a dull moment. The house was full of live creatures, most of them running free. Stuffed animals stood in the hall next to young Frank's rocking horse; snakes and green frogs were kept in cases in the dining-room.

Visitors had to be prepared to eat some strange dishes. Alligator was a rare treat for the Buckland household, mice were frequently served on buttered toast, and the famous anatomist Richard Owen and his wife were regaled with roast ostrich. At two-and-a-half the precocious young Frank was taken to Windsor Great Park, and was not a bit frightened when he was bowled over by the kangaroos he was chasing.

When he was four his mother gave him a small natural-history cabinet which he used throughout his life. He took it with him when he later left home for Winchester, the famous public school. There he would catch, dissect or stuff small animals, sometimes relieving his hunger with delicacies such as squirrel pie or mice in butter. Live pets included an owl, a buzzard, a raccoon, some jackdaws and an evil-looking magpie.

When he went on to Oxford he shared his rooms with snakes, guinea pigs, mice, frogs, a monkey, a dove and a chameleon. His pockets were always stuffed with damp moss for his slow-worms, which had a habit of poking their heads out while he was deep in conversation.

The small courtyard between his room and the canon's garden was turned into a miniature zoo, its inhabitants including a baby bear called 'Tig', a monkey, a jackal and an eagle. Authority would seem to have turned a blind eye, until one day the eagle decided to attend eight o'clock service.

The cloister door had been left open and the huge bird found its way into the church as the *Te Deum* was being sung. The Dean stood petrified as Buckland's bird advanced with menacing cries. It was seized in the nick of time but apparently the Dean looked 'unspeakable things' in Buckland's direction and dealt with him later.

Deciding to become a surgeon, Frank Buckland enrolled as a student at St George's Hospital, London, in 1847. It was a time when antiseptics were unknown, when surgeons operated in any old clothes and carried whipcord for tying arteries. The suffering was appalling, but it brought out the best in Buckland. His kindness and humour made him a great favourite, especially among the poorer patients.

When his father was made Dean of Westminster, Frank returned home to live with his parents. The deanery, chaotic as ever, was a lively centre of scientific and cultural society. One day Queen Victoria's ocultist, Mr White Cooper, came to dinner. After the port Frank invited him down to the cellar to inspect his pet rats. One large black specimen went straight for the reluctant visitor's ankles. 'Look out. He bites!' yelled Buckland, throwing a bag over it. In spite of his distaste, Cooper was impressed by his host's knowledge and the amusing way in which he described his pets' habits and peculiarities.

He urged Buckland to put the information down on paper and promised to find a publisher. Buckland's fascinating article on rats eventually appeared in a magazine called *Bentley's Miscellany*, and proved a landmark. Nobody had written like this about animals, particularly rodents. It was the first of a series later published as *Curiosities of Natural History*.

Though commissioned as an assistant surgeon in the Life Guards, he devoted more and more of his time to natural history, being much in demand as a writer and lecturer. He also became involved in one of the most eccentric schemes ever devised in Victorian England, becoming a founder member of the Society for the Acclimatization of Animals in the United Kingdom.

A rapidly rising population needed new and cheaper sources of meat. Why not fill the great parks of Britain with kangaroos, yaks and bison? Once acclimatized, they would provide juicy steaks for everyone. The capybara, largest rodent in the world, was a fast breeder but perhaps not very appetizing. Chinese sheep were actually imported at a great expense from Shanghai, but for some reason failed to breed.

At the annual dinner of the Society in 1862 Buckland's menu was enormous, including kangaroo stew, wild boar and roast curassow (a tough South American bird). The company chewed its way through the gargantuan feast for two and a half hours; but not all appreciated Buckland's *piéce de résistance*, stewed tripang or Japanese sea-slug. 'They are said to be the most succulent and pleasant food, not unlike the green fat of turtle,' wrote Buckland in gleeful anticipation. In the event even he had to admit they tasted like something between calf's-head jelly and the contents of a glue pot.

Buckland's home life was happy. His house became well known for its peculiar assortment of visitors. Children would climb the railings to gawp at the giants and dwarfs, circus freaks and fairground folk who were asked to tea along with scientists and politicians. He was very fond of the famous Siamese twins, Chang and Eng.

His wife Hannah shared his love of animals, often caring for small, sick zoo animals. One patient was a very tiny, very rare South African red river hog. She managed to rear it, but as it grew it became increasingly boisterous. Its favourite trick was to crawl under a dining-room chair during dinner and raid the table at the first opportunity. As it grew larger it often became firmly wedged. One night a solemn clergyman found himself travelling steadily backwards from the table towards the door. He was furious at the indignity. Clearly the red river hog had to go!

In 1861 Buckland hatched his first perch and began a new career that was to occupy him for the rest of his life – fish farming. He set up a hatchery in his Albany Street home and joked that, as he had hatched 30,000 salmon in his kitchen and since that noble fish always returned to his birthplace, one day there was obviously going to be a problem.

Much of his own money was spent setting up a museum of fish culture in South Kensington. Queen Victoria went to see it and was so impressed she invited him to pay a visit to her home at Frogmore.

In 1867, to his delight, he was appointed Inspector of HM Salmon Fisheries. This took him up and down the country to look into the state of rivers and make sure that the salmon could negotiate weirs and other man-made obstacles on their way to sea. Where necessary, he set up salmon 'ladders' to help them. At one particularly difficult spot he left them a notice: 'No road at present over this weir. Go downstream, take the first turn to the right and you will find good travelling water upstream and no jumping required. F.T.B.'

His stocky, bearded figure became well known on the

railways, but because his fishy luggage smelt so awful he was usually given a carriage to himself.

He cared little for personal comfort. Year after year he waded through icy rivers, testing the force of the current with his chest, building ladders and catching fish eggs for hatcheries. In winter he would rub himself all over with hair oil and wear a waterproof suit, which as often as not froze solid and clung to him like a suit of armour.

In January 1878 the New Zealand Government sent an urgent request for an extra shipment of salmon ova. It was too late in the season for 'ripe' fish, but Buckland went from river to river, sometimes standing for hours in the freezing water, hardly able to see for the driving snow. He caught the steamer in time but the effort proved too much even for his burly frame. As a result of asthma and inflammation of the lungs he had to abandon all outdoor work. When dropsy set in and surgeons wanted to operate, he refused chloroform on the grounds that he wanted to see the operation.

Frank Buckland was only 54 when he died on 19 December 1880. He anticipated his death with characteristic good humour. In his will he wrote: 'God is so good, so very good to little fishes. I do not believe he would let their inspector suffer shipwreck at last. I am going on a long journey where I think I shall see a great many curious animals . . . this journey I must go alone.'

The Duke who Detested Daylight

Like a mole hiding from the light of day, William John Cavendish Bentinck Scott, fifth Duke of Portland, vanished underground when he inherited Welbeck Abbey in the 'Dukeries' country of Nottinghamshire.

Welbeck had always lain low for most members of the Portland family. But it was not low enough for William

John who, after coming into the title in 1854, spent the rest of his life burrowing.

He hated meeting people and never invited anyone to his home – yet he set out to construct a vast complex of subterranean rooms which included the largest ballroom in the country, a 250ft library, a huge glass-roofed conservatory and a billiard-room big enough to take a dozen billiard tables.

He was mad about tunnels. There were 15 miles of them running underneath his park linking the buried rooms with the rest of the Abbey and with each other. One tunnel, a mile and a quarter long, ran from his coach-house to Worksop, enabling him to come and go unseen when he had a sudden whim to catch the London train. It was wide enough to take two carriages and was eerily lit by domed skylights during the day and hundreds of gas jets by night.

The story of the lonely, eccentric Duke, who was seldom seen by anyone but builders during his lifetime, is one of the strangest to be found in the history of the British aristocracy.

Born in 1800, he lived what appeared to be a reasonably normal life as a young man, frequenting London society, holding commissions in fashionable regiments and even, for a short period, representing Kings Lynn in Parliament. But he was awkward in the company of women, and a confirmed bachelor. And gradually his acute shyness, apparently inherited from his mother, took over his whole personality.

From the moment he moved into Welbeck until he died, he went to the most extraordinary lengths to avoid contact with people. He stripped the great rooms of the abbey of all their fine tapestries, carpets, furniture and ancestral portraits, and stowed them out of sight in a jumbled heap. Then he retreated to four or five sparsely furnished rooms tucked away in the west wing, and it was here that he worked out his plans for burrowing.

The door of each room had a double letter-box, one for incoming and one for outgoing notes. His valet seemed to be the only servant allowed near him. When he was ill and needed medical care, the doctor would be asked to stand outside while the valet took the Duke's pulse and reported his condition.

Such secrecy led to the wildest rumours. Some said that he had a hideous skin disease and was not fit to be seen. Others felt sure he had gone raving mad. But in fact a photograph, which he had allowed to be taken in typical Victorian style with his gloves and tall hat on a table by his side, show that he was a pleasant-looking man with a wide, generous mouth, large nose and mutton-chop whiskers. Mr F.J. Turner, the resident agent at Welbeck, who must have come into contact with his employer at some time, told the fifth Duke that he was 'extremely handsome, kind and clever'.

For years he was completely absorbed in building his underground rooms and tunnels. There was no comfort anywhere. The whole place looked like a mammoth construction site with mountains of builders' rubble, wheelbarrows and shovels all over the ancestral pile. His passion for bricks and mortar may well have been inherited from his distant ancestor, Bess of Hardwick, the formidable Elizabethan lady who built some of the greatest houses in England and who acquired Welbeck Abbey for the family in the first place.

Everything he did was on an enormous scale. Hundreds of workmen were employed at a time. The underground ballroom alone measured 174ft long and 64ft wide and had a hydraulic lift able to carry 20 guests at a time from the surface. Two thousand people could have danced with ease under giant chandeliers and a ceiling painted to resemble a glowing sunset.

Why did this lonely man build a ballroom? Presumably,

in his heart the Duke longed to be a different kind of creature altogether – a man who gave parties and balls and received his guests with lavish hospitality. But he never summoned up the courage.

The Duke was said at one time to be one of the best judges of horseflesh in England and his stables at Welbeck held nearly 100 horses, none of which he ever rode. The buildings above ground included a windowless riding school, the second largest in the world, lit by 4,000 gas jets.

For some obscure reason he ordered all the great, bare unused rooms in the Abbey to be painted in a most unsubtle shade of pink and in the corner of each, exposed to full view, was installed a lavatory basin.

As work progressed at Welbeck he was sometimes forced to come into contact with his workmen. But they were given firm orders. On no account must they show by any sign that they had recognized him. If a man touched his cap in deference, he was dismissed. His tenants were told to pass him by 'as if he were a tree'.

The only time he would venture out for a walk was in the dead of night when a woman servant carrying a lantern was sent 40 yards ahead of him, with strict orders not to speak or look behind.

He had a most peculiar style of dressing. Sometimes on sweltering hot summer days he was glimpsed wearing a full-length sable coat. On other occasions he put on three frock-coats of different sizes, all at once, one on top of the other. His trousers were tied up with a length of old string, just above the ankles. Whatever the weather, he carried with him an old umbrella and a heavy topcoat. If someone approached and looked likely to address him, he would immediately cover himself with the coat and snap up the umbrella to hide his face. He took to wearing a dark brown wig – he had boxes of them on his bedroom – and on top of it he would perch a stove pipe hat, nearly 2ft high.

His daily diet was chicken, always chicken. For years he

had one killed every morning and roasted on a spit in the
kitchens above ground. When ready it would be lowered
by lift into a heated truck which ran on rails through one
of the underground tunnels and into the house.

In spite of his strange behaviour he was a good and
thoughtful employer. His workmen were paid good
wages and were given, in addition, an umbrella to protect
them from the rain and a donkey on which to ride to
work.

In the 'pleasure garden' at Welbeck there was a large
skating rink and a man was employed specifically to look
after the skates of every size that were kept there. The
Duke had decided that it would be good for his domestic
staff to have regular exercise and housemaids were sent
skating daily, whether they liked it or not.

The farms, schools and roads in his estate were kept in
excellent condition and his greenhouses were among the
finest in the country. He laid down avenues of fruit trees
and a huge vegetable garden.

When the Duke decided to go up to London, his
departure was contrived with the utmost secrecy. He
would leave Welbeck via the underground tunnel in a
black hearse-like carriage, drawn by black horses. Green
silk blinds completely covered the windows. He would
remain seated in the carriage while it was loaded onto a
railway truck at Worksop station, and he would not leave
it for the entire journey. When he arrived at Harcourt
House, his London residence in Cavendish Square, all the
servants would be ordered out of sight while he climbed
down and hurried through the front hall and into his study.

Precautions were taken to ensure his absolute privacy
by erecting screens all round the garden. For years his
neighbours had been tortured with curiosity and most
were convinced that orgies were taking place.

Welbeck Abbey was in utter chaos when he suddenly
died in his 80th year in December 1879. His cousin,

arriving with his family in a carriage to take up the inheritance, found the drive overgrown with tangled weeds and grasses, and strewn with rubble. Planks had to be fetched to ease the carriage over the debris. When the great front door was thrown open, the sixth Duke was staggered to see that the hall had no floor. He went on to discover the strange pink rooms with the lavatories, and then to find all the treasures of Welbeck stuffed away like worthless bric-à-brac, the tapestries in tin trunks, the ancestral portraits stacked against the wall without their frames.

But the world had not yet finished with the fifth Duke. He had been buried with the utmost simplicity and his grave tucked away in a shrubbery at Kensal Green cemetery in North London when the whispers started.

Had the Duke been leading a double life? Nothing could have been easier for him. His comings and goings were always secretive and few people knew what he really looked like. Rumours had been going round London for years.

It all came to a head in the 'Druce Affair', which provided English society with enough gossip for a decade. A widow named Anna Maria Druce, who lived at 68 Baker Street, London, claimed that the late Duke had been none other than her beloved husband, Thomas Charles Druce, owner of a flourishing shop called the Baker Street Bazaar.

Druce was thought to have died in 1864. But his 'widow' swore that the funeral at Highgate cemetery had been a mockery. The coffin had been filled with lead.

It was, she claimed, no more than a ruse to allow her husband, who had grown tired of his alter ego, to return to his reclusive but aristocratic life at Welbeck. She therefore claimed the title and lands of the Portland family for her son.

The sixth Duke treated the claim with 'supreme

contempt' but enough speculators were found to put up £30,000 in an attempt to fight the case, which dragged on for years.

When it eventually came to court, the Druce family and their supporters committed perjury so many times that the case became a national joke. Eventually in 1907 it was decided to open the alleged Thomas Druce's grave in Highgate. He was found lying there 'aged and bearded' and perfectly in peace.

The case collapsed, the tricksters were sent packing and the fifth Duke was allowed to sink back at last into the obscurity that he had so passionately desired.

Castle Curious

Irishman Johnny Roche built himself a castle in County Cork with nothing more in the way of tools than a spade, a shovel and a rickety old cart.

For three years – from 1867 to 1870 – he sweated and laboured, gathering stones from the river by hand, digging away furiously, and drawing lime in his ancient cart pulled by an equally ancient donkey.

As the castle grew higher and higher he invented a winch to draw up the stones. People came from miles around to stare. They called it 'Castle Curious' and obviously thought its builder mighty curious too.

Johnny Roche dressed in loose, flowing garments spun and stitched by himself, with a wide-brimmed hat pulled low to conceal his bearded face. His passion to possess a castle of his own, when he hardly had two pennies to rub together, convinced the locals he was mad.

They knew him as the son of a carpenter and blacksmith from Walltown, near Mallow, who had emigrated to America to make his fortune, but returned empty-handed. Back in Cork he had tried running a mill beside the Awbeg river and, when that failed, turned his hand to making tombstones. Building castles seemed right out of his league.

But, when the strange building with its labyrinth of tiny rooms was finished, Johnny Roche confounded them all by moving in and living there for the rest of his life.

Today the labyrinth is in ruins, but the framework still stands. It consists of an oval tower 45ft high and 27ft in length, topped by two oval turrets that run at right-angles to the main building. At the base of the tower a slab of granite is engraved with fine lettering: John Roche, 1870.

In his lifetime one of the turrets carried a flag with a flying angel, and the walls were ornamented with gargoyles. He did not encourage callers and, thanks to a private well inside the castle walls, was able to 'pull up his drawbridge' whenever he felt inclined. St Bernard's Holy Well, however, lay only a few feet from the castle walls and Johnny Roche, afraid that his privacy was threatened, would lean out of a tower window and rain down colourful abuse on the heads of pilgrims.

He was, however, by no means a recluse. He travelled about the countryside on a home-made bicycle or else in a ramshackle coach drawn by two mules and equipped with a bed and a stove.

His skills developed as he grew older. It was said he could draw teeth, mend clocks, produce sculpture, play the bagpipes and the violin, dance, whistle and sing.

His best friend, a retired dragoon called Nixon, was so impressed by his talents that he asked Roche to design his tombstone if he should die first. In due course the master builder erected a flagpole over the grave of his friend with the bare inscription 'HERE LIES NIXON'. He planned something more elaborate for himself, but died before he could order his plans to be carried out. However, his own epitaph survives:

'Here lies the body of poor John Roche.
He had his faults, but don't reproach;
For while alive his heart was mellow;
An artist, genius and gentle fellow.'

His Watery Lordship

Had Lord Rokeby been given the option, he would no doubt have preferred to have been born a frog. As it was, he did everything he could to turn himself into an amphibian. Convinced that water was his natural habitat, he stayed immersed for as much of his life as was humanly possible and became the watery wonder of 18th-century England.

He started life in a perfectly normal fashion as plain Mr Matthew Robinson, a member of a respectable and down-to-earth Scottish family who had moved south from Struan and settled in Kent. His father, Sir Septimus Robinson, distinguished himself by being made gentleman usher to King George II.

As heir to the family fortunes, he was given an excellent education and became a Fellow of Trinity College, Cambridge. People were somewhat surprised when he took up politics as an ardent Whig and joined the 'patriots' who called William of Orange to the English throne in order to ensure the Protestant succession. But in every other way he seemed the epitome of the cultured, affluent country gentleman.

In 1754, on the death of his courtier father, the family estate at Mount Morris, near Canterbury, passed into his hands and he devoted himself to the task of farming its wide acres, replacing its deer with black cattle and cultivating the land. He was so much admired for his shrewd good sense and engaging manner that he was chosen to represent Canterbury in parliament. He succeeded to the Rokeby title on the death of his uncle, Richard Robinson, Bishop of Armagh and Primate of Ireland.

Then, one fatal summer, Lord Rokeby decided to spend a holiday in the spa town of Aix-la-Chapelle. He 'took the waters' and blissfully submerged himself in the health-giving baths. It was a revelation! His career as an amphibian had begun.

Home in Kent, he began to make daily trips to the sea to immerse himself in salt water. As time went by it became increasingly difficult to persuade him to come out. He was convinced that water was good for his intestines and, besides, he never felt happier than when bobbing about in the waves.

As though his behaviour was not odd enough, he also took to growing a beard – not the normal sort of affair, but a great wild, woolly appendage which grew until it reached his waist and was so thick it stuck out under his arms and could be seen from behind.

Still an excellent host, he received many visitors who were consumed by curiosity to get a close view of the beard and then to learn more about his addiction to water. Only one thing put them off. He had a passion for reading boring poems of enormous length to any captive audience.

He built himself a little hut on the sands at Hythe, about 3 miles from Mount Morris, and would launch himself into the sea, in all weathers, sometimes bobbing about for so long that he fainted and had to be carried from the water.

The daily procession which set out from Mount Morris to the beach was extremely bizarre. Lord Rokeby walked all the way, very slowly, with his hat tucked underneath his arm. His short, curiously curved figure was half-covered by his extraordinary bush of a beard. His clothes were as plain as those of his poorest tenant. But he insisted on being followed by his carriage and a favourite servant dressed in splendid livery. If it rained, Lord Rokeby made the servant ride in the carriage 'as he might spoil his clothes and catch the devil of a cold'. But his lordship carried on walking.

All along the route to the beach he had built drinking fountains so that his favourite liquid could be close to hand. He kept a number of half-crowns in his pocket and if he came across anyone drinking at a fountain as he passed by he would present them with a coin, together with a homily on the joy of pure water.

After a few years he grew weary of trailing all the way to the beach and decided to build a swimming-pool in the grounds of his mansion. It was under glass and heated by the sun.

Everyone was curious to see Lord Rokeby in his element, but few people managed it. He conducted the whole business with great secrecy and spent the greater part of his day alone in the water. However, there is one eye-witness account by an unnamed gentleman who had 'resolved to procure a sight of this extraordinary character', and it is reproduced in a fascinating book called *Public Characters*, printed in 1799. He describes how, after the necessary inquiries, he was conducted by a servant to a little grove at Mount Morris, in the middle of which was a building constructed of glass.

'The man who accompanied me opened a little wicket and, on looking in, I perceived immediately under the glass, a bath, with a current of water supplied from a pond behind. We then proceeded and, gently passing along a wooden floor saw his lordship stretched on his face at the farther end. He had just come out of the water and was dressed in an old blue woollen coat and pantaloons of the same colour. The upper part of his head was bald, but the hairs on his chin, which could not be concealed, even by the posture he had assumed, made its appearance between his arms on each side. I immediately retired and waited at a little distance until he awoke, when, rising, he opened the door, darted through the thicket, accompanied by his dogs, and made directly for the house . . .'

As his habits became more and more solitary, all kinds of rumours began to circulate about him, one being that he was a cannibal and lived on raw flesh. In fact, his diet was extremely frugal and consisted mainly of beef tea. The cannibal rumour probably sprang from the fact that occasionally he would take a leg of roast veal with him into the water and take a nibble whenever he felt faint from hunger.

On rare occasions, he came out of the water to entertain a special guest. Prince William of Gloucester, travelling through Kent, had expressed a desire to meet him. He was evidently staggered by the luxurious dinner provided by this strange man. The food was magnificent, the choice of wines memorable and the Prince's dessert, it was reported, was accompanied by a fine Tokay that had been maturing in the cellars at Mount Morris for 50 years. Lord Rokeby himself would touch nothing but water. On even rarer occasions, he would take his best clothes out of mothballs and present himself at court. His sister, Mrs Elizabeth Montagu, a sparkling socialite, was terribly embarrassed. After one such appearance she wrote to her husband: 'I am glad he has gone back to the country. He had made a most astonishing appearance at court. I wish the beefeaters had not let him past the door!'

His strange behaviour was a constant source of anxiety to his poor sister, who enjoyed a splendid social life and lived in terror that her inconvenient brother might 'exhibit his amphibious and carnivorous habits at Bath'. For, like most fashionable women, she relished the season at the famous Regency spa town as much as the season in London, and wailed: 'I shall never be able to stand the joke of a gentleman's bathing with a loin of veal floating at his elbows, all the Belles and Beaux of the Pump Room looking on and admiring.'

Rokeby paid not a scrap of attention to her. His beard grew wilder until it nearly reached his knees, and he became extremely obstinate in his ways. He hated fires and refused to have them in the house even in the bitterest weather. His windows were kept open throughout the year. He also hated doctors and refused to be treated by them. Once he fell into a fit and the nephew who was with him at the time became alarmed and insisted that he must call for medical attention. Rokeby gathered his wits together and threatened to disinherit the young man if he let a doctor through the door.

Going to church was another of his pet phobias. He said that God could best be worshipped at the natural altars he had provided for mankind – the earth, the sea and the sky. He also complained that clergymen were too preoccupied with trivia and preached boring sermons, and he would have nothing to do with them.

When he was 83 he stayed at the Chequers Inn at Lenham so that he could vote in the general election of 1796. By now he presented such an astonishing sight that inhabitants from all the nearby villages came to see him. They came to the conclusion that such a strange-looking man could not be an English lord. They decided he must be a Turk.

Old age had not tamed him at all. He was regarded as something of a marvel. His great bush of a beard did not stop him pursuing pretty girls, as he had done in his youth, and he seemed to thrive despite his profound contempt for all 'practitioners of physic'.

When he died peacefully at Mount Morris in December 1800 in his 88th year, he was mourned by many. The only wonder was that he died in his bed – it was a miracle that he didn't drown.

The Elusive Billionaire

In a small, darkened room at the top of the nine-storey Desert Inn, Las Vegas, Howard Hughes, the American billionaire, lay on his bed watching a film. His skinny frame was stark naked apart from a pair of drawstring underpants. His hair and beard hung down to his waist in lank, greasy strands. Every now and them he would reach out a claw-like hand with 2in-long yellowed nails to buzz for someone to come and change the reel. Hughes had been in that room for three months on one of his incredible film-watching marathons and in all that time he ate nothing but candy bars and nuts washed down with glasses of milk. His favourite movies were all-action dramas and he had sat through *Ice Station Zebra* 150 times with the sound turned up so loud that it bounced off the walls.

Many people were surprised that Howard Hughes was still alive in the 1960s, let alone watching films night and day. He had turned himself into one of the great mysteries of the 20th century. For 15 years the once-handsome man about town, who owned most of the casinos in Las Vegas and escorted beautiful women by the score, had shut out the world, living in dark rooms, guarded by men who seldom saw him.

Howard Hughes developed such a dread of coming into contact with people, such a horror of touching anything that other people had touched, that he turned evasion into a science and secrecy into a religion.

He was born rich in Houston, Texas, on Christmas Eve 1905. His father owned an oil-drilling company and when he died he left it to Howard. The young tycoon was then in a position to gratify any fancy that took him. Hollywood was just beginning to catch fire and when he was 21 he decided to shake the dust of Texas off his feet and become part of the new, glamorous world of picture-making.

He became an independent producer and almost immediately made his mark on an industry that never failed to fascinate him. He produced *Scarface*, one of the classic gangster films of all time which made international stars of Paul Muni and George Raft, and *Hell's Angels*, the picture that introduced Jean Harlow to the screen.

Actresses found him hard to resist and Hollywood was littered with apartments he had bought for adoring stars and starlets. He made it perfectly clear that they could stay around as long as they pleased – but only if they reserved their favours for him alone. He soon forgot them. Jean Harlow was dated, given a fabulous apartment, then ignored. In the 1930s and 1940s he often had as many as 20 beautiful girls on his dating list. Film stars liked being seen with him and in his heyday he could take his pick, escorting beauties like Ava Gardner, Elizabeth Taylor, Lana Turner, Ginger Rogers, Mitzi Gaynor and Cyd Charisse.

Signs of his eccentricity came with his discovery of Jane Russell. He found her behind the reception desk when he went to have his teeth seen to, launched her in *The Outlaw* and began to take an obsessive interest in her bust. He wrote pages of notes to cameramen about how her bosom should appear on film and invented a special cantilevered bra to show her shape off to the best advantage.

But films were only part of the scene for Howard Hughes. He was a business tycoon on America's biggest scale and owned two aircraft companies: Trans World Airlines and Hughes Aircraft. He was crazy about planes and a keen pilot. During World War II, he decided to do his bit for the war effort by building planes. The first was a monster called the 'Hercules' – an eight-engined flying boat weighing 200 tons, designed to carry 700 passengers. The plane's wingspan was slightly longer than a football pitch and its tail the height of an eight-storey building.

He put 50 million dollars into the project, but the plane only flew once. Hughes himself took it up and managed to keep it in the air for just 1 mile. The second plane was an experimental long-range reconnaissance design in which he had great faith. But on the first flight, with Hughes at the controls, it crashed. He sustained appalling injuries which left him in pain for the rest of his life and started his dependence on drugs.

Sometimes, tired of his lifestyle, he would disappear for six months. On one of these jaunts he piloted a private plane to Louisiana and was forced to land with engine trouble. He wandered into the nearest town and tried to hire a car to drive on into Florida. He had 1,200 dollars in his pocket but no identification, so the police were called and he was taken to the nearest jail as a vagrant. When he protested that he was Howard Hughes, the policeman looked him up and down and retorted: 'You're a bum.' No wonder. He was unshaven, wore a crumpled, dirty suit with gym shoes and carried sandwiches and a bottle of milk in a paper bag. He was not released until someone was found to identify him.

Hughes married twice. His first wife was Ella Rice; then in 1957 he wed film actress Jean Peters. She later told how she was treated almost like a prisoner in the Bel Air mansion which was their home. From the start, Hughes insisted that they had not only separate bedrooms but also separate refrigerators and facilities for cooking. No one, he insisted, not even his wife, was allowed to touch his food. The marriage came to an end with a one million dollar settlement. Hughes, becoming more and more averse to human contact, retreated to a bungalow in the desert near Las Vegas and hired his famous 'Mormon Mafia', a group of men of Mormon faith whose sole job in life was to protect him from outside contamination.

One of the main reasons for his desperate efforts to isolate himself was a growing terror of germs. He told a newspaperman: 'Everybody carries germs around with them. I want to live longer than my parents, so I avoid germs.'

When visitors drove out to the desert they had to stand in a chalk square drawn on the paving outside, to be inspected before they were allowed near his front door. Even his own doctor was only allowed to 'examine' him from the other side of the room. Beside his chair he kept a huge box of tissues. They were his life-savers, his 'insulation' against the bug-ridden world. He would touch nothing without first covering his hand with a Kleenex.

But, however strange his behaviour in this respect, he remained the old Howard Hughes in business. He had a zest for tough negotiating and loved to hold secret meetings to discuss million-dollar deals.

Robert Gross of Lockheed had every reason to remember his meeting with him over the proposed sale of the Hughes Aircraft Company. Hughes insisted on driving Gross away from the bungalow into the desert so that they would not be overheard. They drove mile after mile in searing heat along roads that threw up clouds of dust. The car windows were firmly shut and Hughes insisted they stayed that way. When they stopped to talk he made Gross stuff handkerchiefs in all the air vents because he thought their conversation might be heard outside the car. The fact that there wasn't a living soul for miles and his companion was fainting from the heat didn't deter him. Once the car was hermetically sealed, he got down to business.

On one occasion, when Hughes discovered his room had been 'bugged', he immediately ordered 20 new Chevrolet cars. Puzzled aides asked him what on earth he was going to do with them all. For one thing, he said, he'd

use a different one every day. 'No one will be able to bug
20 cars and no one will know which one I am going to use.'

By the time he reached his mid-50s even the desert
bungalow was not secluded enough for him. From now on
he led a nomadic existence, wandering from one luxury
hotel to another. Each time, the move was made with utter
secrecy, the whole Hughes entourage scurrying out
through kitchen exits and down fire-escapes before
daybreak, carrying 'the boss' strapped to a stretcher.

At each luxury hotel he took the whole penthouse floor.
Guards who were never allowed to see him were
stationed outside the apartment while TV sets monitored
'dangerous' spots like lavatory windows and fire-escape
doors. His aides and the 'Mormon Mafia' spread
themselves out in the luxurious rooms while he sealed
himself into the smallest he could find. Windows were
darkened and taped, and all furniture removed apart from a
bed and a chair. There were no books, pictures or personal
touches about the room; only the film equipment with a
screen at the end of the bed, and a huge box of paper
tissues.

Nobody knew the truth about those years until after his
death when James Phelan, an American investigative
reporter who had been trying to break through the
'Secrecy Machine' for two decades, was approached by
aides Gordon Margulis and Melvin Stewart who had
been with Hughes right to the end, and at last he was
given the whole incredible story.

They told how Hughes had reduced himself to a
skeleton by an atrocious diet that depended entirely on
whim – and their boss, they said, had a 'whim of steel'.
Sometimes he would live on tinned chicken soup for
weeks, eating it so slowly while he watched the screen
that the same tin would have to be reheated over and
over again. Sometimes he'd go for the candy bar, nuts and
milk menu. For days he would eat nothing but ice-cream,

sticking to one flavour until every ice-cream parlour in the district had run out of it.

Even when he consented to eat normally, he would order the same dinner day after day – steak, salad and peas. The peas were inspected carefully and all those over a certain size pushed to the side of the plate.

He refused point blank to have his hair or nails cut and only submitted twice in ten years to a barber and manicurist. On those rare occasions he insisted that the barber wash and scrub up like a surgeon before being allowed anywhere near him. But the man could hardly complain; Hughes paid him 1,000 dollars for the haircut.

Only three times during 15 years in hiding did Howard Hughes consent to meet someone from the outside world. His hair was cut, his waist-length beard reduced to a smart Vandyke and his nails trimmed back and polished. But he insisted on leaving his left thumbnail about half an inch long and squared off. 'That's my screwdriver,' he explained. 'Don't trim my screwdriver too short.' He used it to flick over pages of business documents, tighten loose screws and make adjustments to his film equipment.

The only clothes he possessed were a dressing gown, a couple of pairs of pyjamas, a pair of sandals, an old-fashioned Stetson and a few pairs of specially made underpants or shorts, fastened with drawstrings. Sometimes he just refused to wear anything and sat stark naked with a napkin over his private parts.

It took an earthquake to force Howard Hughes out into the open. On the night of 23 December 1972, he was holed up in the usual fashion on the top floor of a hotel in Managua, capital of Nicaragua. Most people had gone to bed and everything was quiet when suddenly it started. The whole hotel shook and heaved; the world seemed to be full of screams and horrendous crashes. Melvin Stewart, the devout Mormon aide who had just said his prayers and gone to bed, managed to fight his way through the debris to Hughes's bedside and persuaded him to get dressed. 'He was the calmest man in Managua,' said Stewart afterwards.

They hustled him onto a stretcher and a little group managed to manhandle him through the wreckage to a Mercedes still in one piece in the parking lot. From there he was whisked out to a baseball field, away from the danger of falling buildings.

When the sun came up it was on a scene of utter chaos and destruction, with smoke and dust still rising from the rubble of one of the worst earthquakes of modern times. Hughes muttered something about sending funds to help rebuild the hospitals but otherwise seemed aloof from the hellish devastation around him and wanted to get back indoors. He was taken to President Somoza's house and pushed into a bathing cabin by the side of the swimming-pool. The light, he complained, was hurting his eyes, and someone found a blanket to hang over the window.

An executive jet was sent for and he was flown to Florida, only to insist, within a few hours, on being taken to London. There he took refuge on the top floor of London's Inn on the Park. It looked as though the routine would be the same as anywhere else, but when news came through that after 12 years of bitter wrangling the US Supreme Court had cleared him of imposing self-serving deals on TWA, and had dismissed a 170-million-dollar judgement hanging over his head, he was in unusually high spirits.

His good humour was surprising enough, but nobody was prepared for his staggering announcement that he wanted to pilot a plane again. Everyone rushed about looking for something he could wear. Margulis was sent out for suits and shirts and the rest combed London for an old leather flying jacket and snap-brim Stetson, the sort he wore in his great days as an ace pilot. He was not allowed to take the controls but went up as a co-pilot in a private jet and seemed to revel in the freedom.

It was short-lived. A few weeks later he fell and broke his leg in the bathroom. Though he had four doctors on his payroll and had given millions to medical research, he refused to take their advice and was never to walk again.

Yet he still insisted that, after a brief stay at one hotel, the whole caravan must move on to another and the exhausting business of packing up, strapping his emaciated body onto a stretcher and spiriting him down fire-escapes continued.

Finally, in a darkened room at the Acapulco Hotel in Mexico they knew the end had come. While the rich, the young and the beautiful enjoyed the good life in the rest of the hotel, and superb brown bodies toasted in the sun, a doctor gazed with horror at the famous Howard Hughes. His body, wrecked with drugs and malnutrition, was down to 90lb in weight. His hair and beard had grown again almost to his waist and his nails were like eagles' talons.

Howard Hughes died on the plane taking him back home to Houston, Texas, in one last frantic bid to save him. The secret days were over.

Bookseller Royal

A single gunshot fired from a rickety boat on the River Wye on 1 April 1977 signalled the start of a new era for residents of the small Welsh border town of Hay. Though the salvo did little more than startle the ducks, it meant the beginning of Home Rule and Independence from Great Britain – that, is if you happened to be a supporter of bookseller extraordinary Richard Booth, in future to be known as King Richard I of Hay-on-Wye.

The Mayor and Town Council had pinned up a notice saying they completely disowned him, several elderly residents had threatened him with umbrellas and others had stated publicly that he was off his head. But he had plenty of support from others who, like him, were sick of bureaucratic rule from outside that seemed to be making the ancient town 'poorer and poorer' and in danger of sinking into obscurity.

On Independence Day they sang 'Hay-on-Wye, Hay on High . . .' as their national anthem, to the tune of Colonel Bogey, flew the new Free State flag over the ramparts of King Richard's bookshop, half-roasted an ox (somebody got the cooking time wrong) and cheered as a single-engined plane, hired from the local flying club, came into sight, dipping its wing over the hedges in salute.

It was all very moving, but people kept asking Richard Booth: 'Why are you King?' A rumpled, comfortable-looking man of 38 with dishevelled hair and owlish spectacles, he didn't look particularly regal – for one thing, his trousers were held up with a safety pin and his socks were odd.

'Well, I'm the biggest property owner in town for a start,' he would explain, 'and it *was* my idea. It came to me all of a sudden in a pub . . . some bright spark said if we were going to be independent we would have to have a King, and who better than Booth?'

King Richard owned Hay Castle, a stately pile started in the 11th century, burned down in 1978 and now lovingly restored. But, more important, he also owned a chain of shops in Hay which comprise the biggest second-hand book business in the world. He had drenched Hay in literature and attracted buyers and sellers to the town from all over the world. At one point he had an estimated 1.25 million books resting on miles of shelves.

King Richard's ancestors in the town reached back for generations. He had a typical upper-crust start in life, first going to Rugby, which he loathed, then to Oxford, which he found boring. He was always in trouble because he wouldn't conform. To please his father, who wanted him to go into the City and restore the family fortunes, he joined a firm of accountants for three weeks. He left like a shot when his great-uncle died, leaving the family mansion, Brynmalin, a few miles from the centre of Hay, to his relieved father. Richard now felt free to do what he wanted. More than anything, he liked books, so he promptly opened his first shop in Hay.

His business flourished. But he could see how many small traders and craftsmen in the little town were being driven out of business by big multiple concerns. He declared war on them. With independence, he said, they would have the Hay National Loaf, baked by local bakers. There would also be Hay National Ice-Cream. He even concocted a plan to get dozens of people building wind- and water-powered generators to supply Hay's electricity.

King Richard felt just as strongly about all forms of bureaucracy – 'a tiny place like Hay is swamped with dozens of government departments at work, all choking the life out of it' – and even to abolish the Welsh Tourist Board. Nowadays, on Bonfire Night in Hay, instead of burning Guy Fawkes they set light to a wooden figure with a bundle of forms in one hand and a cup of tea in the other.

'You wait and see,' he promised the sceptics. 'There are lots of things we can do to make life better for people in Hay. For one thing, there are too many outsiders fishing in the Wye, paying fees to wealthy landowners, not to the town. We'll cut off their lines . . . ,' he threatened with a huge grin.

Apart from fine speeches, King Richard had some very practical ideas for raising money for the exchequer. He had passports printed and planned to sell them at 25p to anyone crossing the Wye. He even printed some currency on edible rice paper, but didn't get any further than 50p notes.

But the best money-spinner was his unique method of creating an instant aristocracy for his kingdom by selling Dukedoms for £25, Earldoms for £15 and Knighthoods for a mere £1.50. He found American tourists, especially, couldn't resist the temptation and paid up merrily for the privilege of going home with a title.

Running a kingdom, of course, could not be done single-handedly. He made his gardener, Charlie, Minister of Agriculture, a neighbour who travelled to Hereford every day Minister For Foreign Affairs, and 'a chap I met in a pub' Chancellor of the Exchequer. His horse, Waterton, named after the great eccentric traveller and zoologist, became Prime Minister. But it was the appointment of glamorous April Ashley, who lived in a flat above one of his shops, as film censor that caused consternation among the teacups. Furthermore he proceeded to create her Duchess of Offa's Dyke!

Since UDI, Hay-on-Wye has thrived with more and more people flocking there to buy and sell books and sample a whiff of freedom. Since the Great Day in 1977, the anniversary has been celebrated with considerable panache. In 1978 King Richard declared a national holiday (Hay Day) and invited 200 Gujarati Indians from Leicester, declaring that, from then on, Gujarati was the second official language. Another year, April Ashley gave a kimono party and His Majesty, charmed by the grace of all those geishas, considered turning Hay into a Japanese town.

The Major and Corporation never stopped protesting. 'He's made this town a laughing stock . . . he's upset a lot of elderly people . . . he's a crank.' King Richard just laughed. His réign was established. He now had royal regalia – an orb made from a ballcock and a sceptre from a piece of copper wire.

Clown of Rock

Hotel managers the world over said a silent prayer when they heard that Keith Moon was coming to stay. Moon, wild-eyed drummer with 'The Who' rock group had earned a reputation as the supreme joker of the pop world. Hotels were his favourite target and he didn't care a damn how much his escapades cost.

He had been known to drop a firecracker down the toilet in an American hotel, blowing a great hole in the bathroom floor. Once, when a frantic manager complained about the loud music coming from his room, he blasted the door off. He took an axe to furniture, hurled TV sets through windows and, for a period of ten years, happily wrecked hotel bedrooms in America, Europe and the Far East. His extraordinary behaviour cost him between £150,000 and £200,000 in damages!

To many people's surprise, Keith Moon could explain himself articulately: 'The momentum is still there when I come off stage. I'm like an express train or an ocean liner. it takes me two or thee miles to stop.' Regarded as a clown, albeit a destructive one, he was in many ways the victim of his own reputation. He came to feel everyone *expected* him to be outrageous. Once when asked what he feared most, he admitted: 'Having to grow up.'

Being his friend let you in for some hair-raising experiences. He made Mick Jagger furious on his honeymoon. The Rolling Stones' lead singer and his wife Bianca had gone to bed and were asleep in their 11th-floor hotel room in Hollywood. Jagger was wakened by a rustling movement on the balcony outside and the sound of heavy breathing. He drew a gun from under his pillow and aimed it, thinking they were about to be burgled. Just in time, he heard a familiar voice drawl 'Good evening'. It was Keith Moon, come to offer his congratulations. He had climbed to the 11th storey from balcony to balcony and collapsed with laughter while Jagger, understandably, fumed.

Actor Steve McQueen found it was something of an ordeal living next door to him in Malibu. Moon kept a telescope trained on McQueen's beautiful wife, Ali McGraw, and would sometimes go roaring across the film star's lawn on a motorbike. It was all part of his plan to discomfort the superior 'jet set' of Hollywood.

At home in America or at his smart mews house in London's Mayfair, he could be seen relaxing in a black-velvet, monogrammed dressing gown, swigging Bucks Fizz (champagne and orange juice) out of a mug, like a Regency hell-raiser, born out of time.

Keith Moon, son of a London motor mechanic, was born on 23 August 1947, and all his early years were spent around Wembley and Shepherd's Bush. He went from one job to another until he joined 'The Who', then known under a different name, in the 1960s. He said quite plainly he thought their drummer was no good and that he could do better. When he turned up for his audition, lead singer Roger Daltry remembers he had orange hair and wore a bright orange suit; so they called him 'the gingerbread man'. His audition ended with a crashing finale in which he managed to smash his drum kit to pieces. The group thought he was great. He was hired.

They soon found he was the sort of man who created mayhem out of nothing. Outrageous stories were always circulating about him, some of them quite untrue. But Moon in top gear was a force to be reckoned with. There was a time when he would polish off two bottles of brandy and two of champagne every day, 'just to get things moving'. He once dumped a new Lincoln Continental car in a hotel swimming-pool, then sat back and waited for the reaction.

Sometimes his fellow musicians would take to their

hotel rooms for a bit of peace and quiet. On one occasion when that happened and they refused to let him in, he used an explosive device to blow the doorknobs off.

He spent his money as fast as he earned it. Being court jester to the pop world was an expensive business. His great weakness was for dressing up. He would go out into the street in anything from a nun's habit to a Nazi storm-trooper's uniform. One afternoon in London's Oxford Street, a lilac Rolls-Royce drew up to the kerb and two scar-faced hoodlums in trilbies and striped suits leaped onto the pavement. They headed straight for a bald, middle-aged clergyman, who seemed to be minding his own business, and treated him to a roughing up that would have done justice to an early James Cagney film. Passers-by looked on appalled – as passers-by usually do. The poor vicar was dragged, struggling and kicking into the Rolls and was heard to yell: 'Have you no respect for the Cloth?' While most people stood rooted to the spot with horror as the car drew away, two young men gave chase and saw the abducted vicar pinned down in the back seat, arms and legs thrashing. The car was stopped at a police road block and the unfortunate clergyman released. It was Keith Moon.

Grinning his gap-toothed grin and ruffling his already dishevelled hair, he would plead: 'I love the unexpected – and I love to make people laugh.'

His favourite prank was what he called 'The Trouser Joke'. He would go into a store and ask for a specially strong pair of trousers. A customer who happened to be passing – by arrangement of course – would be asked to help test the trousers before he bought them. They would take a leg apiece and rip the trousers apart. Moon's road manager would then appear on crutches, with one leg cunningly strapped out of sight. 'Ah, that's just what I want,' he would cry out on spotting the single trouser leg. Moon would insist that he accepted both legs as a gift, but insisted that they were wrapped separately. He would then solemnly pay the bill and depart.

He had a passion for explosives. In America, when 'The Who' appeared on TV, it was decided their performance must end with something memorably dramatic. What could be more dramatic than Keith Moon's drums exploding on the final note of their last number? When the time came, the special-effects man arrived with his gunpowder and set up the operation. Unfortunately, according to Keith Moon himself: 'I kept giving the special-effects man more and more drink from my hip flask and he kept putting more and more gunpowder into my drum kit.' When it came to the last note, Moon gave the cue and all hell broke loose. He was hurled backwards through the scenery by the violence of the explosion and lead guitarist Pete Townshend was left standing petrified, his hair on fire. Moon staggered forward to make his bow, covered in blood, with bits of cymbals sticking out of his arms. Screen star Bette Davis, waiting in the wings with Mickey Rooney, took one look at Moon and fainted.

Considering his unprepossessing looks – he was usually half-shaved and bleary eyed – he fascinated women of all kinds from wide-eyed hangers-on to smart society girls. He married his wife, Kim, when he was only 18 and she 16. For publicity reasons, he was persuaded to keep his marriage secret and to pretend that Kim was his sister. Not surprisingly, the marriage ended in divorce.

One night Moon was having a meal at 'Tramp', a fashionable West End haunt for show people, when he saw a beautiful blonde Swedish girl at a nearby table. He was completely bowled over. Calling a waiter, he gave him a substantial tip and arranged for the blonde's escort to be called away. Then he went over and introduced himself to Annette Walter-Lax. If she was angry, she didn't show it. Such was Keith Moon's effect that their relationship carried on from there. She went to live in

California with him and nearly succeeded in training him. Marriage? 'I'm married to "The Who",' he once said emphatically. 'After all the pressures we've been through we're welded together . . .' But friends say he would have married Annette Walter-Lax had he lived.

Moon always predicted that he would die young, so perhaps that was why he was so reckless. With the help of the Swedish girl and the moral support of fellow drummer, Beatle Ringo Starr, he managed to curb his drinking. But he still regarded himself as the Clown Prince and only two months before he died he was thrown off a British Airways jet in the Seychelles when he tried to break into the pilot's cabin and play his drumsticks on the control panel.

One night in 1978 he went to a party. He was in a quiet mood, spent most of his time talking with Beatle Paul McCartney, and announced his engagement to Annette. Next morning, he was found dead; and although there was talk of drug overdose all those closest to him insisted he had died in his sleep of natural causes. One thing would have pleased him. He was last seen in public with a glass of champagne in his hand and a beautiful girl on his arm. It had been a great performance.

Powerful
Passion

Scourge – and Pride – of Venice

In his memoirs Casanova wrote: 'I felt myself born for the fair sex . . .' No one knows exactly how many women the immortal Italian lover seduced, but it was thought to be hundreds. His amorous career started at the age of 16 when he made love to two sisters in the same bed. It progressed through an extraordinary variety of amours including nuns, novices, duchesses, whores, lusty peasants and rich old ladies. He was able to fall madly in love within 15 minutes and no woman he desired had to wait more than a few seconds for the first move in the game. 'I have loved women even to madness,' he wrote.

But Casanova loved his freedom as much as he loved his women, and, though several times he became entangled enough to be within sight of the altar, at the last minute he always escaped. He did it with the greatest subtlety, employing the most ingenious delaying tactics, until the bride-to-be got tired of waiting. When she inevitably made off with someone else he would retire to his bed for a couple of days, grief-stricken, before looking for consolation.

His opening move in an affair was often to provoke a quarrel or argument. He could then apologize, comfort and caress the offended beauty. He firmly believed that celibacy could ruin a healthy man's constitution. His own physique was strong and he had an enormous appetite for rich foods. Often, his seductions were carried out as part of a luscious feast. Crayfish or crab soup was a favourite starter followed by aphrodisiac oysters, which he slid between the breasts of his paramour and ate delicately in situ.

He did, at times, have moments of remorse for his libertine ways and would then consider going into a monastery – but a new beauty always arrived on the scene just in time to save him from his better self.

When his memoirs were first published – and they

appeared in many different versions before the manuscript was at last printed exactly as Casanova had written
it, in 1960 – they were received with disbelief. No man had
ever left such an intimate record of his life. Some people
questioned not only their authenticity but whether in fact
such a man as Casanova ever really existed.

Contemporary portraits are not impressive, though he
was said in his youth to have been exceptionally
handsome. He was tall for an 18th-century Italian –
6ft 1¹/₂in – with a fine head of hair and only three smallpox
scars to blemish his swarthy, aquiline profile. His
fascination probably lay in his enormous stamina and
energy, his commanding presence and air of virility. For
Casanova was not just a profligate. He was one of the
most brilliant figures of his age. Whatever he did, as lover,
scholar, gambler, bon viveur, spy or raconteur, he did with
colossal flair and charm.

He was born in Venice on 2 April 1725, the son of an
actor and actress, in a city given over to sensuality. His
parents neglected him and he was a miserable, sickly child
whose nose was always bleeding. At the age of nine he
was taken to Padua to be educated. He lodged with the
Abbé Gozzi, who taught him to play the violin, and he
studied at Padua University until he was 16.
Astonishingly, he became a priest himself – it was the
most common thing for a man with talent but no money
in those days. Yet Holy Orders did not stop him from
'losing his innocence' to two sisters, Nanette and Marton
Savorghan, daughters of a noble Venetian family. He spent
the night with the pair of them in the same bed! From then
on, he had a penchant for double seductions.

Having left the priesthood, Casanova entered into a life
in which he lived largely by his wits. He was taken into
the service of distinguished men, talked his way into the
most brilliant society and, through letters of recommendation, moved up the social scale. The Prince de Ligne

said he was 'one of the most interesting, odd characters' he had ever met. By the age of 20 he was also completely obsessed by gambling. He would stake his money on any game but Faro was then the rage of Europe and he became a past master. He thought nothing of gambling all night, all day and the next night without a break.

Every woman he desired he pursued with almost comic fervour. Visiting the estate of the wealthy Countess Mont-Real he was attracted by a newly married young woman of exceptional beauty and made advances to her – without success – whenever her husband turned his back. One afternoon Casanova persuaded her to go out riding in a two-wheeled chaise. A terrible thunderstorm frightened her almost to hysteria. 'Using a method of distraction which provided excitement closer at hand, I succeeded in curing her of her dread of thunder,' he wrote, 'although I doubted that she would reveal the secret of my remedy!' Between seductions of a similar nature Casanova went to sacred concerts and wrote Italian verses for church music.

His financial situation fluctuated wildly. At one time he was reduced to playing the violin in a theatre in order to keep himself. His only regular income was from patrons like the noble Venetian, Matteo Bragadin, former Inquisitor of State, who adopted him as a son and gave him a monthly allowance which he received until his protector's death.

However, he had an attitude of contemptuous insolence towards the ruling class in Venice that made him hated by the Establishment. He was even suspected of being a spy. His jealous enemies were ready to seize on anything to get him out of the way and eventually it was a religious satire he had written as a youth that gave them an excuse. On the night of 25 July 1755, he was arrested and taken to The Leads, the infamous Venetian prison, which derived its name from the heavy lead tiles that covered the roof. He was condemned to five years without trial. Perhaps, it was suggested afterwards, the fact that Casanova was wooing the mistress of one of the Inquisitors had something to do with it.

His escape from The Leads 15 months later was one of the classic prison breaks of history. He had managed to get hold of a piece of iron and patiently whittled it away with a fragment of marble until it was an 18in spike. He had made a gaping hole in the floor of his cell and was ready to put his escape plan into action when he was suddenly moved to more spacious accommodation in The Leads. The furious jailer threatened to report him to the authorities, but Casanova managed to keep him quiet. For his next attempt he enlisted the help of a fellow prisoner, a priest called Balbi. One day he called the jailer and asked him to take Balbi a huge Bible as a present. The Bible was to be delivered along with a plate of macaroni which Casanova recommended as being especially delicious. The Bible was placed on top of the macaroni and the jailer was too busy trying not to spill it to notice that the plate was extremely heavy. Casanova had slipped his iron spike into the Bible's parchment cover.

The priest, whose cell was above, bored a hole through Casanova's ceiling and hauled him through. Together the two men then drilled through to the great attic where they were usually taken to exercise, and from there it was easy enough to prise one of the lead sheets away from the roof. They scrambled out – and were away. Casanova hailed a gondola and spent the night in the home of the Chief of Gendarmes, who was out looking for him!

Casanova spent the next part of his life keeping out of the hands of the Venetian Inquisitors. His conquests consoled him. In Constantinople, however, he met with rare defeat. Despite the religious code which demanded the absolute division of the sexes, he had managed to mesmerize a Moslem lady he referred to as 'The Wife of Yussef'. One night he attempted to remove her veil and made her so angry he could do nothing but beat a hasty retreat. Afterwards he realized with chagrin that he had made a foolish mistake and that she would have been willing to take off everything else.

In Paris he was admitted to the most exclusive circles and was appointed a director of the French lottery. His interest in the occult and black magic fascinated certain women of high rank, among them the Marquise d'Urfé. He was her lover, of course, and she supported him lavishly for years but the poor woman, besides being rich, was also incredibly gullible. She was a Cabalist, a believer in a complicated pseudo-religious sect and reincarnation. She was certain that Casanova could communicate with spirits and asked him to transmigrate her soul into the body of a male infant. Casanova set about to oblige by making love to a carefully chosen virgin. If they could produce a son, he assured her, it would be the reincarnation of the Marquise. The mumbo jumbo went on for ages and was the scandal of Paris until Casanova tired of it. While he did not take advantage of the credulous old lady directly, he knew very well that he had power over her and relished it.

To keep up the dazzling life he was leading, however, he needed ever more funds. He decided to go into business. In Paris there was a great vogue for painting patterns on silk after the Chinese fashion. This seemed an elegant enterprise to suit his tastes and he set up an establishment. He engaged 20 girls for the work, interviewing each one himself, to make sure she was attractive. Each girl in turn became his mistress. But, while his love life flourished, his business did not.

As a lavish spender and gambler he was often at a loss for money and to obtain cash he would sometimes pawn his jewels and gold snuff boxes. He spent a fortune on women, anticipating their every whim and showering them with presents of jewels and clothes.

He usually came out of his affairs unscathed, but one encounter in Italy he was never to forget. Visiting the Duke de Matalone in Naples, he was introduced to the Duke's beautiful young mistress, Leonilda. He fell desperately in love with her, so much so that he asked the Duke to grant him her hand in marriage. The Duke affably agreed, amused to see Casanova so truly smitten. All that remained was to send for the girl's mother to put her name to the marriage contract. On the day she was expected to arrive, Casanova went out to deal with some business, returning to the ducal palace in time for supper. Waiting for him in the drawing room he found the Duke, Leonilda and Leonilda's mother, all in a state of happy excitement. When the latter saw Casanova she screamed and fainted. It was one of his old loves, Anna Maria Vallati, who had borne his child 17 years before. There was no doubt about it. He had been about to marry his own daughter.

Overcome with remorse, he offered to make amends and marry his old love instead, but Donna Lucrezia, as he used to call her, knew his character too well, and declined. After making Leonilda a handsome present for her eventual marriage, he set off again on his travels.

Casanova lived in England for nine months. He had been sent to try to set up the French form of lottery. While in London he was introduced to the famous courtesan, Kitty Fisher. He declined to take advantage of her favours for the simple reason that he did not speak English and therefore could not hold a conversation with her. Delicately, he explained that when making love the enjoyment of *all* his senses was necessary.

He played whist with English aristocrats and joined in the lively social life, but at his apartment in Pall Mall he languished alone. Piqued by this unusual solitude, he advertised some of his rooms to let, furnished, and netted a pretty, refined young Portuguese girl who spoke French and kept him company until her boat sailed for Lisbon.

But it was also in England that he had an experience from which he swore he could date his decline. He became involved with a shrewd little prostitute named Marianne Charpillon. To his rage and humiliation, she cost him 2,000 guineas and refused to grant him her favours. When she explained that she was dying of an incurable disease he was so distraught that he went 'laden with lead' to commit suicide in the Thames. Friends stopped him, telling him she was in fact, at that moment, merrily dancing the minuet. As a revenge he bought a parrot and taught it to repeat in French 'Charpillon is a greater whore than her mother'.

Casanova fled from England to avoid debts and returned to Venice in 1772 after years of exile. He was welcomed with open arms and even invited to dinner by the Inquisitors who were dying to know how he had in fact escaped from The Leads.

But, as J. River Childs writes in the biography of Casanova: 'For him, as for Byron, the days of his youth were the days of his glory. He had drunk life to the lees as few men before or after . . .' By now his glitter began to fade. He found he could not earn a living by his pen. His translation of the *Iliad*, though admired, had to be abandoned for lack of funds. In 1776, under the name of Antonio Pratolini, he became a secret agent for the Inquisitors. But the work did not suit his temperament. For a time he lived a quaintly domestic life in a small rented house with a little seamstress called Francesca Buschini, who was very sympathetic and devoted to him. However, he could never keep out of trouble for long and yet another affair of honour, a threatened duel and bitter words drove him from his birthplace once more and for the last time.

Some time in February 1784 Casanova met the Count Joseph Charles de Waldstein, whose great castle in

Bohemia had a library of 40,000 volumes. They shared a love of gambling and the occult and after some persuasion he agreed to become the count's librarian. For the next 13 years, the last years of his life, he was bored to death. Only one thing interested him – the past. He spent hour after hour drafting his memoirs, revelling in his moments of glory, savouring again the conquests of his youth. He held nothing back. Little did he realize that the account of his outrageous amorous adventures, translated into some 20 different languages, would one day be hailed as a literary masterpiece.

Pablo Picasso

Pablo Picasso needed the love of a woman as much as he needed paint and canvas, for the great artist was both a genius and a Don Juan. Every time he fell in love he was inspired by revolutionary ideas and swept along on a tide of creativity. Both the beginning and the ending of his love affairs were reflected in his painting. The seven great loves of his life were each connected with a major period of his work.

Picasso had been born in Malaga on the south coast of Spain on 25 October 1881, the only male child of a family which could be traced back on his father's side to Old Castle at the beginning of the 16th century. His mother, a dark, petite woman, who passed on her looks to her adored son, came from a once-famous family of goldsmiths on Majorca. From his earliest days the only thing that really interested Picasso was drawing and painting. The portraits he painted at the age of ten were astonishing. Their technique was said to be that of an already established artist. Fortunately his family recognized the incredible driving force in him. His father, Don José, a sad, disillusioned, failed artist, sensing the genius in his son, helped and guided him all the way.

The family moved to Barcelona when Pablo was a youth. It was a place bursting with intellectual life and he discovered the true existence of the avant garde movements in Europe. He also discovered his vigorous sexual appetite. He studied in Barcelona and Madrid but knew all along that one day he would have to go to Paris. His first visit was in 1900. He felt lost, awkward, out of place and could speak very little French. It was not until four years later, after several visits, that he felt ready to become part of that colourful, impoverished world that centred on Montmartre.

He moved into a studio in the 'Bateau Lavoir', a ramshackle, almost derelict row of apartments in the rue Ravignan. It was a building which had neither gas nor electricity; it let in the wind in winter and heated up like an oven in the summer. There was only one cold-water tap to serve the whole building and it was there he often met a fellow painter, a student at the Ecole des Beaux Arts. Her name was Fernande Olivier, and she was an extraordinarily beautiful young woman.

One stormy evening Fernande rushed into the Bateau Lavoir dripping wet and bumped into Picasso in the corridor. He was carrying a tiny kitten in his arms. They laughed about the rain and Picasso smiled at her with his enigmatic black eyes and offered her a cup of hot coffee. Before the night was out she was his mistress.

Both of them were experiencing their first genuine passion after many casual experiences. Fernande had posed for several painters and sculptors in Paris, including Dufy, and had become more than a model to some of them. With Picasso she knew instinctively things would be different. At this period of his life he was short and stocky with a face the colour of parchment, magnetic black eyes and a lock of black hair falling over his forehead. He dressed like a workman in blue cotton trousers and jacket but there was something of the aristocrat about him and his features expressed terrific willpower and strength. There was usually a poppy-coloured belt around his hips or a scarlet scarf around his neck, for he styled himself as a bit of a dandy.

Fernande moved in with him. They were desperately poor but their poverty did not worry her. She was a passive sensual creature who spent hours lying on a divan reading newspapers and smoking cigarettes in an amber holder. Picasso did many of the household chores, including the shopping. Like a true Spaniard, he was intensely jealous and did not want her to meet other men unless he was with her.

Their apartment could almost have been described as squalid. Everything was worn-out and shabby, the floor strewn with cigarette ends and squashed tubes of paint. It consisted of a tiny hall, a bedroom almost entirely taken up by a divan and a large studio in which the paint was peeling off the walls and the window panes were tinted blue to reduce glare. It was difficult to move around because of the unbelievable quantity of junk that Picasso had picked up in the flea markets. He was a compulsive collector of bric-à-brac all his life and never threw anything away.

On summer days when the temperature inside became torrid, Picasso would paint with his studio door thrown wide open onto the corridor where other tenants could see him working at his easel, stark naked except for a scarf tied round his loins. He was very proud of his strong, muscular shoulders and his delicate wrists and ankles and enjoyed lingering, appreciative glances from the opposite sex. On bitter, winter days, when it became unbearably cold, Picasso and Fernande would huddle together in bed for warmth.

They were so poor that once when Picasso had been given a commission to paint a still-life of flowers he had to do it without using white because he could not afford a fresh tube of paint. During his love affair with Fernande he painted some of the great pictures of his 'blue period' and, though his output was prodigious, he only got a few francs apiece for pictures he sold.

He cleared out a lumber room adjoining the studio and turned it into a sort of shrine for his love. On a packing case draped with red silk cloth he arranged the souvenirs of their life together: a dark red paper rose, a couple of cheap vases won at a fair, a pair of Fernande's earrings, the blouse she had been wearing the night of the storm.

Though their life was hard they could be heard laughing and singing together and the communal life they shared with other artists softened the harshness of poverty.

Most of the time through this period Picasso was making beautiful drawings and pictures of circus figures: acrobats, tumblers, harlequins and clowns. One day the art dealer Ambroise Vollard came to see him in the rue Ravignan. He spent ages thoughtfully sorting through canvasses then, to Picasso's joy, bought 30 paintings for which he paid 2,000 francs. News spread like wildfire through the art world that Picasso had been taken up by Vollard and his friends began to call him 'maître'.

Connection with Vollard meant security. In the autumn of 1909 Picasso moved an ecstatic Fernande to a comfortable apartment in the boulevard Clinchy where they had hot running water out of the taps and electricity. A new Fernande emerged. Now that Picasso was earning real money she developed a passion for dresses, hats and furs. Once she spent all their housekeeping money on perfume. She also decided that a resident maid was essential. After a time there were quarrels, sulks and reconciliations until Picasso began to think nostalgically of their old days together in the rue Ravignan. It was after one particularly fierce quarrel and passionate reconciliation that he painted his first truly cubist picture.

In the summer of 1912 he was introduced to a friend of Fernande's called Marcelle Humbert, a woman whose refined elegance and delicate beauty completely captivated him. It was love at first sight. Only after a time did Fernande realize that Picasso was being unfaithful to her. She had to do something. Herself in the throes of an infatuation with Italian painter Ubaldo Oppi, she hoped to make Picasso jealous by running away with him. Her action had the opposite effect to what she intended. Picasso, finding himself free, packed his bags and went off to Ceret, taking Marcelle with him. The little town, idyllic in the full beauty of spring, was spoiled when many of their Bohemian friends followed them, to find out how Picasso's affair was progressing.

Eventually Fernande herself arrived, full of remorse and despair. But it was too late. Picasso told his friend Gertrude Stein, the writer: 'I am still spellbound by her beauty but I can't stand her caprices any more.' To bring their relationship to a definite end he left with Marcelle for Avignon. Years later, when he heard Fernande was ill he sent her a million francs to get proper medical treatment. But they were never to meet again. After she died alone in her apartment in 1966, a little heart-shaped mirror that Picasso had once given her was found in a jewel box.

Picasso and Marcelle rented a house in the village of Sorgnes near Avignon. He had a burst of creative energy to celebrate the beginning of his new love. He called Marcelle Eva because she was the 'first woman' in his life, and though he could not paint a realistic portrait of her because he was in the middle of experimenting with cubism he paid homage to her by inscribing two of the pictures he painted in 1912 'J'aime Eva'. She appeared as a figure in some of his works and a picture bearing the inscription 'Ma Jolie' was found on the kitchen wall of their apartment. When Picasso left, Khanweiler, the cubist art dealer, sent a team of experts from Paris to remove the painting from the wall.

After Provence the lovers settled into a well-appointed studio in Montparnasse, but their happiness was to be short-lived. Marcelle began to be racked by fits of coughing. The doctor diagnosed TB and she died at the beginning of 1916. Picasso was grief-stricken by the loss of his graceful, delicate partner and too miserable to work. It was altogether a sad year for him. His father died, too, and as a pacifist he found himself terribly alone and isolated as most of his friends had volunteered to serve in the war then raging over Europe.

He would eat alone at the Café Rotonde in Montparnasse and walk the streets rather than go back to the apartment where he had lived with Marcelle. He moved house again, renting a small suburban villa with an overgrown garden in the rue Victor Hugo in Montrouge. Soon he began to feel the place was ill-fated. It was burgled, flooded and cursed with a chilly atmosphere. Though he took women back there for casual affairs, they meant nothing to him and made him even unhappier.

Jean Cocteau rescued him from this gloom. He asked Picasso if he would design sets and costumes for the controversial, ultra-modern work of *Parade* which was to be staged by the great Diaghilev for the Russian Ballet. Picasso had never worked for the theatre before but he went with Cocteau to Rome where rehearsals were in progress and soon became excited by the ideas which poured from his ever-fertile mind.

At one rehearsal he met Olga Koklova, a dancer with the Russian Ballet. She was the daughter of an officer in the Russian Artillery. Her supple grace, sleek dark hair and almost childlike simplicity intrigued Picasso. In a company with extremely lax morals she displayed a flower-like innocence. He was tired of easy conquests and longed for an intense relationship again. Olga was receptive to his wooing. She was weary of the vagabond life she had to lead with the Ballet and ready to settle down. Picasso seemed to offer her stability and a position in cultured society. Her failure to realize that he was a free spirit and true Bohemian was the root of a great deal of future trouble.

For the moment, however, there was not a cloud on the horizon. Picasso painted Olga in a white mantilla and sent the portrait home to his mother. Then, to show how serious he was, he took his intended bride to Barcelona and introduced her to his family. Picasso's mother made her welcome but, detecting her bourgeois nature, tried to warn by saying: 'I don't think any woman can be happy with him and his way of life.'

They were married on 12 July 1918 with Cocteau, Diaghilev and the poet Apollinaire as witness. Picasso gave himself up to the infinite pleasure of educating his young wife in the ways of love. To please her, he even tried to turn himself into a society artist, dedicated to receptions, elegant dinners and entertaining. He also took a handsome apartment near the Champs Elysées and was quite amused at first by the social strata into which marriage drew him.

As usual his new love brought a new phase of creativity. He amazed the world by his explosion of artistic genius. Still painting for the Ballet, he also produced superb still-life pictures and other canvasses of startling originality. They were happy years. His son Paolo was born in 1921 and he painted exquisite, tender portraits of this adored child.

But slowly, over the years, the naïve sprite of the Russian Ballet turned into a bourgeois with the stiff, formal outlook of her kind. Their apartment was handsome, but it was not the home of an artist. Frustrated by the houseproud Olga, Picasso rented an apartment above their own and kept it as his own domain, a place where he could paint, drop his cigarette ends and collect his incredible junk. By 1924, under the influence of the Surrealist movement, he began to paint deformed portraits in which people had several heads, dismembered legs and eyes and noses in the strangest places. In the future, whenever he faced an emotional crisis he reverted to this style.

Their life together became stormy. Olga would not adapt herself to Picasso's Bohemian habits and did not understand him. He was tired of trying to conform to her way of life. Her scenes of rage, anger and jealousy made him utterly dismayed, but for a long time he tried to placate her for fear of losing his son should they separate.

One day in 1931, walking in Paris near the Galeries Lafayette, he bumped into a tall, fresh-faced blonde with the bronzed, athletic look of a northern goddess. They fell into conversation and he learned she was Swiss, 17 years old, and her name was Marie Thérèse Walter. Her life was devoted to sport, but she had such a jovial, gentle, undemanding personality that Picasso fell in love with her. After the Slavic intensity of his wife she was like a cool, refreshing stream.

Marie Thérèse loved Picasso simply and deeply and did not want any part of his fame. They did not live together very much and he did not introduce her to his friends, but for years she remained a happy, gentle influence in the background. She had a softening influence on his work. The monsters disappeared and he began to paint full, harmonious figures which glorified the female body. Marie Thérèse is seen in the famous 'Femme au Fauteuil', and again in his large sculptures.

In 1935 Picasso left Olga for good. He found it difficult to discuss separation with her. After all she had been part of his life for 17 years. A divorce suit was begun but the decree was never made absolute. A happier event that year was the birth of his daughter Maria at Boisgeloup, the beautiful country house Picasso retreated to with Marie Thérèse in an effort to escape from the still hovering Olga. He would not be free of his first wife for many years. She would follow him to exhibitions, screaming abuse at any woman in his company, hang around the places he often frequented, even appear threateningly on beaches when he swam in the sea.

During this time, however, he found yet another companion who was to live with him in the ten difficult years ahead. He threw himself into the new affair in the autumn of 1935 when he already had two women competing for his attentions. His meeting with Dora Maar was over a bowl of ripe cherries at the famous café, Deux Magots. He was fascinated by the young woman's sensitive face, lit up by the palest blue eyes, and tried to think of ways to get to know her better. She solved the problem for him. She was a photographer, a close friend of great camera artists like Man Ray and André Breton, and she often worked as a freelance journalist. This gave her an excuse to call on Picasso. Commissioned to do a feature article about him, she asked to take photographs in his apartment . . . the affair began.

His love life at this stage has certain elements of farce. He now had two mistresses to keep happy, knowing that Olga could be waiting round any corner, ready to leap out and scream at him. His Swiss love contented him with her sunny temperament and beautiful body but he turned to Dora for the fresh stimulus he needed in order to paint. The two women hated each other. Picasso enjoyed their rivalry and wickedly took pains to provoke their jealousy. One day they flew at each other in his presence and he did nothing to stop the fight.

He rented an enormous loft studio in the rue des Grand Augustins. Dora proved an excellent companion as well as a passionate lover. She fascinated and excited him and inspired the most dramatic period of his life which saw his work rise to tragic heights of greatness.

Two terrible events which were to influence his work were the Spanish Civil War, which broke out in 1936, and the tide of Fascism leading to World War II. Throughout the Spanish war he gave financial support and sold pictures from his private collection to help refugees and children's organizations. On the morning of 28 April Nazi planes helped the Spanish Fascists bomb the little Basque town of Guernica. The casualties were horrifying. Sick with anger and grief, Picasso recorded 'Guernica' for all time in one of the greatest works of its kind ever produced.

When war broke out in Europe he shut himself away. He watched the Germans march into Paris from his studio window. 'They are another race,' he said sadly. The few painters in German uniform he met were not turned away. He talked with them, showed them his work and presented them with postcards of 'Guernica'. He knew Hitler had designated him as a degenerate artist but he was determined to see the war through in Paris with Dora.

During the four years of the occupation he hardly left his studio, holding court there for those who wished to see him. He had tried to cling to his love for Dora but she had a changeable character, which made her subject to fits of depression and sudden rages which ended in tears. Before the war ended another woman entered his life.

He was now in his early 60s but magnificently preserved, his body strong and muscular, his face lean and commanding. When they met in May 1943 Françoise Gilot was only 21, a young painter whose beauty and talent enchanted him. She was graceful and tall, with a slender waist, corn-coloured hair and emerald-green eyes.

Françoise did not capitulate immediately. She played the coquette, sometimes displaying ardour, sometimes indifference. He soon found he was unable to hide his passion, but was determined not to be outwitted by this young woman. He would try to shock her in public by kissing her on the mouth or fondling her breasts in front of their friends. Once he asked her to take off her clothes and lie down beside him only to gaze at her with a cool, professional eye then tell her to get dressed again. She describes their 'prolonged fencing match' in the book she wrote about their love affair. It went on for three years until May 1946 when Françoise gave in, left her grandmother's house and went to live with Picasso on the Côte d'Azur.

When Dora realized what was going on there were terrible scenes. She became subject to hallucinations, and a religious fanatic. Picasso took her to a clinic for the best treatment he could afford but she was lost to her dreams and spiritual visions. Their last meeting was painful. She hurled accusations at him when he insensitively suggested that Dora tell Françoise face to face that it was all over between them.

In the south of France Picasso regained his youth, became bronzed and agile, swimming and sunbathing with his beautiful Françoise. He painted the most marvellous pictures of the female body and also found a new inspiration in ceramics. Working in the little town of Vallauris, completely absorbed in the new medium, he turned out 2,000 pieces in 18 months. Vallauris was suddenly famous. Picasso was made an honorary citizen and they celebrated his birthday each year.

At the end of 1948 he settled down close to Vallauris in a house called 'La Galloise', set in the midst of orange groves. Françoise complained that it was too small and cramped and they had little privacy there, for Picasso was now an international figure and hundreds beat a path to his door. Françoise was also annoyed by the fact that the townspeople, knowing she was not his wife, called her 'La Picasette', meaning Picasso's girl. She did not intend to be laughed at or to play second fiddle to his greatness.

Gradually quarrels and disagreements spoiled their life together. Picasso felt Françoise should have children to fulfil herself and persuaded her to become the mother of his children. His son, Claude, was born in 1947 and his daughter, Paloma, in 1949. He was delighted with them but Françoise, still not satisfied, became assertive. He began painting her in grotesque twisted postures. To cap it all Olga turned up as he bathed in the sea, shrieking at him from the beach that he was still her husband in the eyes of the Spanish law.

Picasso's friends had been expecting something drastic to happen for some time. He had been seeing other women and generally flaunting his amazing fitness and virility. On 30 September 1953 Françoise left with the children and returned to Paris to begin a new life.

There was a bullring in Vallauris and Picasso was able to go to the *toros* again as he had with his father when he was a small boy in Malaga. People noticed that more and more often he was accompanied by a petite brunette with brilliant blue eyes. Her name was Jacqueline Roque and she was a young divorcée with a six-year-old daughter. Picasso began to paint her, a sure proof of his deep interest. He dressed her in Turkish costume, in Provençal dress and as a Spanish woman with a mantilla, but the most famous portrait shows her as 'Madam Z', revealing her natural Mediterranean warmth.

Jacqueline was to be his last love. She was gentle, devoted, adoring and was content to sit for hours watching him work. Moreover she was a good housekeeper and provided him with a comfortable home, well run, with meals on time. She also helped him organize his business life. She dealt with banks, lawyers, dealers and publishers, answered his letters and kept a catalogue of his works.

At 74 he was more vigorous than ever and gaily moved into an extraordinary villa called 'Le Californe', a folly built by a champagne merchant in the hills above Cannes. Not content with that, he also took on the imposing Château de Vauvenarges, an old fortress with four turrets and a fine gateway. He finally settled down at a house in Mougins, built on a hill overlooking the village. His life from then on was confined mostly to his new home, though he would swim occasionally at Golfe Juan or visit a familiar restaurant. His work continued in a steady stream and on his 80th birthday he did a flamenco dance on a table while his friends cheered and clapped.

He married Jacqueline and she was to be the last of his numerous loves, or almost the last. He had always regarded death as a woman and he knew that lady was waiting for him.

Lord Byron

Were Byron and his half-sister, Augusta Leigh, lovers? The question has haunted generations of those intrigued by the romantic poet with the reputation of being 'mad, bad and dangerous to know'.

George Gordon, sixth Lord Byron, born on 22 January 1788, was the son of a handsome rake known to his family as 'mad Jack'. This same black sheep was also the father of Augusta. Byron's mother was a Scottish heiress called Catherine of Gight, a Celt with such a bad temper she once bit a piece out of a saucer. Augusta's mother was the wife of Lord Carmarthen, and she caused a major scandal by eloping with rakish Jack and marrying him after her divorce.

Brother and sister met for the first time in 1802 when Byron was 14 and Augusta 19. To the boy who suffered bitterly from awareness of his club foot and a tendency to stoutness, she seemed like an angel of understanding. Gentle, sensual, dark, with a beautiful curved mouth, she fitted exactly Byron's idea of a perfect woman. But of course she was forbidden fruit. She was also engaged to their cousin, George Leigh. 'Can't you drive this cousin of ours out of your pretty little head?' he begged her. But she went through with her plans, married the horsey Colonel Leigh and settled down to be a country wife in Newmarket.

As the years went by, however, and Byron grew to be one of the most handsome and fascinating men of his day, the two found themselves drawn to each other and their affection developed into an intense passion. Byron called her 'the one whom I most loved' and even confessed to his bride on their wedding night that no woman would ever possess as much of his love as his sister Augusta.

Byron had a miserable childhood and spent most of his life making up for it by indulging his passionate, sensual nature. When he was a boy his mother's moods of depression alternated with bursts of tenderness or fury. She once called him a 'lame brat' and the words seared his soul. He had a thoroughly Scottish upbringing in Aberdeen and was looked after by a Calvinistic nanny who taught him that all people were sinners, predestined to damnation, a harsh doctrine that also left its mark.

When he was ten his great-uncle, always called 'the wicked Lord Byron' because he lived as a recluse with a servant girl he had named 'Lady Betty', died and left him heir to the title. He also left his Newstead Abbey, a magnificent Gothic ruin of a place in Nottinghamshire with a sinister lake and a ghost. Byron loved it. His mother took him to live there and provided him with a pretty young nurse who added spice to her affairs with other servants by occasionally hopping into bed with the young Lord. 'My passions were developed early,' he recalled later. Too early, thought his mother, who dismissed the nurse and sent him away to school.

Byron's first real love was his cousin, Mary Chaworth,

heiress of Annesley Hall, only a few fields away from Newstead. She was already 'promised' and cut him to the quick by saying in his hearing 'Do you think I could care anything for that lame boy!' He said the remark stayed in his heart ike a splinter of ice and it certainly explained a lot of his ruthless behaviour to women in the future. When she married he missed a whole term at Harrow because he was so heartbroken. He wrote lines to her which began, 'Well, thou art happy . . .' and it was years before he completely got over her.

He went from Harrow to Cambridge and threw himself wholeheartedly into the business of becoming a young rake. His mother was worried to death by his extravagance and his drinking. 'Ruined! At 18. Great God!' she exclaimed. But Byron had started to write poetry and that gradually became as important to him as other pleasures. Then, still inclined to stoutness, he began to follow a strict regime which he summarized as follows: 'Much physic, much hot bathing and much violent exercise.'

He emerged from this self-inflicted torture ready to make half the women in Britain swoon, giving the name 'Byronic' to a certain kind of male beauty. His figure was now slim and elegant. Dark curls clustered round his head, his grey eyes were fringed with long, dark lashes; his well-shaped mouth, cleft chin and smooth, pale brow combined to give his face a look of classic nobility.

At Cambridge, however, he had gained a reputation as a profligate and gambler and now he plunged head first into London life. 'I am buried in an abyss of sensuality,' he informed his great and brilliant friend, John Cam Hobhouse, later to be Lord Brougham. But it is important to remember that Byron always liked to exaggerate his wickedness for dramatic effect.

His unfulfilled love for Mary Chaworth lingered on and he had failed to persuade his sister Augusta not to marry, so in 1809 he decided to travel in Europe and the Near

East and forget about them both. After a farewell party at Newstead Abbey he sailed from Falmouth with Hobhouse and did not return to England for two years.

Byron cut his teeth on various love affairs abroad, then once back in London decided to give himself up to his poetry. He only half-succeeded. His club foot, which he did his best to conceal, proved no obstacle to his success with the opposite sex. Women gazed instead at that pale face with its arrogantly sensual lines and were lost. Suddenly, he woke up one morning to find himself famous. On 10 March 1812 the first two Cantos of *Childe Harold* were published. The epic was greeted with near hysteria and sold like hot cakes. Some people tried to identify Byron with his hero and were convinced that he had a hidden life. Mounds of invitations arrived at his lodgings in St James's Street. It was said you could not sit down at a dinner table in London without hearing the constant repetition of his name.

Of course what most fascinated women was the hint of scandal about him. Behind the pale beauty many suspected darkness and mystery. He revelled in the notoriety, and no doubt derived much satisfaction from it. He had a keen sense of humour and satirical wit which permeated a great deal of his work.

One woman who literally threw herself at him was the wild, delicate hoyden Lady Caroline Lamb, daughter of the Earl of Bessborough. At her first meeting with Byron she turned on her heel saying that the very sight of that handsome face made her feel faint. They were introduced again at Lady Holland's and he was entranced by her huge brown eyes, short, tumbled curls and boyish figure. Her tantalizing first rejection of him, then the experience of meeting the pretty creature face to face, was a challenge Byron could not resist.

For a few months he was in love with her then, just as suddenly, cooled off. The wild extravagance of her passion had proved too much for him. He had awakened her sexually. 'The tumult, the ardour, the romance bewildered my reason,' she wrote after one lovers' meeting. She besieged him with her emotions and when they quarrelled tried to stab herself, first with a knife, then with a piece of broken glass. She exposed him to public ridicule, and that he could not forgive. At he beginning of their affair he was telling her that her heart was a little volcano – 'It pours lava through your veins and yet I cannot wish it a bit colder' – and, he assured her, 'I have always thought you the cleverest, most agreeable, absurd, amiable, perplexing, dangerous fascinating little being.' Before long, however, he was moaning, 'this dream, this delirium . . . it must pass away'. She sent him some of her pubic hair, asking for his in return. Her immodesty put him off even more.

When Lady Caroline's mother tried to persuade her to go to Ireland, hoping that with the sea between them the affair would come to an end, Caro asked Byron to elope with her. He took her back to Lady Bessborough as though she were a naughty child and in the end she had to settle for Ireland. From there she bombarded him with letters.

Byron did the only thing possible to stop Caroline pestering him. He took a new mistress, the Countess of Oxford, a beautiful bluestocking who believed in free love and was twice his age. He declared that the autumn of her beauty was preferable to another woman's springtime and when Caro wrote asking for confirmation of his love he replied: 'Lady Caro, our affections are not our own . . . mine are engaged. I love another. I am no longer your love.'

In the midst of all this he met Annabella Milbanke. She, too, was a bluestocking, a clever, intellectual girl who specialized in mathematics, theology and Greek. She was only 20 but liked life to be orderly and systematic. Byron's friends tried to make him see that they were not even remotely suited, but he was in raptures about her 'nut brown looks' and had no doubt added to the list of her charms the fact she was an heiress. Annabella was quite bowled over by his famous looks, came to the conclusion that he needed saving from himself, and she would do the saving. He called her 'my princess of the parallelograms' and proposed. To his amazement, she refused him.

Suddenly Byron's half-sister, Augusta, arrived on the London scene. They had been writing to each other for years, a charming, lively correspondence that showed their affection. But in the hot summer of 1813 Augusta was bored, restless and dissatisfied. Living at Newmarket with her three daughters, she hardly ever saw her husband other than when he appeared for the races. She packed her bags and descended on Byron and he was reminded once again that his sister, with her dark, sensual grace, was his ideal woman.

Byron's whole life had been devoted to satisfying his sensations. Now, it is almost certain, he gave away his desires once again and discovered the sensation of forbidden love. In her biography of the poet, Lady Elizabeth Longford says: 'Gradually, however, there was another sensation not so pleasant as the first – sexual guilt. Ill-treated by her husband, Augusta would do anything Byron wanted. It is as certain as these things can be that she was his lover. Her unthinking acquiescence in his crime must have increased his guilty torment.'

Augusta constantly dominated his thoughts and feelings. At last he could no longer bear the burden without telling someone else. Lady Melbourne seemed the ideal person. She had been acting as a go-between for him with Annabella, but was a modern thinker and feminist. Byron told her how his love for his sister made all other loves seem insipid. Their intentions, he admitted, had been very different and when they failed to adhere to them it had been due to her 'weakness' and his 'folly'. Lady Melbourne was appalled and told him so. Byron had some wild idea about going abroad and taking Augusta with him. Lady Melbourne implored him to go abroad by all means, but to leave Augusta behind.

When Byron celebrated his 26th birthday Augusta was heavily pregnant. For the moment only Lady Melbourne knew of his feelings and she dreaded to think what society would say if the 'truth' came out. The press had already described Lord Byron as 'a deformed Richard III, an atheist rebel and a devil'. What would they do if they found out about his relations with his sister?

Augusta gave birth to a daughter. Could he be the father? Byron himself, apparently, had doubts and he was never as fond of this child, christened Medora, as he was of Augusta's other children who were undoubtedly fathered by Colonel Leigh.

Ten months had gone by since he last saw Annabella Milbanke, proposed to her, and received her refusal. He decided he must try to lay the ghosts of past love affairs and commit himself to a decent marriage. Various candidates were put forward by well-meaning friends but he would not consider them. He became involved with the pedantic bluestocking again and they drifted into a marriage which both were to regret bitterly.

Though he could be a sparkling and charming companion, he behaved abominably on their honeymoon, taunting Annabella with his love for Augusta and hinting that the child she had just given birth to was his.

Marriage was not as bad as he expected. They had some pleasant times together at the Milbanke home at Seaham in the north of England, but Byron began to feel cut off, trapped, and insisted they move back to London. They collected Augusta on the way and Annabella, seeing brother and sister together, had her worst suspicions confirmed. Byron, torn apart by his conflicting emotions, behaved even worse than on his honeymoon. 'There were times,' Annabella wrote later, 'when I could have plunged a dagger into his heart.' Strangely enough his behaviour drew the two women together and Annabella began to have hopes that she could 'save' them both. 'His misfortune is an habitual passion for excitement,' she told Augusta.

When their daughter Ada was born Annabella began to suspect that debts, drunkenness and remorse over Augusta had driven Byron mad. He told her they could no longer afford to live in style in London and she was to go home to her parents at their estate in Leicestershire. They said goodbye for the last time on 14 January 1815. She could take no more and had come to the conclusion that she had fallen in love with Lucifer himself. The truth was, they were ill-matched from the start.

Byron himself seemed to accept her judgement, saying bitterly in one letter to her: 'It is my destiny to ruin all I come near.' Annabella eventually admitted to a confidante that her secret reason for parting with Byron was her growing suspicion of incest. Augusta was pregnant again and this time people were giving voice to their suspicions. She could no longer stay for even short visits at Byron's house in Piccadilly. She went off to resume her duties as a woman of the bedchamber to Queen Charlotte, who would not have believed in such goings on, even if she had been told about them.

The separation of Byron and Annabella caused no little scandal. Female society turned against the poet, though women still peeped from behind their fans, around doors and lace curtains to catch a glimpse of him, and their hearts beat faster at a glance from those cool grey eyes.

It was under these circumstances that Byron boarded a packet for Ostend on 25 April 1816 and left England, never to return alive. He and Augusta said goodbye to one another wretchedly and in tears. They were never to meet again. He wrote to her the exquisite lines beginning:

'Thou wert the solitary star
Which rose and set not to the last . . .'

His friend Hobhouse listened to him curse the hypocrisy and repressiveness of English morality, which was driving him away, and noticed that some inquisitive society women, disguising themselves as servant girls, had gathered on the quay to have one last look at the demon lover.

Byron travelled through Belgium and Switzerland in his dark green Napoleonic coach to join his friend, the poet Shelley, and his wife Mary at their hotel on the outskirts of Geneva. Also waiting for him was a hot-headed girl he hoped he had left behind in England.

At the 11th hour before his departure Byron had become involved with 17-year-old Claire Clairmont, Mary Shelley's stepsister. She was an incurable romantic, jealous of Mary's elopement with Shelley and determined to catch herself a poet. She wrote to Byron, asking for a meeting and making it quite clear she was ready to be his mistress. The meeting took place somewhere near London during his last week in England. Byron had no intention of seeing her again but he had unwisely given her the address in Geneva where she could write. She packed and hurried to Switzerland ahead of him.

Now the party was a foursome. He took the Villa Diodati on the Belle Rive of Lake Geneva while the Shelleys occupied a villa on the hillside above. He spoke of Claire as 'a foolish girl' but she was close to him for a brief spell and gave birth to his daughter.

Switzerland was a watershed in Byron's life. Stimulated by the company of the younger poet and by the drama of the mountains and lakes, he wrote his great poem *The Prisoner of Chillon*. When it was translated into German Byron was taken up by Goethe and his fame began to spread throughout Europe. He also climbed the Alps with Hobhouse and wrote the first two acts of his poetic drama *Manfred*.

For a time it was an idyllic life, but Byron eventually

made a move to end it for he did not want to be tied to Claire. He persuaded the Shelleys to take her home. He still encountered upper-class English tourists in Geneva who stared at him 'as though a devil had come among them'. He wanted to get even further away from his homeland. Italy had a very strong appeal for him. He headed for Venice and the sun.

It did not take him long to find comfortable lodgings over a prosperous baker's shop. The great attraction of these premises was the baker's wife, Marianna Segati, with whom he fell 'in fathomless love'. Her husband saw no harm in taking this English Lord as her lover, in fact he bragged about it. Marianna was a seductive, hot-blooded creature with large, liquid eyes, dark, glossy hair and the grace of a gazelle. She also had a fearful temper which she displayed when she thought her sister-in-law was trying to take her place in Byron's bed.

Rumours of her violent love for the poet travelled all over Venice and, naturally, shocked the resident English. Apart from the affair with Marianna his first few months in the city were comparatively respectable. He was entranced by its ancient narrow streets and canals and loved the Italian working people and shopkeepers whom he found natural, vivid and warmhearted. It was after he installed himself in the Palazzo Mocenigo overlooking the Grand Canal that he gave way to the excesses that impaired his health. The Venice Carnival, with its unspeakably dissolute entertainments, held him captive. Yet it was at this time that he wrote some of his finest poetry including the first Canto of *Don Juan* and *Manfred*, which contained some of his most profound thoughts about man's destiny.

La Segati was followed by baker's wife Margherita Cogni. He met her one day while he was out riding and was immediately drawn to the magnificent, 22-year-old peasant, tall, strong, wild and beautiful. To keep her near him he employed her as housekeeper at his summer villa at La Mira on the river Brenta, 7 miles from Venice. She, too, had a terrible temper and it was said she once took advantage of Byron's lameness and beat him in a fit of jealousy. Certainly after a few months he had had enough of her, but she refused to leave. When he finally managed to dismiss her, she threw herself into the canal from which she was rescued just in time.

This was the most dissolute period of his life. When he celebrated his 30th birthday in 1818 he was beginning to show some of the effects of his self-indulgence. He was said to have founded a harem which cost him £3,000. He boasted that it accommodated 200 women of every nationality, but he was probably exaggerating. He had become, in his biographer Lady Longford's words, 'a puffy Romeo, both comical and sad'. Yet his poetry flooded out to a disapproving world that could not help but recognize his genius, and in his debauchery he wrote one of the most beautiful lyrics in the language:

'So we'll go no more a-roving
So late into the night,
Though the heart be still as loving,
And the moon be still as bright.

For the sword outwears its sheath,
And the soul wears out the breast,
And the heart must pause to breathe,
And love itself have rest.'

At a reception held by the Countess Benzoni the 30-year-old Byron came face to face with the last love of his life. Nineteen-year-old Countess Teresa Guiccioli had been married for just three days when they met. Her husband was an elderly, eccentric landowner and the marriage had been one entirely of convenience. Byron was attracted by this striking Italian girl with golden hair, blue eyes, a fine complexion and magnificent bust and shoulders, but did not at the time foresee what the depths of his feelings for her would be. They discussed Dante together, rode on horseback under the great umbrella pines, strolled through scented gardens on balmy evenings. Soon he was writing to her: 'You have been mine and, whatever is the outcome, I am and eternally shall be yours . . .' She called him 'mio Byron' in public, which was guaranteed to shock.

The Guicciolis moved to their palazzo in Ravenna and Byron was invited to rent the upper floor. He was not entirely happy about it, suspecting that the old man intended to spy on them. Nevertheless he moved in, bringing with him ten horses, five cats, an eagle, a crow and a falcon. After a few months he added five peacocks, two guinea hens and a crane.

Byron and his countess lived in a romantic trance. This time he was really in love. She brought such beauty and intelligence into his life that he was haunted by regrets that they had not met sooner. He quite clearly saw himself as an aging Don Juan.

Count Guiccioli was well aware of his wife's affair with Byron but waited until he caught them together on a sofa one day before reading the riot act. He demanded she should give him up. Her answer was to ask the Pope for a separation. This was eventually granted to her and she went to live under her father's roof at the nearby Palazzo Gamba. Byron was left with her eccentric husband, the poet comically pretending that he could not possibly move out because of his vast menagerie.

Revolution was in the air and politics were soon to change their lives. Teresa's family was well known for its sympathy with the oppressed poor. In 1821, after a fracas in which the commander of the papal troops was killed in the street in Ravenna, the Gambas, including Teresa, had to fly from the Pope's domain. Teresa left Byron in floods of tears, wondering if she would ever see him again.

Three months elapsed before he could follow. Shelley had visited him in Ravenna, finding him popular with the people there who knew he sympathized with their struggles. Byron told his friend that he was 'reformed as far as gallantry goes'.

In October of that year Byron's travel-worn Napoleonic coach rumbled out of Ravenna for the last time. He found a suitable house on the river Arno, near Pisa, only two or three minutes from where Teresa had settled with her family. They formed a new social circle, entertaining in style and giving dinners at which a mellowed Byron played host with wit and irony until the early hours of the morning. Perhaps it was just a shade too domestic, too cosy. When Lady Blessington visited him, he told her 'there is something in the poetical temperament that precludes happiness, not only to the person who has it, but to those connected with him'. To her he confessed his extraordinary presentiment that he would die in Greece.

Greece had been on his mind for some time. He was totally in sympathy with those who suffered oppression of any kind. By the beginning of April 1823 he was afire to help the struggling Greek patriots in their war of independence against the Turks. He did not dare tell Teresa that he was going to war, partly because he feared she would try to stop him. But the young countess knew well enough what was happening and she too had a presentiment that he would not return. Their last hours together almost broke her heart.

Byron was only 35 when he sailed from Genoa to Greece in July 1823 but his constitution was wrecked and his life force spent. When he landed on the beach at Missolonghi, resplendent in scarlet uniform, the Greeks hailed him as a delivering angel. But the enterprise to which Byron was committed was badly planned and ill-conceived. Missolonghi was set on a lagoon rich in malaria. Once the winter rains began the place became a disease-ridden mudbowl. His health weakened by the conditions, Byron had no strength left to fight the rheumatic fever that struck him in the spring following that appalling winter. The end came swiftly on Easter Monday, 19 April 1824, when he fell into a deep sleep after delirium. There were memorial services in every important town in Greece. In England, those who considered him to be a demon lover, Lucifer incarnate, flocked into the streets as the cortège carrying his body made its way home for burial.

Napoleon

Power meant more to him than women. That was the truth of it. But Napoleon Bonaparte had a romantic, passionate nature that could not be denied. So, in the midst of war, he could sit down and write to Josephine Beauharnais: 'Your image and the intoxicating pleasure of last night allow my senses to rest. Sweet and matchless Josephine, how strangely you work upon my heart . . . a thousand kisses, but give me none back for they set my blood on fire.'

His love for the Creole who was to become his Empress poured out in floods of romantic words, classic love letters that are still read today. But when it became necessary for him to re-marry if he was to found a dynasty he did not hesitate to put her aside. 'Be brave,' he told the unhappy Josephine, 'you know I will always be your friend.'

Napoleon had two wives, Josephine and Marie Louise, and at least 12 mistresses. On the whole his attitude to women was tender and uncomplicated. He moved from mistress to mistress, always under the impression that he was genuinely in love.

To the end of his days he remembered every detail of his youthful idyll with Caroline Colombier at a cherry-gathering expedition in Valance in 1786. He was a young officer cadet then, barely 16, newly arrived from Corsica. She was sweet and fresh and lovely; he was thin, lank-haired and gauche. Years later he saw her face in a crowd, recognized her and greeted her with tears.

As Captain Bonaparte, already stirring with ambitions, he asked a Marseilles cloth merchant for the hand of his daughter, Désirée Clary. She was the pretty younger sister of his brother Joseph's wife. But the merchant Clary decided one Bonaparte in the family was enough. Napoleon's wooing had been tepid and Désirée, in love with the Corsican, never forgave him for his lack of determination. She was later to marry his most unrelenting enemy, Count Bernadotte, and become Queen of Sweden.

In the next few years his military career progressed swiftly. He was recalled from the Italian front in 1795 to become Commander of the Garrison in Paris. When he crushed the Royalist insurrection in the capital and saved the Convention, he became a hero.

Among those who watched the Corsican with fascination was Josephine Beauharnais. Her husband had been guillotined during the Terror and she and her two children, Hortense and Eugène, had not long been released from prison.

The 14-year-old boy asked to see Napoleon, told him he was the son of General Beauharnais and asked if he could please keep his father's sword. He returned full of praise for Napoleon's kindness and gentlemanly behaviour towards him. Josephine invited him to call on her so that she might thank him.

Napoleon at once became a regular visitor to her small house in the rue Chantereine and fell madly in love. She was 32, six years older than him, handsome rather than beautiful, graceful, with a pleasant voice and regular features. Napoleon was still quite unsophisticated with regard to the opposite sex, but Josephine was worldly and had developed her sensual life to a fine art. The Vicomte de Barras, Commander of the Army of the Interior, whose mistress she had been, advised Napoleon to marry her. The wedding took place on 9 March 1796 in a registrar's office. Napoleon was two hours late.

Barras handed him supreme command of the army in Italy as a wedding present. Their honeymoon lasted for one day; then Napoleon set off for the south on a journey that would eventually end on the battlefield of Waterloo. The 26-year-old general was distraught at having to leave his beloved Josephine so soon. At every halt he made time to sit down and write to her what were to prove some of the most moving love letters ever composed. He begged her to come to him. 'If you hesitate you will find me ill . . . take wings . . . come . . . come.'

In the Italian campaign Napoleon showed the first signs of his genius in battle. The French went mad with relief. They had found a hero-leader at last. All he needed was her presence by his side. He wrote again and again but she delayed her departure until he could bear it no more and ordered her to come.

She had been enjoying her life in Paris and had no great desire to abandon the receptions and balls at which she had been fêted like a heroine. But once in Italy her eyes were opened. If she did not realize before that she had married a great man, she began to now. He was being treated like a king. Audiences with him were arranged in strict order of protocol, meals were taken in public and there was a constant coming and going of French generals and Italian nobles.

Josephine did not accompany him when he went back in triumph to Paris. She followed a month later. He was still madly in love with her, so did not complain when she started to spend money on their house in the rue Chantereine. Later her attitude to money was to drive him almost mad with frustration.

In the spring of 1798 Napoleon announced that he was going to Egypt. It was to be 18 months before he saw Josephine again. His farewell was tender and loving.

The landing in Egypt was a success and he captured Cairo in July 1798. But while he was deeply involved in the east, Josephine had been amusing herself. She had always been promiscuous and now, lonely without her husband, she had apparently taken a handsome young man called Hippolyte Charles as her lover. A letter from brother Joseph gave Napoleon the news. He said she was at that very moment under the chestnuts at Malmaison in a mansion she had acquired, equipped and redecorated at Napoleon's expense.

Napoleon took the news badly. 'The veil has been torn off once and for all,' he told Joseph with despair. His orgy of self-pity was broken by the sound of a merry laugh. Making inquiries, he discovered that it belonged to a petite, flaxen-haired soldier's wife called Margaret Pauline Foures. Her husband was a newly commissioned officer and she had sailed from Toulon with him dressed in soldier's uniform. Despite the fact she was newly married, Madame Foures became Napoleon's acknowledged mistress in Egypt and wore a miniature of him on a gold chain round her neck.

His return to France was sudden and unexpected. Josephine heard the news while she was dining out, rushed home, dressed in her prettiest clothes and went to meet him. She wanted to explain her conduct before anyone else could get to him. But in her haste she missed his cavalcade and he reached home to find his mother, not Josephine, waiting. His family flocked around telling him of her infidelity and her wild extravagance. He promised to divorce her, rushed up to his room and locked the door.

When Josephine returned, too late, she fell to her knees, begging him to open the door so that she could be heard. He refused. Just as she was about to go away, the maid arrived with her children. Napoleon could not resist them. The door was suddenly flung open and all three were gathered into his arms.

Josephine was never again unfaithful, though Napoleon himself had fleeting affairs with actresses, countesses and adventuresses, not from physical desire alone but to escape for a while from the pitiless pressures of states-manship. He was embroiled in transitory love affairs during the pre-Austerlitz period, and was actually caught in his bedroom with Marguerite Georges, or Georgina, as he called the empty-headed little actress. For once it was Josephine who suffered jealousy.

That Josephine still meant a great deal to him was proved by his insistence on her rights during the weeks preceding their coronation as Emperor and Empress on 2 December 1804. But within two years Napoleon would ask for his freedom.

On his triumphal entry into Warsaw in November 1806 Napoleon was greeted by an 18-year-old Polish countess, Marie Walewska. She was waiting, with crowds of peasants, in the little town of Bronia between his headquarters at Pultsk and Warsaw. He only caught a glimpse of her but the impression of magnolia skin, flaxen hair and blue eyes stayed with him.

He recognized her instantly when she attended a grand ball soon after his arrival and learned that she was the wife of a 70-year-old Polish patriot. He asked her to dance but she declined. He went back to his room and wrote her a note. 'I saw but you. I admired but you, I desire but you. Answer at once and calm the impatient ardour of N.' She refused to answer this note or the notes following until he blackmailed her into submission by promising: 'Your country will be even dearer to me if you have compassion on my heart.'

She gave way to him in the end and she became very precious to him. When she told him she was going to have his child, he came to a decision. He must divorce Josephine, find a royal bride and produce an heir.

He was still very fond of Josephine. They had come a long way together and she had earned his admiration and respect. One night at dinner he broke the news to her. He wanted a divorce. She screamed and fainted and had to be carried bodily to her room. But when the day of her leaving came she made her exit with great dignity.

The way was now open for his marriage to the Archduchess Marie Louise of Austria. She was a fresh-faced princess of 18 who had been brought up in total ignorance of the opposite sex. It was said that even animals with sexual organs had been cut out of her books. Napoleon was so overjoyed at becoming a member of the Hapsburg family that he did not care about her dullness and ignorance. He was so impatient to see her that on the day of her arrival he rode out to meet her, stopped the carriage and escorted her home. The poverty-stricken court at Vienna had been amazed at the trousseau he sent and she was splendidly dressed to meet the French aristocracy.

Napoleon did not demand passion from her. He wanted a pleasant, gentle companion. Marie Louise came out of her shell, happier than she had ever thought she could be. Within a year she presented him with a son and heir, who was given the title of King of Rome.

Within four years Napoleon knew that the dynasty he hoped to start with this son would never materialize. His enemies were gathering round, closing in on him. On 25 January 1814 he saw the Empress and his son for the last time. Shortly afterwards, his downfall was proclaimed and he departed for Elba.

Josephine died of diphtheria on 29 May 1814, and was buried at Reuil. On his last visit to Paris in a final desperate attempt to regain power he made a journey to

Malmaison, visited the room where she died and came out weeping. She had, after all, been the great love of his life. He went alone into exile.

Metternich

Metternich, powerful Chancellor of the Austro-Hungarian Empire, was the most amorous diplomat in Europe. The great peacemaker, instrumental in shaping the destiny of nations, made every woman he met fall in love with him.

He was handsome and elegant, had great wit and charm and was said to be a virile and experienced lover. Typical of his affairs was that with Princess Katharina Bagration, wife of a Russian general. One day she called on him at the legation in Dresden. They had never met before. He opened the door to find 'a beautiful naked angel' standing on the doorstep. She was wearing one of the diaphanous dresses fashionable in high society and standing against the sun she appeared to have nothing on. She was like an exquisite little marble statue. Metternich was so impressed he almost forgot to ask her in. When she looked up at him she saw a handsome fair-haired man wearing an open-necked silk shirt and a purple dressing gown trimmed with sable. In describing him afterwards she exclaimed: 'He was an Apollo descended upon the Earth.' The attraction between them was so powerful that they made love at that first meeting.

Princess Katharina was highly intelligent and beautiful in a delicate oriental way. She had traces of Mongolian ancestry, seen in her high cheekbones and titled almond eyes. Within a few weeks all Dresden knew of the affair. Even the return of his wife, Eleanor, did not make any difference to the intensity of Metternich's feelings.

Within three months the Princess knew she was going to have his child. He decided the wisest thing was to tell his wife immediately. Eleanor, who adored him, said the best solution was for her to accept the child and bring it up as their own. Metternich loved Katharina all his life, but that was the end of the affair.

Count Clemens Metternich of Coblenz was 16 when he went up to Strasbourg University in 1788. The city was full of French aristocrats fleeing from the rumblings of the Revolution. They set up their headquarters at the Inn of the Three Golden Crowns, trying to recreate the atmosphere of the Paris they had left behind. They dined, danced and gambled under vast crystal chandeliers, the women wore all their diamonds and the air was heavy with perfume.

Metternich was taken there one night. As he looked round the room one face stood out from all the rest. He could not take his eyes off Constance de la Force. She was the daughter of the Marquis de Saviale, Keeper of the Seals, one of the most beautiful women in France.

Only 18, she was married to the Duc Caumont de la Force who left her alone a great deal. 'Who is that?' she asked as Metternich entered. 'C'est un enfant', younger even than you, her friends replied. But she insisted on meeting him.

After dinner that night she took him back to her house, pushed him into the depths of a chair and commanded: 'Wait for me.' When she next appeared it was in a white batiste dressing gown edged with soft Valenciennes lace, her small feet in white satin slippers. The champagne and her perfume overcame his senses.

For the rest of his life Metternich said he sought the beauty and perfection of that night. He never found it again in quite the same way but he never stopped looking, even in old age. He wrote: 'I loved her with all the enthusiasm of youth and she loved me with all the simplicity of her heart.' The relationship lasted more than three years.

When Emperor Leopold II died, his son, Archduke Francis, succeeded him. This was good news for Metternich. The new Emperor was a good friend and only four years older than himself. He was created Minister Plenipotentiary at The Hague and sent on a special mission to England. When he returned he was a confident, accomplished, highly attractive young diplomat.

His mother, seeking a good match, chose the Countess Eleanor von Kaunitz. He was not enthusiastic, but they were married on 27 September 1795. They set up house in Vienna and Metternich profited from his wife's social position. She fell passionately in love with him, but as far as he was concerned it remained a marriage of convenience.

When he was 28 the Emperor offered him a choice of diplomatic posts. He asked for Dresden. It was a month before his wife joined him, and in that time he had had his encounter with Princess Katharina Bagration. Though his oriental charmer was never forgotten he was soon delighting in the charms of someone else. The Duchess of Kurland threw herself at him and he 'accepted her as a gift'. She was tall, beautiful, with golden ringlets and dark eyes. She proved a demanding mistress. He often tried to escape from her but she held him under her influence for a long time.

His arrival in Paris as Austrian Ambassador in August 1806 caused a great deal of interest. Metternich disliked Napoleon's politics but admired the man. The feeling was mutual. What Napoleon did not expect was that Metternich would have an affair with his sister. Caroline Murat, the Grand Duchess of Berg, who would one day be Queen of Naples, was just as stubborn as her brother when she knew what she wanted. And she wanted Metternich. She was tall, elegant and possessive. They were seen everywhere together. That did not stop him from carrying on a love affair with someone else. He was quite positive he had the ability to love one, two or even three women at the same time, saying that he cared for them all in a different way and for different reasons. So the 34-year-old dandy, with his startling blue eyes, also courted the Duchess of Abrantés, a tiny feminine woman as lovely as a Dresden doll. Napoleon became very angry, fearing that Caroline had not shown enough discretion. But, before the whole thing could be blown out of proportion, Metternich was recalled to Vienna with his family.

The Congress of Vienna which followed his return was the most brilliant gathering of its time, when for an entire year Vienna became the capital of Europe. Hundreds of beautiful women arrived with their husbands or families, each trying to outdo the other in elegance. But for Metternich there was only one. She was to be the greatest love of his life and her name was Julia Zichy. She was the daughter of Count Zichy, a minor courtier who had been given a post at the Congress. As Metternich got to know her he found a peace of mind and heart that he had not felt for years. She was almost nun-like in her gentle simplicity. When he craved for her physically she told him she would not become his mistress unless he promised he would have nothing more to do with other women.

Metternich was exhausted by the strenuous life he had lived ever since the first campaigns against Napoleon. He needed rest and intended to leave the Congress for a short while to recover. Julia took him to a hunting lodge in the heart of snow-covered mountains and there they walked and talked and he fell in love with her as he had with no other woman. The idea of strict fidelity appalled him at first, but he agreed. He planned a new sort of life in which they would be together for always. But the end came suddenly and tragically. Soon after the Congress Julia had turned deeply religious. She passed hours, even days, in contemplation and prayer. One day, as he was sitting at the desk in his office, Metternich was handed a little box tied with black ribbon. Opening it he found ashes, charred fragments of his own love letters. Julia Zichy was dead. Metternich pillowed his arms on the desk and wept.

His wife Eleanor died, too. But he would twice marry again, from now onwards living for nothing but his family. Both his second and third wife were 20 years younger than himself, but his physical capacity remained and he was as mentally vigorous as ever. His second wife was Marie Antoinette von Leykham. He was blissfully happy with her for a year, then she died in childbirth. But the great lover still had one more triumphant love affair to consummate. He married Countess Melanie Zichy Farraris, a tempestuous, excitable Hungarian. She bore him five children. They were happy together for 22 years, then after a serious illness in March 1854 she died. 'Her last moments,' he wrote, 'might be compared with a light slowly going out.' His own light flickered and died five years later, when he was 86.

Valentino

He was the film world's first romantic idol. They called him 'the Great Lover' and up there on the screen he was certainly that. Women shrieked with ecstasy when he bared his chest in the *The Sheik*. They fainted in the aisles. They read more into his performances than ever he intended. He was the lover of their dreams, the violent exciting lover who never pleaded for a woman's favours but took them as his right. 'Lie still,' he said to Agnes Ayres as he prepared to make love to her in *The Sheik*. 'Lie still, you little fool.' And every woman in the cinema wished she could take her place.

The cult of Valentino lasted for a whole generation. His latin looks and smouldering eyes, enhanced by the costumes he wore and the brutal-tender manner in which he wooed his women, made his films box-office winners.

Yet, in private life, Rudolph Valentino was nothing like the great lover women imagined. His first marriage ended on his wedding night when his bride locked him out of the bedroom. He was deeply in love with his second wife, Natacha Rambova, but she left him to pursue her career. When the sultry Polish star, Pola Negri, clinging to him like a limpet, decided she was going to be the next Mrs Valentino, he hardly noticed.

The truth was that Valentino was basically just a very likeable Italian of peasant stock who by some strange chemistry became a star of magic sensuality on screen. After Nureyev, the great dancer and ballet idol of later times, had played the part of Valentino in Ken Russell's film of that name, he told an interviewer: 'I have watched Valentino's old films. In those days most film actors were very jittery. He was much slower, more sinuous in his movements. He would hold still and just turn his head or move his hands to indicate an emotion. There was a dance quality about his movement, which was completely natural . . .'

They knew nothing about all this in the village of Castellaneta, his birthplace in the south of Italy. To them he was Rodolpho Guglielmi, son of the local vet, the village nuisance as a child and a worry to his mother.

He was born on 6 May 1895. His father died when he was 11 and his mother urged him to learn a trade or even become a lay brother of the church when he left school. Rodolpho did not know what he wanted to do. He only knew he hated Castellaneta, its bare, stony fields, its crumbling poverty. As he entered his teens he spent more and more time wandering through the streets of the nearest town, Taranto. He probably went to agricultural college about this time but it left no impression. Taranto was like a glimpse of the outside world. His mother thought he should be content, but he was determined to see what lay beyond.

Many of the young men he met in the town talked of families who had started afresh in the New World. This, he decided, was what he would do. When he told his mother there were tears and recriminations and once, after he had thrown a violent temper, a beating from a male relative. Eventually she agreed to his emigration and sent him off with her prayers.

On 9 December 1913, Rodolpho Guglielmi joined the steerage passengers sailing for New York with dreams of a better life. As it was bitterly cold and he did not own an overcoat he stuffed sheets of newspaper under his shirt to keep warm. One American dollar was sewn into the lining of his jacket.

His first months in America shattered his illusions. He spent them living with Italian immigrant families, working as a messenger, dishwasher, janitor and shop assistant. He was desperately homesick. But in June 1914 he found work as a gardener on the Long Island estate of wealthy Cornelius Bliss. Here, something traumatic happened to him. For the first time in his life he came close to people who were rich. He became passionately interested in studying them, the way they walked, talked and laughed, the way the men devoted themselves to the pursuit of pleasure and beautiful women. One day, he swore, he too would be rich.

Perhaps he spent too much time dreaming. He lost his job on Long Island and had to take work as a gardener with the Manhattan parks department. But there, too, as he weeded and mowed grass, he watched the rich young men, copying their manners and the way they held themselves. In his leisure time he also discovered the cheap dance halls and cabarets where some of his countrymen congregated. He became increasingly skilful at popular ballroom dancing, his speciality being the continental tango. The tango was the rage of the day and no one could have been better equipped for it than Rodolpho with his dark, Latin good looks and natural grace. Soon his performance was so good people crowded round the floor to watch him.

Word spread about Rodolpho's tango and he was offered a job at Maxim's, one of the most luxurious cabarets in New York along with Delmonico's and the Ritz Grill. Cabarets of this class hired male tango dancers purely for the purpose of keeping their rich, bored women customers happy. Some of them were gigolos, living off their clients, but Valentino was always careful to point out in later years that he never became one. But he happily accepted the silk shirts, expensive toiletries and jewellery that his admirers lavished upon him. He changed his name to Rodolpho Valentino and claimed to have come from a noble Italian family which had fallen upon hard times. The rich American women he danced with loved his foreign accent, good manners and languid grace. He told them incredible stories about his past and they believed him. They shivered with delight as he held them close and brushed their ears with his lips.

Within months he was the most sought-after dancer in Maxim's. The next step was to become an exhibition dancer and for this he demanded more and more professional and accomplished partners as his name became known. He had taken to wearing a corset to give him the lithe figure of a matador and he grew sideboards to emphasize the Latin look. But he was not satisfied.

He managed to get a part in a lightweight musical comedy playing its way across the country to San Francisco. When it reached Omaha, Nebraska, it died a death, but there was just enough money in the kitty to pay for coach tickets back to New York. Rodolpho exchanged his ticket for a ticket to San Francisco.

Most of the show people he had met were talking about one thing – the movies. There were, they told him, marvellous opportunities if you were lucky, and it was all happening down there in California. Life was hard for him at first in San Francisco. He was friendless and unknown. But things looked up when he was asked to replace a dancer in a show called *Nobody Home* and made friends with a young showman called Bryan Foy.

When *Nobody Home* closed he moved to Los Angeles to share an apartment with Foy, excited by the fact that he was going to be right in the centre of filmmaking. Every day about teatime he sauntered into the Alexandria Hotel in Los Angeles where everybody who was anybody in the movie business gathered to talk shop and eat free hot ham sandwiches. He at last managed to get a couple of days work as an extra in a ballroom scene for five dollars a day, but the prospects seemed dismal.

His big break came one autumn afternoon in 1918 when he met Emmett Flynn, who had given him the job as an extra. He had liked the look of Rodolpho and suggested he play the part of a villainous count in *The Married Virgin*. Though he did not like the thought of being typecast as a foreign nasty, a gangster-cum-gigolo, he accepted. His first film roles were all the same.

During the next three years he did everything he could to improve his appearance and his image. Because of a slight physical defect – he was born with a partially cauliflowered left ear – he was turned down for the young romantic roles. Someone hit on the idea of using make-up to completely cover the ear and photographing him from the right instead of the left, but still the better parts evaded him. He learned to ride, fence, swim, play tennis, golf and bridge; he read books to improve his English and shortened his sideburns to look less Latin; had his eyebrows plucked and grew a moustache. But for three years nothing went right for him.

Girls would hover round him all the time but he had not yet learned how to deal with that sort of adulation. His first love affair was with a young actress at Metro called Jean Acker. It was she who suggested he should change his name to Rudolph Valentino as it was less exotic, easier to say.

Within a few days of knowing each other, they decided to get married. The wedding was a simple quiet affair with a supper party following the ceremony. Valentino, as he was now known, seemed very happy with his petite, dark-haired bride. They went to spend their honeymoon night at a Hollywood hotel where Valentino insisted on carrying his bride across the threshold of the bridal suite. But as he stooped to pick her up in his arms she stepped nimbly to one side, dashed into the room and slammed the door in his face. He laughed and knocked, asking to be let in. But Jean told him to go away, that the whole thing had been a terrible mistake. He thumped on the door, pleaded with her, begged to be let in. But she was adamant. Whatever her game was, he knew he would be a laughing stock if the story got out . . . Valentino, locked out of the bridal chamber on his wedding night! He ran from the hotel and was sick under a palm tree.

Miserable and bewildered as to why any woman would want to play such a trick – she never did give any believable reason – he accepted any parts that came his way, and continued life as a bachelor. But one of Metro's best writers, June Mathis, had been keeping a careful watch on his screen appearances and one day rang him to say she had just read a script which had the perfect part for him. It was called *The Four Horsemen of the Apocalypse*, a moving story of the 1914–18 war with most of its scenes laid in France. The president of Metro was not enthusiastic. He saw Valentino only as a young Italian dogged by bad luck. But he listened to June Mathis, whom he respected, and the part was given to Valentino.

As the daily 'rushes' were shown in the projection room, it became clear to everyone that in Valentino they had found a remarkable new star. The film itself was an artistic achievement that won columns of praise in the press, but after its general release the film magazines concentrated on the young Italian. His performance inspired thousands to write asking for pictures of him, asking where he came from, when they would see him again.

Metro's barbers, masseurs and tailors had turned Valentino into a remarkably handsome figure. Many actresses and wealthy women now asked him to spend an evening with them, often inviting him to stay the night. Remembering Jean Acker, the studios warned him of the dangers to young male actors. But he had grown weary of casual affairs and was ready for real love.

Nazimova, the famous Russian star, asked him to play opposite her as Armand Duval in the film version of *Camille*. As she had once cruelly snubbed him in public by referring to him as a gigolo he was not over-anxious. But he agreed in the end for the part was too good to turn down. The set designer for *Camille* was a young woman called Natacha Rambova, a beauty, but an ice queen who like to dominate everything and everyone. Friends told him she was the wrong woman for him, but Valentino did not listen. He could not stop talking about her beauty, her aristocratic bearing, her intelligence. It was obvious to everyone that he was hopelessly in love. His strange marriage to Jean Acker no longer upset him, but it was obviously going to pose a problem if he wanted to marry again.

On 17 January 1921 Jean Acker served notice of her suit against him for separate maintenance. She claimed he had deserted her, refused to live with her, never supported her. He threw such a monumental rage that work on the set had to stop.

When the *Four Horsemen* was generally released he found himself an international star. But the fuss that surrounded him then was nothing to what was to follow.

Valentino had signed a five-year contract with Paramount and they were now wondering what to do with their new star. He was still an unknown quantity in many ways. Then Jesse Lasky, head of Paramount, had a brilliant idea. His company had recently bought a sensational novel by E.H.M. Hull called *The Sheik*. It was sensational because it had been written by a very proper English lady and told a torrid love story which included the rape of an English aristocrat by a passionate Arabian. It was rubbish, but it was a best-seller. Valentino, it was decided, should be cast as the Sheik Ahmed Ben Hassan. He was thrilled. Natacha said the novel was pure trash and it would ruin his career. In fact it made him one of the screen's immortals, the forerunner of all the great screen lovers.

Valentino was a sensation. Women were advised by the film's publicity men: 'Shriek, for the Sheik will seek you too!' They gasped with shock or fainted in their seats as he swooped on Agnes Ayres, eyes burning with the flame of passion. Police had to trace hundreds of runaway girls who left home to find their own Arabian princes; women neglected their homes to see the picture again and again. Valentino himself was bemused by the intensity of this reaction. After *The Sheik* he starred in *Blood and Sand*, his lithe figure encased in the skintight costume of the matador, and once agin there was a tidal wave of hysteria.

Offscreen Valentino's romance with Natacha was blooming. By May 1922 it was obvious to everyone that they would marry. Her real name, it emerged, was Winifred Hudnut and she was the stepdaughter of Richard Hudnut, the millionaire cosmetics manufacturer. On 12 May, accompanied by two close friends, the couple headed south for Mexicali, just across the border in Mexico, and were married by the local mayor. But even before they could return home there were rumours that their marriage was not valid. Valentino, who had an 'interlocutory decree

of divorce' from Jean Acker, should have waited 12
months before marrying again. The seriousness of the
situation was explained to the Valentinos by Jesse Lasky
himself. Rudolph returned to Los Angeles to face the
music, sending Natacha to New York to wait out the
storm. Irving Shulman describes what happened next in
his biography of Valentino: 'On Sunday morning, May 21
1922, Valentino, accompanied by his attorney, W.I. Gilbert,
went to the district attorney's office, where he surrendered
himself and pleaded guilty to a charge of bigamy before a
justice of the peace. Bail was set at 10,000 dollars. Only
half-following the proceedings, Valentino prepared to
leave – and was stopped. His bail was 10,000 dollars. But
it was Sunday, the banks were closed, and he did not carry
such sums on his person. Nor did Mr Gilbert have the
money at hand. Paramount officials could not or would
not provide the bail in cash – as was required. Valentino
was clapped into a cell.'

He beat against the bars, shouting in Italian and
English, but to no avail. He never forgave Paramount this
indignity. Next morning he was hurried from jail past an
army of reporters. His ordeal and the subsequent decision
that he should be freed of the bigamy charge brought him
terrific publicity but he felt he had been humiliated and he
was angry.

Natacha and Valentino were remarried in a quiet, private
ceremony in Indiana on 14 March 1923, then set out on a
European tour that was a honeymoon. For Valentino the
voyage was a personal triumph. Ten years before he had
travelled steerage as an immigrant. Now he strolled about
the first-class deck looking the epitome of elegance and
wealth in a magnificent overcoat with fur collar and cuffs.
He was proud of Natacha whose classic, cool beauty made
every head turn. Their stay in Europe was full of excitement and he indulged his greatest weakness – shopping.
He purchased, among other things, a Voisin racing tourer

with vermilion morocco lining; three dozen silk shirts, several dozen pairs of silk pyjamas, 12 lounging robes and 12 quilted smoking jackets. He also found time to be measured for several dozen sets of fine silk underwear.

When he returned to America it was announced that he would star in *Monsieur Beaucaire*, a costume drama that would put him into knee breeches and powdered wigs and show off his looks dramatically. As soon as it was announced thousands of women besieged the studios asking for jobs as extras. Even wealthy women offered to work as canteen waitresses just to get a glimpse of him on the set. Some offered to work without pay, others offered themselves, sending their photographs taken stark naked. There were letters pleading for just one item of his under-wear, as long he had worn it; letters beseeching him for one hour of love. Paramount publicity did its best to add to these raging fires of passion. They told lovelorn fans that Valentino had become the world's most erotic male because he spent his leisure poring over ancient books of love and from these volumes he had discovered 'the ten ways to infinite delight, indefinitely prolonged till eternity'! Valentino laughed at his publicity. Natacha did not.

He had started throwing money about like a madman, buying everything and anything that took his fancy: books, illuminated manuscripts, large dogs, Persian rugs, old chests, Turkish and Arabic furniture, portraits, dinner services and antique suits of armour. Perhaps it was to take his mind off the fact that his wife was becoming a problem. Natacha fought him constantly, and evenings at home in their sumptuous hilltop mansion, Falcon Lair, became increasingly tense.

She detested his image as the great lover and always thought he should be doing something to increase his stature as an actor. She hated the crowds that pushed around him, though perhaps her aversion was understandable. One night Valentino took a girl who worked in the publicity department of United Artists to the cinema. There was pandemonium. People stood on their seats to get a better look at him. As he left the cinema his police escort was swept away by fans demanding his autograph. He was left struggling, trying to get into his limousine. One woman with a pair of scissors cut the buttons off his coat, others were tearing at his clothes, trying to stroke his hair. His bowtie was snatched off; he lost his handkerchief and scarf along with several gold studs and a glove. Both seams of his coat were torn under the arms where women had pulled at him.

When he went to Europe the scenes were repeated. At the London première of *The Eagle* at the Marble Arch Pavilion, thousands of screaming women were waiting for him and tried to tear the doors off his car. In France they ran amok as he descended from his train on a bitter December day, tearing his clothes and scratching his face.

He looked into the middle distance nowadays when reporters questioned him about his marriage. Natacha, on the other hand, was blurting out to everyone: 'Homes and babies are all very nice, but you can't have them and a career as well – if Valentino wants a housewife, he'll have to look again.' What Valentino really wanted was a home.

Reporters tried hard to find some story of passion that would go with his screen image. But though he escorted many beautiful women there was never any scandal to uncover. He learned when asked questions about his sexual prowess to smile enigmatically and say nothing. When there was an attempt to prove he was effeminate, he answered the slur by taking on his accuser in the boxing ring.

On 18 January 1926, divorce from the one woman he had truly loved was announced. Reporters who pounded him with questions were impressed by his dignity and self-control. But Valentino without a lover was unthinkable. People felt sure there must be some other woman in his life. Romantic rumours linked his name with Mae Murray after he had been seen kissing her hand in a lingering fashion, and Pola Negri, the sultry Polish star, was also placed on the short list, though Valentino said he hardly knew her.

Without Natacha, he began to spend even more wildly and sank further and further into debt. He refused to look at bills, brushing them aside impatiently, and suddenly deciding to replace everything in the house that reminded him of her. He made *The Son of the Sheik* mainly for money. Pola Negri seemed to be always hovering around him, yet it was clear the only woman he really cared for was still Natacha. He sank into deeper and deeper depressions, drove recklessly and seemed almost to be courting a quick and dramatic end. His friends, who were genuinely fond of him, pleaded with him to stop brooding and enjoy life. Pola Negri still clung to him like a limpet and talked about their undying love. But, as far as Valentino was concerned, it was a one-sided affair.

There was an interval of several months before he was due to make his next film and United Artists urged him to spend the summer of 1926 in Europe where he could rest. He ordered a complete set of new luggage and a dozen new suits, then suddenly made an appointment to see Adolph Zukor to patch up his past quarrels with Paramount. Later, friends wondered if he had a feeling something was going to happen.

On Monday 16 August, every major daily paper in America carried the news that Valentino was desperately ill. He was in hospital in New York suffering from an acute gastric ulcer and ruptured appendix. Peritonitis had set in. Thousands of telegrams were sent to the private ward where he had been taken after collapsing in his suite at the Ambassador Hotel. Lorryloads of flowers were delivered, women wept and prayed on the hospital steps and Pola

Negri retired to bed, overcome with grief. The film colony in Los Angeles was deeply shocked when it heard Valentino had had two operations and was fighting for his life. For a time he was conscious and even started to talk about making a film with Gloria Swanson.

But by the morning of 23 August 1926 all hope for him was abandoned as his condition deteriorated and he began to babble deliriously in Italian. Someone found a priest who came originally from Castellaneta and he stood at the bedside holding a crucifix to his lips. At ten minutes past noon, Valentino died. He was 31.

Scenes unprecedented in living memory took place as Valentino's body lay 'in state' at a city funeral parlour. In the end his coffin was closed and hidden. There were fears that it might be stolen.

Errol Flynn

Errol Flynn was a man out of his time. He was a pirate, a buccaneer, a swashbuckling rake who, according to his own highly coloured account of himself, had tasted every vice from Macao to Marseilles. He was a lover of Olympic stature, a seducer and, when it suited his purpose, the most gloriously inventive liar. But he was always completely honest with himself.

This latterday Casanova, one of the most colourful characters ever to come out of the film industry, did everything to excess. Women loved him and men laughingly envied and liked him.

In his prime Flynn was a beautiful man with a magnificent deeply tanned physique, well-cut features and deep blue eyes full of laughter and devilment. He was always in the middle of some fantastic tangle involving women, drink or fighting.

He always styled himself as an Irish Tasmanian. Born in

Hobart, Tasmania, in 1909, he was the son of an eminent biologist, Professor Theodore Thomson Flynn. His mother, said Errol, considered him a very nasty little boy and an even nastier big one, for at 16 he nearly killed another youngster in a fight and was expelled from school.

Work was found for him in a local office but he was sacked when he was discovered dipping into the petty cash for money to bet on horses. There were to be no more office jobs for Flynn. News of a gold strike in New Guinea fired his imagination and at 17 he set out to make his fortune.

The story of the next five years, told in his autobiography *My Wicked, Wicked Ways*, reads like an impossible film script.

First he bluffed his way into the colonial service as a sanitation inspector. Thrown out of that job after being caught in the arms of a high official's wife, he then talked his way into being made manager of a copra plantation. The money was good and soon he had enough to buy a schooner in which he ran freight and passengers along the coast. Twice he tried for a strike in the gold fields, but each time he failed. His greatest success was with the local girls who were stunned by his good looks and devil-may-care ways. But fighting was in his blood and he became known as a tough customer, especially after being hauled before a local court for the alleged murder of a native. He barely escaped prison.

As he had had no luck with the gold and was under constant surveillance after his court appearance, he decided to head back to Australia. In Sydney he took a bizarre job as a 'sniffer' in a bottle factory, sniffing bottles to make sure they were not tainted. As this did not provide him with enough money to live well, he swallowed his pride and became a gigolo. His wealthy, middle-aged mistress, he admitted, 'woke my understanding of the possible wonder and diversity of the female form'. One night he slipped away with all her jewels, leaving a note of apology. He had decided to be an actor and needed the fare for Europe.

After a journey filled with garish incidents, he eventually arrived in London. Though he had no experience he talked a Northampton repertory company into giving him a chance as a juvenile and then, by sheer good fortune, landed a bit part in an English film. By now, with his hair bleached by the sun, his skin the colour of mahogany and his lopsided grin showing perfect white teeth, his physical appeal was dazzling. Jack Warner, the Hollywood film maker, saw him in the bit part and realized the potential of this beautiful young man. In no time he was off to America.

In 1935, at the age of 26, he burst upon the screen in spectacular fashion as 'Captain Blood' and for the rest of his life made millions playing similar swashbuckling costume parts. There were a few exceptions, including a film about World War II in which he saved Burma single-handedly.

They called him 'the Baron' and he lived up to his name by building a mansion and buying a yacht. He kept both of them unusually well stocked with pretty girls. He had already been singled out, however, by a glamorous French actress called Lili Damita, a star of second rank who earned his admiration by her 'boudoir art'. One night she stood on a windowsill, several floors up, and threatened to jump if Flynn would not marry her. He understood and admired that sort of bravado and laughingly agreed. They divorced six years later and she was to cost him a great deal of alimony.

Lili told the divorce-court judge that Flynn paid more attention to his yacht than to her. Or could it be the crew that took up his attention? There were always plenty of willing, lissom young women ready to go sailing with him and cook delicious little suppers before they snuggled into his bunk. His taste for teenage girls got him into trouble on several occasions. His yacht *Zaca* became forbidden territory as far as the mothers of nubile 16-year-olds were concerned.

He met his second wife, Nora Eddington, in 1945. She was small, red-haired, dynamic and determined. She took a job selling cigars in a kiosk so that she could get a chance to talk to him. He was intrigued by her and they were married that year. Flynn's roistering lifestyle proved too much, however, and it didn't last.

Flynn, of course, thoroughly enjoyed flouting convention. He didn't give a damn what anyone thought of him and chose like-minded fellow actors for his companions. But there was a side of him which many did not know. He had a lively and questioning mind and read deeply. His academic father, who was very close to him, saw him quite differently to most people. He saw him as an adventurer who lived the kind of life men would give their eye teeth for and believed him to be basically kind, intelligent and brave.

He was engaged for a time to 20-year-old Romanian Princess Irene Ghika and they planned a spring wedding in the Greek Orthodox Church, but the romance petered out. They were not meant for each other.

He would have hated life among the minor European royals. He was happier sailing round the ports of the Mediterranean, meeting up with old friends like David Niven and Peter Finch and roaring the night away drinking vodka and reminiscing. He always said that among his fondest memories were the number of times he had ducked alimony and the night he kicked Hedda Hopper, the vitriolic Hollywood columnist.

During the latter part of his life, Flynn discovered two great loves: Jamaica, and his third wife, Patrice Wymore. His love affair with Jamaica began in 1947 when he was forced by bad weather to put into harbour there. He thought he had found paradise. For the first time he really felt that he wanted to put down roots. He bought an estate for £33,000 and for ten years his parents helped him to run it. He needed to make regular visits to America but he regarded New York as a violent place and got away from it as fast as he could. Hollywood had became 'total anathema' to him over the years but he was realistic enough to know he had to make his living there.

It was on the set, making a film called *Rocky Mountain*, that Errol Flynn met Patrice Wymore, the beautiful red-haired actress who was to be his third and last wife. He said she was the only woman he really loved. They were married in October 1950 and she had 'seven wonderful years' with him before he drifted off again.

Though she looked elegant and ladylike she had enough spirit to join with him in his hectic lifestyle. She was seldom surprised by anything he did. Once Flynn bought a new Jaguar car and was so excited he could hardly wait to show it to her. He zoomed round the corner where they lived and yelled for her to come out. 'I'll take you for a spin round the block,' he said. They got back ten days later. Instead of going round the block, he headed for Mexico. 'In each year with him I packed in more fun, more real living than some wives get in 40 years,' she said without bitterness when he had gone.

By the 1950s he was drinking vodka at the rate of a bottle a day and had got himself into the news by joining Fidel Castro for five hair-raising days behind the Cuban rebel lines in the war against Batista. He was asked whether the rumours that he had given up drinking after his experience were true. 'Malicious gossip!' roared Flynn.

He was only 50 when he died in Vancouver. He had gone there to sell his yacht *Zaca* as plans were going ahead for a house in Jamaica. He had a heart attack on the morning of 15 October 1959 and died in the hotel. He was not alone. His latest girlfriend, a pretty young starlet called Beverly Aadland, was by his side. Patrice Wymore wept bitterly for him. She said there was a sadness about him as the swashbuckling started to come to an end. And a tragic realization in his eyes that he'd thrown so much away.

The Profumo Scandal

The biggest scandal in British public life took place, ironically, in the Swinging Sixties, when everyone was supposed to be having a lot of sex and having a good time – apart from government ministers that is. When it was discovered that the Minister of War, John Profumo, had been sharing a prostitute with the naval attaché at the Russian embassy and had lied to the House of Commons about it, he was forced to resign. But that was not the end of the matter. Soon after, the Prime Minister, who had been seriously damaged by the affair, resigned and the following year the Conservative government was swept from power.

The scandal centred around Christine Keeler who, at the age of 15, quit her home in the Buckinghamshire village of Wraysbury for the bright lights of London. Within months, her self-confidence and good looks had taken her from being a waitress in a Greek restaurant to being a part-time model and a topless dancer in Murray's Cabaret Club in Soho, where she earned £8.50 a week. There, fellow show-girl Mandy Rice-Davis, a perky 17-year-old from Birmingham, introduced her to her friend Stephen Ward.

Ward was a thin and elegant man in his late 40s. He was a talented artist but earned his living as an osteopath. He numbered among his clients several high-ranking members of the establishment. These included Lord Astor, who rented him a cottage in the grounds of his Cliveden estate for the peppercorn rent of £1 a year, and Sir Colin Coote, Editor of the *Daily Telegraph*, who associated with the head of MI5, Sir Roger Hollis – whom Peter Wright later named as the fifth man in the Cambridge spy ring.

Ward liked doing favours for people. He also liked drugs and the company of pretty women, including prostitutes. Christine Keeler and Mandy Rice-Davis moved in with him in his London flat in Wimpole Mews and would go with him to Cliveden at weekends for parties in his cottage.

In June 1961, over lunch at The Garrick, Coote introduced Ward to the Soviet naval attaché, Yevgeny Ivanov. MI5 had singled out Ivanov as a man who might easily succumb to the temptations of the West. They thought that a weekend party with some of Ward's attractive young female friends might be just the thing to turn him. The defection of such a high-ranking Russian official would be quite a prize. Specifically, MI5 wanted Ward to 'honeytrap' Ivanov with Keeler.

Ward invited Ivanov down to Cliveden on Sunday 9 July 1951. He took Keeler down there the night before when the Astors were holding a dinner party in the house. Keeler wanted to go swimming and Ward dared her to go in the nude. When she did, he stole her swimming costume.

Lord Astor and John Profumo were out in the gardens for an after-dinner stroll when they spotted the beautiful, naked 19-year-old in the swimming pool. Christine realized that they were coming and struck out for the edge of the pool. She emerged nude and grabbed a small towel to cover herself, moments before the two men caught up with her.

The two middle-aged men were fooling around with the near-naked girl when suddenly the floodlights were turned on. The rest of the guests – including Profumo's wife – came out into the garden, too. Christine was introduced. Later, Profumo managed to give her a guided tour of the bedrooms at Cliveden.

At 46, Profumo was a rising Tory politician. The son of a successful barrister, he was independently wealthy and lived the life of a Tory squire. Educated at Harrow and Oxford, he served on the staff of General Alexander during World War II, rising to the rank of lieutenant-colonel. He was elected to Parliament for Stratford-upon-Avon in 1950 and joined the government in 1952, rising to the position of Secretary for War in 1960. In 1954, he had married the actress Valerie Hobson.

The day after Christine met Profumo, Ivanov turned up at Cliveden. Ward laid on a swimming party as a way of introducing him to Christine. She fancied Ivanov immediately. She told the *News of the World*: 'He was MAN. He was rugged with a hairy chest, strong and agile.'

However, when they decided to have a piggy-back fight in the pool, it was Jack Profumo's shoulders she clambered on to, not Ivanov's. That evening, Christine left with Ivanov, but not before Profumo had asked her for her phone number. Christine was flattered and told him to contact Ward.

Back at Ward's Wimpole Mews flat, Christine and Ivanov demolished a bottle of vodka. Then he kissed her.

'Before I knew what was happening, I was in his arms,' she said. 'We left serious discussion and I yielded to this wonderful huggy bear of a man . . . He was a wonderful lover.'

Two days later, Profumo phoned and came round. On his third visit, he began to kiss her and soon 'I was returning his kisses with everything that I suddenly felt for him,' she said.

Profumo would always call first before he came round for what Keeler called a 'screw of convenience'. They had to be discreet. With Ivanov, she went out on the town, but Profumo could not risk being seen out with her in a pub or restaurant. Occasionally though they went for a drive. As well as having sex at Ward's flat, they had it in Profumo's red mini and a black car he borrowed from the Minister of Labour, John Hare. And once, when his wife was away in Ireland, Profumo took Christine back to their house in Nash Terrace near Regents Park. It was late and the butler and staff were asleep. Profumo took her directly to the bedroom.

Profumo had no idea that he was sharing his mistress with Ivanov. He was deeply attached to her. But she did not share his feelings. For her, sex 'had no more meaning than a handshake or a look across a crowded room', she said. Meanwhile, Profumo showered her with expensive gifts and money – ostensibly to buy her mother a birthday present.

After a month, MI5 learnt about Profumo's affair with Keeler. Fearing that it compromised their entrapment of Ivanov, Hollis asked the Cabinet Secretary, Sir Norman Brook, to warn Profumo. On 9 August 1961, in panic, John Profumo wrote a note to Christine Keeler:

Darling,
In great haste & because I can get no reply from your phone. Alas something's blown up tomorrow night & I can't therefore make it. I'm terribly sorry especially as I leave the next day for various trips & then a holiday so won't be able to see you again until some time in September. Blast it. Please take care of your-self & don't run away.
Love J

I'm writing this cos I know you're off the day after tomorrow & I want you to know before you go if I still can't reach you by phone.

It was this note that sealed his fate.

Despite the warning, Profumo continued seeing Christine Keeler for another four months. During that time, he took amazing risks. One evening an army officer turned up at the flat looking for Ward.

'I had to introduce him to the War Minister,' said Keeler. 'The colonel couldn't believe it. Jack nearly died.'

Profumo only broke it off in December because Keeler refused to move out of Ward's flat and into a discreet love nest that he was going to buy for her.

MI5 began to lose interest in the plan to honeytrap Ivanov. They were finding Ward increasingly unreliable. Keeler had moved on, too. While scoring marijuana for Ward, she had met West Indian jazz singer, Lucky Cordon, and, through him, another West Indian named Johnny Edgecombe. She had begun sleeping with both of them. This had led to a fight at an all-night club in Soho in October 1962, where Cordon got his face slashed. Keeler moved in with Edgecombe briefly. When things did not work out, she moved back into Ward's flat. One night, Edgecombe came round to try to win her back. It was late and she would not let him in. He pulled a gun and blasted the front door. The police were called and Edgecombe was arrested and charged with attempted murder.

After this incident, Ward asked Keeler to leave the flat. She turned to one of his patients, solicitor Michael Eddowes, for help. She told him that she and Ward had actually been spying for the Russians and that Ward had asked her to find out from Profumo about British plans to arm West Germany with nuclear weapons.

She told the same story to former Labour MP, John Lewis, who had a personal dislike of Ward. He passed the information on to George Wigg, a Labour MP who disliked Profumo after he had bested him in the House. In January 1963, Paul Mann, a journalist, took Keeler to the

Sunday Pictorial. Keeler showed the *Pictorial* the note that Profumo had written and the paper offered her £1,000 for her story.

However, the newspapers were exceedingly cautious at the time. The previous year, the exposure of the spy John Vassall, an admiralty clerk who had been passing secrets to the Soviets, had led to a Tribunal of Inquiry that had investigated the role of the press in the affair. In the course of it, two journalists had been sent to prison for refusing to name their sources.

The *Pictorial* contacted Ward, who managed to convince the paper that Keeler's story was a pack of lies and publication was dropped. This annoyed Keeler so she went to the police and told them that Ward procured call-girls for his rich clients. A few days later, Profumo found himself being questioned by the Attorney-General Sir John Hobson, the Solicitor-General Peter Rawlinson and the Chief Whip Martin Redmayne. He denied any impropriety with Keeler. Although sceptical, they chose to accept what he was saying.

Prime Minister Harold Macmillan was briefed. A man of the world, he said that if Profumo had had an affair with Keeler he had been foolish, but sleeping with a pretty young woman, even if she was alleged to be a prostitute, was hardly a sackable offence. Everyone hoped that that was the end of it. But, on 8 March 1963, a small-circulation newsletter called *Westminster Confidential* ran a piece about the story that the *Pictorial* had dropped. It repeated the allegation that both the War Secretary and a Soviet military attaché, one Colonel Ivanov, were the clients of the same call-girl.

On 10 March, George Wigg, who by this time had a bulging dossier on the relationship between Profumo and Keeler, took it to the Labour leader, Harold Wilson. Wilson urged caution, but events now had a momentum of their own.

On 14 March, Johnny Edgecombe came up for trial at the Old Bailey. The key witness, Christine Keeler, was on holiday and it was rumoured that she had been whisked out of the country to keep a lid on the scandal.

The next day, the *Daily Express* ran the headline 'WAR MINISTER SHOCK'. It claimed that John Profumo had tendered his resignation for 'personal reasons'. Down the page was a picture of Christine Keeler under the headline 'VANISHED'.

The *Express* later claimed that the juxtaposition of the two stories was purely coincidental. But everyone put two and two together.

On 19 March, during a debate on the Vassall case, George Wigg, under the protection of parliamentary privilege, raised the rumours circulating about the War Minister. He was supported by Barbara Castle and the Labour frontbencher Dick Crossman. The government was flustered. The Home Secretary, Henry Brooke, told the Labour critics that if they wanted to substantiate their accusations they should use a different forum, one that was not shielded from the laws of libel by the cloak of privilege.

Profumo had one supporter though – backbench Labour MP Reginald Paget.

'What do these rumours amount to?' Paget asked rhetorically. 'They amount to the fact that a minister is said to be acquainted with an extremely pretty girl. As far as I am concerned, I should have thought that was a matter for congratulation rather than an inquiry.'

Profumo was then grilled again by the Chief Whip, the Leader of the House Iain Macleod and Bill Deedes, Minister without Portfolio and future editor of the *Daily Telegraph*. Profumo again insisted that he was innocent. He then made a parliamentary statement. In it he admitted knowing Christine Keeler, but said he had not seen her since December 1961. He also said that he had met Stephen Ward and Yevgeny Ivanov. He denied that he was in any way responsible for her absence from the trial and stated categorically: 'There was no impropriety whatsoever in my acquaintanceship with Miss Keeler.' He threatened anyone who repeated the allegations outside the House with a writ.

A few days later, the newspapers caught up with Christine Keeler in Madrid. She confirmed what Profumo had said, but George Wigg would not leave it at that. He went on the *Panorama* TV programme and said that Ward and Ivanov were security risks. The next day, Ward met Wigg and tried to convince him that it was not true. He failed. More than ever, Wigg believed that Profumo had lied. He wrote a report of his meeting with Ward and gave it to Harold Wilson, who passed it on to Macmillan.

Although the Vassall case was keeping the British press subdued, there was no such reticence in the foreign papers. Profumo issued writs against *Paris Match* and *Il Tempo Illustrato*, which both said that he had been 'bonking' Christine Keeler.

In an attempt to salvage the situation, the Home Secretary told the Metropolitan Police to try to find something on Ward. This was highly irregular. The police are supposed to investigate crimes and find out who committed them, not investigate people on the offchance they have committed a crime.

It soon became clear to Ward's friends and clients that he was in serious trouble. They deserted him in droves. Mandy Rice-Davis was arrested on trumped-up charges and held in prison until she agreed to testify against Ward.

Ward desperately wrote to everyone he could think of, protesting his innocence. Harold Wilson received a letter. He showed it to the Prime Minister, who agreed to set up a committee of inquiry under Lord Dilhome. Profumo was on holiday at the time. When he returned, he realized that the game was up. He could not face a committee of inquiry and lie again, so he went to see the Chief Whip and Macmillan's Parliamentary Private Secretary, told them that he had lied and resigned.

His letter of resignation and Macmillan's reply were published the next day.

'I misled you, and my colleagues, and the House,' Profumo wrote; but, he explained: 'I did this to protect my wife and family.'

Macmillan's terse reply said: 'I am sure you will understand that in the circumstances I have no alternative but to advise the Queen to accept your resignation.'

The very day this exchange appeared in the papers, 5 June 1963, there was more drama. Christine Keeler's other West Indian boyfriend, Lucky Cordon, came to court on the charge of assaulting her outside a friend's flat. Keeler turned up at court in a Rolls-Royce.

From the dock, Cordon accused her of giving him VD. She responded with an outburst from the public gallery. The newspapers lapped it up. Cordon was sent down for three years, which was overturned on appeal.

Ward appeared on TV on 9 June and denied that he had encouraged Christine Keeler to have an affair with John Profumo because he had a friend in the Soviet Embassy. The following day he was arrested and charged with living on immoral earnings.

By this time, newspapers worldwide were running the scandal on the front page. Mandy Rice-Davis told the *Washington Star* about society orgies in London. She mentioned that at one dinner party a naked man wearing only a mask waited on table. The hunt for the masked man was on. Was it a senior judge, a cabinet minister or a member of the royal family?

Under the headline 'PRINCE PHILIP AND THE PROFUMO SCANDAL, the *Daily Mirror* vehemently dismissed the 'foul rumour' that Prince Philip was involved. The Queen's Consort was a member of a gentleman's association called the Thursday Club, which also boasted Stephen Ward among its membership.

Allegations flew thick and fast. Everyone in any position in society was now a target. The Bishop of Southwark, Mervyn Stockwood, appealed for calm.

Politically the question came down to: how had John Profumo managed to lie about his affair for so long? Macmillan, who had taken a lenient attitude to the matter back in January, was now in the firing line. Colleagues began to sense that his tenure of office was drawing to a close. Lord Hailsham quit his title to become a contender for the premiership. He threw his hat into the ring by appearing on television and condemning Profumo for lying. Again, Reginald Paget rallied to Profumo's defence.

'When self-indulgence has reduced a man to the shape of Lord Hailsham,' he said, 'sexual continence involves no more than a sense of the ridiculous.'

Milking the situation for all it was worth, Mandy Rice-Davis told the *Sunday Mirror* that the Soviet military attaché and the War Minister had missed bumping into each other at Ward's flat by a matter of minutes on a number of occasions.

Michael Eddowes issued a press statement, saying that he had warned the Prime Minister of the security risk as early as 29 March. Meanwhile, Christine Keeler sold her 'confessions' to the *News of the World*, which began serializing them.

The Times attacked the Conservative government for its lack of moral leadership. To this, Lord Hailsham responded petulantly: '*The Times* is an anti-Conservative newspaper with an anti-Conservative editor.'

Even the *Washington Post* got in on the act, saying that 'a picture of widespread decadence beneath the glitter of a large segment of stiff-lipped society is emerging'.

Labour went on the offensive. In a debate in the House of Commons on 19 June, Harold Wilson said that the Profumo scandal had 'shocked the moral conscience of the nation'. Pointing the finger at the Prime Minister, he said that for political reasons he was gambling with national security.

Macmillan could not even count on the support of his own backbenchers. Conservative MP, Nigel Birch, stated the simple facts of the case.

'I must say that [Profumo] never struck me as a man at all like a cloister monk,' he told the House. 'And Miss Keeler is a professional prostitute. There seems to me to be a basic improbability that their relationship was purely platonic. What are whores about?'

Addressing the Prime Minister directly, he said: 'I myself feel that the time will come very soon when my Right Honourable Friend ought to make way for a much younger colleague.'

Macmillan survived the debate but was badly wounded. Four days later, he announced an official inquiry under Lord Denning. It did not save him. Macmillan resigned in the early autumn, shortly before the party conference. He was replaced by Sir Alec Douglas-Home, but the Conservative government was tainted by the scandal and was swept from office the following year.

Although Lord Denning was supposed to look into possible breaches of security caused by the Profumo scandal, like Ken Starr, he concentrated on the salacious aspects – so much so that, when he cross-questioned witnesses, he often sent the official stenographer out of the room to save her, or perhaps his own, blushes.

When Ward went on trial at the Old Bailey, the world's media were there in force. Again, the salacious details were played up. One newspaper in New Zealand was prosecuted for indecency for merely reporting the case.

The star of the show was undoubtedly Mandy Rice-Davis, whom the judge mistakenly addressed as Marilyn Monroe. When it was put to her that Lord Astor had denied that he had met her at his house parties at

Cliveden, she said: 'Well, he would, wouldn't he?' That remark is now in the *Oxford Dictionary of Quotations*.

In his summing up, the judge pointed out that none of Ward's highborn friends had come to testify on his behalf.

'One would have thought from the newspapers that this country has become a sink of iniquity,' he told the jury. 'But you and I know that the even tenor of family life over the overwhelming majority of the population goes quietly and decently on.'

He might as well have been putting the noose around the defendant's neck. The judge was implying that Ward was not just guilty of introducing rich and powerful people to a couple of attractive and available girls, but that he was responsible for the general loosening of moral standards that many people felt was engulfing the country. Ward knew that he was being made a scapegoat.

'This is a political trial,' he told a friend. 'Someone had to be sacrificed and that someone is me.'

On the night of 3 July 1963, Ward took an overdose of sleeping tablets. He left a suicide note saying that, after the judge's summing-up, he had given up all hope. He asked that resuscitation be delayed as long as possible, adding, bizarrely, that 'the car needs oil in the gearbox'.

With Ward unconscious in St Stephen's Hospital, the jury found him guilty on two counts of living on immoral earnings. He died on 3 August, without regaining consciousness. Even after he was dead, the newspapers kept vilifying him.

There were only six mourners at Stephen Ward's funeral and only two wreaths. One came from his family. The other was from Kenneth Tynan, John Osbourne, Arnold Wesker, Joe Orton, Annie Ross, Dominick Elwes and Penelope Gilliatt. The card on it read: 'To Stephen Ward, victim of hypocrisy.'

When the Denning report was published in October 1963, it was an instant best-seller, selling over 4,000 copies in the first hour. It, too, laid the blame squarely at the door of Stephen Ward, who was in no position to answer back.

Profumo left political life and threw himself into charity work, for which he was awarded the CBE in 1975. He remained married to Valerie Hobson. Christine Keeler was jailed for six months for contempt of court for failing to appear at the trial of Johnny Edgecombe. Her autobiography *Scandal* was published in 1989 and was made into a successful movie.

Mandy Rice-Davis wrote a series of novels, became a film actress, opened two clubs in Israel and married a millionaire. George Wigg became chairman of the Horse Race Betting Levy Board and later pleaded guilty to soliciting for prostitutes in Soho.

Boris Becker – an Expensive Five Seconds

In July 1999, Boris Becker had sex with a Russian model in the broom cupboard of an upmarket London restaurant. The German former tennis superstar admitted that the encounter which led to the birth of a daughter, Anna, was the most expensive one-night stand of his life. It lasted just five seconds but it cost him a reported £2 million settlement, plus maintenance of £25,000 a month. 'It wasn't even an affair,' said Becker, 32 at the time, whose fortune was estimated to be in excess of £60 million. 'It was a mistake which will haunt me for the rest of my life.'

Speaking on German television, Becker recalled how his meeting with Angela Ermakowa, who was to become little Anna's mother, followed a day of wild drinking. He had just lost the last match of his career at Wimbledon and had had a row with his then wife Barbara.

'I lost at lunchtime to Pat Rafter on the Centre Court at

Wimbledon,' he said. 'Then, after 2pm, I began drinking one after the other. All through the rest of the day and the whole evening. Then of course, there was a huge "discussion" with Barbara which I don't want to go into.' Mrs Becker stayed in their hotel while Boris went to Nobu, an expensive Japanese restaurant in Park Lane, Mayfair. It was there that he met 33-year-old Miss Ermakowa, and they reportedly had sex in the cupboard, an act which according to Boris 'lasted five seconds'.

Becker admitted: 'Never seen her before. Didn't see her again. But it was me who took the final step. I continued drinking and completely lost control. It was the first time in my life that had happened, only on this one day. The result is brutal for me, but also particularly for my wife, my children, my mother.'

Reminded by the German TV interviewer that his wife had been expecting their second child Elias at the time Boris replied: 'This is a thing I will have to live with for the rest of my life. There is no real explanation.'

Becker had previously insisted that baby Anna's arrival was not the reason why he and his wife of seven years split up. After several months of acrimony the couple reached a multi-million-dollar settlement and divorced in January 2001. In the television interview Becker went on to talk about his attitude to women in general.

'I have lost a little respect for women,' he declared. 'When you grow up for years in a sweet shop, it eventually gets too sweet and doesn't taste any more. Then you need something with a heart. The Hollywood star Paul Newman once said: "I get hungry outside and eat the juicy steak at home." That's similar to how I see things.'

After parting from his wife, Becker embarked on an affair with the German rap singer Sabrina Setlur. He allowed them to be photographed together and even gave an interview about the new relationship, describing it as a delicate plant that needed tending. Nevertheless, it lasted only a matter of weeks. Then he claimed that intense media interest in his love life was ruining his chances of meeting anyone new and forming a serious relationship.

'I can no longer get to know a woman normally,' he complained. 'If I go out with a new friend it is in the newspapers the next day, and hardly any woman can cope with that.'

All this non-stop attention made living in Germany difficult for him, he admitted, but he was not thinking of leaving. He owns a big Mercedes dealership in Germany as well as a string of homes around the world. 'I am free and have courage to live after the divorce,' he said.

However he added that he was getting on well with his 34-year-old ex-wife and was able to visit her in Miami, where she lives with their two sons Elias and Noah, every two or three weeks. Since his retirement from competitive tennis in 1999, Becker – who at 17 became the youngest man ever to win Wimbledon – has been adding to his fortune with a series of lucrative TV advertising deals and has also become involved in sports marketing.

Royal
Lovers

François I

Night after night in 16th-century Paris a tall figure would slip through a back gate of the royal palace and into the shadows. A single servant would accompany him on his wanderings through the narrow streets. They would arrive at some half-timbered house to be received with low bows and ushered inside. Throwing aside his cloak, François I, that most virile of French Kings, was revealed out on his nocturnal prowl.

Not content with his adoring Queen, his harem of well-born French women and his official mistress, François could never resist the thrill of a secret assignation, a carefully concealed affair. He wandered the streets at night prepared to risk everything for the thrill of making love to a pretty woman.

Yet François I, for all his philandering, was a great prince as well as a great lover. He towered above his contemporaries both physically and otherwise. He was a Valois, 6ft tall, high-spirited with a magnificent presence and powerful body. His face was not classically handsome, but pale, with rather curious almond-shaped eyes, a long nose and thick lips, But his looks were enhanced by a pleasing voice and smooth chestnut hair worn close into the nape of his neck like a page. His clothes were always splendid, strewn with pearls and diamonds, fastened with gold buttons and buckles. His shirts were kept in a case of scented Russian leather and the scabbard of his sword was jewel-encrusted white velvet. Everything about him, it was said, flashed and sparkled.

François was above all a man of action, happiest when riding to hounds, tilting at the joust or making love. Stories about his love of women were being circulated with relish even in his lifetime – they grew to legendary proportions after his death. One report sent back to the

English court, said: 'The King is a great womanizer, and readily breaks into others' gardens and drinks at many sources.' It was alleged that he had a mistress at the age of ten, that he had incestuous relations with his sister and that he built the great château at Chambord simply to be near a woman he desired. There is certainly evidence that at the time of his accession he was having an affair with the wife of an eminent Parisian barrister, and even Mary Tudor complained that he had been 'importunate with me on diverse matters not to my honour'. Successive generations have not been able to resist adding their own stories until the only thing left was to turn him into fiction. He became the royal lecher in Victor Hugo's *Le Roi S'Amuse* and the Duke of Mantua in Verdi's *Rigoletto*.

Though undoubtedly he usually thought first of satisfying his sensual appetite, he also loved women as works of art, considering them an integral part of the decoration of his great palaces. He liked to see them beautifully dressed and from time to time would order trunkfuls of magnificent gowns for his favourites so that they could grace his personal landscape. It was estimated once that he spent 300,000 gold crowns a year – a vast amount – on presents for women.

Historically, he transformed the cultural life of France and ushered in the Renaissance. 'After a long succession of dreary kings he burst forth like the sun,' says his English biographer, Desmond Seward. As supreme patron of the arts he had Leonardo da Vinci and Andrea del Sarto as court painters. Leonardo actually died in his arms. Benvenuto Cellini was his jeweller and he bought the works of Raphael and Michelangelo for his palaces. The library he put together became the Bibliothèque Nationale.

This astonishing King came from a line that had reigned from the 10th century. He was born in 1494 and brought up in the palatial château at Amboise, growing to be a wilful, high-spirited youth, spoiled by the adoration of his

mother and sister. Fortunately, he also had great qualities
of courage and intelligence. At 16 he jumped at the chance
to become a courtier at the palace of Louis XII.

By this time he had already taken part in his first sexual
adventures and after barely two years at court his mother
was writing with great horror of a disease in her son's
private parts. He had, apparently, contracted syphilis in
the arms of a generous lady called La Belle Ferronière. He
was completely cured and warned to be more careful in
future.

King Louis was childless so François, as senior Prince of
the royal blood, was heir presumptive. He was made Duc
de Valois and given several magnificent royal residences.
He was the hero of the young nobility who despised King
Louis' meanness and frugality. They applauded wildly
when François rode out to tournament resplendent in
cloth of silver, cloth of gold and crimson velvet, and
crowed with delight over his nocturnal escapades.

Louis died on New Year's Day 1515 and the coronation
of François I that followed dazzled the world. From this
time on, whatever happened in his private life, François
never forgot the mystic grandeur of the ceremony that
made him King, never forgot that in some strange way he
was France.

When the time came for him to marry, his bride was
Claude, Duchess of Brittany in her own right. She was
nothing like the King's ideal woman. Though renowned
for her sweetness and kind nature, she was very small and
dumpy, and walked with a pronounced limp. At first he
took very little interest in her save as the mother of his
children. Over a period of nine years she bore him three
sons and four daughters. But the charm of her manner
made her popular with everyone and François grew very
fond of her. She adored him, bearing his infidelities with
resignation. Unfortunately her life was short, no doubt
due to such intensive childbearing, but when she died at

Blois on 26 July 1524 he felt pangs of regret and said that if he could bring her back by giving his own life he would gladly do so.

The King's favourite mistress in the year he came to the throne was 17-year-old Jeanne de Coq, wife of an eminent Paris lawyer, Maître Disomme. By all reports she had a lovely face, skin like a peach and a perfect figure. But Maître Disomme was elderly, had a vile temper and was fiercely jealous. The King had to be very discreet. He usually entered the lawyer's house through the garden of a neighbouring monastery, sometimes being forced into Matins by encounter with the monks. They thought him a very devout young man. On one occasion he was caught by the astonished lawyer. What on earth was the King doing in his house at that time of night? François hastily explained that he had long wanted to make the acquaintance of such a distinguished man but, his days being so full, he was forced to come at this hour!

Quite early in his reign, François, a fine soldier, twice led his army into war. At the historic battle of Marignano, when he astonished Europe by giving the Swiss their first real beating and recovered Milan for the French, he made his entry into the Italian city 'wonderfully fine and triumphant, sword in hand, clad in blue velvet sewn with gold fleurs de lis'. Marignano was instantly recognized as one of the great victories of French history and a medal was struck showing him in profile, wearing a plumed hat and looking younger than his 22 years. After Marignano François was, for a time, the most admired ruler in Christendom.

Over on the other side of the Channel, another young hotblood, Henry VIII of England, had been closely watching his rival. Henry, too, was in his prime. And he was eaten with curiosity. He had heard François was a great lover. Could he possibly be a great warrior too? When Henry first heard of the victory at Marignano, he refused to believe it. He asked French diplomats endless questions about François. Was he really as amorous as they said he was? Were his legs shapely? How much did he spend on clothes?

Early in 1518 François had acquired the first of his great official mistresses – Françoise de Foiz, Comtesse de Chateaubriant. Now about 23, she was a handsome, dark woman with a forceful personality, both demanding and promiscuous. The relationship between them was one long saga of jealousy and reconciliation. Françoise infuriated the King by flirting with his great friend, Bonnivet, Grand Admiral of France, and by hinting how much she enjoyed the Admiral's company. Once, on his own way to sleep with her, the King almost caught her in bed with him. Bonnivet just had time to hide in the fireplace which, as it was summer, was filled with greenery. François unwittingly got his revenge by relieving himself in the fireplace and drenching his rival.

The affair did not stop him from sleeping with other women. A modern biographer has written: 'He was as amorous as a cat, amorous and inconstant.' His favourites were members of 'La Petite Bande', a group carefully selected for their beauty and charm. Among them was the delightful Madame de Canaples, whose portrait hangs in the Scottish National Gallery. Like most of the women François admired, she was a brunette with a pretty, rounded figure and sparkling eyes.

His nocturnal wanderings often got him into hot water. One time, when he was 'madly in love' with a lady of the court, he made his way to her bedroom only to find her husband waiting with a sword, obviously prepared to kill him. François very cleverly turned the tables by pointing his own sword at the wretched husband's throat and, commanding him to do the lady no harm, added that if he as much as moved the King would have no alternative but to kill him. François then coolly sent the husband off into the night and climbed into his bed.

Restless by nature, François seldom stayed in any one place for more than three months. Moving the French court about was like moving an army, but he never counted the cost. When he rode from one place to another, as many as 18,000 people followed him, 12,000 on horseback.

He was by nature extravagant, and in the spring of 1520 he had a chance to show off as he had never shown off before. Henry of England was coming to France to see him, a visit that had been strongly advised when their two countries signed the Treaty of 1518. Hearing that François had grown a beard, Henry swore he would not shave until they met. The contest had begun.

The site of this historic meeting, for ever after known as 'The Field of Cloth of Gold' was in a valley known as the Val Doré, about 6 miles from Calais. Henry landed at Calais, at that time British soil, with Queen Catherine and a retinue numbering 5,000. François was waiting with 5,000 courtiers and nearly 5,000 horses.

Their camps vied with each other in fabulous splendour. The French King's own pavilion was almost 60ft high, supported by huge masts and hung with cloth of gold, striped with blue velvet and sewn with gold fleurs de lis. Inside, the pavilion was lined with blue velvet, the ceiling fringed with gold. It was divided into rooms, some of which were hung with black velvet to show off the royal silver and crystal. There were 400 similar, smaller tents – 'an entire town of silver and gold, silk and velvet and floating tapestries, shining in the sun'. Henry, determined to outdo his rival, erected a castle of wood and canvas, hung with green and white silk, Henry's personal colours, and with cloth of gold and silver.

It was a full week before the Kings met, in the late afternoon of Thursday 7 June, the Feast of Corpus Christi. François was a magnificent sight. His doublet was of cloth of silver, slashed with gold and embroidered with diamonds, pearls, rubies and emeralds. Over this he wore a cloak of gold satin shot with purple, and round his neck the plain gold collar of St Michel. His long boots were soft, white leather, his hat black-plumed and sparkling with jewels. Henry matched his magnificence, wearing the jewelled Order of the Garter round his neck. They galloped towards each other at the agreed signal and after a period of great nervousness and doffing of hats, still in the saddle, they embraced each other heartily.

For a fortnight there was jousting and carousing and great feasting, then the exchange of rich presents and a Pontifical High Mass celebrated by Cardinal Wolsey. Their meeting on the Field of Cloth of Gold had little lasting effect politically but François and Henry formed a genuine regard for each other which they never quite lost. Years later, when François heard that the English King was dead he had a mass said for his soul.

François made his court a centre of learning and art, persuading the aged Leonardo da Vinci to come to France and bring with him some of his greatest paintings including the *Mona Lisa* and the *Virgin of the Rocks*. Desmond Seward in his life of the great Prince describes the full Renaissance glory of his background. The floors of his châteaux and palaces were of marble or parquet and strewn with fine carpets instead of rushes. His tables were covered with cloths of gold, rich plate flanked by Venetian glass, dishes of majolica and enamel, cups, bowls and ewers of agate and crystal, lapis lazuli and amber, sardonyx and jade. Rooms hung with rich tapestries were lit by flaming torches in burnished gold or silver sconces, by candles in crystal holders and by scented logs of juniper, apple and pear burning in great hearths.

Against this background, François arranged his collection of beautiful women in their rich silks and satins, glowing in Renaissance colours. But the French people began to count the cost of having such a flamboyant, spendthrift King. It took a decade to pay for the Field of Cloth of Gold alone. In the 1520s everything seemed to go wrong for him. Soon after his meeting with Henry, Charles V of Spain, the Holy Roman Emperor, was to challenge him, beginning a rivalry that was to last all his life. There were private griefs, including the death of Queen Claude. Then at the battle of Pavia on 24 February 1524 the glorious François was captured and humiliated by the Spaniards. Less than two hours after they had started fighting, 8,000 Frenchmen and their mercenaries had been killed. François, unhorsed, fought by himself, swinging a great gold-hilted sword, until he was eventually forced to surrender. Surrender also meant that he was the prisoner of Charles V, now the most powerful man in Europe.

The captured King wrote courteous letters to the Emperor, which were ignored. However, his entry into Madrid was almost a march of triumph. Dressed in his usual splendour and riding a magnificent horse, he was received with wild enthusiasm. The Spaniards were impressed by their prisoner. Some of the ladies, who it appeared particularly admired his legs, visited him every day, bringing flowers and gifts.

So lulled was he by this reception that he actually had the nerve to ask for the hand of the Emperor's sister in marriage, but it was refused. A rude shock awaited him in Madrid after all the flattering processions; Charles ordered his imprisonment in the tower of the Alcazar.

He almost died of fever, then of humiliation as one by one he gave in to Charles' terms for his freedom. He was to give up Burgundy, Flanders and Artois and he had to abandon his claims on Naples and Milan. He was told he could return to France provided his two elders sons were sent as hostages. Surprisingly the Emperor then said he would give him his sister, Eleanor, as his bride. François solemnly kissed her on the mouth to seal their betrothal.

On 15 March 1526 François crossed the frontier into France to be greeted with great joy. 'Now I am King again,' he cried out. He spent several months travelling in a leisurely fashion through southwest and central France, showing himself to his people. It was probably about this time that he met Anne d'Heilly who was to take the place of Françoise de Foiz.

He felt he needed a woman in his life. Claude was dead, he was tired of Françoise, he had been forced to be celibate in Spain and he was in no hurry to tie the marriage knot with Eleanor. Anne, he learned, was the daughter of Guillaume d'Heilly, Seigneur de Pisseleu, a nobleman from Picardy who had married three times and had 30 children. She was only 18, maid of honour to Louise of Savoy, and he was enchanted by her cool blonde elegance and her sensitive appreciation of the arts. Within the year the King had added her to his 'Petite Bande'.

Françoise de Chateaubriant was at home in Normandy when she heard of the King's release and his return to court with a new mistress. Françoise hurried to Paris where she sought out Anne d'Heilly and among other things called her a 'fuzzy chit'. Hearing of her jealous rage and her attacks on Anne, the King lost his royal gallantry and called his former beloved a 'rabid beast'. He ordered her to leave court and retire to her husband's estates.

Anne asked the King to take back all the gold ornaments he had given his former mistress as they were engraved with words of undying love. But on receiving the King's messenger Françoise sent all her gold jewellery to be melted down and returned them as ingots. The King was impressed. 'Return them all to her,' he ordered. 'She has shown more courage and spirit than I would have expected from a woman in her position.'

After the death of Louise of Savoy in 1531 Anne became governess to the King's daughters, Madeleine and Marguerite, as a pretext to have her near him. He married her off to Jean de Brosse, Seigneur de Penthievre, three years later and made the willing cuckold Duc d'Etampes in order to provide Anne with a title. Eleanor had arrived to claim François as her husband but only duty and politics made him take her to his bed. Tall, with a long, sallow face, she was not unpleasant to look at but, while she was only in her 30s, she seemed middle-aged, placid and colourless.

The shocked English ambassador reported that when Queen Eleanor made her ceremonial entry into Paris in 1531 the King and Anne d'Heilly sat in a window together, laughing and talking before thousands of people. Though he was still sometimes unfaithful, Anne was the woman he loved for the rest of his life. Like all great mistresses she held him by virtue of her intelligence, not only her sensual beauty. He was also amused by her vivacity though her wilfulness began to be resented after a time. When he built Fontainebleu, thought by many to be the finest house in Europe, Anne was given a magnificent bedroom next to his. He also provided her with magnificent châteaux at Etampes and Limours. She remained golden-haired and attractive but portraits also show her shrewd eyes and firm little mouth.

Since he was a child François had burnt the candle at both ends. Now 52, he continued to take violent exercise in the day and to sleep with his mistresses at night. But life was catching up with him. His last years had been plagued by trouble and he never got over the misery of losing Boulogne to the English. Like many others in the family, he was tubercular, and he sometimes suffered from old injuries sustained in war. His life was wearing out.

When François died in the early hours of 31 May 1547, the Marshal de Tavannes, a shrewd observer, said: 'Ladies more than years caused his death.' Strangely enough, just before he died he had dismissed Anne d'Heilly with a wave of his hand and she had fled from him in hysterics. Also, strangely, for one who was so promiscuous, he had once written a couplet with a diamond on a window at Chambord. Translated, it read: 'Woman is often fickle; Mad is he who trusts her.'

The Six Wives of Henry VIII

There have been few more scandalous monarchs than Henry VIII. He changed the religion of a Kingdom in order to divorce his first wife and had two subsequent wives executed. With six wives he had the reputation of being a great stud. In fact, with two of them he was almost certainly impotent. He only married so much in an effort to secure an heir. At the time it was seen as a political imperative to avoid plunging England back into the 30 years of internecine feuding that had preceded his father's reign, which have come to be known as the Wars of the Roses.

Henry Tudor, Henry VIII's father, had won the Wars of the Roses by defeating Richard III at the Battle of Bosworth Field and was crowned Henry VII. A Lancastrian, Henry VII ended any further struggle by marrying the daughter of the other great rival dynasty, Elizabeth of York.

As a Prince, Henry VIII was brought up chastely. A studious lad, he wrote the religious tract called *Assertio septem sacramentorum adversus Martin Lutherum*, a reply to Martin Luther's 95 theses nailed to the church door in Wittenberg that started the Protestant Reformation. As a result, Henry was awarded the title *Fidei Defensor*, or 'Defender of the Faith', by the Pope.

The first scandal of his reign centred on the marriage of his brother, the 15-year-old Arthur, to the 16-year-old Spanish Princess, Catherine of Aragon. Arthur had died soon after and Henry was encouraged by his father to take an interest in Catherine. A marriage between the heir to the English throne and Spain was important for English foreign policy, so Henry VII pushed for a dispensation from the Pope to allow Henry to marry his brother's widow – which was technically incest – on the grounds that her marriage to Arthur had never been consummated.

Henry VII came to the throne at 18 and, two months later, he married Catherine. Although she was six years older than him, he genuinely loved her. They enjoyed hunting, hawking and making music together, and the grooms who escorted him from his bedchamber to the Queen's reported that he made the trip regularly.

For five years, he was faithful. In that time, Catherine produced a number of stillborn children, a son who lived just two months and a daughter, Mary. Then Henry's attention began to wander. At first, his attention alighted on Lady Anne Hastings. He used one of the Grooms of the Bedchamber, Sir Henry Crompton, as his go-between. But Sir Henry promptly seduced Lady Anne himself.

When they were interrupted by Lady Anne's husband, Sir George Hastings, Crompton claimed that he was making love to Lady Anne not for his own sake but for that of the King. In the resulting scandal, Lady Anne was sent to a nunnery by her irate husband, and Henry banished her brother, the Duke of Buckingham, and Sir George's sister, Elizabeth, from court for spreading gossip. This did not prevent the news from reaching the ears of the Queen and the Spanish ambassador.

While the Queen remained vexed, Henry moved on to Jane Popincourt, the Flemish-born mistress of the Duc de Longueville, a French noble long held hostage in the English court. Her reputation was notorious. Louis XII personally crossed her name off the list of maids-of-honour who were coming to France with Henry's sister, Mary, saying that he would rather see Popincourt burn at the stake than attend his young bride.

Henry returned de Longueville to France to clear the way for his affair. And, when he tired of Jane, he gave her £100 to follow her lover. He had already transferred his affections to 18-year-old Elizabeth 'Bessie' Blount.

The daughter of a Shropshire knight, Bessie had come to court at the age of 13 when her dancing had brought her to the King's attention at a masque. The Queen was so taken by their performance that she had them repeat their *pas de deux* in her chamber by candlelight.

At 18, Bessie became Henry's mistress and in 1519 she presented him with a healthy living son, Henry Fitzroy. Bessie was quickly married off to Gilbert Talboys, one of the wards of the Chancey. The happy couple were given Rokeby Manor in Warwickshire as a wedding present.

Later, Henry considered marrying his illegitimate son to Mary to secure the line – albeit incestuously – but Henry Fitzroy died of tuberculosis while still a teenager.

The next woman to bear Henry a child was Mary Boleyn, Anne's older sister. Both Mary and Anne had been maids-of-honour in the licentious French court, but Mary, it seems, had out-performed the local talent. An Italian diplomat described her as the 'greatest and most infamous whore', while the King of France himself called her a 'hackney'.

Back in England, Mary was Catherine of Aragon's lady-in-waiting when Henry seduced her. Her compliant husband was rewarded with a knighthood. Henry named a ship in his new navy after her, but he dropped her without a penny when he grew tired of her.

Mary's father, Thomas Boleyn, was an ambitious man. It was said that he had even offered his own wife to Henry, who refused her, saying: 'Never with the mother.' Mary's younger sister, Anne, was more to Henry's taste. But Anne wanted nothing to do with him and proclaimed her intention to marry one James Butler.

However, fate – perhaps in the form of Thomas Boleyn – took a hand. Anne was picked to be one of eight ladies to take part in a masque at Cardinal Wolsey's London home, York Place. They were to represent Virtue and had to defend their castle against eight masked men, representing Desire, by dousing them with rose water and pelting them with fruit.

The outcome was predictable. After a few minutes of mock combat, Virtue succumbed. The ladies then danced with their assailants. When the gentlemen unmasked themselves, Anne found her suitor was none other than the King.

But Anne was not to be won over so easily. She took up with a married man, the poet Sir Thomas Wyatt, to protect herself from Henry's advances. Then she received a proposal from the Earl of Northumberland's heir, Sir Henry Perky. But, knowing the King's interest, Cardinal Wolsey put a stop to that match.

Henry stopped sleeping with the Queen and, in a series of passionate love letters, promised to make Anne his sole mistress 'rejecting all others'. This came as a bit of a shock to the court as Anne was no great beauty. She had an unsightly mole on her neck which she hid with high collars, and she wore long sleeves to hide the tiny sixth finger that she had on each hand. But it was her pert young bosom that took the King's fancy – 'those pritty duckys I trust shortly to kysse,' he wrote. 'Ducky' is a medieval word for breast.

Anne still did not succumb. She did not want to suffer the short shrift that Henry had meted out to her sister Mary. But Henry was growing desperate to have a son and he thought Anne might provide him with one. He needed a legitimate heir, however, so he would have to marry her.

Henry began to contend that the dispensation the Pope had given Catherine to marry him had been obtained under false pretences. That was why God had cursed their union and it had failed to give him the son he craved.

Henry persuaded the Dowager Duchess of Norfolk to testify that Catherine had indeed slept with his older brother, Arthur. The marriage had therefore been consummated, making her marriage to Henry incestuous and illegal.

Unfortunately for Henry, the Pope was being held hostage by Catherine's nephew, Charles V, at the time and did not see it that way. All Cardinal Wolsey's attempts to seek an annulment failed. Anne, who was still sore at Wolsey for preventing her marriage to Sir Henry Perky, demanded his dismissal. Wolsey retired to York and died on his way back to London, summoned there to face a charge of treason.

Sir Thomas More took over as Chancellor, but he was against the divorce and wanted to fight what he saw as the Lutheran heresy. He was replaced by the ambitious Thomas Cromwell, who saw that the way to give Henry the divorce he wanted was for him to reject the authority of Rome and make himself head of the English Church.

After holding out for six years, Anne finally succumbed. By January 1533, she was pregnant. On 25 January, Henry and Anne were married secretly. In May, a new Archbishop of Canterbury, Thomas Cranmer, presided over an ecclesiastical inquiry into Henry's first marriage, and on 23 May a special Act of Parliament declared it null and void. At Whitsun, Anne was crowned Queen, and in September she gave birth – to Princess Elizabeth. The Pope's response was excommunication. It bothered no one.

Disappointed at the birth of a daughter, Henry began indulging himself with other lovers. Anne herself complained to her sister-in-law, Lady Rochford, that Henry was neither skilful at love-making nor very virile. Nevertheless, she kept entertaining him in her bed in the hope that she would produce the male heir he so desperately wanted. Anne fell pregnant three more times – although she miscarried on each occasion. Anne blamed one of her miscarriages on Henry's dalliance with a pretty maid.

Anne turned for advice to her Lady of the Bedchamber, the sly Lady Rochford – whom Henry banished from court. In desperation, Anne tried to interest Henry in her own cousin, Madge Shelton. When Henry found out that Anne was trying to manipulate his love life, he dismissed Madge from court, too – after bedding her first, of course.

But Henry was slowing down. He suffered occasionally from bouts of impotence. To his doctors, he complained: 'I am 41 years old, at which age the lust of a man is not as quick as in lusty youth.' This was in the days before Viagra.

Even so, Anne became pregnant again. Henry, then 44, was delighted. But the prospect of being a father again did not stop him from turning his attentions to Anne's maid-of-honour, the beautiful and nubile Jane Seymour.

In January 1536, Catherine of Aragon died and Henry held a joust to celebrate. During the action, Henry was thrown from his horse. He was stretchered from the tournament field and for two hours he lay unconscious. Anne suddenly realized how precarious her position was. If the King died without a son, England would be thrown back into civil war and she would be the first for the chop. Her anxiety triggered premature labour. She gave birth to a son – dead.

Rumours quickly spread that the foetus was deformed, a sure sign that she had been involved with witchcraft. When Henry revived, he denied paternity. In his eyes, the deformed foetus proved that his second marriage, too, was cursed by incest. After all, Anne's sister, Mary, had been his lover before their marriage.

With Catherine now dead, Anne was in a very vulnerable position. Henry could now simply declare that his first marriage had been legitimate after all. That would reconcile him with the Catholic Church, rid him of Anne and allow him to find a new wife.

Anne was also isolated. Those courtiers who had maintained a loyalty to Catherine called her 'the concubine' and
'the goggle-eyed whore'. In an attempt to find allies, Anne
flirted. Enemies spread rumours that she had lovers. This
played into Henry's hands. He encouraged the scandal by
boasting that his wife had slept with a hundred other men.

'You never saw a prince, nor a man, who made a greater
show of his cuckold's horns,' one observer said.

On 2 May 1536, Anne was arrested for adultery, incest
and plotting to kill the King. Sir Henry Norris, a
Gentleman of the Privy Chamber, the grooms Sir Francis
Weston and William Brereton, along with a handsome
young musician named Mark Smeaton, were also
arrested. The first three denied having sex with Anne, but
Smeaton confessed, after torture. The four of them were
found guilty of treason and paid a terrible price. They
were hanged at Tyburn, cut down while still alive,
castrated, disembowelled and, finally, had their limbs cut
off. It was a gruesome way to go.

Anne's brother, Lord Rochford, was also arrested. The
two of them were tried together in the Great Hall in the
Tower of London. Their chief accuser was Rochford's
wife, good old Lady Rochford, who alleged that her
husband had always been in his sister's room. Other
maids gave their own accounts of the 'pastimes of the
Queen's chamber'. Lady Rochford also testified that there
had been an 'undue familiarity' between brother and
sister. The implication was that, since Anne had been
unable to produce the male heir Henry craved with Henry
himself, she had tried to conceive one with other lovers.
Her own brother lent a hand, as it were, because his
position depended on being the brother-in-law of the
current King and the uncle of a future monarch.

As evidence of incest this was less than convincing, but
there was no crossing the King. The judge, who was

Anne's own uncle, the Duke of Norfolk, shed a tear when he delivered the guilty verdict. For treason, the death sentence was mandatory. But whether they were to be burned or beheaded was a matter for the King's pleasure.

Henry was merciful. Rochford was beheaded on Tower Hill. Perhaps in deference to the great love he had once had for Anne, Henry spared her the axe. He paid £24 to bring an expert swordsman over from Calais to dispatch his love on Tower Green.

Curiously, two days before Anne was executed, Henry divorced her. He had their marriage annulled on the grounds that she had previously been contracted to marry Sir Henry Perky. The annulment technically nullified the charge of adultery. And with no adultery there was no treason – and, thus, no reason to execute her. No one mentioned this to Henry. He was too busy having fun.

While Anne was preparing to die, Henry began a round of parties where he pursued any woman he found remotely attractive. He was now 45 and not in the best of health, but he compared his new-found freedom with a man who had disposed of 'a thin old vicious hack in the hope of getting soon a fine horse to ride'.

It did not take him long to find his new mount. On 13 May 1536, just 11 days after the death of Anne Boleyn, he married her pretty maid-of-honour, Jane Seymour. Although Jane had been in Henry's debauched court for several years, she was still reputed to be a virgin – a neat trick in a court where it was held 'a sin to be a maid'. As Queen, Jane imposed her modest demeanour on others. She forbade Anne Basset to wear 'French apparel' and insisted that she use 'chests', material that covered the plunging necklines.

Already, the rumour was that the King was impotent, but something about Jane must have inspired him. In February 1537, it was announced that the Queen was pregnant and on 12 October she gave birth to his long-awaited son, Edward.

Twelve days later, she died.

Henry was heartbroken. But now he had sired a Prince of Wales, he was eager to sire a Duke of York, too, a younger brother for the sickly Edward.

There was a problem though. Since there was now no Queen at court, most of the eligible young ladies-in-waiting were home in the country.

The English ambassador to the Netherlands, John Hutton, was commanded to draw up a list of eligible women. These ranged from a 14-year-old lady-in-waiting to the Queen of France to a well-preserved 40-year-old widow. Hutton's recommendation, however, was the 16-year-old Duchess Christina of Milan. Henry was now aged 48.

However, Henry was interested in the current crop of French Princesses and suggested a beauty pageant of five girls in Calais. The French ambassador said that if the Princesses were to be paraded like ponies why did His Majesty not go one step further – mount them in turn so he could pick out the best ride? The idea was dropped.

The artist Hans Holbein was sent to Italy to paint a portrait of Christina of Milan. Henry was impressed. The young lady was also experienced in the ways of love. At 13 she had been married to the Duke of Milan, who had died a year later. The wedding arrangements were set in hand, but the wily Lord Chancellor Thomas Cromwell was against the marriage. Politically, an alliance with Protestant Germany would be more advantageous.

Holbein was sent off again, this time to Germany, to paint a portrait of Anne of Cleves. The English envoy who went with him protested that Anne and her sister, Amelia, were so well covered that Holbein could see neither their figures nor their faces.

'Why, would you have them naked?' replied the Chancellor of Cleves.

Knowing which way the political wind was blowing,

Holbein turned in an exceedingly flattering portrait of Anne. Henry did not find it displeasing and, bowing to the political exigencies, agreed to marry her.

It was noted that the King was very lusty at the time and, despite a gouty leg, he rode on horseback from Greenwich to Rochester to greet his bride. But, when he set eyes on her, he was appalled by her ugliness and quickly dubbed her his 'Flanders Mare'. To make matters worse, she spoke no English.

After their first night together, Henry told Cromwell: 'I liked her before not well, but now I like her much worse.'

She was 'not as reported', he said. Her breasts were slack and droopy – he liked small pert ones like Anne Boleyn's – and other parts of her body were 'in such a state one suspected her virginity'. She was apparently in such bad nick that Henry complained that never in her company could he be 'provoked or steered to know her carnally'.

Eight days later, he complained to his doctors that even though he had slept with his new wife each night she was 'still as good a maid . . . as ever her mother bore her'. And it was not his fault, he claimed. During the nights he had had a number of nocturnal emissions.

Anne was blissfully unaware of the problem. When Lady Rutland made discreet enquiries about the physical side of their marriage, Anne said: 'When he comes to bed, he kisses me and taketh me by the hand and biddeth me "Farewell, darling". Is that not enough?'

Lady Rutland tried to explain that a little more was expected of Anne if England was to have its Duke of York. But Anne would not listen. She regarded such talk as shameful.

Failing to get much stimulation from his new wife, Henry's amorous attentions quickly turned to Anne of Cleves's 18-year-old maid-of-honour, Catherine Howard, a cousin of Anne Boleyn. She was neither modest nor pious. She had been brought up in the crowded house of the Dowager Duchess of Norfolk in Horsham in Sussex, with numerous young relatives. There they had midnight feasts that often ended in communal sex.

Catherine took her first lover at 14. His name was Henry Manox and he was a young music teacher hired to teach her, ironically, the virginal. She later claimed that full sex had not taken place but he was persuasive and, she said: 'I suffered him at Sunday times to handle and touch the secret parts of my body which neither became me with honesty to permit nor him to require.'

But, when the family moved to Norfolk House in Lambeth, she met another young man named Francis Dereham. He set about seducing her and they were soon calling each other 'husband' and 'wife'.

'Francis Dereham,' said Catherine later, 'by many persuasions procured me to his vicious purpose and obtained first to lie upon my bed with his doublet and hose, and after in the bed; and, finally, he lay with me naked and used me in such sort as a man doth his wife many and sundry times, but how often I know not.'

They were not alone. Dereham would come to the maiden's chamber at night with Edward Waldegrave, where they would stay until dawn with their respective loves – Catherine and Joan Bulmer. According to Joan, Dereham and Catherine would 'kiss and hang by their bellies as if they were two sparrows'. Love tokens were exchanged and, in the dark, Joan heard a great deal of 'puffing and blowing'.

Catherine, despite her young years, was advanced. Joan said she knew 'how a woman might meddle with a man and yet conceive no child unless she would herself'.

Another member of the household, Katherine Tylney, later admitted that on occasions she had joined Dereham and Catherine in what the *Sun* today would call a 'three-in-the-bed love romp'.

Catherine's behaviour was widely known, but her colourful past was quickly hushed up when Henry took an interest. He described Catherine as 'a blushing rose without a thorn' and a 'perfect jewel of womanhood'. He took her as his mistress, but the powerful Howard family had greater ambitions. They were Catholics and wanted to rid the realm of its Protestant Queen.

The diplomatic need for Henry's German marriage had passed. Thomas Cromwell now backed the King's desire to sire more children. He began to arrange for Henry a divorce from his 'Flanders Mare'.

A convocation of clerics was set up to investigate the validity of the marriage. Anne's blushes were not spared when she was asked to repeat her conversations with Lady Rutland in front of the committee. Henry's doctors were also called to give evidence. After the scandal of two very public divorce cases centring on incest, the people of England were treated to hilarious testimony concerning the King's inability to get it up. But this was just a foretaste of the even more juicy scandal that was to follow.

The clerics quickly found that 'there had been no carnal copulation between Your Majesty and the said Lady Anne, nor with that just impediment interceding could it be possible'. The King's inability to perform, they ruled, resulted from a troubled conscience concerning the fact that Anne of Cleves had previously been promised elsewhere. The marriage was quickly annulled.

Anne remained in England and hit the bottle. She took other, more virile, lovers. Rumour had it that she became pregnant twice and gave birth to an illegitimate child.

There was another impediment to Henry's marriage plans, however. Since Catherine was Anne Boleyn's cousin, marriage to Catherine was technically incest. The Archbishop of Canterbury, Thomas Cranmer, quickly arranged a dispensation and the marriage went ahead. Catherine was already pregnant, but who was the father? Henry was fat, 50 and sick, and his waist had swelled out to a massive 54in. Nineteen-year-old Catherine had already shown her preference for younger, slimmer men.

Henry's court was soon packed with Catherine's adolescent playmates, including Joan Bulmer and Katherine Tylney. But, unfortunately, one of them had been overlooked. Her name was Mary Lassels. She had been one of the gentlewomen in the service of the Duchess of Norfolk, who had shared Catherine's communal bedroom at Norfolk House and had witnessed Catherine's youthful indiscretions. Egged on by her brother, a Protestant who sought to end the influence of the Catholic Howard family, Mary spilt the beans to the Archbishop of Canterbury, Thomas Cranmer.

Under torture, both Francis Dereham and Henry Manox admitted their sexual encounters with Catherine. Although he denied that he had known Catherine 'carnally', Manox admitted making advances to her in the small sacristy behind the altar in the Duchess's chapel. Both had ceased any sexual involvement with Catherine before she was married. However, it was revealed that Thomas Culpepper, a Gentleman of the King's Privy Chamber, had succeeded Henry in Catherine's affections.

Culpepper was one of Henry's favourites. According to the French ambassador, as a youth Culpepper had shared the King's bed. Plainly, the Frenchman added mischievously, he 'wished to share the Queen's bed too'.

It was not the first time that Culpepper claimed that Catherine's attendant, Lady Jane Rochford – who had given such eloquent testimony against Anne Boleyn – had 'provoked' him into a liaison. But even under torture he continued to deny that he had ever enjoyed full carnal knowledge of the Queen. When questioned, Catherine also accused Lady Rochford of encouraging her to flirt and, like Culpepper, denied actual intercourse. Meanwhile, Lady Rochford condemned them both as adulterous, while simultaneously maintaining that she had no knowledge of the affair. Soon, the dungeons of the Tower of London were so full that the royal apartments had to be turned into a jail to accommodate the new influx of prisoners.

The trial was a juicy affair. It was Katherine Tylney's evidence that tipped the scales. She said that the Queen often strayed out of her chambers at night and ran up the stairs to Culpepper's room, where they stayed until two in the morning.

Dereham and Culpepper were both convicted of treason at the Guildhall and sentenced to be hanged, drawn and quartered. Culpepper's had been the lesser crime. Dereham, on the other hand, had besmirched his bride by taking her precious virginity. He had to pay the full barbaric forfeit. Afterwards, both their heads were fixed on poles on London Bridge, where they were still to be seen, stripped of their flesh, four years later.

Catherine was stripped of her royal titles for a 'carnal copulation' with Dereham. She was indicted for having led 'a voluptuous and vicious life'.

Charles II

Of all the English Kings none could equal Charles II, the 'Merry Monarch', as a lover of staggering virility. He was the Don Juan of royalty, the supreme rake among rakes. His 17th-century court was the most sexually promiscuous ever known and he led it with untiring vigour.

The number of children born to Charles, apart from those he acknowledged, has never been known for certain but once, when he was addressed pompously as the 'father of his people', Lord Rochester was heard to mutter: 'Of a good many of 'em.'

But he was also a witty, tolerant and kind man who treated all classes of society with the same amiability and courtesy. Even Dr Johnson, who was a stern moralist, found a good word to say for him, excusing his excesses 'because his complexion is of an amorous sort'. It has been said that he was one of the best loved and one of the worst Kings England ever had.

Physically he must have been very impressive, though he had little personal vanity. Once, while his portrait was being painted, he asked the artist if the likeness was good. The artist assured him that it was. 'Then, odds fish,' he exclaimed, 'I must be an ugly fellow!' The King's features were large and heavy, his complexion dark, but the quizzical good humour on his face made him extremely attractive. He was tall, had a dominating voice and dressed magnificently in silk, velvet and great froths of snowy-white lace. Strangers found him formidable.

The trouble with Charles was that he enjoyed ease and luxury too much. His court was turned into something resembling a Turkish harem and he spent hours lolling around on cushions, flirting with his mistresses or strolling through his parks with his courtiers and a troop of the pretty little spaniel dogs to which he gave his name. He had great capacities, which he never used to the full. Science was his favourite topic and he enjoyed talking to scientists and attending meetings of the Royal Society. He also had a sympathetic love and understanding of the arts, of poetry, painting, sculpture and the theatre.

It was his love of the theatre that led him to the mistress most people associate with him – Nell Gwynne. To her, he owed a great deal of his popularity. For Nell was no pampered, greedy courtier, versed in etiquette and protocol and determined to get all she could from the liaison. Nell was a common cockney actress, a seller of oranges, a good-natured bawd who made Charles laugh and loved him faithfully as no other mistress had ever done. As long as he lived he treated her with an affectionate regard that was never given to some of his more aristocratic beauties.

His life had not always been soft, self-indulgent and amorous. His childhood was spent in the formal, austere court of his father, Charles I, a monarch who was utterly faithful to his devoted wife, Henrietta. Charles II could never have inherited his hot-blooded instincts from them. He was only 12 when the civil troubles in England came to a head and his father signalled the opening of the Civil War by raising his standard over Nottingham Castle on 22 August 1642. For three years he was kept close to his father, riding through England in the wake of the Royalist army, seeing battle after battle fought between Roundheads and Cavaliers. Sometimes he hardly knew where his next meal was coming from. Sometimes he came near to death. When he reached 15, his father decided he must be sent to France and safety.

From 1646 until 1660 Charles lived in exile on the Continent. These were years of wandering and waiting for news, broken only by a few rash visits to England, one of which ended with Charles – who would otherwise have been King – hiding from Cromwell's men in the branches of what became known as 'The Boscobel Oak'. As an 18-year-old prince, he made one noble gesture that should be set against future failings. Hearing that his father's life was in the balance, he sent a Carte Blanche to Parliament. This document, still preserved, consisted of a sheet of blank paper with his seal and signature at the bottom, signifying that he was ready to do anything to save Charles I from his executioners.

At this stage he was by no means the debonair gallant of later fame. Tall, gangling, taciturn and heavy-browed, he was ill at ease among the brilliant French courtiers and so impoverished he could not afford his own carriage. But as the years went by he discovered his power over women and life improved. He became a past master in the art of seduction and wherever he went, during those years of exile, there was always a pretty woman, ready to hop into his bed. There is no precise information about the number of mistresses he had in France but at one stage the diarist Pepys remarked that Lady Byron must be his 17th and before he left the number had risen, in some estimates to 40! Charles liked his women to be sophisticated enough to enjoy his favours without demanding too much of his emotions. His favourite was Isabelle Angélique, Duchesse de Châtillon – his 'Bablon' as he called her – who was an enchanting companion without demanding fidelity.

On Oliver Cromwell's death on 3 September 1658, England stirred uneasily and wondered what would happen next. Cromwell's son, Richard, was found to be totally inadequate for the role of Lord Protector and people feared anarchy in the unstable conditions that developed. It was decided to call King Charles home to restore the monarchy.

Flags flying, a squadron of ships set out from England to fetch him. Charles had taken up residence at The Hague in order to be ready. His condition was so desperate that it was reckoned the value of what he stood up in, added to the cost of his servants' clothes, was not more than £2. He was given an immediate allowance of £50,000 so that he could return to his kingdom in style.

As he set foot on English soil again, no longer a fugitive, on 26 May 1660, church bells rang out and people danced in the street. London had never seen such scenes of joy and celebration as this restoration of the monarchy after years of puritan gloom.

After King Charles had listened to hours of speech-making he retired thankfully to bed where the luscious Barbara Palmer was waiting for him. Formerly Barbara Villiers, daughter of Lord Grandison, she was a dark-haired tempestuous beauty whose sexual prowess was to keep him enslaved for nearly ten years.

They first met at his court in exile at Bruges, just before the Restoration. Her husband, Roger Palmer, was a minor diplomat with strong Royalist sympathies and she accompanied him when he went to the Continent to swear loyalty. Charles found her a fascinating creature. She had already been mistress of the notorious rake Lord Chesterfield, a fact which made him madly jealous, and had acquired a taste for wealth, luxury and jewels, which poor Roger Palmer could not hope to satisfy.

During the time she was his mistress Barbara exercised incredible power over the King. She could behave like a fishwife when thwarted and subjected the rest of the court to her imperious will and bad temper. But he would hear no evil of her. In the end, he tired of her demanding ways and her greed, but when he first returned to England she flourished and Samuel Pepys, who was hypnotized by her beauty, confessed to his diary that when he went to bed at night he dreamed that Barbara Palmer was there and he fell asleep in her arms.

Though Charles would have been happy enough to spend his days dallying with his mistress and other beauties of the court, it was soon made clear to him that he must choose a Queen. During his exile many Princesses had been approached as possible partners, but they had not been eager to ally themselves with a penniless King without a throne. He had been humiliated several times. Now, he was in a position to choose.

After some deliberation, he plumped for Catherine de Braganza, Infanta of Portugal, a young lady whose dowry included Bombay, Tangiers and a vast amount of money. She was totally different to the sort of women Charles was used to, though pleasant in appearance with an affectionate nature. She did her best to please him. Only pregnancy kept the seething Barbara from coming to court and establishing her supremacy. Queen Catherine had been warned about the King's mistress before she left home. She knew well enough that Barbara dominated Charles, was the proud mother of one royal bastard and at that very moment expecting another.

Everybody dreaded Barbara's return to court. The King, hoping to mollify her, gave the much-cuckolded Roger Palmer a title, so that she could call herself Lady Castlemaine. Actually, after four months of playing the devoted husband Charles was ready to welcome his mistress back to bed with open arms. So glad was he, in fact, to see her that he committed an act of quite appalling insensitivity.

Knowing full well that his Queen dreaded even the thought of meeting Lady Castlemaine, Charles insisted that his mistress be appointed to the Queen's bedchamber. Catherine protested, but Charles would not listen to her. One day he led Barbara into the Queen's presence and begged to be allowed to present her. The Queen did not know who she was. When her courtiers began sniggering, however, she realized she was holding the hand of the dreaded Lady Castlemaine and fell, fainting, to the ground.

Even this appalling behaviour did not kill Catherine's love for Charles. She knew now that she could never change him and taught herself to accept his amorous, wayward nature. Realizing that she had to put up with Lady Castlemaine, whether she liked it or not, she made the best of things and to the relief of everyone approached her in a friendly manner.

Queen Catherine's deepest grief was that she could not give this fertile King a single child, whereas Lady Castlemaine had three sons and two daughters eventually recognized by their royal father. Statesmen pleaded with Charles to divorce Catherine and marry someone who could give him an heir. But he would not. Whatever his faults, after the bedchamber disaster he always insisted on her dignities as Queen and gave her what affection he could. When Lady Castlemaine once insulted her, he turned on her in anger.

Nothing, however, was permitted to interfere with the royal pursuit of pleasure. Love, to Charles, was an absorbing game in which his emotions took second place to his powerful sexual urge. He seemed to have no conscience, nor did he feel any moral need to curb his desires. His court, brilliant though it was, became increasingly decadent. The King in his maturity was exceptionally attractive and none of his women, and there were many besides his official mistress, could be angry with him for long after they had been discarded. He would be sure to make them laugh and could always manage to laugh at himself.

Queen Catherine had ceased to complain about them. She was discreet and rarely visited the King's bedroom uninvited. A delightful story is told about one occasion when she broke the rule and surprised him. Laughing when she discovered an embroidered silk slipper by the side of the bed, she then withdrew at once so that 'the pretty fool' could come out of hiding.

Charles began to tire of Lady Castlemaine. Their relationship was by no means over but her temper, her greed and her volatile personality were beginning to get on his nerves. Fate sent him a delightful antidote in the shape of his distant cousin, Frances Stuart. As soon as he saw her he was bowled over. Tall, slender, graceful, with a classic profile and a soft, sweet voice, she was also virginal and determined to remain so. Pepys tells how 'besotted' Charles was with his pretty cousin, how he would manoeuvre her into corners and kiss her in full view of the court. But that was as far as he was allowed to go. He did everything he could to win her, organizing balls and fêtes in her honour and writing poetry in praise of her virtues. But, though he was terribly in love, for once he had encountered a woman who could withstand his amorous onslaught. She had no intention of climbing into the royal bed. Charles had her beauty immortalized by the goldsmith Jan Roettiers and for three centuries the coinage of Britain bore her profile in the image of Britannia.

Then, suddenly, 'La Belle Stuart' eloped with the somewhat unprepossessing Duke of Richmond. The court was shaken by the King's fury. He swore he would never speak to either of them again. But when the Duchess became the victim of smallpox Charles could not bear to think of her being ill and sent his own physician to attend her. She recovered and begged his forgiveness for any hurt she had caused him. Eventually be accepted both the Richmonds back at court; some said Frances then granted him favours she had denied him before.

Lady Castlemaine did not remain in favour for very long after this. Her eclipse came in 1667, very soon after that of Clarendon, England's great Lord Chancellor, whose downfall she had schemed for and gloried in. She found herself paid off with an estate and the title of Duchess of Cleveland. Knowing full well that her star had set, she wisely decided to cross the Channel and live in France.

The King had widened his amorous circle to include ladies of the acting profession. One was Moll Davis, who claimed she was a bastard of the great Howard family, the other Nell Gwynne.

Nell had no pretensions to grandeur; she was a cockney born and bred. Brought up in a tavern in the rough area around Covent Garden, she first worked as a barmaid, before moving up the social scale to sell oranges to patrons of the London theatre. She first appeared on stage as a comedy actress at the age of 17 when she became the mistress of Lord Brockhurst, afterwards Earl of Dorset. It was while she was under his protection that the King saw her for the first time at the Theatre Royal, Drury Lane.

Charles could not resist her with her sweet, curly head, joyous laugh, cockney wit and wonderful good nature. At first Nell's visits to Whitehall were fleeting. Then, in the spring of 1670 a new play by Dryden, in which she was to take part, had to be postponed because she was pregnant.

The King admitted he was the father and she became his acknowledged mistress with apartments of her own and a title – the Duke of St Albans – for her son.

About this time another ravishing beauty captured him. The King first saw Louise de Kéroualle in the train of her sister Henrietta Maria when she came to England to negotiate the secret Treaty of Dover between him and Louis XIV. He thought her a frail and lovely creature, but she was only 16 and his sister refused to leave her in his tender care. Henrietta Maria died and King Louis sent Louise back to England. The official reason was that he wished to place her in Queen Catherine's household. But many suspected she had been sent as a spy.

When Louise de Kéroualle arrived in England she and Nell became great rivals for the King's love. Nell spared no one her wit. She had nicknames for nearly everyone at court, which highly amused the King. She noticed that Louise, though very beautiful, had a slight cast in one eye and promptly christened her 'Squintabella'.

Charles gave Nell a fine house in Pall Mall but the French enchantress was made Duchess of Portsmouth and given apartments in Whitehall. These apartments were the cause of a great deal of controversy. They were made so luxurious that, even in a court used to finery, people began to talk angrily of the vast amounts of money spent. But the frail Louise had Charles under her spell and soon proved herself as skilful at intrigue as she was in love.

To the end of his life she fascinated and cheated him more than any other woman. She aroused great feelings of resentment for many reasons. To start with, many people suspected that she was spying for the French King, others feared her Catholic influence on Charles, yet others felt that she was draining him financially. One day a carriage which people thought carried the Duchess of Portsmouth was attacked by a crowd. But a merry, curly head popped out of the window. It was Nell Gwynne who called out:

'Good people, be civil. I am the protestant whore!'

Louise was also a snob, and although only the daughter of a minor nobleman, liked to claim kinship with the older and nobler families of France. When she went into deepest mourning for one supposed cousin, Nell also put on black and said she was weeping for 'The Grand Cham of Tartary'. Nell took comparatively little from Charles compared with the fortunes extracted from him by his other mistresses. But she was always ready to use those in need and is known to have given money for prisoners in Whitecross Jail.

Both had to learn to share him with other women. One of these was Hortense Martini, an Italian beauty, niece of the all-powerful Cardinal Mazarin. The King's passion for Hortense was intense but soon burned itself out. She was dark-haired, turbulent, fascinating, but she also had a wandering eye and this Charles could not tolerate. Her errant fancy wandered from him to the Prince of Monaco who was paying a visit to England and, before she could protest her innocence, she was out of favour.

Charles, not yet 55, and seemingly in good health, was looking forward to discussing with Sir Christopher Wren plans for his new palace to be built at Winchester. Then on Sunday 2 February 1665 he rose from his bed looking pale after a restless night. As the barber began to fix the linen for his shave, Charles had a 'violent fit of apoplexy'. He asked for the Queen directly he had recovered from his first attack. She was present when his condition worsened and was so overcome that she had to be helped back to her room. It was now, in his manner of dying, that one sees the best of Charles II.

Queen Catherine sent a message asking him to forgive her for any wrongs she had done him. 'Alas, poor woman,' was his reply. 'She begs my pardon? I beg hers with all my heart: take back to her that answer.' He apologized to his attendants for being 'such an unconscionable time a-dying' and bore with astonishing humour all the primitive attempts of his doctors to save him. His last words were a request to his brother James, entreating him to be kind to the Duchess of Portsmouth and his children and 'Let not poor Nelly starve'.

Louis XIV of France

The reputation for debauchery of Louis XIV of France, the 'Sun King', was despised and envied across the whole of Europe. However, he was not quite as bad as he was made out to be. Instead of exploiting any extramarital opportunity that presented itself, he practised serial adultery, maintaining one favourite at a time whom he replaced when his passion waned.

When he came to the throne in 1661, Louis XIV was married to the Infanta Maria Theresa, the daughter of Philip IV of Spain. Although the marriage was contracted in order to shore up a peace treaty between the two countries, Maria Theresa was deeply in love with her husband, which was a shame. She was short and swarthy and Louis found her dull in the extreme, preferring hunting, gambling and even the business of government to her company.

He began his reign with an affair with his sister-in-law, which was so scandalous that it almost brought down the monarchy. Then he turned to her lady-in-waiting, Louise de la Baume-Leblac, whom he created Duchess de la Vallière. She was the first of four long-term mistresses who bore him 12 illegitimate children in all.

La Vallière produced four. It was only then that the magnetic effect she had had on the King began to flag. He then fell for the beautiful Françoise Arthenais de Mortmart, Marquise de Montespan. The King was used to the routine of dropping around to the house he had bought la Vallière when he wanted sex. Being a creature of habit, he ordered de Montespan to move in with her rival. This was too much for la Vallière, who quit the court and went into a convent.

De Montespan was Louis's mistress for 12 years and produced seven children, whom Louis had legitimized. Like the offspring of Charles II in England, they formed the backbone of the aristocracy. She lost her position in the King's affections when the 18-year-old Duchesse de Fontages came to court with the specific intention of seducing the King.

De Fontages gave birth to a son who died after a month. Then she herself took ill. Poison was suspected. France was in the grip of what was known as the Age of Arsenic at the time. This had begun in 1673, when two priests told the Paris Police Commissioner, Nicholas de la Reynie, that they had heard a number of disturbing confessions from wealthy men and women. A number of them had admitted to murdering their respective husbands and wives. The priests would not break the sanctity of the confessional and name names, but de la Reynie decided to investigate the matter.

He began by trying to track down the suppliers of the 'succession powders' – so called because they were usually used to ensure the succession of the poisoner. Suspicion fell on a fortune-teller named Marie Bosse. De la Reynie sent an undercover policewoman to consult the clairvoyant on the best way to deal with her troublesome husband. Madame Bosse sold her some arsenic and was arrested, along with her husband, her two sons and another fortune-teller named La Vigoureux, who admitted sleeping with all the members of the Bosse family. A huge cache of poison was found in the Bosses' home. Facing torture, La Vigoureux and the Bosse family provided a list of their clients. These included a number of prominent members of Louis XIV's court.

Plainly, this was a very delicate matter politically, but de la Reynie explained that, although an investigation might embarrass a number of important courtiers, with the epidemic of poisoning that was going on, Louis might find himself the next victim. Louis set up a commission of inquiry.

Officially known as *La Commission de l'Arsenic*, it was known to those who appeared before it as *L'Affaire de la Chambre Ardente*, because de la Reynie, with theatrical flair, conducted the investigation in a room draped in black and lit solely by candlelight. In *La Chambre Ardente*, Marie Bosse and La Vigoureux admitted they were part of a devil-worship cult headed by one La Voisin – real name Catherine Deshayes.

Madame Deshayes was the wife of a failed haberdasher, who had set up in business making skin-cleansing treatments which, at that time, contained a lot of arsenic. Her experiments had led her to learn about chemistry and she had developed preparations that, she claimed, promoted 'inner cleanliness'.

As a sideline, Madame Deshayes worked as an astrologer. Her clients were rich and aristocratic. To lend weight to her predictions, she had developed a network of informants throughout French society. These were exclusively women and many, including La Vigoureux, took pseudonyms.

As an astrologer, La Voisin would predict that a woman's husband, say, was going to die suddenly. If the woman seemed pleased at the prospect, La Voisin would then supply some poison to hasten the event.

The business was so profitable that La Voisin could afford to pay £30,000 for a secluded house in a run-down area of Paris. It was hidden by trees and protected by a high wall. She lived there with her husband, now a successful jeweller, her 21-year-old daughter, Marie-Marguerite Montvoison, and their lodger Nicholas Levasseur – an executioner by trade.

De la Reynie put the house under surveillance. One of his agents, working under cover, overheard one of Deshayes' assistants in a bar drunkenly describing acts of devil worship. The police then picked up two people who had attended meetings at Deshayes's house.

Under interrogation, they said that Deshayes and a 66-year-old priest, L'Abbé Guibourg, regularly conducted black masses there. During the service, a naked woman would act as an altar table. She would lie in front of the altar with her legs splayed. The Abbé, wearing an alb with black phalluses embroidered on it, would rest the chalice and wafers on her body. He would intone the Catholic Mass with the words 'infernal lord Satan' substituted for 'God' and 'Christ'. A child would urinate in the chalice and the contents would be sprinkled over the congregation. Then the wafer would be pressed against the breasts and vulva of the woman. As he inserted a wafer into the woman's vagina, the Abbé would chant: 'Lord Satan sayeth "in rioting and drunkenness I rise again. You shall fulfil the lusts of the flesh. The works of the flesh are manifest – they are drunkenness, revelling, immodesty, fornication, luxury and witchcraft. My flesh is meat indeed".'

This was the cue for an orgy of indiscriminate sex.

The police raided Deshayes's house. In a pavilion in the garden, they found a room draped in black with an altar in it. The candles on the altar were made from the fat distilled from human flesh.

Deshayes's daughter, Marie-Marguerite, told the police that animals had been sacrificed and their blood drunk. Then, under intense questioning, she admitted that there had been human sacrifices too.

She described how, at one ceremony, the Abbé had said: 'Astaroth, Asmodeus, prince of friendship, I beg you to accept the sacrifice of this child which we now offer you.'

Then Guibourg had held the child up by its feet and slit its throat. The blood had spurted into the chalice on the belly of the naked woman. The Abbé had then smeared the blood on his penis and the vagina of the woman, and had sex with her.

One of the children had been Deshayes's own goddaughter, Françoise Filatre. Others had been supplied by the inner circle of devotees or a compliant midwife. Madame Deshayes had had another sideline, as an abortionist, and had often supplied living foetuses ripped from her clients. Victims' entrails were distilled for occult use and the rest of their bodies were burned in a stove.

It turned out that one of the worshippers was none other than the King's mistress, the Marquise de Montespan. Fearing that she was losing the King's favour to the young Duchesse de Fontages, she had attended three of the 'love masses' to try to win back his favour by acting as the nude altar table.

Catherine Deshayes and the Abbé Guibourg admitted to murdering hundreds of children over a career in Satanism that spanned 13 years. Some 150 courtiers were arrested for poisoning and sentenced to death, slavery in the French galleys or banishment. Madame Deshayes herself was burned at the stake in 1680. However, the Marquise de Montespan returned, briefly, to favour.

She was eventually replaced – not by a ravishing beauty but by the middle-aged governess the King had employed to bring up de Montespan's children. Her name was Madame de Maintenon and she had been born in prison. At 17, she had married the elderly poet, Paul Scarron. When he died, she was left penniless and went into a convent before being summoned to court as a governess.

Although she had once been a great beauty, the hardships of life had left her wrinkled and worn. When Queen Maria Theresa died, Louis married de Maintenon morganatically. She was the first and only one of his consorts to have any political influence over him. This proved disastrous.

She urged him to persecute France's Protestants, which led to their mass exodus and also provoked war with England, Spain, Russia, Holland and most of the rest of Europe.

The Court that Louis XIV established at Versailles was a synonym for scandal. Louis XIII had bought a hunting lodge there in 1624, buying up the entire village in 1632. When Louis XIV came to the throne in 1643 at the age of five, he found himself continually surrounded by intrigue. The solution to prevent this, he discovered in later life, was the magnificent court he built at Versailles, which employed some 22,000 architects, gardeners, craftsmen and labourers. Life there was tightly regulated, from the lever – the ceremony that attended the King getting up in the morning – to the coucher – which attended his going to bed at night. Meals were public ceremonies where courtiers had to remove their hats when speaking to or being spoken to by the King. Officers of the state, lesser royals, army officers and members of the nobility – numbering 15,000 in all – were required to attend court. With so much leisure time on their hands, the cream of society gave itself up to promiscuity and had little time to plot against the King.

Contemporary chronicler, Bussy-Rabutin, remarked : 'Debauch reigned more supremely here than anywhere else in the world. Wine-drinking and unmentionable vice were so fashionable that their evil example perverted the intentions of the virtuous, so they succumbed to the lure of viciousness.'

Even though noblewomen gave themselves freely, a lot of courtiers gave themselves up to homosexuality. This, too, was useful to the King, who could elevate lowly lovers by marrying them off to gay courtiers without running the risk that they might sleep with their husbands. Louise de la Baume-Leblac became the Duchesse de la Vallière, by marrying the notorious homosexual, the Duc de la Vallière. He once tried to seduce a visiting Italian lad named Primi Visconti by observing: 'In Spain, monks do it; in France the nobility do it; in Italy everyone does it.'

Court homosexuals formed themselves into a society, whose leaders were selected according to the size of their sexual organ. Bussy-Rabutin recorded an incident that took place in a brothel where 'they seized hold of a prostitute, tied her wrists and ankles to the bedposts, thrust a firework into the part of her body that decency forbids me to mention, and put a match to it.'

The resulting scandal meant more Princes and noblemen had to be banished from court.

Louis XIV was succeeded by his great-grandson, Louis XV, who came to the throne at the age of five. At 15, he married the 23-year-old Princess Marie of Poland. She gave him ten children in ten years. Then she called an abrupt halt to their sex life, forcing the 25-year-old King to seek his pleasures elsewhere.

Louis's first scandalous liaison was with the four de Nesle sisters, who came to his bed one after another. Then, when his young mistress, the Duchesse de Chateauroux, died suddenly in 1744, came Jeanne-Antoinette Poisson, the cultivated wife of Charles-Guillaume Le Normant d'Étoiles. Madame d'Étoiles moved into rooms under the roof at Versailles and gradually became the King's firm favourite. He created her Marquise de Pompadour, although she is universally known as Madame de Pompadour because she was looked down on by the courtiers as a bourgeois. Through her natural guile and an ability to make herself agreeable to everyone at court, she began to grow in influence. The King was shy and introverted and had trouble communicating with his courtiers. Madame de Pompadour became his private secretary and moved out of her attic into regal apartments. When she fell out of favour sexually, she maintained her influence by procuring an endless stream of other lovers for him.

She was a patron of the leading artists and architects of the day, and a friend of Voltaire's. She also acted as an agent for the Empress Maria Theresa of Austria. Madame de Pompadour's protégé, the Duc de Choiseul, reversed France's old alliances, realigning France with Austria against the German principalities and England. This led to the Seven Years War, which left France crushed in Europe and Canada in English hands. These defeats were laid at her door. They left her depressed and Madame de Pompadour died in the royal apartments soon after the end of the war in 1764.

Next Louis moved further down the social scale, taking as his mistress the illegitimate daughter of low-class parents – Jeanne Bécu, a hostess in a gambling house. She was the mistress of Jean du Barry, a Gascon nobleman. However, she could not become the King's official *maîtresse en titre* unless she was married to a nobleman. So Jean du Barry generously married her off to his brother Guillaume, the Comte du Barry. The King then moved her into apartments directly above his own in Versailles. The Comtesse du Barry then outstripped even Madame de Pompadour in extravagance. Every day, she bought new jewels and dresses, costing the French treasury the equivalent of £40 million over five years.

She also fancied herself as the equal of Madame de Pompadour in political intriguing. Although she allied herself with the faction that brought down the Duc de Choiseul, she succeeded in putting everyone's backs up – including those of Louis's heir and his chief minister. Nevertheless, thanks to Louis's dependence on her, she maintained her place at court. He only sent her away five days before his death as an act of penitence.

When Louis XVI came to the throne, he confined du Barry to a nunnery. Despite her humble origins, the Comtesse du Barry aided aristocratic émigrés after the French Revolution, was branded a counter-revolutionary and perished on the guillotine in 1793.

Secrets and
Mysteries

The Missing Earl

He did it – English law in the form of a coroner's jury decreed that Lord Lucan killed his children's nanny on that dark winter's night. The Edwardian-looking Earl with a penchant for gambling and a disdain for modern life wielded the hammer that killed pretty Sandra Rivett. But what has puzzled policeman hunting for him ever since the murder in November 1974 is the secret of what happened to him. Is he dead? Is he alive? More importantly, do his friends know his fate? Perhaps even the most outrageous theory of all is that he is innocent and took to the life of a fugitive because no one would ever believe otherwise. What are the secrets of Lord Lucan?

The story starts, of course, with the murder; when a panic-stricken Lady Veronica Lucan ran from her home in the pouring rain to a local pub and yelled to the astonished drinkers: 'Murder, there's been a murder. He murdered the nanny.' On Lady Veronica's head was an extremely deep wound which poured blood, mingling with the rain running down her face and into her nightclothes.

Officers forced their way into the home at 46 Lower Belgrave Street where they found the lower half of the mews in darkness. Police Sergeant Donald Baker, directed by the light of his torch, saw, at the end of the stairs leading to the basement, smears of what looked like blood on the wallpaper. Gritting his teeth, he advanced further. The police then made their way upstairs where they found the Lucan children. After comforting them the police officers went to the basement. There, on the hard floor, in a canvas Post Office mailbag, was the body of Sandra Rivett.

The murder weapon was found half an hour later – a 9in, 2¼lb length of lead piping wrapped in medical plaster. Lady Frances Lucan, the eldest child, ten years old, told police that she had been watching TV with her mother in the main bedroom when Sandra went downstairs to make some hot drinks. She was gone 20 minutes when Lady Lucan spoke with Frances and told her to watch TV alone while she checked on what had happened to the nanny. She reappeared with a wound on her head . . . with her husband, Lord Lucan. It was the last time that little Lady Frances ever saw him.

Lady Lucan, in hospital after the ordeal, told police this story; that she found the half-landing in darkness when she went to search for the nanny. She called out Sandra's name and there was no reply. She then heard a noise in the cloakroom behind her. She turned – and then a gloved hand grasped her throat and a rain of blows were delivered to her head. Panicking, she said she grabbed the attacker by his genitals and squeezed hard. The man forced her to the ground and tried to gouge out her eyes – releasing the pressure, as the pain from Lady Lucan's grip forced him backwards, she said she looked up and saw the face of her husband.

Lady Lucan claimed he told her that he had killed the nanny, mistakenly thinking it was her. She said she saved her own life by reasoning with him that she would help him to get away. They went upstairs to a bedroom and she lay down on the bed while he went to find some wet towels to bathe her wounds. 'While he was gone I got up and dashed out of the house,' said Lady Lucan. That was her frantic dash to the pub which signalled the beginning of one of history's most intriguing murder cases.

Later that night, 7 November, Lucan's mother, the Dowager Countess Lucan, arrived at the house to meet the police. She said that her son had telephoned, asking her to be there. She told detectives that he had said a 'terrible catastrophe' had occurred, in which his wife Veronica and the nanny Sandra had been hurt by an intruder whom he had disturbed. It was his mother who revealed the first of many secrets about the mysterious Earl. She informed the officers that her son and Lady Veronica had separated and the children were wards of the court. Many of Lucan's friends were unaware of this because of the outward appearance of a conservative, family man was one he both nurtured and cherished.

Checks at the nearby flat he kept and another mews home which was his did not reveal any clues about his whereabouts or what had gone on earlier that evening. police found Lord Lucan's passport in his flat together with a suit that was laid out on the bed as if he was meaning to pack it. But from the way the evidence was shaping up it seemed as if Lady Lucan's story was true; the police began to think that Lucan had bludgeoned the nanny to death after mistaking her for his wife. Sandra Rivett, 29, died because she did not take the usual evening off – the evening that Lucan presumed she would not be in the house.

Police began to chip away at the facade of the Earl who behaved as if he belonged in another century. Outwardly he displayed all the signs of a privileged life, with his fine homes, live-in nanny, membership of gentleman's clubs, a Mercedes car and Savile Row suits in the wardrobe. He was a high-roller on the backgammon and card tables of private gambling clubs where his considerable prowess with the cards earned him the nickname of 'Lucky' among his friends. It was not unusual for 'Lucky' to scoop £5,000 in an afternoon of gambling at the tables of his most exclusive club, the Clermont in London. He held bank accounts in Rhodesia and the Bahamas and was generally reckoned to be financially sound, having inherited family funds, as well as silver and land in Ireland when he succeeded to the title of Earl of Lucan in January 1964. But Lucan's outwardly affluent lifestyle was, police learned, not quite as financially sound as it seemed.

Lucan had frittered away much of his money. He had a fixed income of £7,000 per annum from a trust and spent large sums in legal fees in his bid to gain custody of his children in a court case in January 1973. At one stage he was spending £400 a week for a private detective to watch his wife as he hoped to find illicit liaisons which might convince a judge that the youngsters would been better off under his wing. Another time, his beloved Clermont Club in London's ritzy Berkeley Square once withdrew his credit facilities for a time because he bounced a cheque there for £10,000. In short, Lord Lucan was going broke, and was being eaten away with an almost pathological hatred for his wife which, police surmised, he thought he could exorcise with a swift, clean, simple murder.

Police began to trace his movements prior to the killing and the attack on Lady Lucan. The night before, he had dined with 40 other people at a formal dinner. On the day of the murder itself, he had lunch with friends at the Clermont, met a literary agent to talk over an article he was planning for a magazine on gambling, and at around 8.30pm phoned the Clermont to book a table for four people for dinner.

He arrived at the club some 16 minutes later, spoke with the doorman, and then drove off. His guests arrived but he – the host – was never seen again.

On the Saturday morning, 9 November, police discovered that Lucan had posted two letters to his friend, millionaire amateur jockey Bill Shand Kydd. The letters were postmarked Uckfield, Sussex, and had blood on the envelopes. One read: 'Dear Bill, the most ghastly circumstances arose tonight, which I have described briefly to my mother when I interrupted the fight at Lower Belgrave Street and the man left.'

'V (for Veronica) accused me of having hired him. I took her upstairs and sent Frances to bed and tried to clean her up. She lay doggo for a bit. I went into the bathroom and left the house.'

'The circumstantial evidence against me is strong in that V will say it was all my doing and I will lie doggo for a while, but I am only concerned about the children. If you can manage it I would like them to live with you. V has demonstrated her hatred for me in the past and would like to see me accused. For George (his son) and Frances to go through life knowing their father had been accused of attempted murder would be too much for them.'

'When they are old enough to understand explain to them the dream of paranoia and look after them.' He signed himself 'Lucky'.

The second letter carried the heading 'financial matters' and outlined a sale at Christie's he had arranged for family silver.

Finally police spoke with Susan Maxwell Scott at the estate she shared with her husband, Ian Maxwell Scott, on the outskirts of Uckfield – the place where the letters had been posted from. Lord Lucan had told them the same story as the one he recounted to his mother – that he had gone into the home to act as his wife's rescuer and found himself being accused by her of Sandra Rivett's murder. He drove away from her home at 1.15am in a dark saloon car and has never been seen again.

Or has he? Part of the unanswered enigma surrounding the Earl has been his flight. One theory put forward was that he hopped on a cross-channel ferry and threw himself into the cold water from the deck of the Newhaven-Dieppe ship. Another was that he went to a private airfield and flew out of the country with a friend at the controls. Other flights of fancy suggest that he changed his identity, took the small amount of capital he had in a Swiss bank account and set out to embark on a new life away from justice and the stigma of murder.

But Scotland Yard detectives are never satisfied with

untidy ends. One of the toughest nuts to crack had been Lucan's tight circle of aristocratic friends, many of whom seemed bound to Lucan by a code of loyalty and honour rarely found in 20th-century Britain. A code, some policemen think, which may even have transcended society's most heinous crime – murder. One source close to the investigation once said that he believed that up to five of Lucan's friends knew that he hadn't taken the coward's way out and killed himself. The obvious suggestion is that Lucan's friends, an elite mafia of the rich and privileged, kept his secret and somehow assisted his flight and bolstered the start of his life as a fugitive. It is only a theory and no one has ever been charged with aiding and abetting the flight of a wanted criminal. But in the minds of detectives who are only happy when the loose ends are tied up it is one that comes back frequently to haunt them. Until all the answers are known, Lord Lucan's final secret remains safe.

Jack the Ripper

In 1888 the British Empire was at its zenith. The sun never set on this glorious imperial bastion which spanned the globe, embracing peoples of every race, creed and colour. But in London, the centre of this huge domain, there was a place where the sun never shone. The East End was a disgrace to the Empire and to civilized values. People lived in squalor, poverty and filth. Child deaths were double the national average and prostitution and drunkenness, as well as sexual abuse of minors and murders, were rife. It was the sordid environment for a killer whose notoriety lives on unabated to this day. Jack the Ripper made the mean streets of the East End his killing ground. Even now, with most of the crumbling slums gone, the taverns of his day replaced with office blocks and the gas lamps ripped out in favour of electric ones, the East End has become a lurid shrine for Ripper enthusiasts, fascinated by the macabre killer's violent deeds. But the question remains: just who was Jack the Ripper? His crimes were not all that remarkable, given the 20th century. He butchered five women, admittedly in a gruesome manner. It was the question of identity, with all the suspicions that Jack the Ripper may have been someone highly placed in British society, which made the 'Monster of the East End' a creature of intrigue and ensured that his dastardly deeds are never far from the public's mind.

Jack the Ripper may have gone down as history's most famous murderer but his reign of terror was a short one. He first struck on 31 August 1888. Mary Ann Nichols, a prostitute who frequented the Whitechapel area of the East End to ply her trade was found butchered in one of the area's many dark alleyways. 'Pretty Polly', as the 42-year-old whore was known, was a chronic drunkard and well-known inhabitant of the gin palaces in the area.

Police think Mary Ann approached a tall stranger with the time-honoured 'Looking for a good time, mister?' By the time the man had dragged her into the shadows, it was too late. A hand went around her throat, and in seconds she was cut from ear to ear. 'Only a madman could have done this', said a police surgeon who was to examine the body later. 'I have never seen so horrible a case. She was ripped about in a manner that only a person skilled in the use of a knife could have achieved.'

Murders in that deprived – and depraved – area were not uncommon. Police were happy to put the murder down to a single frenzied attack – until just one week later, on 8 September, 'Dark Annie' Chapman, also a prostitute, was found in Hanbury Street near Spitalfields Market with her few pitiful possessions neatly laid out alongside her disembowelled corpse. Although there was no obvious sign of rape, with this murder as with the first there was every indication that the killer was motivated by some terrible sexual rage as he cut and slashed with grotesque abandon. The dissection of 'Dark Annie', with all her entrails laid out next to the corpse, indicated a knowledge of anatomy or surgery not found in the everyday sex killer.

After the second murder, on 25 September a mocking letter was sent to a Fleet Street news agency. It read: 'Dear Boss, I keep on hearing that the police have caught me. But they won't fix me yet. I am down on certain types of women and I won't stop ripping them until I do get buckled. Grand job, that last job was, I gave the lady no time to squeal. I love my work and want to start again. You will soon hear from me with my funny little game. I saved some of the proper stuff in a little ginger beer bottle after my last job to write with, but it went thick like glue and I can't use it. Red ink is fit enough I hope. Ha! Ha!'

'Next time I shall clip the ears off and send them to the police, just for jolly.'

The sick message was signed Jack the Ripper.

Victim number three was Elizabeth Stride, nicknamed 'Long Liz' because of her height. A policeman found the body of 44-year-old Liz in Berner's Street, Whitechapel, on 30 September near some factory gates. Like the others her throat had been cut from behind, but she did not suffer mutilation or sexual savagery. This led police to think that the murderer had been disturbed in his gruesome work – for on the same day they discovered victim number four a few streets away in Mitre Square. Catherine Eddowes, 43, was disembowelled and her face practically hacked off.

By the time of this fourth murder, Ripper hysteria had gripped London and was ravaging faster than the plague in the dark, damp passageways of the East End. Women began arming themselves with knives and whistles to attract the police; the *Illustrated Police News* speculated that well-to-do ladies were arming themselves with pearl-handled pistols in case the Ripper was tempted to move up the social scale in his search for bloody satisfaction.

The Eddowes murder disturbed the police greatly. Her body was by far the most mutilated of all the victims and there was a trail of blood leading to a wall where, scrawled in chalk, was the message: 'The Jewes are not men to be blamed for nothing.' Sir Charles Warren, the head of the Metropolitan Police Force personally removed the notice – and thereby may have destroyed some vital evidence. He was concerned with the influx into the area of Jews from Eastern Europe – and racial tensions already beginning to bubble – this note could have led to savage reprisals.

The rumours about who the murderer was circulated like wildfire. Some of the frightened wretches who lived in the East End said it was a policeman in his nightly rounds, his job giving him the perfect alibi to be out at night on those cold, dark streets. One suspect was a Russian-born doctor called Michael Ostrog, rumour having it that he was sent by the Tsarist secret police to stir up hatred against the expatriate Jews who fled Russia from persecution; others that it was a mad surgeon, or even Sir Charles Warren himself – a leading freemason who removed the notice to protect a freemason killer.

The final death came on 9 November when Mary Kelly, aged 25 and also a prostitute, was grotesquely mutilated in her squalid rented home. On the morning of 10 November Henry Bowers, her landlord, knocked on her door to collect unpaid rent. The previous evening the attractive blonde girl had been seen approaching strangers asking them for cash. The last one she approached – tall, dark, with a moustache and a deerstalker hat – was her killer. Bowers saw the remains of Mary and later told the police: 'I shall be haunted by this for the rest of my life.'

Mary's death was to be the last. One hundred years later, the puzzle of the Ripper's bloody but brief reign has still not been solved. It was with the passage of time that more and more people grew intrigued by the Ripper mystery. One suspect who has continued to cause violent debate was Queen Victoria's grandson Prince Albert Victor, Duke of Clarence. The finger was pointed at him because he was said to be mad, incarcerated in a mental institution after he had committed the murders because the scandal would have been too great had it ever been revealed to the world.

However, Inspector Robert Sagar, who played a leading part in the Ripper investigation, said before his death in 1924: 'We had good reason to suspect a man who lived in Butcher's Row, Aldgate. We watched him carefully. There was no doubt that this man was insane. After a time his friends thought it advisable to have him removed to a private asylum. After he was removed there were no more Ripper atrocities.'

Another prime suspect is one favoured by several authors, namely Montagu John Druitt, whose body was found floating in the Thames a few weeks after the murder of Mary Kelly. In their book *The Ripper Legacy*, authors Martin Howells and Keith Skinner say that this impoverished barrister was the man that the police of the day reckoned to be the guilty party. They point to the fact that after his death there were no more Ripper murders. But those writers who favour the Duke of Clarence are swift to point out that there were no more slayings after he was incarcerated. Nevertheless, Druitt's family had a history of mental illness and had acquired basic medical skills as a young man. The arguments rage unabated.

John Stalker, who retired in 1989 as Deputy Chief Constable of Greater Manchester, delved into the Ripper files and declared: 'There is still not a shred of real evidence sufficient for a court of law to prosecute anyone.

The truth is that Jack the Ripper was never in danger of capture. The police, I am certain, came nowhere near him.'

'The Metropolitan Police of 1888 were dealing with something quite new: the first recognized series of sexual murders committed by a man who was a stranger to his victims. And 100 years on those are still the most difficult crimes of all to investigate.'

The Green River Killer

Police say he could be anyone. He could be a doctor, a lawyer, a car repairer, a shoe salesman. He could be sitting next to you as you read this and he would walk away out of your life without a word passed or a glance exchanged. But his secret is the darkest one yet to be discovered in American criminal history – for he is the Green River Killer, a demonic monster who makes the Yorkshire Ripper look like an amateur apprentice and has, so far, ruthlessly accounted for the lives of at least 42 women. The secret of his success, say detectives, is that he is so ordinary . . .

It was back in July 1982 that two little boys were out on a fishing trip along the Green River – a stretch of water which meanders slowly near the Seattle–Tacoma Airport in Washington state. The children were bicycling along with their fishing gear, intent on an afternoon of fun by the river, when they made the discovery. One of the boys saw what he thought was a log floating in the shallows, near the iron girders of Peck Bridge. He waded in and rolled it towards himself with his foot before reeling back in horror. He had found the body of 16-year-old Wendy Coffield, the first known victim of the Green River Killer.

Over the next weeks, months, years, Green River's good name – which for generations had signified peace, tranquillity and beauty, was gone; stolen by the killer who used it as his grisly trademark.

At first, King County Police Lieutenant Jackson Berd thought he was dealing with a straightforward sex killing – the man with too much to drink picks up a pretty girl, is denied what he wants, uses violence, panics, kills and dumps the body. It was a gruesome crime, but far removed from the kind committed by the most daunting criminal who plagues police forces – the serial killer. He is the most feared of all wanted men because there is no apparent logic, no method or pattern to his madness which could leave valuable clues for lawmen to follow up.

Wendy Coffield was a child-prostitute runaway from a nearby town, who had been missing for three months when she was discovered by the boys fishing on 15 July 1982. Five weeks later a one-off sex crime turned into the beginning of the nightmare that has yet to end for the petrified residents of King County. For in a single day three more bodies of young women were found in the river at separate locations.

Over the following years the bodies of women aged between 15 and 36 were found all over King County, and in neighbouring Northern Pierce County, and the remains of two were discovered in the state of Oregon, which borders Washington. Police believe that for once the killer deviated from his practice of preying on the small towns and kidnapped his victims to butcher them elsewhere. So far the largest single operation in US history to capture one man has failed. It has cost in the region of £14 million, involved detectives from seven police forces and the FBI, and has drawn a huge blank. The deck, say police, is stacked hugely in the killer's favour.

Now in the Seattle phone book is a permanent listing for a government agency that did not exist before that bright sunny day in July 1982. It is a seven-digit number for the Green River Task Force which waits night and day for new information which could lead to the capture of the killer. Fae Brooks, a spokeswoman for the group which had been formed especially to try to track down the psychopathic sex killer, said: 'In terms of statistics, the guy doesn't stop until he is dead or until he's caught. In fact, if anything, it may be that he has gotten more clever over the years.'

Some of the problems the police faced lay not in overcoming the ruthlessness or cunning of the killer, but in the attitude of the local population. Although petrified that a killer was stalking the Ivy League fields, mountains and ravines of the communities, police say the local populace developed an unhealthy, complacent attitude towards the murderer because so many of his victims had been involved at some stage of their lives with prostitution. One of the missing girls, 19-year-old Tracy Winston, a young prostitute, is now thought to have fallen victim to him in 1983. Her mother summed up the feelings of the grieving parents when she said that attention was being diverted away from catching the killer with the public demanding action against prostitution instead. 'Our kids are being penalized again,' she said. 'It sounds silly, but how can you be penalized any more after you've been murdered? We admit freely and openly that our kids had problems but Tracy didn't deserve to die because she wasn't living what was perceived to be a perfect life. The issue was and is this maniac out there, not the lives that some of his victims were leading.'

Lieutenant Dan Nolan of King County Sheriff's Department is a patient man who has been in the police force all his life, and at 52 looks more like a businessman than a policeman. He has worked on every case from traffic offences to first-degree murder, and is regarded by his colleagues as a patient, thorough policeman who leaves no stone unturned in his quest for justice. He is second-in-command of the Green River Task Force whose lives have centred on catching this man over the years. He says: 'The man we are looking for is a shade of grey. He is very innocuous, fits right into the community. That is what makes him so very dangerous.'

To protect the investigation the police have revealed little about their suspect, apart from issuing a photofit and these scant details: he is thought to be middle-aged and an outdoors-type who knows the mountains, ravines and streams like the back of his hand. He is remarkably strong, being able to carry the body of a fully grown woman for some distances. On a few occasions witnesses have glimpsed the victims with strange men shortly before they were discovered dead. From these sketchy sightings, police believe that the killer could drive a light-blue pick-up truck speckled with primer paint covering rust spots.

He is a sexual psychopath, his mind tormented perhaps, say experts, by some dark secret from his childhood which induces the terrible anger he vents on his innocent victims. Police will not comment on how he kills his victims, although one psychologist who has worked with them to build up a picture of the death says that the killer probably favours strangulation so he is able to watch his victims suffer as he snuffs the life from them.

The Green River Killer is, above all, very clever. He has turned lush meadows and lonely woodlands within a 45-mile radius of Seattle into 'cluster dumps' for his victims. Bodies have been found by mushroom-pickers, hunters and joggers, by boy scouts and apple-pickers, by bottle-scroungers and boys with fishing rods. In one case an amiable psychic said she was drawn straight to the skeleton of one victim after seeing visions of the dead girl over a seven-day period. So far there have been 10,000 tips telephoned into the Green River Task Force centre, a handful of bogus confessions from sick glory-seekers and 1,000 suspects quizzed – everyone from a devil-worshipper to a police officer himself. So far, nothing. Even the faces of two unidentified bodies have been re-constructed by a film expert who worked on the feature film *Gorky Park*. In the film the faces of murder victims in Moscow are reconstituted to help authorities discover their identities. The practice was copied on the two dead women, but it has revealec neither their identities nor the identity of the killer.

Lieutenant Nolan, who had been second-in-command of the hunt for the killer since 1984, says that police officers on the team have learned to live with the disappointment that they have not yet managed to capture the killer. 'The feeling was certainly that we would solve it within a year. When that didn't happen I think we were all frustrated and certainly pretty disappointed. We kind of hit the wall in January 1985. A lot of people started pointing inwardly and saying: "Am I doing my job well enough? Is it possible to solve?" We got clinical psychologists to come out and talk to us about the stress we were going through. We got to a point where we agreed that this was the most difficult investigation that we had ever been involved with and, by God, it certainly was worth it and we were going to stay with it until it was solved.'

There is a grudging respect within the Task Force that their quarry is a man who picks his victims well, leaving his hunters with little in the way of witnesses or clues. Unless the police are holding back, apart from the *modus operandi* of their deaths, there is little the killer leaves behind to point them in the right direction. Nolan went on: 'Because he conceals the bodies, because he doesn't want them found quickly, he is very clever. Very, very clever. It makes determining death more difficult, leaves no clues.'

The killer has now not struck for three years. Why? Nolan speculates: 'The possibility exists that's he in jail, that he's dead, that he has moved out of the area or out of the country – or that he has quit killing. That is probably the least likely – someone who would commit this number of killings isn't suddenly likely to find his appetite sated.'

He added: 'I would love to capture him, to get him to sit down and tell me just why he did this, what drove him. I don't have any idea what this guy's going to tell me, what his secret is. He is still out there, a man with such terrible secrets . . .'

The Man in the Iron Mask

The great novelist Alexander Dumas immortalized him in his novel of the same name – the story of the wretch kept imprisoned in a mask of iron, his identity shielded from the world, the secret of his crime lodged only with the King and perhaps a few of his trusted advisers. He wore the mask for 30 years, ate with it on, slept with it on. Even at his death the contraption stayed on his face. Who is he? What was the secret of his crime? It is a mystery that has endured to this day with many theories put forward but few concrete answers.

It was on the personal command of the Sun King, Louis XIV, ruler of France, builder of the great Palace of Versailles, that the identity of the man in the iron mask was kept secret – not only from his subjects but also from his court and the jailors. To that end, for three decades, he lived in solitary confinement in different prisons, ending his days in France's most infamous jail, the Bastille. In 1703 when he died, the furniture in his cell was burned, the whitewash on the walls was repainted to erase any pathetic epitaph to the world and the metalwork of his mask was melted down. Those who had kept his identity secret in life were determined that he should remain anonymous even when he was dead.

The rumours of the man in the iron mask abounded in France before the revolution. Louis was a deity, a divine ruler, whose harsh laws sentenced bread stealers to years of servitude aboard the galleys and death for stealing apples from the royal orchards. Even in an illiterate society, as France was at that time, it was no wonder that word of the strange prisoner in the bowels of the Bastille spread across the land. What was he guilty of that spared his life – but condemned him to this living death, trapped in a mask of iron? No correspondence exists between prison officials and court functionaries, but the people had their own fantastic theories. One was that he was Louis XVI's twin brother, who was shut away on the orders of the vainglorious Emperor in order to preserve the throne and its privileges for himself. Another theory suggested that he was the illegitimate child of a farm girl, born after a dalliance with the King, and that his resemblance was so close to that of his father that he was imprisoned for ever.

It was not until 50 years after his death that historians began to probe into the identity of this strange man, and to discover what his crime had been. In 1753, exactly 50 years after he died in the Bastille, a journal kept by one Etienne du Jonca surfaced in Paris. Du Jonca was a lieutenant of the King; literate, educated – and curious. He recorded that in 1698, when the unfortunate man had already spent nearly 30 years behind bars, he was sent to the prison as the King's emissary. He recorded the following: 'Thursday 18 September at 3.00 o'clock, Monsieur de Saint-Mars, governor of the Château of the Bastille, made his appearance, coming from the command of the Iles-Sainte-Marguerite Pignerol with a prisoner, whom he always caused to be masked, whose name is not mentioned.'

Five days after recording his arrival at the Bastille, du Jonca wrote of the man's death, saying that his removal from the cell and the subsequent burning of his furniture and clothes was carried out with 'great haste'. The King's lieutenant also noted that the prisoner wore a mask of black velvet and not of iron when he saw him laid out for burial in an unmarked grave. (Whether this was done as a belated attempt at decency by the authorities or not – saving him from burial in the infernal mask – we shall never know.) Etienne du Jonca then testified that the man was buried under the false name of Marchioly. No prison official was allowed to gaze at the face beneath the mask as the corpse was transported from the Bastille under cover of darkness to an unmarked grave somewhere in the vicinity of the city. It is not even known whether or not he received a Christian burial, but it seems likely, for du Jonca also noted that the prisoner received one privilege not usually afforded to inmates of the Bastille – the right to a Bible and Christian worship.

At Villeneuve, in the Bourbonnais region of France, more clues surfaced about how closely guarded the secret of the man's identity was. Peasants there spoke of how, on his journey with the masked prisoner, the governor stopped with his charge at his own château for a meal. Peasants who glanced through the window saw how de Saint-Mars sat opposite his prisoner with two loaded pistols next to his plate, ready to discharge them if the captive made one attempt to reveal his identity to the domestic servants in the château.

Up until the French Revolution in 1789, it was presumed that only de Saint-Mars and the King knew the identity of the prisoner. It was certainly not passed on within the House of Bourbon for neither of Louis's successors knew who he was – and the last ruler of France, Louis XVI, began a frantic search for it at the request of his wife, Marie Antoinette.

When the French Revolution overturned Europe's established order in a tidal wave of change, numerous government agencies were ransacked by rising politicians such as Robespierre. Often the aim was to find information valuable for their own ends; however, papers found in the Minister of War's office in Paris shed intriguing light on the secret of France's most celebrated captive.

It transpired that for years de Saint-Mars had corres-
ponded with a man named Louvois, a functionary of
some kind in the prison service. In July 1669, Louvois
wrote to de Saint-Mars: 'The King has commanded that I
am to have the man named Eustache Dauger sent to
Pignerol. It is of the utmost importance to his service that
he should be most securely guarded and that he should in
no way give information about himself nor send letters to
anyone at all. You will yourself, once a day, have to take
enough food for the day to this wretch and you must on
no account listen for any reason at all to what he may
want to say to you, always threatening to kill him if he
opens his mouth to speak of anything but his necessities.'
Then another letter, from the King himself, was also
unearthed in the War Minister's archives, written to de
Saint-Mars, which said: 'I am sending to my citadel of
Pignerol, in the charge of Captain de Vauroy, sergeant
major of my city and citadel of Dunkirk, the man named
Eustache Dauger. You are to hold him in good and safe
custody; prevent him from communicating with anyone at
all, by word of mouth or writ of hand. So be it.'

Up until the discovery of these letters it was widely
believed that the false name he was buried under,
Marchioly, was a bastardization for Mattioli, an envoy of
the Duke of Mantua who had once incurred the King's
wrath. Mattioli did indeed end up in penal servitude in
Pignerol, but he and the man in the iron mask were two
separate people.

Nineteenth-century research into Eustache Dauger
proved this: he was one of six brothers, four of whom fell
in battle. He came from the northern French fishing port
of Dunkirk and was believed at one time to have been a
lieutenant in the elite King's Guards – a feat made possible
by virtue of his brother's elevation to the nobility.

With his brother circulating in court circles, and himself
guarding the heart of the realm, Eustache came close to

the wicked Madame de Montespan, the King's mistress and a dabbler in black magic. Those close to the royal circle knew that de Montespan was strong medicine for the King, and that he tolerated her heretical indulgences because he was fascinated by her. It is possible, therefore, that Eustache Dauger became entranced by her, went to a black mass, and was discovered by the King. He could not have him spreading the word that the King's concubine indulged in devil worship. Perhaps that was the reason for the years in jail. Perhaps he was merely jealous, paranoid that a mere soldier was set to steal his sweetheart from him. But why not have him executed? Louis was, after all, a monarch with absolute power.

To this day the secret of the man in the iron mask remains as steadfast as the forged metal which kept his face from the world for over 30 years.

The Double Life of Rock Hudson

The Hollywood dream factory is a remarkable thing. It can recreate the parting of the Red Sea on a studio backlot, turn a sound stage into a galactic war zone, or make Fred Astaire dance on the ceiling. But in Tinsel Town, where they hand out awards for trickery and deception, things are seldom as they appear.

So it was with Rock Hudson. For almost 40 years, this master of the silver screen lived a secret, double life. In public he was the most dashing screen hero of his generation – a rugged, macho love god idolized by women and envied by men all over the world. But in private he was a far cry from the debonair lady-killer of his films. He was a homosexual, whose lusting for taboo love eventually cost him his life . . . and shattered the image he had carefully cultivated throughout his career. It was a secret Rock had dearly wanted to take with him to the grave – and probably would have, had he not fallen victim to the disease society has labelled the 'gay plague'.

Even after AIDS was first diagnosed, Rock tried to continue living the lie, and swore his closest friends to secrecy. Eventually, of course, neither he nor they could remain silent, once the devastating effects of the disease became obvious. And so, just a few weeks before his death, the screen giant reluctantly admitted the secret he had kept hidden for so many years.

Back then, Rock Hudson, film star, was just plain Roy Fitzgerald, navy veteran, vacuum-cleaner salesman and would-be actor. He worked hard, saving what money he could, and whenever he had a spare moment would stand outside the gates of the movie studios, waiting to be discovered. It was a lonely time for Roy, as he recalled many years later: 'It was very difficult for me to make friends. People weren't friendly like they were in the Mid-West.'

But by the following year the struggling actor made some friends . . . friends who would change his life forever: the gay community of nearby Long Beach. It was natural for Roy to feel at home among his own kind. Ever since his days in the navy, he had preferred the company, and sexuality, of men. But Roy got more than sex and friendship from those he met – he also got his first break on the way to becoming an international sex symbol.

Some of his fellow gays had connections in show-business and, at a party in 1948, Roy was introduced to Henry Willson, a fellow homosexual and head of talent for the David O. Selznick Studio. Willson, who could spot that elusive 'star quality' at a glance, signed Roy to a studio contract and changed his name to Rock Hudson.

It was during this time that Rock also met two fellow gays, George Nader and Mark Miller. The three would remain close friends all their lives. Mark, a one-time singer, had given up his career in order to become Nader's business manager. Nader, like Rock, was exceptionally good-looking and wanted a career in the movies. But all three knew that if he and Rock were ever going to make it they could not allow even a hint of scandal about their sexual preferences to get into print. Rock went to some bizarre lengths. He always made sure he had two phone lines in his apartment, and his room-mate was never allowed to answer Rock's, lest someone discovered that Rock was living with another man. He and George also developed code-words to talk to each other in public. 'Is he musical?' was a code for 'Is he gay?'

In 1953, Rock, who had already appeared in several films, though was not yet considered a star, met Jack Navaar, a 22-year-old friend of Nader's. The two hit it off immediately and, within a few weeks, the dynamic-looking couple were lovers and room-mates. But Rock could never publicly show any affection for Jack, and even when his first big film, *Magnificent Obsession*, premiered the following year, he was forced to bring a script girl from the studio as his date. Jack, who arrived in a separate car, was also given a female escort. Studio bosses knew they had a potential superstar on the rise, and they didn't want the press to get a whiff of scandal. 'Universal invested a lot of money in Rock, and it was important for his image to remain that of a lady-killer', said Mamie Van Doren, a friend of Rock's.

Unfortunately for Jack, however, fame soon went to Rock's head, and the once-happy couple began to argue bitterly about anything and everything. To make matters worse, Jack couldn't even go out to dinner with his lover any more, because *Magnificent Obsession* had made Rock a huge celebrity. Inevitably, within 12 months, the affair was over – and Hudson, his career booming, would not live with another man for a decade.

But in 1955, despite Rock's intricate precautions, the Hollywood scandal sheet *Confidential* was threatening to write an exposé of his taboo love affairs – which would not only destroy his career but financially cripple the studio as well. To kill the story, the studio and Rock decided that he should get married, which he did on 9 November.

The hastily arranged nuptials, to his agent's secretary, Phyllis Gates, saved his career. Unfortunately for Phyllis she was never told the marriage had been planned by the studio bosses, or that Rock was gay. Many years later, she recalled that Rock had managed to keep his homosexuality from her until the very end of the relationship, which lasted almost three years.

By 1960, Rock was the world's number one box-office attraction, and had just completed his first comedy, *Pillow Talk*, with Doris Day. It was about this time that he began to be driven more by sex than his career. After all, he had now made it to the top, and all those years of self-sacrifice and self-discipline were about to be abandoned. Rock even confided to friends that he thought about having sex all the time during this period, even while driving his car or rehearsing his lines.

In the next ten years, he had numerous lovers, but still managed to keep his secret from the public, thanks to loyal friends and discreet colleagues within the industry. It was a precaution he had to take. Even a malicious gag could almost end a career, as Hudson found out in the early 1970s. A vicious hoaxster sent out invitations to gossip columnists, inviting them to the 'wedding' of Rock and good friend Jim Nabors. The tasteless prank ruined Nabors's career, whose prime-time variety series was cancelled soon after, even though he and Hudson were never more than friends.

The experience left Rock even more paranoid about his secret life, and he avoided Hollywood's bright life more and more. Instead, he would entertain guests at his Beverly Hills mansion, where a string of handsome young men would lie around the pool waiting to offer their services.

In 1973, Rock again took a full-time housemate and lover – Hollywood publicist Tom Clark, whom he'd met ten years earlier. Clark, a far cry from the pretty boys that had walked in and out of Hudson's bedroom over the years, would become the most important person in the actor's life. They were inseparable for many years, and spent wonderful times doing things they both loved – drinking, cooking, travelling, watching football and making love. But, in Tom, Rock had also found something very special. For the first time in his life, he had a man with whom he could walk down the street, and whom he could take to restaurants and studio parties. Tom, you see, had become Rock's personal manager and publicist . . . a legitimate connection.

'I can take him anywhere,' Rock confided to friends. 'I can even introduce him to Princess Margaret.'

In 1975, Rock turned 50 – and Tom threw him the 'prettiest party we ever had.' As the guests mingled in the party room, the hired band struck up *You Must Have Been a Beautiful Baby*. Down the staircase came the birthday boy, wearing only a nappy, as the guests whistled and cooed.

Of course, there were many other parties at Rock's mansion over the years. Once, in 1977, just before he returned home from a three-month tour, he called secretary Mark Miller and said: 'I want a beauties' party when we get home. Could you arrange it? Have a party waiting for me at the house.'

Miller obliged. He invited ten of Rock's closest friends, and 50 handsome young men! One of the guests later recalled: 'There were some of the best-looking men I'd seen in my life.'

But the pleasures of the party were short-lived. That same year, Rock hit rock-bottom, drinking all day, worrying about his age and sliding career, and he even took to touring homosexual clubs in San Francisco where anything went. Ironically, it was at this time that the AIDS virus was taking a foothold within the gay community. Rock's sex and drinking binge lasted almost four years, until, in November 1981, he was forced to undergo bypass surgery on his heart. It was, quite literally, a sobering experience.

'He woke up from the drunkenness of the '70s,' said old friend George Nader. 'The meanness and sniping fell away, and he was returning to the Rock we had known in 1952 – a warm human being who laughed and played games.'

But he was no longer devoted to Tom Clark. In 1982, Rock began to have a lusty affair behind Tom's back with a much younger, more virile man, Marc Christian. Within a year, Tom was thrown out of the house, and Marc moved in. It was to be Rock's most passionate, and final, relationship.

In 1984, Rock was invited to a White House dinner, where he gladly posed for pictures with the President and Mrs Reagan. A few weeks later, the photographs arrived at his office, personally signed by the First Couple. As he and secretary Miller looked at the photos, they noticed a red sore on Rock's neck. It had been there for over a year, but it had become bigger.

Under Miller's constant nagging, Rock eventually decided to see a doctor about the sore . . . and on 5 June 1984 he received the news he had dreaded. It was AIDS. But Rock still wasn't about to let his secret out; not yet, anyway. Those few friends he did tell were sworn to secrecy, as the dying actor vainly sought a cure. Marc Christian didn't know Rock had AIDS until February 1985, even though they continued to have sex. Rock had lived a lie for so long that he couldn't even bring himself to tell the truth to those closest to him. It wasn't until the end was near, when death was certain, that he finally revealed his dreadful secret.

Fans around the world were understandably shattered,

and yet they responded to his plight with sympathy and renewed curiosity about this mystery disease. Suddenly, AIDS was on the front pages of newspapers around the world; research funds were set up; the United States Congress vastly increased efforts towards finding a cure; the United Nations hosted conferences on it; everywhere, people wanted to learn more about the disease which had taken their idol.

Ironically, the secret Rock felt he could never share with the world spurred the same world to take action. Rock's defeat may just become his victory.

Robert Maxwell – the Last Tycoon

Robert Maxwell was one of the last of the post-war tycoons – now a rare breed in Britain. He died on 5 November 1991. His body was later recovered from the sea off the Canary Islands after he had been reported missing from his private yacht – but no one has yet cleared up the mystery of his death.

The kind of life that Robert Maxwell enjoyed now seems to have belonged to another era, one of excess, ridiculous extravagance and outrageous behaviour. Largely speaking, it does belong to another era – the 1980s. Flying around London and the world by helicopter or private jet, seeking meetings with heads of state, throwing lavish parties in his own honour, splashing his exploits across the *Daily Mirror* newspaper, Maxwell's behaviour was showy and brash.

Tony Delano, a Mirror Group director until 1985, recalled: 'One of the charming things about Bob was that he did not know how to behave.' He may have plundered the pension funds to help his ailing companies, but it was also to finance a lifestyle for which he had long since stopped counting the pennies.

BBC economics editor Peter Jay – who worked for him from 1986 to 1989 as chief-of-staff – recalled shaving about £1,400 from a bill for a one-night stay in a hotel in Portugal, with the final bill still reaching some £3,000. 'There was no rhyme nor reason about his behaviour. He was like some huge, primitive animal that plodded on its way, or charged on its way, neither good nor bad . . . just random,' Jay said.

Jay contends, as others have before, that Maxwell only understood two relationships – buyer and seller and master and slave. 'Where he thought he was a seller and someone else was a buyer, he could be positively obsequious. He treated anyone whom he thought was a buyer with reverence and flattery,' he said.

Those who weren't holding a chequebook were treated slightly differently. 'The Maxwell technique depended very heavily on bullying and intimidation, almost of a physical kind. He was a very large man and he had a way of approaching people, nudging them with his belly and breathing into their nostrils,' Delano described.

His sons were among those bullied, dismissed and humiliated. His employees were at his beck and call, night and day. He would sometimes realize that the whole weekend stretched ahead and would be filled with a great feeling of boredom. He would tell the *Mirror* switchboard to get people on the phone and tell them to have a meeting. By the time everyone got there, he had forgotten what it was for, and everyone had to slope off home again.

Tony Delano – now at the London College of Printing – indicated that many of his employees could brave out some of Maxwell's criticism. 'You soon saw that a lot of bluster and bravado was fairly meaningless . . . (if he said) give me a full report on that by next Tuesday, you could be confident you could forget about it, because he would forget about it.'

For bullies to get what they want, they need cowards and Maxwell did succeed in surrounding himself with people prepared to do as he said. 'He had a very high level of low cunning, he learnt about British ways, and British values, he saw how eminently corruptible the British were and how cheap they were to corrupt,' Delano said. 'You didn't have to spend a great deal of money buying their consent or their presence on a board. You simply had to give them a job or a salary . . . he never had any difficulty in attracting these kind of people,' Delano added.

Greed may have been good – at least for Maxwell – but it doesn't seem to have been much fun. Living alone in a flat above his office, he could lay claim to few friends, having formally separated from his wife and being at odds with some of his children.

'He didn't talk about his childhood very much. You had a very strong sense that no one could have been as gross as he was, were he not running away from some hideous poverty,' Jay said. In fact, Jay contends that 'the great key to him was that he lived in constant terror of boredom'.

In seeking to explain Robert Maxwell's actions in later life, many commentators point to the extreme poverty and deprivation of his childhood. The media mogul once claimed that he did not have a pair of shoes until he was seven.

Born in Czechoslovakia, Robert Maxwell succeeded in building a publishing empire that spanned the world. His death in November 1991 at the age of 68 prompted a series of eulogies for his achievements. But in the weeks that followed and as more news emerged of the true state of his company's finances – and his critics gained courage now that their fiery and unpredictable nemesis was dead – he was damned by press and public alike for the way he ran his businesses.

Robert Maxwell was born Jan Ludvik Hoch in Slatinske Dolt in the Carpathian mountains, an area of extreme poverty, in Czechslovakia on 10 June 1923. His orthodox Jewish parents were victims of the Nazis, and he only just managed to escape the concentration camps to arrive in Britain in 1940. Describing himself as 'self-educated', he spoke several languages and by the end of the war he had emerged as a British army officer with commendations for bravery. After the war, he was located in Berlin, where he decided to publish scientific journals and set up Pergamon Press.

Pergamon was quickly and hugely profitable and the now-married Maxwell decided to turn his attentions to politics. As one of the few businessmen who liked to proclaim his socialism, Maxwell stood for the Labour Party in Buckinghamshire in 1964. He won and held his seat until 1970. His relationship with the Labour Party was an uneasy one, with the political party wary of angering the man who owned newspapers sympathetic to Labour principles. Many people cowered from criticizing him, not least because of his readiness to confront his critics in the libel courts. However, even when he was a Labour MP, signs were emerging of his dishonesty.

In 1969, Maxwell agreed a takeover bid for Pergamon from Leasco, an American financial and data-processing group. However, when Leasco questioned Pergamon profits, the talks fell apart and Maxwell was subjected to a DTI enquiry. The inspectors found that Pergamon's profits depended on transactions with Maxwell-family private companies.

The DTI report said: 'We regret having to conclude that, notwithstanding Mr Maxwell's acknowledged abilities and energy, he is not in our opinion a person who can be relied on to exercise proper stewardship of a publicly quoted company.' Few business people could recover their career after such comments, let alone carry on to build a global publishing company.

Dust had gathered on the DTI report by the time

Maxwell came to take over the troubled British Printing Corporation in 1980, renaming it Maxwell Communications Corporation. Maxwell had long hoped he would be able to take over a national newspaper, but had twice lost out to Rupert Murdoch, who succeeded in taking over the *Sun* and the *News of the World*. He got his chance to run a national newspaper when he bought Mirror Group Newspapers (MGN) in 1984 from Reed International. The purchase of America's Macmillan publishers dragged his company further into debt.

In 1991, he floated MGN as a public company, desperate to raise cash because the rest of the company was veering towards bankruptcy with debts of over £2 billion. Exactly how desperate he had become was not clear until after his death, when it transpired that he had taken money from pension funds to keep his companies afloat and boost the share price. More than 30,000 pensioners were left wondering what happened to their pensions when the Maxwell empire collapsed.

Shortly after Maxwell's death in November 1991, it emerged that about £440 million was missing from the funds which were to provide pensions for employees of Maxwell Communications Corporation and Mirror Group Newspapers. After a three-year campaign by the pensioners, the funds were largely recovered, thanks to a £100 million government pay-out and an out-of-court settlement for £276 million. But the fear they would lose their pensions and the stress of the long campaign hit many people hard. The settlement was reached in February 1995.

Investment banks, accountants and what was left of Maxwell's media companies agreed to pay the pensioners, following 18 months of negotiation with government-appointed arbiter Sir John Cuckney. Coopers & Lybrand, Goldman Sachs and Lehman Brothers were among those who paid compensation. Altogether 32,000 people were affected by the pension-fund theft. One campaigner said that Maxwell bought and sold so many companies that some people didn't even realize they worked for him until his death and the pension theft emerged.

Ken Trench, former chairman of the Maxwell Pensioners Action Group said: 'The hardship they experienced was the worry that they were going to lose their pensions. There were husbands who had worked 30 years feeling they were secure, who thought that when they died their wives would receive or carry on receiving their pension. Any Maxwell pensioner who died during those four years, died feeling that he had not properly provided for his wife. That must have been terrible.'

Ironically, even before Robert Maxwell's death, some pensioners had suspected that something was amiss with the pension funds and had started a court case. Tony Boram, whose study is still stacked with legal papers from that time, is chairman of the Association of Mirror Pensioners. He said: 'We started chasing Maxwell a year or two before he died. We were concerned because he wasn't giving us increases we thought we were entitled to. There were rumours that he had received pension money to finance redundancies.'

In the months prior to his death, Robert Maxwell, aware that Boram was organizing a legal action about the pension fund, rang him whenever a negative article appeared in the press. 'He would constantly phone and harass me – I had retired and hadn't worked for him – he would ring me up at eight o'clock in the morning and say, "Why are you doing this to me, it is all lies",' Boram recounted. 'Unlike many other Maxwell pensioners, Mirror Group pensioners did have the background protection of the Mirrror Group company. Those who were most anxious were the members of smaller schemes who didn't have the protection we had,' Boram added. 'It was stressful . . . Many of them had worked for a company all their lives and faced the prospect of pensions disappearing completely,' he said.

'I own the pension scheme,' Robert Maxwell once declared. Considering statements like that, it is no surprise that one day he decided to take what he wanted from his employees' pension fund to prop up his failing business empire. As the pension-holders fought for compensation, legislators considered how best to reduce the chance of this happening again. Even when the DTI report was published, the question still remained whether there were enough checks and balances in place to ensure that no one could steal money from the 119,000 active pension schemes in the UK. Many people lost faith in company pension schemes after 1991, when Robert Maxwell was found to have stolen more than £400m from 32,000 scheme members.

A House of Commons select committee, chaired by Frank Field, called for widespread reform of pensions law, blaming city watchdogs and professional advisers for failing to see what was happening. Many investment banks, lawyers and accountants failed to question Maxwell on irregularities in the way he did business, in part because they accepted his word. The DTI report made several recommendations for ensuring that it could not happen again.

It recommended placing severe sanctions on companies which did not report fraud and guidance on auditing business empires. The report concluded that: 'The most important lesson from all the events is that high ethical and professional standards must always be put before commercial advantage . . . The reputation of the financial markets depends on it.'

The 1995 Pension Act was put in place, in part to calm fears that something like this could happen again. Under that Act, if money has been removed dishonestly from a pension scheme, an employer must make sure enough money is put back into the scheme to pay future benefits.

If the employer is insolvent and unable to restore the funds, the pension scheme will be able to claim compensation of up to 90% from the Pensions Compensation Board.

Trustees now have to make sure that no more than 5% of the pension fund's assets are invested in the employer's shares. If pension-fund-holders do fear the worst, they can now contact the Occupational Pensions Regulatory Authority (OPRA), responsible for ensuring that those who run occupational pension schemes meet their legal obligations. Scheme auditors and actuaries will have to act as whistle-blowers and tell OPRA if they think something is wrong. Under separate financial services legislation, custody of assets is now regulated, ensuring the activities of those who hold the pension funds is monitored.

Opinions vary as to whether this is too much, too little or the wrong kind of regulation.

Most people agree that what happened with Maxwell could quite easily happen again.

'While the government has tightened up trustee management of pension funds, if Maxwell came back to life, he could do it again. It might be a little bit more difficult for him, that's all,' Ken Trench, former chairman of the Maxwell pensioners action group said.

Like many self-made men, Robert Maxwell wanted to build a dynasty. He had nine children, and two followed him into his business, Kevin and Ian. Their life story thus far has been a story of before and after. Before their father died in November 1991, they both held high-level positions in the Maxwell group. After his death, they were embroiled in a lengthy, expensive court case from which they were acquitted. Since then, they have both run their own businesses.

Many tycoons seek to build dynasties and many fail. It is clear that, in his relationship with his sons, Robert Maxwell dominated, placing them under tremendous pressure. In a letter to his father in 1988, quoted by Tom Bower in *Maxwell, the Final Verdict*, Kevin Maxwell wrote: 'You are my teacher and all my life you have tried to demonstrate the principles underlying every action or inaction . . . Above all, you have given me the sense of excitement of having dozens of balls in the air and the thrill of seeing some of them land right.'

Kevin's whole world, and that of his brother Ian, crashed down around them when their father died in November 1991 and it emerged that the company's debts vastly outweighed its assets and the pension scheme had been plundered. Less than a month after Robert Maxwell's death, the Serious Fraud Office began investigating the management of the Mirror Group pension fund, and the company's finances.

In 1996, after an eight-month trial, Kevin and Ian Maxwell and Larry Trachtenberg were cleared of charges of being involved in a conspiracy to defraud company pensioners. It took the jury 48 hours and 17 minutes across 11 nights to deliver their verdict. The trial lasted 131 days, with the final bill of some £25 million and the reputation of the Serious Fraud Office in tatters.

Kevin spent 21 days in the witness box, many of them describing his father as a bully.

At the trial, Kevin said: 'I missed him, his presence and his ability to dominate.' He emerged from that trial – acquitted of all charges – to set up business with one of the co-defendants, Larry Trachtenberg. Now chairman of Telemonde, a telecoms supplier, the company website says that he has specialized in the telecoms industry since 1993. In 1999, shortly before his new company Telemonde was to float on the Nasdaq, he pledged to compensate victims of the pensions scandal:

'The moral burden that I bear, I will bear for the rest of my life. It doesn't go away. The fact that, technically, my bankruptcy has been discharged, and I'm not legally responsible, in no way minimizes the moral burden that I carry. At the present moment, I'm not in any condition to make a contribution, large or small, but obviously I hope that in the future I may be in a position to do something,' he said.

David Rupert:
MI5 Double Agent

At 6ft 4in and 20 stones, David Rupert was not an obvious candidate for a double agent. A giant of a man, he told people he was descended from German immigrants and Mohawk Indians. The story convinced the Irish-American community in Chicago that he was an outsider who had every reason to hate authority. Exactly when he was recruited by MI5 to infiltrate the Real IRA is unclear.

From the moment he turned up to meetings of the Irish Freedom Committee (IFC) in Chicago in 1997, he was an enigmatic figure. A trucker from Illinois, he had no permanent home; it seemed he lived in his 'rig', an articulated lorry in which he crisscrossed the Midwest of America, hauling loads.

He spoke little of his background and nobody was even sure of his real name. He confided in the few people he spoke with that he had stolen the identity of an American soldier who died in Vietnam. His real name was Scott Post, he said.

It has been established, however, that he was born in Madrid, New York State, in 1951 and attended the local high school, where he was regarded as a loner. He drifted between jobs and travelled frequently to the Irish Republic, where for a brief period he had a tenancy on a bar in Tullaghan, Co Leitrim. With his wife Maureen, he later set up a haulage business in Illinois, but became disillusioned and sold his lorry.

He got involved in the Irish Republican movement in 1997 and at some stage after that the British and American security services. For at least three years he spied on the activities of fund-raisers. The intelligence he passed back to his MI5 and FBI handlers was used to intercept funds being sent to dissident Republican groups.

Rupert's air of mystery only enhanced his status among Irish Republican supporters. Secrecy, even paranoia, was the watchword. The FBI was referred to as 'the Front for British Intrigue' because fund-raising groups were convinced they were under surveillance by the FBI at the behest of British Intelligence agencies. Their suspicions were correct, but nobody realized Rupert was the Front for British Intrigue. 'I don't know much about him,' said Joe Dillon, the acting head of Chicago IFC. 'He used to own some pubs in Ireland years ago, I think.'

Even as he was collecting funds and rousing support, Rupert was reporting back to his handlers in the FBI and MI5. His motives were unclear but his effectiveness was beyond question. He passed on details of fund-raising activities, bank accounts, and transactions and membership lists of action committees and support groups that stretched from Pennsylvania and Massachusetts to Rhode Island and New York. The money trail led MI5 to accounts in Ireland used for financing arms purchases and terrorist operations.

By 1999 Rupert was a pivotal and trusted figure in the movement. He networked between rival factions vying for the backing of Irish-American donors. One side supported Republican Sinn Fein, a group that split from Sinn Fein in the 1980s, and its paramilitary wing the Continuity IRA.

Another faction supported the 32 County Sovereignty Committee and its paramilitary wing, the Real IRA, blamed for the 1998 Omagh bombing and the attack on the BBC's West London headquarters. With a foot in both camps, Rupert spied on both sides, playing one off against the other. He struck up a close relationship with Martin Galvin, a New York lawyer who had headed Noraid, the American fund-raising arm of the Provisional IRA. Galvin was a linchpin of the movement. When Galvin transferred his loyalty to the 32 County Sovereignty Movement, Rupert did the same.

Other members of the movement were delighted and he was made the group's main representative in America. He was given the codes to access and control the 32 County Sovereignty Committee's website, one of its main propaganda tools and a device for soliciting funds. Soon other Republican websites carried a warning that the movement's internet services had been infiltrated. 'We wish to state that the website www.32csc.org has been compromised by sinister elements, and as such is no longer representative of our movement,' they warned.

Money raised by Rupert was channelled into Ireland. The FBI and MI5 monitored the funds as they were passed through an account in the Allied Irish Bank in Dundalk, a border town in the Irish Republic where Michael McKevitt, thought to be leader of the Real IRA, lived with his wife Bernadette Sands.

On one of his frequent trips across the Atlantic, Rupert spoke at a Real IRA rally in Dundalk in November 1999. 'There is growing support for the prisoners in Boston, New York and Chicago,' he told his audience to loud applause. Rupert had already met Sands during her trips to America to rally support and collect donations. She was by all accounts impressed. The big man exuded calm and confidence. Sometime early in 1999 Rupert met McKevitt in Ireland. To demonstrate his credentials and financial clout Rupert made a donation of £10,000. Anxious to draw Rupert further into the movement, McKevitt invited him to meet other senior figures in the Real IRA, including, eventually, members of its army council. The move was a costly mistake for McKevitt, but a triumph for the FBI, MI5 and the Garda, the Irish police, who were playing an increasingly important role. Rupert tipped off the authorities about a series of top-level Real IRA meetings. The Garda are understood to have planted listening devices and taken surveillance pictures.

The turning point in the operation came in 2000 when McKevitt allegedly tried to entice Rupert into committing a terrorist offence. Details were passed to the Irish authorities. State prosecutors in Dublin insisted that to charge McKevitt with membership of an illegal organization Rupert would have to appear as a witness.

Rupert's MI5 and FBI handlers met him to talk it over. It would mean burning a valuable source inside the dissident Republican movement and it would change for ever the life of Rupert and his wife. They would be given new identities and a new home. A factor in the decision to end his double life was that Rupert had already become the target of media interest. Dissident republicans had spoken of a 'godfather figure' in America and a number of newspapers including *The Sunday Times* had tried to track Rupert down through the registered address of the 32 County website. The trail led to a number of addresses in Chicago and Indiana that were registered in Rupert's name, though neighbours had never seen him there. One of the false addresses, significantly, was in Wheatfield, Indiana, a tight-knit community known locally for the number of FBI officers living there.

Rupert at the time was living in a safe house, where he was expected to stay until any trial. McKevitt personally took Rupert into his trust and introduced him to senior members of the terrorist group. McKevitt faces life imprisonment if convicted. He is the first person to be charged with directing terrorism under legislation introduced in the Irish Republic after the Omagh bombing in 1998. Irish police have always hinted that they had a 'secret weapon' in the case against McKevitt.

Joe Ruddy, Principal at the high school from which Rupert graduated in 1968, said he had a 'rebel' streak, a word used to describe him in his class yearbook. Rumours that he had a business in Ireland and was wealthy further increased his stature and reputation in his home town. 'This is a very staid rural farm community,' said Ruddy. 'David had a De Lorean sports car. You remember a man of his size trying to get out of a car with gull-wing doors!'

Little more is known about MI5's most unusual agent. His two sisters, to whom Rupert was reputedly close, may have been the only people other than his wife and his handlers to know about his double life. One of them recently declined to talk about him. 'Yes. he's my brother,' she said, 'but I haven't seen him in a long time. You want to know what he looks like? He's a little short guy, he's got curly hair and one leg shorter than then other. I'm not going to tell you anything. Goodbye.'

The Zodiac Killer

A brutal assassin who styled himself the 'Zodiac Killer' stalked the Bay area around San Francisco for over ten years. Like Jack the Ripper, he taunted the police with letters and clues. Also in common with the Ripper, he, too, was never caught and may even have moved on, to kill again.

His reign of terror began on a chilly, moonlit night at Christmas in 1968. A teenage couple had drawn up in their car in an open space next to a pump house on the Lake Herman road in the Vallejo hills overlooking San Francisco. This was the local lovers' lane and David Faraday and Bettilou Jensen were indifferent to the cold. Indeed, they were so wrapped up in each other that they did not notice another car pulling up about 10ft (3m) away. Their amorous reverie was then rudely interrupted by gunfire, however. One bullet smashed through the back window, showering them with glass, while another thudded into the car's bodywork. Bettilou threw open the passenger door and leapt out. David, who was trying to follow her, had his hand on the door handle when the gunman leant in through the driver's window and shot him in the head, causing his body to slump across the front seat. Bettilou's attempt at flight was futile: as she ran screaming into the night the gunman ran after her; she had covered just 30ft (9m) when he fired five shots at her. After she had collapsed and died the gunman walked calmly back to his car and drove away.

A few minutes later another car drove down the quiet road. Its driver, a woman, saw Bettilou's body sprawled on the ground, but did not stop, instead speeding on, towards the next town, Benica, to get help. On the way, she saw the flashing blue light of a police car approaching her and frantically switched her headlights on and off to try to attract the driver's attention. The car stopped and she told the patrolmen what she had seen. They then followed her back to the pump house, arriving there about three minutes later. Although Bettilou was dead David was still alive, but because he was unconscious he could not give them any information about what had happened. He died shortly after his arrival at the hospital to which they had rushed him.

There was little for the police to go on: the victims had not been sexually assaulted and nothing was missing (the money in David's wallet was still there). Detective Sergeant Les Lundblatt, of the Vallejo County police force, investigated the possibility that they had been murdered by a jealous rival, but there were found to be no jilted lovers and no other amorous entanglements. The two teenagers were ordinary students whose lives were an open book. Six months later Bettilou Jensen and David Faraday's files had become just two of a huge number relating to unsolved murders in the state of California.

On 4 July 1969 their killer struck again. At around midnight at Blue Rock Park – another romantic spot, just 2 miles (3km) from where Bettilou and David were murdered – Mike Mageau was sitting in his car with his girlfriend, the 22-year-old waitress Darlene Ferrin. They were not entirely alone because other courting couples had also parked their cars there. Like Bettilou and David before them, Mike and Darlene were too engrossed in each other to notice when a white car pulled up beside them. It stayed there for only a few minutes before driving away, but then it returned and parked on the other side of the road. A powerful spotlight was suddenly shone on Mike's car, whereupon a figure approached them. Thinking that it was a policeman, Mike reached for his driver's licence. As he did so, however, he heard the sound of gunfire and saw Darlene slump in her seat; seconds later a bullet tore into Mike's neck. The gunman then walked unhurriedly back to the white car, paused to fire another four or five shots at them and then sped off, leaving the smell of cordite and burning rubber in his wake.

A few minutes later a man called the Vallejo County police station and reported a murder on Columbus Parkway, telling the switchboard operator: 'You will find the kids in a brown car. They are shot with a 9mm Luger. I also killed those kids last year. Goodbye.' When the police arrived Darlene was dead, and although Mike was still alive the bullet had passed through his tongue and he was unable to speak.

There was another lead for the police to follow, however. Four months earlier Darlene's babysitter had noticed a white car parked outside Darlene's flat. Thinking that it looked suspicious, she asked Darlene about it. It was plain that the young mistress knew the driver: 'He's checking up on me again', she told the babysitter. 'He doesn't want anyone to know what I saw him do. I saw him murder someone.' The babysitter had had a good look at the man in the white car and told the police that he was middle-aged, with brown, wavy hair and a round face. When Mike could talk again he confirmed that the gunman had had brown hair and a round face. After that, however, the clues to the killer's identity petered out.

Then, on 1 August 1969 – almost two months after the shootings of Darlene and Mike, three local newspapers received handwritten letters. They all began: 'DEAR EDITOR, THIS IS THE MURDERER OF THE 2 TEENAGERS LAST CHRISTMAS AT LAKE HERMAN & THE GIRL ON THE 4TH OF JULY . . .' (Like David Berkowitz's letters, they went written in capital letters and contained basic errors in spelling and syntax.) The author gave details of the ammunition that he had used, leaving no one in any doubt that he was indeed the gunman. Each letter also contained a third of a sheet of paper covered with a strange code, which the writer demanded that the papers print on their front pages; if they did not, he warned, he would go on 'killing lone people in the night'. The letters were signed with another cipher – a circle with a cross inside it which looked ominously like a gun sight.

All three of the newspapers complied with the writer's demands and the coded message was also sent to Mare Island Naval Yard, where cryptographers tried to crack it. Although it appeared to be a simple substitution code, the US navy's experts could not break it. Dale Harden, a teacher at Alisal High School in Salinas, however, could. Having had the idea of looking for a group of ciphers that might spell the word 'kill', he managed to locate them and after ten hours' intense work he and his wife had decoded the whole of the message, which read: 'I like killing people because it is so much more fun than killing wild game in the forest because man is the most dangerous of all to kill . . .' The killer then went on to boast that he had already murdered five people in the San Francisco Bay area and added that after he had been reborn in paradise his victims would become his slaves.

After the murderer's cryptic message was made public a tidal wave of information was offered by ordinary citizens: over 1,000 calls were received by the police, but none of them led anywhere. So the killer helpfully volunteered another clue, this time revealing a name; or rather a nickname, that he knew would attract the attention of the headline-writers. Writing again to the newspapers, he began his letters 'DEAR EDITOR, THIS IS ZODIAC SPEAKING . . .' He again gave details of the slaying of Darlene Ferrin that only the killer could have known. Yet although the killer's strategy increased his publicity profile the police were still no nearer to catching him.

On 28 September 1969 the 20-year-old Bryan Hartnell and the 22-year-old Cecelia Shepard – both students at the nearby Seventh-day Adventists' Pacific Union College – went for a picnic on the shores of Lake Berryessa, some 13 miles (21km) north of Vallejo. At around 4.30pm they had finished eating and were lying on a blanket, kissing, when they noticed a stocky man, with brown hair, walking towards them across the clearing. Having disappeared momentarily into a copse, when he re-emerged he was wearing a mask and carrying a gun. As he came closer Bryan saw that the mask had a symbol on it: a white cross within a circle.

The man was not particularly threatening in his manner and his voice was soft. 'I want your money and your car keys', he said. Bryan explained that he only had 76 cents, but said that the masked man was welcome to that. The gunman then began to chat, telling them that he was an escaped convict and that he was going to have to tie them up with the clothesline that he had brought with him. Having forced Cecelia to tie up Bryan, he then trussed her up himself.

The gunman talked some more before calmly announcing 'I am going to have to stab you people', whereupon Bryan begged to be stabbed first, saying 'I couldn't bear to see her stabbed'. Having quietly agreed to this, the gunman sank to his knees and stabbed Bryan repeatedly in the back with a hunting knife. Although he was feeling dizzy and sick, Bryan was still conscious when the masked man turned his attention to Cecelia. Having initially appeared calm, after the first stab he went berserk, plunging the hunting knife into her body again and again while she frantically twisted and turned beneath him in a futile attempt to escape the blows. When she was finally lying still the man regained his composure. He got up, walked to their car, pulled a felt-tip pen from his pocket and then drew something on the door before strolling away.

A fisherman who had heard their screams ran towards them, to find both Bryan and Cecelia still alive. Napa Valley police officers were already on their way, having been alerted by an anonymous phone call in which a man's gruff voice had said 'I want to report a double murder', then going on to give the precise location at which the bodies could be found before leaving the phone hanging from its cord.

When the police arrived Cecelia was in a coma; she died two days later, in hospital, without having regained consciousness. Bryan recovered slowly and was able to give a full description of their attacker, but the police had already guessed who he was, for the sign that the killer had drawn on the door of their car was a circle with a cross within it. The police also located the phone booth from which the killer had reported the murder; it was less than six streets away from the headquarters of the Napa Valley Police Department. They furthermore managed to lift three good-quality fingerprints from it, although their owner's details were unfortunately not found among the police's records.

On 11 October 1969, just two weeks later, a 14-year-old girl was looking out of a window of her home in San Francisco when she witnessed a crime in progress. A taxi was parked on the corner of Washington and Cherry streets and she could see a stocky man, who was sitting in the front passenger seat, going through the pockets of the driver, who appeared to be dead. She called to her brothers to come and watch what was happening and together they observed the man getting out of the taxi, leaving the cab driver lying slumped across the seat, and wiping the door handle with a piece of cloth before walking off in a northerly direction. Although the children promptly called the police they did not give their evidence very clearly and the telephone operator who took the call (which was logged at 10pm) made a note that the suspect was an 'NMA' – Negro male adult – even though he was, in fact, white. Indeed, after the police had put out a general alert, a patrolman actually stopped a stocky man near the scene of the crime and asked whether he had seen anything unusual; the man replied in the negative and because he was furthermore white the patrolman waved him on his way.

A stocky man was later seen running into the nearby Presidio – a military compound that contains housing and a park – whereupon the floodlights were switched on and the area was searched by patrolmen with dogs, but with no success. When they inspected the taxi the police found the driver, 29-year-old Paul Stine, lying dead from a gunshot wound to the head. The motive for his killing, they thought, was robbery.

Three days later the *San Francisco Chronicle* received a

letter from Zodiac. 'THIS IS THE ZODIAC SPEAKING', it said. 'I AM THE MURDERER OF THE TAXI DRIVER OVER BY WASHINGTON ST AND MALE ST (sic) LAST NIGHT, TO PROVE IT HERE IS A BLOOD STAINED PIECE OF HIS SHIRT.' (The piece of cloth enclosed with the letter was indeed found to match the shirt of the murdered taxi-driver. The bullet that had killed Stine was also identified as a .22 that had been fired from the same gun that had been used to kill Bettilou Jensen and David Faraday). The letter went on to say: 'I AM THE SAME MAN WHO DID IN THE PEOPLE IN THE NORTH BAY AREA. THE S.F. POLICE COULD HAVE CAUGHT ME LAST NIGHT', it taunted, before concluding: 'SCHOOL CHILDREN MAKE NICE TARGETS. I THINK I SHALL WIPE OUT A SCHOOL BUS SOME MORNING. JUST SHOOT OUT THE TIRES AND THEN PICK OFF ALL THE KIDDIES AS THEY COME BOUNCING OUT.' The letter was signed with the now-familiar circle containing a cross.

The description of the man supplied by the children, as well as by the policeman who had stopped the stocky, white male as he was leaving the scene of the crime, matched those given by Darlene Ferrin's babysitter, Mike Mageau and Bryan Hartnell. A new composite image of the Zodiac Killer was now drawn up and issued to the public by San Francisco's Chief of Police, Thomas J. Cahill. It depicted a white male, 35 to 45 years old, with short, brown hair, which possibly had a red tint; he was described as being around 5ft 8in (1.75m) tall, heavily built and a wearer of glasses. This 'wanted' poster was plastered around San Francisco.

The Zodiac Killer's appetite for publicity seems to have been insatiable. At 2am on 22 October 1969, 11 days after the murder of Paul Stine, a man with a gruff voice called the Police Department in Oakland just across the bay from San Francisco. After introducing himself as Zodiac he said: 'I want to get in touch with F. Lee Bailey. If you can't come up with Bailey I'll settle for Mel Belli. I want one or other of them to appear on the Channel 7 talk show. I'll make contact by telephone.'

The men for whom he had asked were the USA's two leading criminal lawyers, and although F. Lee Bailey was not available at such short notice Melvin Belli agreed to appear on Jim Dunbar's talk show at 6.30 on the following morning. At around 7.20am a man called in and told Belli that he was Zodiac, although he preferred to be called Sam. Then he said: 'I'm sick. I have headaches.' The mystery caller was eventually traced to Napa State Hospital and proved to be a psychiatric patient.

The actual Zodiac continued his correspondence, however, writing to Inspector David Toschi, of San Francisco's homicide squad, and threatening to commit more murders. In another letter he claimed to have killed seven people – two more than the Zodiac Killer's official body count up till then. He later said that he had murdered ten, taunting the San Francisco Police Department (SFPD) with the score line 'ZODIAC 10, SFPD 0'. He furthermore gave cryptic clues as to his real name and shared his fantasy of blowing up schoolchildren with a bomb with the recipients of his letters.

The following Christmas Melvin Belli received a card saying: 'DEAR MELVIN, THIS IS THE ZODIAC SPEAKING. I WISH YOU A HAPPY CHRISTMAS. THE ONE THING I ASK OF YOU IS THIS, PLEASE HELP ME . . . I AM AFRAID I WILL LOSE CONTROL AND TAKE MY NINTH AND POSSIBLY TENTH VICTIM.' Another piece of Paul Stine's bloodstained shirt was enclosed. Forensic handwriting experts feared that Zodiac's mental state was deteriorating.

On 24 July 1970 the Zodiac Killer wrote a letter that included the words 'THE WOEMAN (sic) AND HER BABY THAT I GAVE A RATHER INTERESTING RIDE

FOR A COUPLE OF HOWERS (sic) ONE EVENING A
FEW MONTHS BACK THAT ENDED IN MY BURNING
HER CAR WHERE I FOUND THEM'. The afore-
mentioned woman was Kathleen Johns. On the evening of
17 March 1970 she was driving in the Vallejo area, with her
baby in the car with her, when a white Chevrolet drew up
alongside her. The driver indicated that there was
something wrong with her rear wheel, so she pulled over
and the other driver also stopped; according to Kathleen
he was a 'clean-shaven and neatly dressed man'. He told
her that her wheel had been wobbling and offered to
tighten the wheel nuts for her, which she gratefully agreed
to. When she drove off, however, the wheel that he had
said that he had fixed came off altogether, whereupon the
driver of the Chevrolet offered her a lift to a nearby service
station. She again accepted his offer of help, but when they
reached the service station he drove straight past it,
replying to her query as to why he had done so in a
chillingly calm voice. 'You know I am going to kill you,' he
said.

Kathleen managed to keep her head, however, and
when her abductor slowed down on the curve of a
motorway ramp she jumped from the car while holding
her baby in her arms, ran off and hid in an irrigation ditch.
The driver then stopped the Chevrolet and started to
search for her, using a torch that he taken out of the booth
of the car. Fortunately for Kathleen, he was approaching
the ditch in which she was cowering with her child when
he was caught in the beam of a lorry's headlights. An hour
later, having watched him drive off, Kathleen made her
way to a police station to report what had happened to her.
On seeing Zodiac's 'wanted' poster pinned to the wall of
the police station she identified him as the man who had
threatened to kill her. When the police drove her back to
her car they found that it was now a burned-out shell – it
seemed that the Zodiac Killer had returned to set it alight.

Despite the new leads that Kathleen Johns had provided the police were still no nearer to catching the Zodiac Killer, although the Vallejo County police believed that he was now the driver of a new, green Ford. The reason behind their suspicion was that the driver of such a car had once stopped and ostentatiously watched a highway patrolman who was parked on the other side of the motorway. After the patrolman had decided to ask him what he was doing and had driven through an underpass to reach him he had found the green Ford gone: it was now parked on the other side of the motorway, exactly where the squad car had been moments before. Zodiac subsequently played this cat-and-mouse game every day for two weeks.

Detective Sergeant Lundblatt was becoming increasingly convinced that the Zodiac Killer was a man named Andy Walker. Walker had known Darlene Ferrin and Darlene's sister had also identified him as the man who had waited outside Darlene's flat in the white car. He bore a marked resemblance, too, to the description of the man who was seen near Lake Berryessa when Cecelia Shepard was stabbed to death. Walker was also known to suffer from bad headaches and to get on badly with the women with whom he worked. He had furthermore studied codes while in the army.

However, neither did his fingerprints match the one that had been left in Paul Stine's taxi nor did his handwriting equate to that on Zodiac's notes. The police then discovered that Walker was ambidextrous, which meant that his handwriting would change depending on which hand he used to write with. They also formulated the theory that the murder of Paul Stine had been so meticulously planned that the Zodiac Killer may have used the severed finger of an unknown victim to plant fingerprints in the taxi and thereby throw the police off his scent.

The police decided that they had to obtain Walker's palm prints in order to see if they matched those that had been found on the telephone that had been left dangling after the Paul Stine killing. An undercover policeman therefore asked Walker to help him to carry a goldfish bowl, but although Walker obliged the palm prints that he left were smudged. Walker soon realized that he was being targeted by the police, however, and approached a judge, who issued a court order which forced them to stop harassing Walker.

Letters from Zodiac threatening more murders were received; some were authenticated, but rendered few new clues. The only thing that the police could be sure of was that Zodiac was a fan of the comic operettas of Gilbert and Sullivan. He had taunted them with a parody of 'The Lord High Executioner', listing those people whom he intended to kill and using the refrain 'Titwillo, titwillo, titwillo', and there were furthermore no letters on killings during the entire run of San Francisco's Presentation Theater's *The Mikado*.

The police also deduced that Zodiac had a curious connection with water. Not only did all of the names of his crime scenes have some association with water, but in one of his letters he had claimed that the body count would have been higher if had not been 'swamped by the rain we had a while back'. The police therefore reasoned that he lived in a low-lying area that was susceptible to flooding or that he perhaps had a basement in which he kept equipment for making his long-threatened bomb.

Next a K-mart shop in Santa Rossa, California, was evacuated following a bomb threat made by a man who identified himself as the Zodiac Killer. Two months later Zodiac wrote another letter to the *San Francisco Chronicle* claiming to have killed 12 people and enclosing a map with an 'X' marking the peak of a mountain in Contra Costa Country, across the bay from San Francisco, from which an observer, he said, would be able to see the entire panorama of the area in which the murders had taken place. When detectives examined the location more closely, however, the spot marked was found to be within the compound of a naval relay station, to which only service personnel with security clearance were granted access.

The letters, which continued to come, now demanded that everyone in the San Francisco area wear lapel badges bearing the Zodiac Killer's symbol. When they did not comply he threatened Paul Avery, the *San Francisco Chronicle*'s crime writer who had been investigating the Zodiac story, whereupon journalists (including Avery), began wearing badges saying 'I am not Paul Avery'. Avery, who was a licensed private eye and a former war correspondent in Vietnam, also started carrying a .38 and practised shooting regularly at the police firing range.

An anonymous correspondent then tied the Zodiac slaying to the unsolved murder of Cheri Jo Bates, an 18-year-old college student who had been stabbed to death after leaving the college library in Riverside, California, on Hallowe'en in 1966. Although the police could not rule out a connection they could not prove a concrete link either. When Avery investigated it, however, he discovered that the police had received what they considered to be a crank letter from 'Z'. In a series of typewritten letters the author furthermore gave details of the murder that only the killer could have known. He also threatened more killings and wrote of a 'game' that he was playing. Handwritten letters were received, too, whose writing matched that of Zodiac's. Armed with this evidence, Avery managed to persuade the police to re-open the Bates case in the light of the Zodiac murders.

During 1971 there were a number of murders which could have been committed by Zodiac. Indeed, letters purporting to have come from him confessed to them, but he could easily have been claiming the credit for other people's handiwork.

At around 9 pm on 7 April 1972 the 33-year-old Isobel Watson, who worked as a legal secretary in San Francisco, got off a bus in Tamalpais Valley. She had just begun walking home, up Pine Hill, when a white Chevrolet swerved across the road and nearly hit her. After the car had come to a halt the driver apologized and offered to give her a lift home; when Isobel declined he got out of the car, pulled out a knife and stabbed her in the back. Her screams alerted her neighbours, who came running out of their homes, whereupon the man jumped back into his car and sped off. After Isobel had recovered she gave a description of her attacker: he was a white man in his early 40s, around 5ft 9in (1.78m) tall, and he had been wearing black-rimmed reading glasses. The police believed that there was a better than 50-50 chance that he was the Zodiac Killer.

As time went by, many of the detectives working on the Zodiac case were reassigned, and eventually only Inspector David Toschi was left. Agents from the Federal Bureau of Investigation (FBI) looked at the files, but even they could take the case no further. Zodiac's correspondence now ceased for nearly four years, but although psychologists believed that he was the type to commit suicide Toschi was not convinced that he was dead. He reasoned that Zodiac got his kicks from the publicity that his murders generated rather than from the killings themselves and that he would therefore have left a note or some other clue that he was Zodiac if he had killed himself. Then, on 25 April 1978, Toschi received confirmation that Zodiac was still alive when the *San Francisco Chronicle* received a letter from him. The letter mentioned Toschi by name and said that the writer wanted the people of San Francisco to know that he was back.

Robert Graysmith, the author of the book *Zodiac*, deduced that the eponymous murderer was a film buff. In one of his cryptograms, for example, he had mentioned the 'most dangerous game', which is the title of a film, in another calling himself the 'Red Phantom', which is also the name of a film. He furthermore frequently mentioned going to the cinema to see *The Exorcist* or *Badlands*, the latter a fictionalized account of the murderous spree of the Nebraskan killer Charles Starkweather.

The police used the information supplied by Graysmith, as well as the Zodiac Killer's obvious love of publicity, to try to trap him. When a film about the Zodiac killing was shown in San Francisco a suggestion box was installed in the lobby of the cinema, into which the audience was invited to drop notes containing any information or theories that they may have had regarding the murders. Inside the huge box was hidden a detective, who read every note by torchlight as it fell through the slot; he had been ordered to raise the alarm if any looked as though they could have come from the Zodiac Killer, but none did.

The Oakland police thought that they had captured the Zodiac Killer at one point. The suspect was a veteran of the Vietnam War who had seen the Zodiac film three times and had been apprehended while masturbating in the cinema's lavatory after a particularly violent scene. They were soon proved wrong, however, for his handwriting did not match Zodiac's. Amid a welter of recrimination Toschi was transferred from homicide following (baseless) accusations that he had forged the Zodiac letters for self-promotion. The police in the Bay area now began to believe that the Zodiac Killer was either dead or serving time for another crime in a prison outside the state. On the other hand, maybe he reckoned that his time was running out, having nearly been caught following the killing of Paul Stine.

Robert Graysmith was not convinced by these theories, however. He had managed to link the Zodiac killings with the unsolved murders of 14 young girls, usually students or hitchhikers, in the Santa Rosa area during the early 1970s. Although most of them had been found naked, with their clothes missing, they had generally not been sexually molested. Each had been killed in a different way, as if the murderer had been experimenting to ascertain which method was best. Graysmith now reckoned that Zodiac's body count could be as high as 40.

Graysmith believed that Zodiac's symbol – a cross within a circle – was not intended to represent a stylized gunsight, but rather the projectionist's guide that is shown on screen during the lead-in to a film. He traced a promising-sounding suspect through a cinema in San Francisco on whose ceiling the constellations were painted: the man, Graysmith was told, had filmed some murders and kept the gruesome footage in a booby-trapped can. Another suspect of Graysmith's was a former boyfriend of Darlene Ferrin, who had also been a resident of Riverside at the time when Cheri Jo Bates was murdered. He lived with his mother, whom he loathed, and dissected small mammals as a hobby. During the crucial 1975 to 1978 period, when the Zodiac Killer had been quiet, he had been in a psychiatric institution after having been charged with molesting children at the school where he was employed. Graysmith could not pin the Zodiac murders on either of his suspects, however. He published the story of his investigation in 1955.

In 1990 a series of murders was perpetrated in New York by someone who claimed to be Zodiac. Although descriptions of the New York killer did not match those given by the witnesses to the Zodiac murders in California, a man can change a lot over 20 years. Who can tell where he may strike next?

Michael Hutchence

No superstar death in recent years has caused as much speculation as that of the INXS lead singer, Michael Hutchence. He left behind a web of mystery in the circumstances surrounding his death in a Sydney hotel room in November 1997.

Born on 22 January 1960 in Australia, Michael Hutchence spent the early years of his life living in Sydney. However, as a result of his father's job, Hutchence's family left Sydney for Hong Kong when he was just four years old. For a child, Hong Kong was an exotic location in which to grow up, but more notably it was the place where a toy company gave Hutchence his first paid singing assignment.

The family moved back to Australia in 1972, settling in Sydney once more. Hutchence's teenage years were spent in the city, growing up with Andrew Farris (later a band-member of INXS) as a best friend. But times were not all good. Hutchence's parents divorced when he was just 15; his father remained in Sydney while his mother relocated to America. Forced to choose a home, Hutchence went to the USA with his mother. However Hutchence soon moved back, once more, to Sydney and took up residence with his father. Back at the same high school with his friends, Hutchence joined an extra-curricular band 'The Farris Brothers' with Andrew, Tim and Jon Farris, along with Garry Beers and Kirk Pengilly. The boys took the band seriously, and, when the time came two years later to leave high school, they remained as a group, concentrating on writing new material and practising for small gigs in the city.

The group went from strength to strength and in 1980 they signed their first contract with a record company. The group also changed their name to the more marketable

INXS. Over the next four years, INXS gained experience, record sales and, more importantly, publicity.

In 1987, and six albums later, INXS were one of the most popular and marketable bands of the time. They had received increasing critical acclaim for their music and Michael Hutchence was recognized as an international superstar in his own right. The late 1980s were without doubt the peak of INXS's pop life. But fame and fortune had its drawbacks. Hutchence, like many similar pop stars cum superstars of the time, threw himself into the arms of the world that encapsulated sex, drugs and rock'n'roll. He became as famous for his prolific drug-taking and supposedly wild sex life as he did for his music. He had a string of beautiful and famous girlfriends, most notably the Australian singer Kylie Minogue and the Danish supermodel Helena Christensen.

As a superstar in his own right, Hutchence considered leaving INXS to pursue a solo career, but soon rejoined the band to record their seventh album, *X*, a successful album by any standards but not as popular as their previous album had been. The resounding success of the group's late 1980s music had become their benchmark, and new material, although selling extremely well, was not quite as popular as it had once been. The early 1990s was an increasingly difficult period for Hutchence, knowing that INXS had had their heyday. In 1995, his personal fortunes changed when he met Paula Yates and entered into an affair with the then wife of Sir Bob Geldof. The affair rapidly became public knowledge and Geldof wasted no time in filing for divorce. The courts granted this but a more involved question remained – who would retain custody of Yates' three children by Geldof?

In what became a much-publicized and fought-out custody battle, the future of the three children was for the time being undecided. Yates and Hutchence had a child of their own – Heavenly Hiraani Tiger Lily – in July 1996.

The couple lived together with their child in London, with the custody battle continuing in the mean time. In 1998, the band members celebrated 20 years of INXS by undertaking a world tour, the final leg of which was in Australia. The last two days of Hutchence's life, 21 and 22 November, were spent in Sydney at the end of the tour. But they are two days which have been greatly scrutinized and speculated upon as no one, it seems, can comprehend why Michael Hutchence died there and then.

On the evening of the 21st, Hutchence spent time with his father, who has since stated that his son seemed fine that evening and certainly did not show any cause for concern. Back in his hotel room later that evening, Hutchence was contacted by Yates with the news that she and the four children could not come out to Australia to visit him due to restrictions of the court case. The events of the remainder of the evening have been pieced together from the telephone calls that Hutchence made and also from the recollections of two friends who spent the evening in the hotel room with the singer until the early hours of the following day.

The following morning, Hutchence's naked, lifeless body was found crumpled behind the door of his hotel room. He had seemingly died as the result of hanging. A coroner ruled a verdict of suicide.

The coroner's report, for the most part, should be taken as read and accepted as an end to what is a sad, tragic and wasteful loss of a talented life. Hutchence had been on medication for depression and there was speculation that his marriage to Paula Yates was hitting a rocky patch, especially with the pressure of the custody battle. The news that his wife and the children would not be able to fly out to Australia probably added to the cloud of sadness that Hutchence was apparently under.

But even the coroner had to base his opinion and verdict on a set of circumstances which he chose to interpret in his own, ultimately partially subjective way. So, if another person were to consider the same circumstances, reports and evidence, would they have arrived at the same conclusion?

It was even suggested that Hutchence may have died as a result of a wild sexual act that went wrong. Two people – Kym Wilson and Andrew Rayment – spent most of the night of the 21st with Hutchence in his hotel room, and remained there until the early hours of the following morning, leaving just hours before Hutchence's body was discovered. Both stated that Hutchence had seemed worried about the court case, but otherwise nothing else appeared different about his character. All three consumed a variety of drinks that evening.

Several close associates received calls from Hutchence on the evening of the 21st and on the morning of the 22nd. One was Michelle Bennet, who actually came round to the hotel to visit Hutchence on the morning of the 22nd, anxious to make sure he was OK after he had seemed 'upset' during the conversation they had had earlier that morning. Despite knocking loudly on the hotel-room door and phoning him, Bennet was unable to see Hutchence at all. Little did she know at the time why this was so. Hutchence's personal manager, Martha Troup, and Bob Geldof were also contacted earlier by Hutchence. Both, like Michelle Bennet, expressed concern with the sound of his voice on the telephone.

A medical report of Hutchence's body showed that alcohol, cocaine and prescription drugs were present in his bloodstream at the time of death. Some of the prescription drugs were those given to him for the treatment of his depression, which, incidentally, was considered 'minor' by his doctor.

Hutchence was discovered by the chambermaid slumped behind the door in his hotel room. A belt had been used for the purpose of hanging, but this had eventually snapped under the weight of the body, hence the discovery of Hutchence on the floor.

Since no one can link together the pieces of the jigsaw surrounding Hutchence's troubled death with absolute certainty, his death is still shrouded in mystery. The coroner's report has laid to rest much of the speculation and suggestions that the media put forward, but the coroner's opinion is still ultimately open to subjection.

Doctor Death

An 84-year-old retired doctor died in July 1983 in the genteel Sussex seaside resort of Eastbourne. His passing might have warranted no more than a paragraph in the local paper, but for one thing . . . the doctor, John Bodkin Adams, was believed by many to be a man who literally got away with mass murder. And it was only upon his death that newspapers could safely produce their dossiers on the astonishing case, in which Adams was tried at the Old Bailey for the murder of one of his patients, Edith Morrell, a 72-year-old widow. If he had been convicted he would have been charged with further murders. Two other charges had been prepared and the Crown believed it had sufficient evidence to prosecute three other cases.

Early in the investigation one of the policemen involved, Scotland Yard Detective Chief Superintendent Charles Hewitt, believed Adams killed nine of his elderly patients. He later increased his estimate to 25, believing that Adams had probably 'eased' many others out of this world after influencing them to change their wills in his favour.

But none of this came to light at the Old Bailey. Adams was acquitted after a classic courtroom duel between the then Attorney-General, Sir Reginald Manningham-Buller QC, and a brilliant defence lawyer, Geoffrey Lawrence.

Lawrence disliked his client intensely but he fought

tigerishly, turning the Attorney-General's over-confidence against him in a brilliant tactical coup which is still recalled and admired by lawyers. Manningham-Buller was certain he would destroy Adams once he had him in the witness-box. Lawrence simply told Adams to exercise his right to remain silent – and thus avoid cross-examination. It was that, the police and prosecution believed, that saved him from the rope. For, with the linchpin of the Crown's case snatched away, the jury took just 45 minutes to find him not guilty.

The trial was such a disaster that the Director of Public Prosecutions lost confidence that a conviction on any other charge could be procured. So he announced there would be no further action.

What the jury never knew – and could not in law be told – was that the police had investigated the deaths of a further 400 of his patients. They had also exhumed the bodies of two of the women who had not been cremated. They had prepared cases on the deaths of nine patients and had evidence pointing to the murders of many others.

The police knew that, over his 35 years of practice in Eastbourne, Adams had been the beneficiary of 132 wills, amassing £45,000 in cash – worth ten times that today – antique silver, jewellery, furniture and cars, including two Rolls-Royces, from the bequests of dead patients.

So was John Bodkin Adams merely a plausible rogue or was he the most cunning mass murderer of the century?

He was certainly the most fashionable doctor in Eastbourne, a town where the elderly could spend their last days peacefully in genteel retirement. He had arrived there virtually straight from medical school in his native Northern Ireland and built up a good practice with the cream of the town as his patients.

He was an ugly man, only 5ft 5in (1.7m) tall and weighing almost 18 stones (114kg), with a pink fleshy face, small eyes and thin lips and a rolling chin that sagged over the celluloid collars he wore. But to his elderly women patients he was charming. He caressed their hands and combed their hair.

However, the picture painted by the year-long investigation by Mr Hewitt, then a sergeant, and his 'governor' Detective Chief Superintendent Bert Hannam of the Yard's Murder Squad, was as follows.

Adams made his victims dependent on his drugs. They craved his morphine and heroin and became addicts. He influenced them to change their wills in his favour. Then they died.

His method, the police claimed, was not startling, shocking or gory. He eased them gently out of life with an overdose of drugs.

Scotland Yard's investigations showed that, of all the patients for whom Adams signed death certificates, he explained an improbable 68 per cent as being due to either cerebral haemorrhage or cerebral thrombosis.

Even before the war there was gossip that Adams did his rounds with a bottle of morphia in one pocket and a blank form in the other. In 1936 he had been the beneficiary in the will of Mrs Alice Whitton, to the extent of £3,000 – a substantial amount then. Her niece contested the will in the High Court but Adams won and kept the money.

The tongues continued to wag into the mid-1950s. But it was not until 1956 that police investigations actually began and the evidence started to build, much of it circumstantial.

There was the case of William Mawhood, a wealthy steel merchant, who was such a long-standing friend of Adams that he lent him £3,000 to buy his first house. As Mawhood lay dying, Adams asked his wife Edith to leave the bedside for a moment. She heard Adams say: 'Leave your estate to me and I'll look after your wife.'

Mrs Mawhood rushed back into the bedroom. She said later:

'I grabbed my gold-headed walking stick and struck out at the doctor and chased him around the bed. He ran out of the room and as he dashed down the stairs I threw my stick at him. Unfortunately it missed, and broke a flower vase. I shouted to him to get out of the house. It was the last I wanted to see of him. I certainly would not tolerate the idea of Adams trying to get into my husband's will.'

There was the case of Emily Mortimer, whose family had a strict tradition, designed to keep its fortune intact. Whenever a Mortimer died, the bulk of the estate was divided among the surviving members of the family.

Adams persuaded Emily to break the tradition. In the year she died, she added a codicil to her will, transferring £3,000 worth of shares from the family to the doctor. Shortly before her death, she changed the will again so that Adams received £5,000 and members of the family were cut out. Adams signed the death certificate – the cause of death 'cerebral thrombosis'.

Police discovered the case of the two old women who were persuaded by Adams to let him sell their house and move into a flat for the good of their health. He then refused to hand over the money from the house sale until forced to do so by a writ two years later.

Statements from local solicitors and bank managers on the doctor's insistent concern with the wills of his patients revealed a host of questionable activities: visits to banks with patients to change details of wills already made; telephone calls to solicitors insisting on their immediate attendance to change or draw up a new will; a comatose patient who signed his altered will only with an X; wills changed on several occasions so that the deceased were cremated instead of buried as originally stipulated; and 32 cheques for the doctor amounting to £18,000 drawn on one old lady's account in the last few days of her life – and with highly suspect signatures.

Odious as such unprofessional behaviour was, it was not evidence of intent to murder. There was, however, plenty of other evidence . . .

Clara Neil-Miller was an elderly spinster who had lived in genteel retirement with her sister Hilda for 13 years. When Hilda died she left everything to Clara. When Clara died, 13 months later, she bequeathed the bulk of her estate – £5,000 – to Adams.

Three years later the police exhumed both bodies and the post-mortem showed that Clara had died of pneumonia, not coronary thrombosis as Adams had put on the death certificate. Then one of the other guests in the rest home for the elderly where she died told the police:

'Dr Adams was called to Miss Clara the night before she died. She was suffering from influenza. He remained in her bedroom for nearly 45 minutes before leaving. I later became worried as I heard nothing from the room. I opened the door and was horrified by what I saw.'

'This was a bitterly cold winter's night. The bedclothes on her bed had been pulled back and thrown over the bedrail at the base. Her nightdress had been folded back across her body to her neck. All the bedroom windows had been flung open. A cold gush of wind was sweeping through the room. That is how the doctor had left her.'

Police found that, in addition to the £5,000 bequest, Clara had, in the weeks before her death, made out cheques for £300 and £500 to the doctor. The purpose was not clear. It could not be for medical treatment as, apart from the flu, she was not ill. Nor did she receive much in the way of medicines.

Adams had a financial interest in the rest home and sent many patients there. A potential key witness was the woman who ran it, Mrs Elizabeth Sharp. Ex-Detective Chief Superintendent Hewitt recalled:

'Mrs Sharp was on the point of talking when we left Eastbourne for a week's conferences with the Attorney-

General in London. She was the witness we needed. She knew much of what went on between Adams and his patients. She knew where the bodies were buried and she was scared and frightened. When we left, she was about to crack.'

'One more visit was all we needed, but when we were in London she died. When we got back to to Eastbourne and heard the news, she had already been cremated on the doctor's instructions.'

'I always had a feeling, but no positive clue, that Adams speeded her on the way. It was too much of a coincidence when she died.'

Then there was the case of Julia Bradnum, a strong and healthy 82-year-old until one morning when she woke up with stomach pains. The doctor was called and remained in the room with her for five minutes. Ten minutes later she was dead.

Her body was also exhumed but it was too decomposed to show much more than that she had not died of the cerebral haemorrhage Adams' certificate claimed.

Only a few weeks before she died Adams had brought her a new will. He said something about her other will not being legal, she later told a friend, Miss Mary Hine. 'She asked me if I would witness the new one,' Miss Hine said. 'Dr Adams pointed to a spot on the paper where I was to sign. I turned over the paper to see what I was witnessing, but Dr Adams put his hand on the writing and turned it back.'

Another of the doctor's patients was Harriet Maud Hughes, aged 66, whom Adams had started to treat only three months before her death of 'cerebral thrombosis'. She spoke of changing her will in his favour. A few weeks before her death, she became ill but then recovered sufficiently to go to her bank with the doctor, who asked the bank manager in her presence to make him the executor of her will. Afterwards, she told her domestic help: 'You should have seen the bank manager's face. He was most surprised at my choice of executor.'

After her death it was discovered that she had added two codicils to her will. The first decreed that she should be cremated. The second, added a month later, left £1,000 each to a Mr and Mrs Thurston, acquaintances of Dr Adams. After the death, the police discovered Adams received 90 per cent of the bequests – giving the Thurstons 10 per cent for the use of their name.

Then there was the case of James Priestly Downs, a wealthy retired bank manager and widower who in his last days tried nine times to sign his will while in a drugged state. On the tenth occasion he signed it with an X. Adams guided his hand. The will left the doctor £1,000. All Mr Downs was being treated for was a fractured ankle. After a fortnight of the treatment, however, he was in a coma. A month later he died.

Annabelle Kilgour was a widow who had been ill for several weeks and was being looked after by a State Registered Nurse, Miss Osgood. One night Adams arrived and said he would give an injection to help her get a good night's sleep.

The nurse was astounded as she watched the doctor give what she regarded as being greatly in excess of the normal dose. 'This will keep her quiet,' he said, and left.

It did. She immediately fell into a coma and died the next morning. When Adams arrived, the nurse told him: 'Mrs Kilgour is dead. You realize, doctor, that you have killed her?'

The nurse later told the Yard men: 'I have never seen a man look so frightened in all my life.'

Once again Adams gave the cause of death as cerebral haemorrhage. In her will, Mrs Kilgour left the doctor a sum of money and an antique clock.

Margaret Pilling, a member of one of Lancashire's richest cotton families, was suffering from nothing more serious than flu when Adams was called to her. Within a fortnight she was practically in a coma. But her family insisted she should go to stay with them.

Her daughter, Mrs Irene Richardson, said later:

'At first we thought she was dying of cancer and that the doctor was being kind by not telling us. But we held a family conference and decided we were not satisfied with the treatment. Whatever her illness, she was definitely being drugged. Her condition was deteriorating rapidly.'

'We took a house for her at Ascot, near one of her relatives. Within a fortnight she was on her feet and at the races. Had I not taken her away, I am quite satisfied she would have died.'

But the case that really clinched the matter, as far as the police were concerned, was when Bobbie Hullett, a friend of the Chief Constable Richard Walker, died. Mrs Hullett, a vivacious woman of 49, widowed four months earlier, was not even really ill.

Late in 1955 her husband Jack, a retired Lloyds under-writer, became ill. 'Thank God I have a good doctor,' he told one of his nurses. When he was stricken by a heart condition one night in March the next year, the 'good doctor' sat on his bed and injected a dose of morphia. Seven hours later Jack Hullett died. In his will he left Adams £500. The residue went to Bobbie, who was shocked and grief-stricken. Friends rallied round – none more so than Adams, who prescribed drugs to help her sleep. In four months she was dead.

Perhaps in the beginning the sleeping drugs were a wise practice. But as the weeks passed the dosage was not cut down. The domestic staff said later: 'She staggered downstairs most mornings as though she was drunk.'

One of her closest friends was comedian Leslie Henson. He said: 'Her death shocked me greatly. My wife and I saw her turning into a drug addict. We invited her to our home to get away from everything, but she rushed back after 24 hours to get to her pills again. We saw her disintegrating mentally through them.'

After her death another of her friends, Chief Constable Walker, began to make a few discreet phone calls. It was established that, two days before Bobbie fell into the coma from which she never recovered, she gave Adams a cheque for £1,000. He immediately drove to the bank and asked for a special clearance. Within hours the amount was credited to his account. At the time, Dr Adams' bank accounts had £35,000 in them. With his investment holdings amounting to a further £125,000, he was not exactly in urgent need of money.

At the inquest, Adams was severely criticized by the coroner for his diagnosis and treatment. A number of penetrating questions were asked. Why had he not told his co-doctor, called in for a second opinion, of his patient's depressive medical history? Why had he failed to get proper daytime medical attention for her or had her put in a nursing home? Why, after 34 years as a doctor, did he take the advice of a young house surgeon in administering a new drug? Why had he failed to call in a psychiatric consultant? And why had he persisted in his diagnosis of a cerebral catastrophe after a pathologist had suggested it might be poisoning?

The doctor replied: 'I honestly did what I thought was best for her.'

The coroner was unimpressed. 'There has been an extraordinary degree of careless treatment,' he said.

And that was the moment that Chief Constable Walker called in Scotland Yard.

So what went wrong? Why, in the face of all this evidence, was John Bodkin Adams not charged with other offences? Why did the prosecution choose to concentrate on the case of Edith Morrell, the 72-year-old widow of a wealthy Liverpool shipping merchant?

One prosecution lawyer said afterwards: 'We chose it because it was such a clear and obvious case of murder that I should have thought no jury could have regarded it in any other way.'

But Mr Hewitt says:

'Adams was allowed to escape because the law made an ass of itself. I will never forget the conference we had with Manningham-Buller in the Attorney-General's office at the House of Commons. Bert Hannam and I felt sick with disbelief when he announced he was going for Mrs Morrell. It was madness when we had so many better cases, with more specific evidence – and, what's more important, with bodies.'

'Mrs Morrell had been cremated. This meant we could not use evidence of the best forensic scientist of the day, Dr Francis Camps. But Manningham-Buller was so arrogant he would not listen to his junior counsel, Melford Stevenson and Malcolm Morris, or Mr Leck of the Director of Public Prosecutions' office.'

'He knew the doctor was a worried man and he would destroy him in the witness-box. But it never happened because Manningham-Buller never considered for a moment that Adams might not be called to give evidence.'

Adams came to trial on 25 April 1957 – six years after Mrs Morrell's death. Prosecution witnesses testified that, over a period of six weeks, Adams had prescribed a massive dose of more than 4,000 grains of barbiturate and heroin for Mrs Morrell.

The British Pharmaceutical Association's recommended maximum daily dosage was a quarter of a morphia grain. But on the last day of her life Adams injected into his barely conscious patient 18 grains of the drug, they said.

But Geoffrey Lawrence managed to discover the nurses' daily record books which gave a more accurate account of the medicine Adams prescribed than the memories of the nurses themselves. Then came his master stroke of not putting Adams into the box.

Three months after his acquittal Adams appeared at Lewes Assizes and pleaded guilty to 14 charges, including the forgery of National Health Service prescriptions and failing to keep a record of dangerous drugs. He was fined £2,400 and ordered to pay costs. In November that year he was struck off by the General Medical Council.

On 22 November 1961, at the age of 62, he was re-admitted to the medical register, an event which went largely unnoticed. Only the Home Office retained some doubts: his licence to dispense dangerous drugs was never returned.

His practice in Eastbourne picked up again, although never to its previous size. In 1965, a grateful patient left £2,000 to Adams in her will.

Shortly before his death Adams was interviewed at his Eastbourne home. He refused to talk about his personal life. 'I don't want any more publicity,' he said. 'I have had too much of it. God knows, I have.'

Jim Morrison

'There's the known. And there's the unknown. And what separates them is the door, and that's what I want to be. I want to be the door.' – Jim Morrison, 1967.

There is a man living in the Amazonian rainforests who has one hell of a past, should he care to own up to it.

Or, alternatively, there is a bath tub in a flat in Paris that could tell a few stories.

Nobody knows what happened on the night of 2 July 1971; nobody who is alive today saw Jim Morrison's dead body. All that is known for certain is that during his 27 years on the earth he changed for ever the way rock music is presented on stage, totally redefined the concept of rock singer as messiah to a subservient generation, and completely rewrote the book on the matter of rock lyrics.

As a poet in a bluesy, gutsy rock group, as a melodramatic and dangerous performer, as a tortured artist, he appeared to be the god of several different religions, all committed to the same goal: 'the breaking away or overthrowing of established order . . . revolt, chaos, especially activity that seems to have no meaning.'

James Douglas Morrison was born on 8 December 1943, in Florida, the son of a fastidiously upright high-ranking naval officer. A hyperactive, intelligent child, the young Jim bewildered his peers and thrilled his teachers by quoting extensively from Joyce, Kerouac and Nietzsche while still in high school. His genius IQ and craving for the classics went hand in hand with a magnetic personality. Pretty soon he was engaging in verbal duels with his English teacher.

A keen writer himself, he was a sucker for the Rimbaud legend. Rimbaud had written all his poetry by the end of his teens and vanished into a life of slave-trading in Africa. He had also put forth the increasingly popular proposition that the true poet – as opposed to the would-be poet – must risk personal ruin on every level in order to stand a realistic chance of seeing the unknown, the mad, the beautiful.

Turned on to rock music by friends at UCLA, where he was studying cinematography, Morrison started to set his words to music. He met up with organist Ray Manzarek, and the latter's reaction 'Those are the greatest lyrics I've ever heard' propelled them both into a serious rock career. The whole thing gelled when guitarist Robbie Krieger and drummer John Densmore enlisted. In 1965 The Doors began to play in public.

Months of rehearsals and useful practice gigs in deserted bars helped to perfect the act. In it the hitherto shy Morrison, skinned down to a lean, confident 10 stones, was behaving increasingly dramatically, serving up his lyrics with theatrical moves and overt, sexual poses. He began to consider very seriously the role of poet/leader/visionary, and gobbled tabs of LSD to open up a few more doors. Lest the American interest in matters Vietnamese put a dampener on the exciting new proceedings, Morrison pleaded homosexuality to dodge the draft.

The blatant sexuality of his stage act in the formative months, which called for maximum friction between groin and microphone stand, was offset by the epic soundscapes that The Doors were building around his lyrics. Morrison's obsessions with potent poetic images of sex, death, fire, speed, intimacy and distance, reptiles, violence and love were pretty articulate for one so possessed. What he was screaming had meaning. At this point the audience hysteria was a source of inspiration to him. Later he would be repulsed by it.

The Doors' most traumatic song at this stage was called 'The End'. It included an approximation of the Oedipal conflict, in which Morrison sang – or screamed – the following words:

And he came to a door
And he looked inside.
'Father.'
'Yes, son?'
'I want to kill you.'
'Mother!'
'I want to ffffuuuuuuuuuuuuuuuck youuuuuuuuuuuuuu.'

The Doors' eponymous debut album was a mighty triumph on its release in 1967, and necessitated some sort of hackneyed biography for magazines to quote from. Bored with the usual 'favourite colour' scenario, Morrison cobbled together a few random notes along with scant biographical histories of the four Doors. He described his own attitude to being in The Doors as 'the feeling of a bow string being pulled back for 22 years and suddenly let go'. Further down the page he claimed that his parents were dead. As the focal point of the band, Morrison's life was becoming more and more complex. A natural drinker, one who drinks to drink rather than to socialize, he started to knock back greater and greater quantities of liquor, mixing it with perilous wedges of dope and frequent acid excursions. He was fairly settled into a relationship with a girlfriend, Pamela Courson, but enjoyed outbreaks of promiscuity. The faster the rollercoaster, the more he drank to stay in focus. Drink gradually usurped drugs. One night he visited Jac Hoizman, the head of his record label Elektra, and threw up all over his front porch. It was a common occurrence for him to go on stage tanked to the limit. Every night a different binge.

An incident in New Haven, Connecticut, towards the end of 1968 marked a swift decline in the quality of Doors performances. An argument backstage with a particularly unartistic cop resulted in Morrison being sprayed in the face with a can of mace. Morrison proceeded to relate the story on stage, suitably embellished, and was arrested for a breach of the peace.

Already exhibiting impatience with the mindless, stoned teenagers who he felt were desecrating the performances, he treated his audiences with more and more contempt, attempting to spur them into some kind of action, even if it had to be violent and negative.

Meanwhile his drinking had reached saturation level. His fridge had been stripped of food in order to accommodate more beer and he was banned from several bars in the Los Angeles area, where the group was based. He seemed to be drunk all the time. At a recording session for the song 'The Unknown Soldier' he needed 130 takes before he got it right.

His hatred of blanket audience conformity drove him

over the edge. Being obviously drunk hadn't moved them, spitting at them hadn't moved them, and swearing at them had only excited them. He resolved to put into action a plan he had conceived many years before. He would instigate a riot, then stand back and observe at first hand the gut reactions of the rabble.

It is quite easy for a rock band to start a riot. All one has to do is play one's most provocative material very quickly, without a break, while raising personal hell up there on stage.

Therefore, one night in Chicago, Morrison deliberately cued in the revolutionary 'The Unknown Soldier', the inflammatory 'Five To One' and the cataclysmic 'When The Music's Over'. All the while he gyrated to the music in a display of such terminal anguish that the audience charged the stage the minute he left it.

Encouraged by the toadying attentions of his entourage, he began to behave in arch poetic style – as practised years earlier by Dylan Thomas and Brendan Behan, to the detriment of both – and drank himself under every available table, emerging only to vomit or hassle some pretty waitress. His looks suffered, his weight shot up and, worst of all, his voice deteriorated.

The second riot came in New York. This time he went straight for the jugular. Right from the beginning of the set he did his epileptic contortionist's dance, clamping one fist on his crotch, the other on the microphone, writhing on the stage in a state of frenzied ecstasy. The result was a pitched battle between police and audience when the kids attempted to envelop the crazy man on stage.

He explained away the riots in playful fashion: 'We have fun. The kids have fun. The cops have fun.'

Still, the riots were becoming just another expected facet of The Doors' stage act. No longer were they a novelty. There was a depressing 'roll up, roll up, come and see the freaks' attitude in the minds of the kids.

Morrison felt that he had resolved the dilemma when he came into contact with a radical drama group called The Living Theatre. They were getting into areas of direct confrontation, using shock tactics like nudity and repetition to stun the audience and slap them out of their complacency. Morrison was starting to assimilate these ideas, wondering how to introduce them into a Doors show.

The fact that he failed miserably was put down at the time to alcohol, but it remains an extremely grey area. What he did in an effort to move a crowd was a depressing display of at worst egotistical machismo, at best puerile petulance. Faced, in Miami, with a typically stultifying audience, he resorted as usual to some preliminary abuse:

'You are all a bunch of fucking idiots. Your faces are being pressed into the shit of the world. Take your fucking friend and love him. Do you want to see my cock?'

He then, it was alleged, 'did lewdly and lasciviously expose his penis in a vulgar or indecent manner with intent to be observed, did place his hand on the penis and shake it, and further . . . did simulate the acts of masturbation upon himself and oral copulation upon another.'

Although he did not know it at the time, there was a warrant out for his arrest.

The hell-raising did not abate. A film he had an idea for went to the rehearsal stage. One scene involved him dancing along a 17th-floor ledge without a safety net. He did this, despite the howling protests of friends, and finished by urinating down onto the street below.

The Doors were now about as popular as Henry VIII in a singles' bar. The remaining gigs on their schedule were cancelled by the local authorities for fear of further riots, and they only managed to secure immediate work by agreeing to what Morrison called a 'fuck clause' – in other words, one hint of an unzipped fly and the cops get to join in on the chorus.

While awaiting trial for the events in Miami, Morrison was arrested a second time, for being drunk and disorderly on an aeroplane. In the wake of various hijacking attempts, security around airports had tightened and this was now a very serious charge. It was compounded by a new charge, 'interfering with the flight of an aircraft'. The offence carried ten years.

He was a wreck by now, unstable, teetering. He no longer bothered to find a toilet when he needed to pee. Just used the carpet. A lucky break at the 'hijacking' trial – the key witness didn't recognize him – took care of one legal matter. But the Miami affair was still outstanding and it seemed likely that no amount of hip legal rhetoric from the Morrison camp would be able to persuade the judge that Jim Morrison was actually bang in tune with the mores of the time.

In the mean time he married a witch. She was called Patricia Kennely and she edited one of Morrison's favourite American rock papers. In a formal witches' wedding, they signed their names in their own blood.

The Miami affair came to trial. Seventeen prosecution witnesses of pristine, virginal disposition took the oath and claimed to have been outraged/shocked/disgusted by Morrison's behaviour on the night of the alleged offences.

He was found guilty, to nobody's surprise, of profanity and indecent exposure. The sentence was six months in jail and a $500 fine. An appeal was lodged.

Morrison had been getting heavily into cocaine. His love of the quick high, the delirious rush, was satisfied perfectly by the effects of this drug, and he combined it with alcohol to produce a state of heightened neutralized glee.

Around this time he was approached by members of an

anti-drug campaign and asked to record a personalized message warning his impressionable teenage fans about the dangers of speed.

'Hello, 'he began, 'this is Jim Morrison of The Doors. I just want to tell you that shooting speed ain't cool . . . so snort it.'

Taking a major breather from the band, the trials and all his worries, Morrison fled to Europe with his on-off girlfriend Pamela. He never returned.

On Monday 5 July 1971, several calls were put through to the English offices of Elektra Records. Everybody wanted to know the same thing – was it true that Jim Morrison was dead?

The calls were shrugged off. It was perfectly in the nature of things to dodge rumours of Morrison's tragic demise. It happened every time he went on a weekend binge. The rumours, however, were gathering pace and this time there was no Morrison in the office to nullify them. So The Doors' manager called Pamela in Paris and received an oddly muted instruction to come over as soon as possible. Arriving the following day he found the flat; in it he found Pamela, a sealed coffin and a signed death certificate attributing the death of James Douglas Morrison to a heart attack. The coffin was interred the following day.

Immediately the stories began to circulate. It was pointed out that Pamela was the only one who saw the body apart from the doctor who signed the death certificate, and he couldn't be found. Suspicions were aroused that Morrison could have suffered anything so, well, mundane as a heart attack.

Jim Morrison died in a bath tub. This happens to be the common place for victims of a heroin overdose to end up (in the hope that the water will shock them back to life). Morrison had been seen hanging around notorious Parisian heroin dealers in the days leading up to his death.

To this day Paris believes that Morrison died of an overdose.

The only one who could have settled the matter once and for all is now no longer in a position to do so: Pamela died in 1974.

Therefore, it is a case of whom you believe: a qualified Parisian doctor, albeit one who ran to ground and stayed there; the woman who was virtually his wife; or a few close friends who were privy to Morrison's most bitter attacks on the music business and the unspeakable evil of the dumb Pavlovian audiences. And they mention the marvellous, madcap plan he thought up one day as far back as 1967 – how, when it all got too hectic and too useless, he'd relocate to the jungle, lose his bearings in the new sensations and gradually forget the bad times. Then, when he was good and ready, he would make contact with his friends again, using the cryptic nom-de-guerre Mr Mojo Risin . . . which crossword lovers will instantly recognize as an anagram of Jim Morrison.

Kurt Cobain

The tragic death of rock band Nirvana's Kurt Cobain on 5 April 1994 sent shock waves around the world's music industry. His apparent suicide rocked the heart of youth culture, as his name was added to the list of stars who were too young to die.

Cobain's early life certainly influenced his later outlook on life and perspective of the world. Born on 20 February 1967, Kurt Cobain spent his early childhood years in the sleepy town of Aberdeen in the state of Washington. By nature a weak, often sickly child, Cobain's childhood memories were not, for the most part, happy ones, especially when his parents divorced around his seventh birthday. This, by his own account, was a turning point in his life. Gone were the ideal securities and united love of his family and Cobain reacted to this sadness by emerging into an increasingly difficult and troublesome child. After the divorce, Cobain was passed around from relative to relative, effectively without a permanent address most of the time.

Cobain's teenage years in Aberdeen, like most young people's, were heavily influenced by music. He and friend Krist Novoselic (who also later became a band-member of Nirvana) were enormous fans of the Sex Pistols and other similar punk bands whose aggressive lyrics and hard, fast music fired the imagination of many at that time.

By 1985, Cobain was ready to move on. At 18, he moved to Olympia and began forming rock band after rock band of his own. Nirvana was formed in 1986 and consisted of Cobain, Novoselic and Dave Grohl. They performed strong, meaningful songs from the start, earning themselves early recognition. By 1988 Nirvana had produced their first album, *Bleach*.

Heavy promotional work led to them gaining rapid international fame, particularly across the Atlantic in Britain. When, in 1991, they released their second album, *Nevermind*, the band was propelled into megastardom.

Cobain was the principal songwriter of the group. He confessed his lyrics came out of the anguish of his childhood years, and the anger that he needed to release after his parents all but rejected him. The tracks on *Nevermind* were musically and lyrically stronger than those on *Bleach*, and the first single which they released from the second album, *Smells Like Teen Spirit*, became an anthem for Nirvana fans around the world.

As an overnight millionaire and a critically acclaimed songwriter and musician, Cobain was pushed into the public eye under the microscopic gaze of the world's media. Still fundamentally an insecure and often sickly man, Cobain did not cope with the pressure well. Even today, many consider his disbelief at Nirvana's success did nothing to prepare him for the fame and fortune of rock'n'roll.

Cobain's passionate lyrics and his perpetual desire to relieve his angst through his music fuelled his surprise at the following Nirvana gained. The pressure of just how much his music influenced others, and how little he could control just whom it influenced, affected Cobain greatly. He was easily upset when his music was misinterpreted and began to rely heavily on heroin to deal with the pressures of rock star life, and also to overcome the pain of the continual medical problems he had been unable to leave behind with his childhood.

In the early 1990s, Cobain found love in the form of fellow rock star Courtney Love. They were married in Hawaii in February 1992. Courtney Love was already pregnant when they were married, and gave birth to Frances Cobain later in the year. Their marriage from the start had huge ups and downs. Its endurance was reportedly often shaky, but they remained together, both unified in their love for their young daughter.

In early 1993, Nirvana released the well-received album *In Utero*, which contained material more personal and more passionate than Cobain had written before. Shortly after, Nirvana's *Unplugged* tour was to be the last recording the band made together. Cobain became increasingly wary of the influence his music had on people, and at the same time more dependent on heroin. An avid gun-collector, Cobain had pursued an interest in handguns for some time, and possessed a collection of them.

Part-way through Nirvana's European tour in 1994, Cobain was taken ill and the band cancelled a number of scheduled performances. While recovering from his illness, Cobain attempted suicide. He was rushed to hospital having consumed a large amount of strong painkillers, washed down with champagne. The suicide bid was covered up as an accident (so much so that close friends and relatives did not hear about it) and he soon returned home to Seattle. Courtney Love convinced Cobain to start a detox rehabilitation programme upon his homecoming. Cobain did so, but checked himself out after only a few days into the programme. This was the last time Cobain saw his family; after he checked himself out of the programme, he was officially reported as missing.

An electrician who was visiting his mansion found his body on 7 April 1994. The workman simply wanted to install a new security system, and when no one answered the front door he went around the back of the property. Peering in at the window of the annexe-room at the back of the mansion, the stunned electrician saw Cobain lying on the floor. He called the police who discovered Cobain's body crumpled on the floor with a shotgun pointing to his chin. Post-event medical reports state that Cobain killed himself two days earlier on 5 April, by putting a shotgun in his mouth. Found near to the body was a suicide note addressed to his wife and his little girl.

Cobain's death came as shock to most. Distraught fans, his grieving family and the stunned music world all paid tribute alike to the talented musician and songwriter whose work had affected so many. Some fans took the death to heart. A memorial a couple of days after the discovery of Cobain's death was far from peaceful, and police were needed to cope with the angry and disbelieving crowd.

For some fans, the news of Cobain's death was too much. He had represented so much to so many and several cases of copy-cat suicides across the world were reported. Nirvana, Kurt Cobain and youth culture are still synonymous today. The impact their music had on fans was, and is still, overshadowed by the media's desire to highlight all that was bad about Cobain's heroin-filled existence and his angst-filled music.

For some, Kurt Cobain's 'suicide' never happened. They feel the circumstances surrounding the rock star's death are far from clear and a flawed police investigation, and a misrepresentation by the media have led to a debatable verdict. Was Kurt Cobain's tragic loss of life, and the end of so much talent, really the result of suicide or could it have been murder? Or was his tortured existence finally too much for Cobain to take, fuelling his death wish to its ultimate conclusion? His status as a rock legend enhanced and elevated in death like so many other 'too fast to live, too young to die' icons of our time, the death of Kurt Cobain will remain an unsolved mystery for ever.

The Monster of Florence

In 1968 Antonio Io Bianchi was making love to Barbara Locci in the front seat of his car when they were both shot dead, Barbara's husband being subsequently arrested and convicted of the murders. It would be six years before Signor Locci could prove his innocence and establish that the double murder was the first atrocity committed by a serial killer who preyed on courting couples in Tuscany who later became known as the 'Monster of Florence'.

While Signor Locci was languishing in jail another courting couple was killed in a car. The police established that they had been shot with the same .22-calibre Beretta pistol that had been used in the Bianchi and Locci murders; the female victim had furthermore been mutilated. During the course of the next year two more people were killed in a similar manner. Although a German couple was murdered, too, neither of them was mutilated (they were homosexuals and their killing was probably a mistake).

Upon Signor Locci's release the Monster of Florence

appeared to suspend his activities. He struck again in 1981, however, stabbing his female victim some 300 times. Four months later, in October 1981, another woman was murdered and mutilated. The Monster of Florence continued to wage his campaign of murder over the next four years. The slayings followed a rigid pattern: all of the men were shot through the driver's window before the women were killed, their bodies then being dragged from the car and mutilated with a knife (their left breasts were generally hacked off). Ballistics tests revealed that all of the 67 bullets that were fired in a total of 16 murders came from the same gun, all also being marked with the letter 'H'. The Monster of Florence's final attack, in 1985, differed slightly from the rest, however. He slaughtered his last victims – a French couple – in their tent, cutting off a section of the woman's genitalia (which he later posted to the police) during his grisly mutilation of her body.

The Florence police handled the case badly. Numerous false accusations were made and one man who had been named as the killer committed suicide by cutting his throat. Another five were jailed for the killings, three of whom were released when the Monster struck again while they were behind bars; because there was no evidence against a fourth a judge released him, while the fifth man remained the subject of controversy.

During the course of the Monster of Florence's bloody reign of terror the police received scores of anonymous notes identifying Petro Pacciani as the killer. Pacciani was a peasant farmer who had been convicted of murder in 1951 and jailed for 13 years for killing a rival in love. (Pacciani had followed his 16-year-old fiancée upon seeing her going into the woods with another man; when he could no longer stand the sight of them making love he had stabbed the man 19 times before raping the terrified girl next to the mutilated corpse.) The police speculated that if he was indeed the Monster of Florence the embittered Pacciani had sought to avenge himself on other couples. Key to their thinking was the theory that it had been the sight of his fiancée's exposed left breast during her seduction that had triggered Pacciani's initial attack and that this was also why the Monster usually amputated the left breasts of his female victims. Pacciani had again come to the police's attention in 1987, subsequently being convicted of molesting his two daughters and accordingly being jailed.

His name was fed into a computer, along with those of more than 100,000 people who had the opportunity of carrying out the Monster of Florence's crimes. The computer identified just one suspect, however: Pacciani. Convinced that Pacciani was the perpetrator of the murders, the police searched his farm in minute detail for evidence, but nothing was found. They were on the point of giving up when a bullet was unearthed which was later found to match those that had been used in the murders.

Although a weapon was never recovered Pacciani was charged with murder. His trial dragged on for six months before the jury finally convicted him, whereupon he was jailed for life in 1994. Subsequently, however, a judicial review reassessed the flimsy evidence against him and after its ruling that his conviction was unsafe Pacciani was released from prison in 1996. As far as anyone knows the Monster of Florence is still at large.